Counseling Individuals With Eating Disorders

An Intersectional Approach

A Volume in An Intersectional Approach to Counseling and Health

Series Editors

Jennie Park-Taylor and Merle A. Keitel
Fordham University

An Intersectional Approach to Counseling and Health

Jennie Park-Taylor and Merle A. Keitel, Series Editors

Counseling Individuals With Eating Disorders: An Intersectional Approach (2025)
edited by Merle A. Keitel, Melinda Parisi Cummings, and Jennie Park-Taylor

An Intersectional Approach to Counseling Children and Adolescents With Health Conditions (2024)
edited by Jennie Park-Taylor and Merle Keitel

Counseling Individuals With Eating Disorders

An Intersectional Approach

edited by

Merle A. Keitel
Fordham University

Melinda Parisi Cummings
Holy Family University

Jennie Park-Taylor
Fordham University

IAP

INFORMATION AGE PUBLISHING, INC.
Charlotte, NC • www.infoagepub.com

Library of Congress Cataloging-in-Publication Data

CIP record for this book is available from the Library of Congress
http://www.loc.gov

ISBNs: 979-8-88730-859-3 (Paperback)

979-8-88730-860-9 (Hardcover)

979-8-88730-861-6 (ebook)

Printed in the United States of America

CONTENTS

PREFACE

Jennie Park-Taylor,
Merle A. Keitel, and Melinda Parisi Cummings

Counseling Individuals With Eating Disorders: An Intersectional Approach was written to provide mental health professionals and students of counseling, medicine, psychology, social work, nursing, and other helping professions with useful information and suggestions for their work with individuals with eating disorders. The chapter authors rely on an intersectional understanding of the human experience and specifically focus on how individuals with various intersecting identities experience, understand, and seek support for their disorders. We are so grateful to the diverse group of authors who collectively contributed their professional expertise to create this culturally-centered, engaging, and interdisciplinary resource. We strongly believe that our book fills a unique gap in the currently available texts that address these issues because case examples are included that are embedded in a specific sociocultural context. It is important to note that, although a range of illnesses are represented, the book is not comprehensive. The chapters that we did include, however, represent eating disorders that are frequently encountered in clinical settings and each chapter has great practical significance and utility for mental health practitioners as well as students in training.

Throughout the book, there is a strong emphasis on Crenshaw's (1989) conception of intersectionality as a way to better understand the dynamic relationships between societal and individually-based drivers of health behaviors and outcomes. Crenshaw's work in the early 1990s that explored

Counseling Individuals With Eating Disorders: An Intersectional Approach, pp. vii–ix

Black women's compounding experiences of discrimination in the United States served as foundational for her articulation of the concept of intersectionality, which describes how systems of oppression overlap to create distinct experiences for people based on their multiple identity categories. Considering contemporary research that has outlined some of the ways in which individuals' multiple social identities interconnect and interact to compound experiences of illness, health psychology researchers would benefit from applying an intersectional understanding of health in their explorations of the micro- and macro-level variables that influence pathways towards health and illness for different groups (Heard et al., 2020). For mental health practitioners, an intersectional lens will more likely lead to innovative and inclusive interventions. Furthermore, an intersectional approach to treating individuals with eating disorders requires that helping professionals are aware of, attuned to, and skilled at addressing their diverse clients' multiple experiences of oppression. This is critical given that social ills (e.g., racism, ageism, gender discrimination, religious discrimination) can and are experienced together, produce material and social disadvantage, and serve to maintain health disparities (Heard et al., 2020; McGibbon & McPherson, 2011).

Counseling Individuals With Eating Disorders: An Intersectional Approach includes chapters that focus on general topics, such as intersectionality and ethics, counseling individuals with specific eating disorders, counseling special populations, and counseling parents. Each of the disorder-specific chapters in the book begins with a description of the disorder, research regarding prevalence rates across diverse groups, and evidence-based treatments. Most chapters include an extended case vignette that highlights considerations relevant to a client's intersectional identity, followed by an analysis of the vignette from the perspective of a theoretical approach or approaches supported by empirical research. Chapters conclude with future directions for treatment, research, theory, and policy, as well as four to five questions for discussion.

Of course, meaningful differences exist within various cultures, and we recognize that the way authors have conceptualized diverse groups may not apply to all individuals in those groups. Given page limitations, we were unable to include all groups or examples of clients with all intersecting identities. That said, we are confident that our book is an initial step toward acknowledging the importance of considering intersectionality in clinical work and will be of great use to mental health practitioners and students who plan to or are currently working with individuals with eating disorders. Readers of the book can focus on a specific eating disorder and develop their knowledge, skills, and awareness of cultural and systemic considerations.

REFERENCES

Crenshaw K. (1989). Demarginalizing the intersection of race and sex: A Black feminist critique of antidiscrimination doctrine. *University of Chicago Legal Forum, 1,* 139–168.

Heard, E., Fitzgerald, L., Wigginton, B., & Mutch, A. (2020). Applying intersectionality theory in health promotion research and practice. *Health Promotion International, 35*(4), 866–876. https://doi-org.avoserv2.library.fordham.edu/10.1093/heapro/daz080

McGibbon, E., & McPherson, C. (2011). Applying intersectionality and complexity theory to address the social determinants of women's health. *Women's Health & Urban Life, 10*(1), 59–86.

CHAPTER 1

INTERSECTIONALITY AND EATING DISORDERS

Natasha L. Burke, Julia Yermash, Tatyana Bidopia, and Yvette Karvay

The exact term "intersectionality" is credited to Kimberlé Crenshaw, a United States civil rights advocate and critical race theorist (Crenshaw, 1993). Though some erroneously consider this the beginning of intersectionality, it was only the introduction of the term, which also spurred discourse in the academic realm (Collins & Bilge, 2020). Though there are myriad ways scholars, practitioners, and activists may define intersectionality, the following definition captures the intricacies of the construct:

> Intersectionality investigates how intersecting power relations influence social relations across diverse societies as well as individual experiences in everyday life. As an analytic tool, intersectionality views categories of race, class, gender, sexuality, class [*sic*], nation, ability, ethnicity, and age—among others—as interrelated and mutually shaping one another. Intersectionality is a way of understanding and explaining complexity in the world, in people, and in human experiences. (Collins & Bilge, 2020, p. 2)

As such, intersectionality acknowledges mutually dependent social categories operating within the context of larger political, economic, and cultural structures that differentially predict experiences and outcomes. Importantly, the ethos of intersectionality involves social justice advocacy.

Counseling Individuals With Eating Disorders: An Intersectional Approach, pp. 1–24

Intersectionality has existed—even if not named as such—since at least the 19th century. Examples of intersectionality at work in the 1800s include Savitribai and Jyotirao Phule's political activism in India confronting casteism, classism, sexism, and religious inequalities and Sojourner Truth's civil and women's rights activism confronting slavery at the crossroads of race and sex in the United States (Collins & Bilge, 2020).

In the United States, it was the activism of Black feminists in the 1960s and 1970s, and the scholarship and activism of critical race theorists, that brought the ethos of intersectionality into the broader social discourse (e.g., Beale, 1970; Crenshaw, 1993; Hill Collins, 1990). During the 1960s and 1970s feminist movement in the United States, Black women felt they were not adequately represented. Indeed, the historical, political, and economic policies of the United States resulted in unique—and often oppressive and detrimental—experiences for Black women that had not been addressed in the prevailing feminist rhetoric. Black feminists called for changes in that discourse, arguing that their multiple social identities (e.g., race and gender) operated both independently and interactively to determine their risk of discrimination, disadvantage, and disparity (Cole, 2009).

Intersectionality recognizes that an individual's interlocking aspects of identity operates within existing systems of power, privilege, and oppression that differentially influence and predict one's experiences and outcomes. Categories of identity are, in large part, determined by the social structures that create and house them. Additionally, individuals present to the world as one entity—not individual aspects of identity (e.g., gender, race, class, etc.)—and these socially-constructed identities and the power differentials that create them are mutually dependent and impact daily life. Therefore, Black feminists advocated for their voices to be heard, which meant society's recognition that their race and their gender together (i.e., the distinctive aspects of being a Black woman) resulted in unique and compounding experiences of discrimination, disadvantage, and disparities not fully accounted for by their race only (i.e., being Black) or their gender only (i.e., being a woman). Each social category afforded its own "-ism"—racism and sexism—that, when combined for Black women, were more detrimental than the sum of their parts. Though considerations of intersectionality historically occur within the context of social justice and advocacy, intersectionality acknowledges privilege and power, in addition to oppression. As such, it could equally help in considering how some in a given population may be disproportionally *advantaged* for various outcomes and opportunities within a given sociocultural context, depending on the combination of their various identities, though this focus is more readily used as a benchmark highlighting disparities for other, relatively disadvantaged, groups.

Intersectionality's Relevance for Mental Health

A prerequisite to adequate mental health treatment inherently includes understanding the complexity of people, human nature, and the human experience. As such, governing professional organizations in the fields of psychology, medicine, and social work have issued guidelines emphasizing the importance of a taking a multicultural stance to improve our understanding of how sociocultural context influences the human experience and mental health (Clauss-Ehlers et al., 2019; National Association of Social Workers, 2015; U.S. Department of Health and Human Services Office of Minority Health, 2016). The American Psychological Association's *Task Force on Re-envisioning the Multicultural Guidelines for the 21st Century* pinpointed intersectionality as the most important guideline for multicultural psychological treatment (Clauss-Ehlers et al., 2019). Though each of the guidelines harken to intersectionality-informed practices, Guidelines 1, 5, and 8 from the *Multicultural Guidelines* are particularly salient.

> **Guideline 1.** Psychologists seek to recognize and understand that identity and self-definition are fluid and complex and that the interaction between the two is dynamic.

To this end, psychologists appreciate that intersectionality is shaped by the multiplicity of the individual's social contexts. (American Psychological Association, 2017, p. 4)

Though identity is often implicitly conceptualized as static (Derlan Williams et al., 2020), it is fluid across social contexts and across the life course. Importantly, how one is perceived by others versus how one perceives themselves is just as complex and can similarly change across social contexts and throughout development. As a result, as the guideline implies, how our clients present to treatment, how we perceive them presenting to treatment, and our case conceptualization are all influenced by our own social contexts and identities. Accordingly, as clinicians, we need to be aware of and actively address our potential blind spots in the assessment and treatment context.

> **Guideline 5.** Psychologists aspire to recognize and understand historical and contemporary experiences with power, privilege, and oppression. As such, they seek to address institutional barriers and related inequities, disproportionalities, and disparities of law enforcement, administration of criminal justice, educational, mental health, and other systems as they seek to promote justice, human rights, and access to quality and equitable mental and behavioral health services. (American Psychological Association, 2017, p. 4)

> **Guideline 8.** Psychologists seek awareness and understanding of how developmental stages and life transitions intersect with the larger biosociocultural context, how identity evolves as a function of such intersections, and how these different socialization and maturation experiences influence worldview and identity. (American Psychological Association, 2017, p. 5)

The crux of intersectionality and mental health is contained in these two guidelines. Intersectionality-informed approaches help clarify and address culturally relevant social categories that confer risk (or protection) secondary to systemic, structural, and individual factors. Such approaches allow for understanding the possibility that the effect of one socially-constructed category depends upon the existence of one or more other categories. Understanding such intricacies of identity and experience can then positively influence assessment, diagnosis, and treatment towards effective and equitable client care. APA's *Multicultural Guidelines*, therefore, behoove psychologists and mental health practitioners to operate with a social justice and advocacy lens, following the same spirit that intersectionality discourse in the United States and elsewhere came into being.

Intersectionality's Relevance for Eating Disorder Treatment

Considering intersectionality in the field of eating disorders (EDs) is critical as, along with other mental health conditions, it has important. implications for risk, assessment, diagnosis, treatment, and outcomes (Burke et al., 2020). The categories suggested by Collins and Bilge (2020) in their definition of intersectionality (e.g., race, gender, age) are certainly relevant to EDs. However, others are likely as salient, including weight status, socioeconomic status, immigration status, and acculturative stress, among others (Burke et al., 2020). Such aspects of identity are also potential modifiers of health risk, treatment, and outcomes. However, in consideration of the APA *Multicultural Guidelines*, clinicians would be remiss if they did not consider the historical and cultural context of ED diagnostic criteria that spurred inequities in assessment and diagnosis from their foundation.

Culture, Eating Disorders, and the DSM

Culture is composed of the distinctive knowledge, customs, values, attitudes, norms, and beliefs of a society or community that are passed down over time and form the foundation of daily behaviors and practices including one's language and understanding of health and illness (American Psychiatric Association, 2022). Although culture is often treated as a static construct, like identity, culture is dynamic and changing over time. It informs daily life, the organization of family and community, and broader economic and political domains (American Psychiatric Association, 2022). The ED diagnostic criteria in the Diagnostic and Statistical Manual of Mental Disorders (DSM; American Psychiatric Association, 2022) were developed through a Western-focused lens, and primarily around White, relatively young, and economically advantaged women (Rodgers et al., 2018). Thus, individuals outside of these categories were at a disadvantage from all aspects of care—from screening and assessment to diagnosis and treatment—and these disparities continue (e.g., Coffino et al., 2019; Sonneville & Lipson, 2018). The most recent text revision of the DSM, the DSM-5-TR, acknowledges that current ED diagnostic profiles started as "cultural syndromes," but states such profiles have been adopted widely based on their clinical and research utility (American Psychiatric Association, 2022). Still, clinicians can enhance the cultural sensitivity and relevance of their care by understanding that no demographic, cultural group, or intersection of identities is immune to EDs, and EDs may present differently for individuals of various cultural and demographic groups.

Longstanding stereotypes regarding the demographics of those who do—and do not—have EDs is both a barrier to care and seeking treatment (Sonneville & Lipson, 2018). For example, historical stereotypes framed EDs as diseases of affluence (Gard & Freeman, 1996); however, EDs occur across the socioeconomic (SES) spectrum. It is posited that clinician bias based on these stereotypes contributes to disparities in ED diagnosis and care among those from economically disadvantaged backgrounds (Becker et al., 2003). The same stereotypes permeate society more broadly, and are likely why those from economically disadvantaged backgrounds are also less likely to perceive a need for treatment (Sonneville & Lipson, 2018). Studies indicate risk for EDs may actually be *higher* for those of lower SES (Burke et al., 2022). Conditions related to SES, such as food insecurity, are also predictive of binge eating over time (Hazzard et al., 2022). In 2021, 10.2% of U.S. households experienced food insecurity, which included nearly 13% of households that contained children (Coleman-Jensen et al., 2022). Notably, food insecurity disproportionately affects marginalized groups (e.g., Black and Hispanic individuals; Coleman-Jensen et al., 2022), placing these multiply marginalized youth and adults at greater risk for eating pathology. For example, data indicate Hispanic adolescents with food insecurity are more likely to engage in binge eating compared to non-Hispanic adolescents (Kim et al., 2021). Aspects of culture can influence how eating behaviors and food insecurity interact. For example, in times of food shortage, Bangladeshi girls are expected to restrict their food intake and sacrifice meals so that the boys of the family have enough to eat (Blum et al., 2019). In this case, cultural expectations by gender impact dietary restraint patterns influenced by food insecurity. Overall, data point to a strong link between binge-eating behaviors and other types of disordered eating behaviors in children and adolescents, highlighting the need to (a) not equate lack of food with lack of potential ED pathology, and (b) assess for ED pathology in youth with food insecurity (Bidopia et al., 2023). Mechanisms for understanding these connections are currently being investigated (e.g., Stadterman et al., 2022).

Other stereotypes have similarly persisted, which have dire implications for those not fitting the "skinny, White, affluent girl" (aka "SWAG," a term popularized by the media; Sonneville & Lipson, 2018) demographic. Indeed, for some African American adolescents, ED symptoms were totally ignored or dismissed by clinicians due to the erroneous belief that EDs were rare in African American populations (Becker et al., 2010). Epidemiological data dispute the erroneous belief that racial and ethnic minorities are not at risk for or experience EDs (Cheng et al., 2019). Racial and ethnic disparities in healthcare access are well known, and utilization of mental health services are lower among racial and ethnic minority groups due to systemic, social, and sometimes culturally specific barriers that remain unaddressed (Atdjian & Vega, 2005; Cook et al., 2017; Marrast et al., 2016; Planey et al., 2019; Udo & Grilo, 2018). As one example, South Asian women described judgement by members of their community, in the forms of general mental health stigma and social stigma, as significant barriers that maintain the taboo nature of speaking about and receiving treatment for EDs and mental health issues more broadly (Goel, Thomas, et al., 2022). Understanding the social barriers to care encountered by individuals with EDs is an essential step toward eliminating disparities in assessment, diagnosis, and treatment access. A study that hoped to understand the racial and ethnic disparities in treatment receipt among children and young adults found that Black and Hispanic youth receive outpatient mental health and substance use services at half the rate of non-Hispanic White youth, citing cultural values and a paucity of treatment providers as potential explanations (Marrast et al., 2016).

Other non-"SWAG" populations have also suffered from these disparities and oversight, including men and nonbinary individuals (Hartman-Munick et al., 2021; Strother et al., 2012), older adults (Mangweth-Matzek & Hoek, 2017), and those at the higher end of the weight spectrum (Kennedy et al., 2017). Though the DSM-5-TR includes significant revisions in the "Culture-Related Diagnostic Issues" sections for each ED, clinicians should be aware that the acknowledgement and understanding of such issues are still in the nascent stages and will inevitably evolve over time. Despite an increase in the recognition and exploration of culture in the context of EDs (Soh & Walter, 2013), our understanding of culture and EDs is still developing, which some believe prohibits our ability to provide culturally- sensitive treatment (Ramirez et al., 2018). As culturally adapted interventions produce greater reduction and remittance of symptoms across a range of psychological disturbances (Hall et al., 2016), continued work of this nature is critical for improving outcomes in underserved and underrecognized populations that may be overlooked by approaches that fail to account for the impact of marginalized and intersecting identities.

Extant Research on Eating Pathology and Intersectionality

Extant research supports the tenets of intersectionality theory as it relates to EDs. Specifically, research indicates ED prevalence among groups with multiple marginalized identities may be disproportionate to the prevalence noted with each individual identity in isolation (Burke et al., 2021; Rodgers et al., 2017). As one example, intersectional approaches have indicated that the intersection of gender and Latinx identities produces specific vulnerabilities; Latina adolescent girls' risk of purging behaviors is significantly greater than would be expected based on their ethnicity or gender alone, and significantly greater than their White female, White male, and Latino male peers (Beccia et al., 2019). Similarly, research examining the intersection of sexual orientation and race/ethnicity indicates a particularly high prevalence of EDs among Latinx and Black sexual minority individuals (Feldman & Meyer, 2007).

Which combinations of identities are held may differentially predict risk (e.g., multiracial individuals are not a monolith and experience differential risk depending on identity; Burke et al., 2021). As stated previously, the intersection of these socially-based identities within a given cultural context has implications for risk, assessment, and treatment (Burke et al., 2020). Those with multiply marginalized identities, secondary to historical, structural, and cultural influences, may be especially vulnerable (e.g., racial/ethnic, gender, and sexual minorities, those of lower socioeconomic status; Burke et al., 2022; Burke et al., 2020). Therefore, clinicians would be well advised to engage patients with an interview approach, such as the Cultural Formulation Interview, which provides an avenue for eliciting the clinically relevant features and experience of a patient's social identity (American Psychiatric Association, 2022). Such culturally appropriate evaluations consider both the sociocultural context and the individual living within that context (Kirmayer, 2016).

Risk/Prevalence

Eating Disorder Pathology

The importance of understanding the risk and prevalence of EDs in multiply marginalized individuals has been noted (Calzo et al., 2017; Smolak & Piran, 2012). Since EDs and subclinical disordered eating behaviors emerge most commonly during adolescence and persist into young adulthood (Neumark-Sztainer et al., 2011), a handful of studies have been conducted to understand how intersecting identities affect ED risk in young people. Early research in this area explored ED risk among young people by assessing whether risk associated with one identity was modified by a second identity. While some of this early literature did not find increased risk among multiply marginalized U.S. high school students using this approach (Austin et al., 2013), potentially due to using additive versus intersectional statistical models (Burke et al., 2020) or low sample size, there were increased ED behaviors in racial/ethnic and sexual minority groups independently (Austin et al., 2013). Contrastingly, recent work has indicated that ED prevalence may be higher among young people when accounting for their multiple identities than when accounting for each identity separately (e.g., Burke et al., 2021; Rodgers et al., 2017). As mentioned previously, Latina adolescent girls in the U.S. are at a higher risk of purging when considering the combined effects of their ethnic and gender identities (Beccia et al., 2019). Additionally, Asian adolescent boys in the U.S. of higher weight status are twice as likely to engage in dieting and overeating behaviors when considering their racial identity and weight status (Rodgers et al., 2017).

In a study of U.S. undergraduate and graduate students conducted by Burke and colleagues (2022), receiving a positive ED screen was significantly more likely among lower SES students than among higher SES students. The robustness of the relationship between screening positively for EDs by SES varied across social identities (gender, sexual orientation, race/ethnicity) and was especially notable among participants with intersecting marginalized identities. For example, ED prevalence was higher in lower SES Latinx sexual minority individuals and in Latinx sexual minority individuals, regardless of SES, when compared to Black and White sexual minority individuals (Burke et al., 2022).

In a study among South Korean male university students, sexual identity and university prestige (dichotomized into low- and high-prestige universities), were explored in relation to Korean men's cultural consonance to examine the risk of developing an ED (Monocello & Dressler, 2022). When cultural consonance, defined as the approximation of specific cultural domains in one's beliefs and behaviors (Dressler et al., 2017), was added to a model including sexual identity and university prestige, all were significantly associated with ED. Gay and bisexual men reported higher DE compared to heterosexual men overall. However, heterosexual men from low-prestige universities reported a higher association of cultural consonance and ED risk than high-prestige university men of all sexual identities. Yet, no differences in the association of cultural consonance and ED risk were found between gay, bisexual, and heterosexual men in the high-prestige university group (Monocello & Dressler, 2022). Altogether, this highlights how university prestige, sexual orientation, and aspects related to identity, such as cultural consonance, intersect to determine DE risk for South Korean men. Of course, understanding South Korean culture related to educational status, sexual orientation, and cultural expectations is needed to place these results in context. With all of our clients, it is critical to seek consultation and guidance when engaging with clients whose cultural backgrounds and experiences are different from our own.

Other studies have focused on the experience of gendered racism and its effects on DE among Asian American individuals (Le et al., 2022; Le et al., 2020). Le and colleagues (2020) were the first to investigate gendered racism in relation to DE behaviors in a sample of Asian American women. While racism and sexism were not independently associated with DE, gendered racial microaggressions were positively related to DE (Le et al., 2020). These findings exemplify why it is crucial to prioritize intersectional identities when exploring the effects of discrimination (e.g., racism, sexism) on DE behaviors, because solely looking at sexism or racism would not have revealed the complete picture. With regard to Asian American men, there has been limited ED literature that considers their intersecting identities. Through an online survey, Asian American men in the U.S. answered a variety of questions about gender, racism, and muscularity-oriented DE behaviors. In parallel with the previous study on Asian American women (Le et al., 2020), gendered racism was positively correlated with muscularity-oriented DE behaviors. However, racism alone was not associated with muscularity-oriented DE behaviors (Le et al., 2022), which aligns with previous work with Asian American men (Cheng et al., 2016). Researchers exploring muscularity-oriented DE behaviors in another sample of Asian American men speculated that this may serve as a way to increase self-esteem when experiencing gendered racism, which can lead to feelings of self-doubt and inadequacy (Liao et al., 2020). In sum, the association between gendered racism and DE for both Asian American women and men clearly highlights the importance of understanding the combination of race and gender in relation to DE symptoms and treatment.

Using a large national epidemiological dataset with a significant portion of sexual minority participants (National Epidemiologic Survey on Alcohol and Related Conditions-III; Grant et al., 2014), Shepherd and colleagues (2022) found that U.S. sexual minority men were more fearful of gaining weight when at their lowest weight, experienced more loss of control when overeating, and were more likely to be categorized as underweight when compared with their heterosexual counterparts. For female participants, sexual minority women reported "ever having a binge-eating episode" and "binge eating weekly for at least three months" more often than heterosexual women (Shepherd et al., 2022). Others have found more ED symptoms among sexual minority men and women than their same-gender heterosexual counterparts, with these discrepancies appearing more consistent among male participants (Calzo et al., 2017).

Qualitative research is well-suited to examining and understanding intersectionality and EDs. It allows for a deep and often nuanced exploration of identity, experience, and any related pathology. Still, researchers are starting to apply novel methodological approaches in the ED field that are well-suited for quantitative intersectionality research, including multilevel analysis of individual heterogeneity and discriminatory accuracy (MAIHDA). MAIHDA allows researchers to use two-level multilevel modeling to observe any socio-demographic inequities and their magnitude (Merlo, 2018). A study utilizing the MAIHDA method examined the intersection of gender identity with gender expression, sexual orientation, and weight status (Beccia et al., 2021). The authors had two goals: (a) to find social patterns and (b) to question the focus on gender in the ED field. Regarding the latter point, gender identity is relevant in ED research, but the authors argued that gender may be prioritized more than necessary and should be examined in a more intersectional way (Beccia et al., 2021). Additional findings of the study indicated that individuals with intersecting marginalized identities (i.e., gender nonconforming expression and sexual minority) had increased severe ED pathology compared to individuals with one minority identity (Beccia et al., 2021).

In the context of weight status, researchers used Ecological Momentary Assessment (EMA), a research technique that uses repeated assessment of participant behaviors and thoughts over time within their naturalistic environments (Shiffman et al., 2008), to explore minority stressors among sexual minority women in the U.S. with overweight/obesity. Multiple minority stressors (i.e., internalized homophobia, sexual orientation concealment, and weight bias experiences) led to more episodes of overeating and binge eating within the 5-day EMA period (Panza et al., 2021). Given the high prevalence of obesity and DE behaviors among sexual minority women in comparison to heterosexual women (Eliason et al., 2015), future work should further explore these intersecting identities as they relate to DE.

In the therapeutic context, understanding the risks for individuals at the higher end of the weight spectrum with other socially marginalized identities warrants special assessment and attention. In addition to sexual identity, weight status has been studied in connection to race in a sample of military-dependent and civilian youth. In a sample of youth with overweight and obesity, findings indicated Black military-dependent youth had more DE behaviors than Black civilian youth, a pattern not found among White participants (Higgins Neyland et al., 2022). Additionally, White civilian youth with overweight/obesity had higher levels of DE than Black civilian youth with overweight/obesity (Higgins Neyland et al., 2022). These results may stem from the specific experience of being a Black adolescent military-dependent at the intersection of three marginalized identities (i.e., having overweight/obesity, being a member of a racial minority group, and being a military-dependent). Additionally, these youth may be receiving conflicting messages in terms of their identities. For example, military appearance and fitness expectations (i.e., muscular and lean body; Tanofsky-Kraff et al., 2013) may counter the acceptance and celebration of a variety of body types within some Black civilian communities (Cassidy et al., 2013). While Rodgers and colleagues (2017) found a similar pattern among a female adolescent sample, Black adolescent males with overweight had higher levels of dieting behaviors when compared to their White male peers with overweight (Rodgers et al., 2017). Altogether, identifying with multiple marginalized identities and specific cultural groups results in specific experiences with disordered eating. Given these findings and the extant research pointing to increased DE behaviors among racial minority young people in the U.S. (Beccia et al., 2019; Beukes et al., 2010; Croll et al., 2002; Neumark-Sztainer et al., 2002), further research is needed to understand the intersection of weight status and race during adolescence and beyond. These individual-level findings represent larger systemic and structural factors (e.g., power, oppression), that need to be understood to identify how experiencing stigma or discrimination based on having multiple marginalized identities influences the risk of DE behaviors. Discussing such experiences in a supportive way may be particularly beneficial for clients presenting for treatment for an ED.

Researchers have also investigated *perceptions* of DE, rather than DE symptoms specifically, at the intersection of weight status and race. In an experimental study, college students in the U.S. were given a vignette of a female student varying in weight status and race that disclosed a range of DE symptoms (Osa et al., 2021). While reported symptoms varied based on the weight status in the vignette, results indicated no significant interaction effects between weight status and race. As the authors noted, the data collection method (i.e., vignette) may not have fully communicated or captured the interconnection between weight status and race (Osa et al., 2022). The goal of the experimental study design using the vignette was to frame identity categories (i.e., weight status and race) as stimuli to represent individuals with intersectional identities and capture perceptions of these identities. While this may be able to provide information about how college students perceive weight status and race together, this study design is unable to capture the lived, nuanced experiences of having these identities. A qualitative exploration of these intersecting identities may be needed to fully capture the impact on DE symptoms and the perceptions of others experienced by multiply marginalized individuals.

Body Image

Body dissatisfaction is a consistent and robust predictor of EDs. Intersectionality-focused literature on body image and body satisfaction, however, is scarce. Extant research in this area has primarily explored risks for and prevalence of body image issues in Black female populations (Awad et al., 2015; Capodilupo & Kim, 2014). In one study of Black female college students in the U.S., researchers conducted focus groups to identify factors relevant to Black women's body image since discussion about body image in psychological discourse has historically been based on experiences reported by White women (Awad et al., 2015). The themes that emerged were categorized into four domains (hair, skin tone/colorism, body type, and messages/sources) that were aligned with characteristics identified to be relevant to body image issues for Black women in previous literature (Grabe & Hyde, 2006). Without looking at race and gender in conjunction with one another (i.e., without looking at these identities through an intersectional lens), capturing the racialized context underlying Black women's body image that has resulted from many years of oppression is not possible (Awad et al., 2015). While Awad and colleagues (2015) focused on college women, many of whom may be of higher socioeconomic status or have potential for upward mobility (Awad et al., 2015), Capodilupo and Kim (2014) explored similar ideas with a community sample of women in a metropolitan U.S. city. The primary category that emerged from the interviews was body/self-image, which was similarly informed by feelings about hair, skin, weight, shape, and attitude. These findings emphasized the importance of looking past what is often discussed in relation to U.S. beauty standards (i.e., weight and shape) and focusing on physical characteristics that Black women may find more pertinent (i.e., hair and skin tone) to understand the source of body image issues for this group of women. Numerous studies have found that Black women feel pressure to adhere to specific ideals like light skin tone, long hair, and a small nose that have historically been associated with Eurocentric, White features (Capodilupo & Kim, 2014; Kendi, 2016; Wilfred & Lundgren, 2021). Notably, both aforementioned studies utilized qualitative methods to capture the participants' perspectives within their sociocultural contexts, with the intention of avoiding grounding their experiences in the previous literature that has focused chiefly on White, Eurocentric beauty ideals (Awad et al., 2015; Capodilupo & Kim, 2014; Parker et al., 2022).

The intersecting effects of race and gender on body image have also been studied in adolescent populations. In adolescence, the bodily changes that occur during puberty result in increased focus on body image and comparison to peers (Voelker et al., 2015), so understanding adolescents' unique experiences may help to prevent later development of DE. For example, Black adolescent girls in the U.S. with greater skin color dissatisfaction reported more binge-ED symptoms and were at increased risk for binge-ED. This relationship was mediated by body dissatisfaction, indicating that skin color dissatisfaction plays a significant role in body image for Black adolescent girls and may also be related to binge eating (Parker et al., 2022). As mentioned previously, research exploring body image among Black girls and women should utilize an intersectional framework that prioritizes the historical and sociocultural context in which Black girls/women understand their bodies (Awad et al., 2015). This stands true for individuals across genders and ethnicities, among other factors.

COVID-19

The coronavirus (COVID-19) pandemic uniquely impacted individuals with ED pathology and body image-related issues (Devoe et al., 2023; Schneider et al., 2023). Indeed, research and clinical observations indicated that symptoms associated with ED pathology were exacerbated during the COVID-19 pandemic (Czepczor-Bernat et al., 2021; Giel et al., 2021; Rodgers et al., 2020), secondary to a myriad of psychosocial shifts in society (e.g., food availability, limited social behavioral activation; Cooper et al., 2022) and lessened access to ED treatment (Cooper et al., 2022). Furthermore, during the pandemic, individuals experienced dysregulated eating behaviors in general (Karvay et al., 2023) and were subjected to increased bias toward weight gain and body size (Schneider et al., 2023). These effects may have been exacerbated for individuals at the intersection of certain socially-relevant identities (e.g., body size, gender, sexual orientation, race/ethnicity), particularly as related to pandemic-specific experiences including fear of exposure, threats of discrimination, and risk perception. Indeed, a study conducted by Brownstone, Greene, and colleagues (2022) examined these concepts within a diverse (in terms of racial/ethnic identity, body size, and sexual orientation) U.S. subclinical sample of cisgender individuals who reported experiencing DE during COVID-19. Out of the five main themes identified by the authors, the idea of bodies being vulnerable, defined as "an internalized and externalized experience of identity and the pandemic" varied the most by participants' intersecting identities. Individuals who identified as BIPOC, large-bodied, or queer most commonly reported the impact of body vulnerability on patterns of restrictive and binge eating, exercise patterns, and so on, whereas BIPOC and large-bodied participants were most likely to emphasize how social distancing and mask-wearing reduced public visibility, which decreased the amount of discrimination they experienced (Brownstone, Greene, et al., 2022). Another study aimed to highlight the distinct body- and eating-related experiences of transgender and gender nonbinary individuals in the U.S. during the pandemic. All participants reported increased reflection about their intersecting identities during the pandemic due to more time spent alone. For some, this reflection led to worsened body dissatisfaction and/or gender dysphoria, whereas, for others, it resulted in positive self-exploration (Brownstone, Kelly, et al., 2022). These studies highlight the unique experiences of individuals with (multiple) marginalized identities, while reflecting that no particular group has the same exact experiences. Therefore, understanding how intersecting identities influence experiences is helpful as a general guidepost, but it is not a specific navigational compass. No one group is a monolith.

Assessment

Most tools and measures used to assess EDs were initially developed and validated in White women, which may, as a result, prevent them from fully capturing symptoms in other groups (e.g., Burke et al., 2017; Murray et al., 2017). The Eating Disorder Examination Questionnaire (ED-Q; Fairburn & Beglin, 1994), a commonly used self-report measure of ED pathology in research, is no exception. Different factor structures of the EDE-Q have been created and tested with various populations. However, it is still unclear what factor structures best measure ED pathology at the intersection of multiple facets of identity, as the EDE-Q is often examined by looking at individual elements of identity in isolation. McEntee and colleagues (2021) aimed to address this gap by using an intersectional approach to examine U.S. group differences in ethnicity (Latinx vs. non-Latinx) and gender (men vs. women) to test the measurement and construct validity of the EDE-Q at the intersection of those identities. They also compared the original and modified factor structures of the EDE-Q given the psychometric issues with the original factor structure reported in the literature (Grilo et al., 2015; Schaefer et al., 2018). In line with previous work, only the modified, seven-item EDE-Q was found to be a valid way to measure eating pathology across gender identity and ethnicity. There were independent effects of gender and ethnicity, and a significant interaction on the Shape Concerns subscale (McEntee et al., 2021), underscoring the need to develop and use measures that accurately assess ED symptoms in groups other than non-Hispanic, White women. Although some studies have demonstrated measurement validity for alternate factor structures of the EDE-Q in groups that have been historically excluded in the ED literature (e.g., Goel, Burnette, et al., 2022; McEntee et al., 2021), findings also indicate norms and ED symptoms differ by intersecting marginalized identities (Kambanis et al., 2022). Therefore, it is vital to establish norms for measures among individuals who hold multiple marginalized identities to ensure proper assessment and diagnosis of ED pathology, as these types of guidelines are often the basis of clinical interventions.

CONCLUSION

More research is being conducted prioritizing intersecting identities in relation to ED pathology and body image, which will ideally serve as a complement to clinical work in this area. Indeed, we recommend clinicians, researchers, and those with lived experience engage in ongoing dialogue to best guide assessment, measurement, and interventions to best serve individuals with and at risk for EDs. As suggested by Burke and colleagues (2020), a more comprehensive range of identities needs to be incorporated in future ED research and clinical work using an intersectional framework. Simultaneously, strengths-based approaches are needed to pinpoint identity-related factors that might be protective and utilized in treatment (Burke et al., 2020). Importantly, at the heart of the matter is better understanding and seeking to change the systems of oppression and privilege that contribute to health-related disparities, and the tenets of intersectionality are aligned to do just that (Bowleg, 2012).

DISCUSSION QUESTIONS

1. In what ways does your social position (your lived experience and intersection of identities) influence how you approach treatment and interact with your patients?
2. What systemic factors influence the development of EDs, and how might that differ for individuals from multiple marginalized backgrounds?
3. With changing political and social climates, what actionable steps can you take to keep abreast of and address factors influencing the lived experiences of your clients from marginalized communities?
4. How might mental health stigma be particularly detrimental to those at the intersections of multiple marginalized identities, and what might help to ameliorate this?

REFERENCES

American Psychiatric Association. (2022). Culture and psychiatric diagnosis. In *Diagnostic and statistical manual of mental disorders* (5th ed., text rev.). https://doi.org/10.1176/appi.books.9780890425787.Culture_and_Psychiatric_Diagnosis

American Psychological Association. (2017). *Multicultural guidelines: An ecological approach to context, identity, and intersectionality*. http://www.apa.org/about/policy/multicultural-guidelines.pdf

Atdjian, S., & Vega, W. A. (2005). Disparities in mental health treatment in U.S. racial and ethnic minority groups: Implications for psychiatrists. *Psychiatric Services, 56*(12), 1600–1602. https://doi.org/10.1176/appi.ps.56.12.1600

Austin, S. B., Nelson, L. A., Birkett, M. A., Calzo, J. P., & Everett, B. (2013). Eating disorder symptoms and obesity at the intersections of gender, ethnicity, and sexual orientation in U.S. high school students. *American Journal of Public Health, 103*(2), e16–22. https://doi.org/10.2105/ajph.2012.301150

Awad, G. H., Norwood, C., Taylor, D. S., Martinez, M., McClain, S., Jones, B., Holman, A., & Chapman-Hilliard, C. (2015). Beauty and body image concerns among African American college women. *Journal of Black Psychology, 41*(6), 540–564. https://doi.org/Beauty

Beale, F. (1970). Double jeopardy: To be Black and female. In T. Cade (Ed.), *The Black woman: An anthology* (pp. 90–100). Signet.

Beccia, A. L., Baek, J., Austin, S. B., Jesdale, W. M., & Lapane, K. L. (2021). Eating-related pathology at the intersection of gender identity and expression, sexual orientation, and weight status: An intersectional Multilevel Analysis of Individual Heterogeneity and Discriminatory Accuracy (MAIHDA) of the Growing Up Today Study cohorts. *Social Science & Medicine, 281*, 114092. https://doi.org/10.1016/j.socscimed.2021.114092

Beccia, A. L., Baek, J., Jesdale, W. M., Austin, S. B., Forrester, S., Curtin, C., & Lapane, K. L. (2019). Risk of disordered eating at the intersection of gender and racial/ethnic identity among U.S. high school students. *Eating Behaviors, 34*, 101299. https://doi.org/10.1016/j.eatbeh.2019.05.002

Becker, A. E., Franko, D. L., Speck, A., & Herzog, D. B. (2003). Ethnicity and differential access to care for eating disorder symptoms. *International Journal of Eating Disorders, 33*(2), 205–212. https://doi.org/10.1002/eat.10129

Becker, A. E., Hadley Arrindell, A., Perloe, A., Fay, K., & Striegel-Moore, R. H. (2010). A qualitative study of perceived social barriers to care for eating disorders: Perspectives from ethnically diverse health care consumers. *International Journal of Eating Disorders, 43*(7), 633–647. https://doi.org/10.1002/eat.20755

Beukes, M., Walker, S., & Esterhuyse, K. (2010). The role of coping responses in the relationship between perceived stress and disordered eating in a cross-cultural sample of female university students. *Stress & Health, 26*(4), 280–291. https://doi.org/10.1002/smi.1296

Bidopia, T., Carbo, A. V., Ross, R. A., & Burke, N. L. (2023). Food insecurity and disordered eating behaviors in children and adolescents: A systematic review. *Eating Behaviors, 49*, 101731. https://doi.org/10.1016/j.eatbeh.2023.101731

Blum, L. S., Khan, R., Sultana, M., Soltana, N., Siddiqua, Y., Khondker, R., Sultana, S., & Tumilowicz, A. (2019). Using a gender lens to understand eating behaviours of adolescent females living in low-income households in Bangladesh. *Maternal and Child Nutrition, 15*. https://doi.org/10.1111/mcn.12841

Bowleg, L. (2012). The problem with the phrase women and minorities: Intersectionality-an important theoretical framework for public health. *American Journal of Public Health, 102*(7), 1267–1273. https://doi.org/10.2105/AJPH.2012.300750

Brownstone, L. M., Greene, A. K., Kelly, D. A., Maloul, E. K., Norling, H. N., Rockholm, R. H., & Izaguirre, C. M. (2022). "Are people thinking I'm a vector ... because I'm fat?": Cisgender experiences of body, eating, and identity during COVID-19. *Body Image, 40*, 256–266. https://doi.org/10.1016/j.bodyim.2022.01.002

Brownstone, L. M., Kelly, D. A., Maloul, E. K., Dinneen, J. L., Palazzolo, L. P. A., Raque, T. L., & Greene, A. K. (2022). "It's just not comfortable to exist in a body": Transgender/gender nonbinary individuals' experiences of body and eating distress during the COVID-19 pandemic. *Psychology of Sexual Orientation and Gender Diversity, 9*(4), 434–445. https://doi.org/10.1037/sgd0000519

Burke, N. L., Hazzard, V. M., Karvay, Y. G., Schaefer, L. M., Lipson, S. K., & Rodgers, R. F. (2021). Eating disorder prevalence among multiracial U.S. undergraduate and graduate students: Is multiracial risk different than the sum of each identity? *Eating Behaviors, 41*, 101501. https://doi.org/10.1016/j.eatbeh.2021.101501

Burke, N. L., Hazzard, V. M., Schaefer, L. M., Simone, M., O'Flynn, J. L., & Rodgers, R. F. (2022). Socioeconomic status and eating disorder prevalence: At the intersections of gender identity, sexual orientation, and race/ethnicity *Psychological Medicine*, 1–11. Advanced online publication. https://doi.org/10.1017/S0033291722001015

Burke, N. L., Schaefer, L. M., Hazzard, V. M., & Rodgers, R. F. (2020). Where identities converge: The importance of intersectionality in eating disorders research. *International Journal of Eating Disorders, 53*(10), 1605–1609. https://doi.org/https://doi.org/10.1002/eat.23371

Burke, N. L., Tanofsky-Kraff, M., Crosby, R., Mehari, R. D., Marwitz, S. E., Broadney, M. M., Shomaker, L. B., Kelly, N. R., Schvey, N. A., Cassidy, O., Yanovski, S. Z., & Yanovski, J. A. (2017). Measurement invariance of the Eating Disorder Examination in Black and White children and adolescents. *International Journal of Eating Disorders, 50*, 758–768. https://doi.org/10.1002/eat.22713

Calzo, J. P., Blashill, A. J., Brown, T. A., & Argenal, R. L. (2017). Eating disorders and disordered weight and shape control behaviors in sexual minority populations. *Current Psychiatry Reports, 19*(8), 49. https://doi.org/10.1007/s11920-017-0801-y

Capodilupo, C. M., & Kim, S. (2014). Gender and race matter: The importance of considering intersections in Black women's body image. *Journal of Counseling Psychology, 61*(1), 37–49. https://doi.org/10.1037/a0034597

Cassidy, O., Sbrocco, T., Vannucci, A., Nelson, B., Jackson-Bowen, D., Heimdal, J., Mirza, N., Wilfley, D. E., Osborn, R., Shomaker, L. B., Young, J. F., Waldron, H., Carter, M., & Tanofsky-Kraff, M. (2013). Adapting interpersonal psychotherapy for the prevention of excessive weight gain in rural African American girls. *Journal of Pediatric Psychology, 38*(9), 965–977. https://doi.org/10.1093/jpepsy/jst029

Cheng, H.-L., McDermott, R. C., Wong, Y. J., & La, S. (2016). Drive for muscularity in Asian American men: Sociocultural and racial/ethnic factors as correlates. *Psychology of Men & Masculinities, 17*(3), 215–227. https://doi.org/10.1037/men0000019

Cheng, Z. H., Perko, V. L., Fuller-Marashi, L., Gau, J. M., & Stice, E. (2019). Ethnic differences in eating disorder prevalence, risk factors, and predictive effects of risk factors among young women. *Eating Behaviors, 32*, 23–30. https://doi.org/10.1016/j.eatbeh.2018.11.004

Clauss-Ehlers, C. S., Chiriboga, D. A., Hunter, S. J., Roysircar, G., & Tummala-Narra, P. (2019). APA Multicultural Guidelines executive summary: Ecological approach to context, identity, and intersectionality. *American Psychologist, 74*(2), 232–244. https://doi.org/10.1037/amp0000382

Coffino, J. A., Udo, T., & Grilo, C. M. (2019). Rates of help-seeking in U.S. adults with lifetime DSM-5 eating disorders: Prevalence across diagnoses and differences by sex and ethnicity/race. *Mayo Clinic Proceedings, 94*(8), 1415–1426. https://doi.org/10.1016/j.mayocp.2019.02.030

Cole, E. R. (2009). Intersectionality and research in psychology. *American Psychologist, 64*(3), 170–180. https://doi.org/10.1037/a0014564

Coleman-Jensen, A., Rabbitt, M. P., Gregory, C. A., & Singh, A. (2022). *Household food security in the United States in 2021*. U.S. Department of Agriculture.

Collins, P. H., & Bilge, S. (2020). *Intersectionality*. John Wiley & Sons.

Cook, B. L., Trinh, N. H., Li, Z., Hou, S. S., & Progovac, A. M. (2017). Trends in racial-ethnic disparities in access to mental health care, 2004-2012. *Psychiatric Services, 68*(1), 9–16. https://doi.org/10.1176/appi.ps.201500453

Cooper, M., Reilly, E. E., Siegel, J. A., Coniglio, K., Sadeh-Sharvit, S., Pisetsky, E. M., & Anderson, L. M. (2022). Eating disorders during the COVID-19 pandemic and quarantine: An overview of risks and recommendations for treatment and early intervention. *Eating Disorders, 30*(1), 54–76. https://doi.org/10.1080/10640266.2020.1790271

Crenshaw, K. (1993). Demarginalizing the intersection of race and sex: A Black feminist critique of antidiscrimination doctrine, feminist theory and antiracist politics. In D. K. Weisbert (Ed.), *Feminist legal theory: Foundations* (pp. 383–395). Temple University Press. (Original work published 1989)

Croll, J., Neumark-Sztainer, D., Story, M., & Ireland, M. (2002). Prevalence and risk and protective factors related to disordered eating behaviors among adolescents: Relationship to gender and ethnicity. *Journal of Adolescent Health, 31*(2), 166–175. https://doi.org/10.1016/s1054-139x(02)00368-3

Czepczor-Bernat, K., Swami, V., Modrzejewska, A., & Modrzejewska, J. (2021). COVID-19-related stress and anxiety, body mass index, eating disorder symptomatology, and body image in women from Poland: A cluster analysis approach. *Nutrients, 13*(4), 1384. https://www.mdpi.com/2072-6643/13/4/1384

Derlan Williams, C., Byrd, C. M., Quintana, S. M., Anicama, C., Kiang, L., & Umaña-Taylor, A. J. (2020). A lifespan model of ethnic-racial identity. *Research in Human Development*, *17*(2-3), 99–129 https://doi.org/10.1080/15427609.2020.1831882

Devoe, D. J., Han, A., Anderson, A., Katzman, D. K., Patten, S. B., Soumbasis, A., Flanagan, J., Paslakis, G., Vyver, E., Marcoux, G., & Dimitropoulos, G. (2023). The impact of the COVID-19 pandemic on eating disorders: A systematic review. *International Journal of Eating Disorders*, *56*(1), 5–25. https://doi.org/10.1002/eat.23704

Dressler, W. W., Balieiro, M. C., & Dos Santos, J. E. (2017). What you know, what you do, and how you feel: Cultural competence, cultural consonance, and psychological distress. *Frontiers in Psychology*, *8*, 2355. https://doi.org/10.3389/fpsyg.2017.02355

Eliason, M. J., Ingraham, N., Fogel, S. C., McElroy, J. A., Lorvick, J., Mauery, D. R., & Haynes, S. (2015). A systematic review of the literature on weight in sexual minority women. *Women's Health Issues*, *25*(2), 162–175. https://doi.org/10.1016/j.whi.2014.12.001

Fairburn, C. G., & Beglin, S. J. (1994). Assessment of eating disorders: Interview or self-report questionnaire? *International Journal of Eating Disorders*, *16*(4), 363–370. https://doi.org/10.1002/1098-108X(199412)16:4

Feldman, M. B., & Meyer, I. H. (2007). Eating disorders in diverse lesbian, gay, and bisexual populations. *International Journal of Eating Disorders, 40*(3), 218–226. https://doi.org/10.1002/eat.20360

Gard, M. C., & Freeman, C. P. (1996). The dismantling of a myth: A review of eating disorders and socioeconomic status. *International Journal of Eating Disorders*, *20*(1), 1–12. https://doi.org/10.1002/(SICI)1098-108X(199607)20:1<1::AID-EAT1>3.0.CO;2-M

Giel, K. E., Schurr, M., Zipfel, S., Junne, F., & Schag, K. (2021). Eating behaviour and symptom trajectories in patients with a history of binge eating disorder during COVID-19 pandemic. *European Eating Disorders Review*, *29*(4), 657–662. https://doi.org/https://doi.org/10.1002/erv.2837

Goel, N. J., Burnette, C. B., Weinstock, M., & Mazzeo, S. E. (2022). Eating Disorder Examination-Questionnaire: Evaluating factor structures and establishing measurement invariance with Asian/Hawaiian/Pacific Islander, Black, and White American college men. *International Journal of Eating Disorders*, *55*(4), 481–493. https://doi.org/10.1002/eat.23696

Goel, N. J., Thomas, B., Boutté, R. L., Kaur, B., & Mazzeo, S. E. (2022). "What will people say?": Mental health stigmatization as a barrier to eating disorder treatment-seeking for South Asian American women. *Asian American Journal of Psychology*. https://doi.org/10.1037/aap0000271

Grabe, S., & Hyde, J. S. (2006). Ethnicity and body dissatisfaction among women in the United States: A meta-analysis. *Psychological Bulletin*, *132*(4), 622–640. https://doi.org/10.1037/0033-2909.132.4.622

Grant, B. F., Chu, A., Sigman, R., Amsbary, M., Kali, J., Sugawara, Y., Jiao, R., Ren, W., & Goldstein, R. (2014). *National Epidemiologic Survey on alcohol and related conditions-lll (NESARC-lll).* National Institute on Alcohol Abuse and Alcoholism.

Grilo, C. M., Reas, D. L., Hopwood, C. J., & Crosby, R. D. (2015). Factor structure and construct validity of the Eating Disorder Examination-Questionnaire in college students: Further support for a modified brief version. *International Journal of Eating Disorders, 48*(3), 284–289. https://doi.org/10.1002/eat.22358

Hall, G. C. N., Ibaraki, A. Y., Huang, E. R., Marti, C. N., & Stice, E. (2016). A meta-analysis of cultural adaptations of psychological interventions. *Behavior Therapy, 47*(6), 993–1014. https://doi.org/10.1016/j.beth.2016.09.005

Hartman-Munick, S. M., Silverstein, S., Guss, C. E., Lopez, E., Calzo, J. P., & Gordon, A. R. (2021). Eating disorder screening and treatment experiences in transgender and gender diverse young adults. *Eating Behaviors, 41*, 101517. https://doi.org/https://doi.org/10.1016/j.eatbeh.2021.101517

Hazzard, V. M., Hooper, L., Larson, N., Loth, K. A., Wall, M. M., & Neumark-Sztainer, D. (2022). Associations between severe food insecurity and disordered eating behaviors from adolescence to young adulthood: Findings from a 10-year longitudinal study. *Preventive Medicine, 154*. https://doi.org/10.1016/j.ypmed.2021.106895

Higgins Neyland, M. K., Shank, L. M., Lavender, J. M., Burke, N. L., Rice, A., Gallagher-Teske, J., Markos, B., Faulkner, L. M., Djan, K. G., Kwarteng, E. A., LeMay-Russell, S., Parker, M. N., Schvey, N. A., Sbrocco, T., Wilfley, D. E., Ford, B., Ford, C., Haigney, M., Klein, D. A., ... Tanofsky-Kraff, M. (2022). Examination of the Interaction between parental military-status and race among non-Hispanic Black and non-Hispanic White adolescents with overweight/obesity. *Journal of Pediatric Psychology, 47*(7), 743–753. https://doi.org/10.1093/jpepsy/jsac008

Hill Collins, P. (1990). *Black feminist thought: knowledge, consciousness, and the politics of empowerment* [Bibliographies, Non-fiction]. Unwin Hyman.

Kambanis, P. E., Bottera, A. R., Mancuso, C. J., Spoor, S. P., Anderson, L. M., Burke, N. L., Eddy, K. T., Forbush, K. T., Keith, J. F., Lavender, J. M., Mensinger, J. L., Mujica, C., Nagata, J. M., Perez, M., & De Young, K. P. (2022). Eating Disorder Examination-Questionnaire and Clinical Impairment Assessment norms for intersectional identities using an MTurk sample. *International Journal of Eating Disorders, 55*(12), 1690–1707. https://doi.org/10.1002/eat.23799

Karvay, Y. G., Helion, C., Vafiadis, A., Smith, D. V., & Jarcho, J. M. (2023). Stress, trauma, and perception of eating behavior changes during the first weeks of the COVID-19 outbreak. *International Journal of Eating Disorders, 56*(1), 169–181.

Kendi, I. X. (2016). *Stamped from the beginning: The definitive history of racist ideas in America*. Bold Type Books.

Kennedy, G. A., Forman, S. F., Woods, E. R., Hergenroeder, A. C., Mammel, K. A., Fisher, M. M., Ornstein, R. M., Callahan, S. T., Golden, N. H., Kapphahn, C. J., Garber, A. K., Rome, E. S., & Richmond, T. K. (2017). History of overweight/obesity as predictor of care received at 1-year follow-up in adolescents with anorexia nervosa or atypical anorexia nervosa. *Journal of Adolescent Health, 60*(6), 674–679. https://doi.org/https://doi.org/10.1016/j.jadohealth.2017.01.001

Kim, B. H., Ranzenhofer, L., Stadterman, J., Karvay, Y. G., & Burke, N. L. (2021). Food insecurity and eating pathology in adolescents. *International Journal of Environmental Research and Public Health, 18*(17), 9155. https://doi.org/10.3390/ijerph18179155

Kirmayer, L. J. (2016). The future of cultural formulation. In R. Lewis-Fernández, N. K. Aggarwal, L. Hinton, D. E. Hinton, & L. J. Kirmayer (Eds.), *DSM-5 handbook on the cultural formulation interview* (pp. 267–285). American Psychiatric Publishing.

Le, T. P., Bradshaw, B. T., Pease, M., & Kuo, L. (2022). An intersectional investigation of Asian American men's muscularity-oriented disordered eating: Associations with gendered racism and masculine norms. *Eating Disorders, 30*(5), 492–514. https://doi.org/10.1080/10640266.2021.1924925

Le, T. P., Kuo, L., & Yamasaki, V. (2020). Gendered racial microaggressions, feminism, and Asian American women's eating pathology: An intersectional investigation. *Sex Roles, 83*, 127–142. https://doi.org/10.1007/s11199-019-01100-5

Liao, K. Y.-H., Shen, F. C., Cox, A. R., Miller, A. R., Sievers, B., & Werner, B. (2020). Asian American men's body image concerns: A focus group study. *Psychology of Men & Masculinities, 21*(3), 333–344. https://doi.org/10.1037/men0000234

Mangweth-Matzek, B., & Hoek, H. W. (2017). Epidemiology and treatment of eating disorders in men and women of middle and older age. *Current Opinions in Psychiatry, 30*(6), 446–451. https://doi.org/10.1097/yco.0000000000000356

Marrast, L., Himmelstein, D. U., & Woolhandler, S. (2016). Racial and ethnic disparities in mental health care for children and young adults: A national study. *International Journal of Health Services, 46*(4), 810–824. https://doi.org/10.1177/0020731416662736

McEntee, M. L., Serier, K. N., Smith, J. M., & Smith, J. E. (2021). The sum is greater than its parts: Intersectionality and measurement validity of the Eating Disorder Examination Questionnaire (EDE-Q) in Latinx undergraduates in the United States. *Sex Roles, 84*, 102–111. https://doi.org/10.1007/s11199-020-01149-7

Merlo, J. (2018). Multilevel analysis of individual heterogeneity and discriminatory accuracy (MAIHDA) within an intersectional framework. *Social Science & Medicine, 203*, 74–80. https://doi.org/10.1016/j.socscimed.2017.12.026

Monocello, L. T., & Dressler, W. W. (2022). Cultural consonance, body image, and disordered eating among young South Korean men. *Social Science & Medicine, 314*, 115486. https://doi.org/10.1016/j.socscimed.2022.115486

Murray, S. B., Nagata, J. M., Griffiths, S., Calzo, J. P., Brown, T. A., Mitchison, D., Blashill, A. J., & Mond, J. M. (2017). The enigma of male eating disorders: A critical review and synthesis. *Clinical Psychology Review, 57*, 1–11. https://doi.org/10.1016/j.cpr.2017.08.001

National Association of Social Workers. (2015). *Standards and indicators for cultural competence in social work practice*. NASW Press.

Neumark-Sztainer, D., Falkner, N., Story, M., Perry, C., Hannan, P. J., & Mulert, S. (2002). Weight-teasing among adolescents: Correlations with weight status and disordered eating behaviors. *International Journal of Obesity and Related Metabolic Disorders, 26*(1), 123–131. https://doi.org/10.1038/sj.ijo.0801853

Neumark-Sztainer, D., Wall, M., Larson, N. I., Eisenberg, M. E., & Loth, K. (2011). Dieting and disordered eating behaviors from adolescence to young adulthood: Findings from a 10-year longitudinal study. *Journal of American Dietetic Association*, *111*(7), 1004–1011. https://doi.org/10.1016/j.jada.2011.04.012

Osa, M. L., Kelly, N. R., & Calogero, R. M. (2022). Disordered eating symptoms as a function of perceived weight status and race: An intersectional examination. *Body Image*, *43*, 337–347. https://doi.org/10.1016/j.bodyim.2022.09.012

Osa, M. L., Siegel, J., Meadows, A., Elbe, C., & Calogero, R. M. (2021). Stigmatizing effects of weight status on lay perceptions of eating disorder-related distress. *Eating Disorders*, *30*(1), 99–109. https://doi.org/10.1080/10640266.2020.1855571

Panza, E., Fehling, K. B., Pantalone, D. W., Dodson, S., & Selby, E. A. (2021). Multiply marginalized: Linking minority stress due to sexual orientation, gender, and weight to dysregulated eating among sexual minority women of higher body weight. *Psychology of Sexual Orientation and Gender Diversity*, *8*(4), 420–428. https://doi.org/10.1037/sgd0000431

Parker, J. E., Endersa, C. K., Mujahidb, M. S., Laraiac, B. A., Epeld, E. S., & Tomiyamaa, A. J. (2022). Prospective relationships between skin color satisfaction, body satisfaction, and binge eating in Black girls. *Body Image*, *41*, 342–353. https://doi.org/10.1016/j.bodyim.2022.04.004

Planey, A. M., Smith, S. M., Moore, S., & Walker, T. D. (2019). Barriers and facilitators to mental help-seeking among African American youth and their families: A systematic review study. *Children and Youth Services Review*, *101*, 190–200. https://doi.org/10.1016/j.childyouth.2019.04.001

Ramirez, A. L., Trujillo-ChiVacuán, E., & Perez, M. (2018). Considerations in the treatment of eating disorders among ethnic minorities. In L. K. Anderson, S. B. Murray, & W. H. Kaye (Eds.), *Clinical handbook of complex and atypical eating disorders.* (pp. 344–362). Oxford University Press.

Rodgers, R. F., Berry, R., & Franko, D. L. (2018). Eating disorders in ethnic minorities: An update. *Current Psychiatry Reports*, *20*(10), 90. https://doi.org/10.1007/s11920-018-0938-3

Rodgers, R. F., Lombardo, C., Cerolini, S., Franko, D. L., Omori, M., Fuller-Tyszkiewicz, M., Linardon, J., Courtet, P., & Guillaume, S. (2020). The impact of the COVID-19 pandemic on eating disorder risk and symptoms. *International Journal of Eating Disorders*, *53*(7), 1166–1170. https://doi.org/https://doi.org/10.1002/eat.23318

Rodgers, R. F., Watts, A. W., Austin, S. B., Haines, J., & Neumark-Sztainer, D. (2017). Disordered eating in ethnic minority adolescents with overweight. *International Journal of Eating Disorders*, *50*(6), 665–671. https://doi.org/10.1002/eat.22652

Schaefer, L. M., Smith, K. E., Leonard, R., Wetterneck, C., Smith, B., Farrell, N., Riemann, B. C., Frederick, D. A., Schaumberg, K., Klump, K. L., Anderson, D. A., & Thompson, J. K. (2018). Identifying a male clinical cutoff on the Eating Disorder Examination-Questionnaire (EDE-Q). *International Journal of Eating Disorders*, *51*(12), 1357–1360. https://doi.org/10.1002/eat.22972

Schneider, J., Pegram, G., Gibson, B., Talamonti, D., Tinoco, A., Craddock, N., Matheson, E., & Forshaw, M. (2023). A mixed-studies systematic review of the experiences of body image, disordered eating, and eating disorders during the COVID-19 pandemic. *International Journal of Eating Disorders*, *56*(1), 26–67. https://doi.org/10.1002/eat.23706

Shepherd, B. F., Brochu, P. M., & Rodriguez-Seijas, C. (2022). A critical examination of disparities in eating disorder symptoms by sexual orientation among U.S. adults in the NESARC-III. *International Journal of Eating Disorders*, *55*(6), 790–800. https://doi.org/10.1002/eat.23717

Shiffman, S., Stone, A. A., & Hufford, M. R. (2008). Ecological momentary assessment. *Annual Review of Clinical Psychology*, *4*, 1–32. https://doi.org/10.1146/annurev.clinpsy.3.022806.091415

Smolak, L., & Piran, N. (2012). Gender and the prevention of eating disorders. In G. McVey, M. P. Levine, N. Piran, & H. B. Ferguson (Eds.), *Preventing eating-related and weight-related disorders: collaborative research, advocacy, and policy change.* (pp. 199–222). Wilfrid Laurier University Press.

Soh, N. L.-W., & Walter, G. (2013). Publications on cross-cultural aspects of eating disorders. *Journal of Eating Disorders*, *1*(1), 4. https://doi.org/10.1186/2050-2974-1-4

Sonneville, K., & Lipson, S. (2018). Disparities in eating disorder diagnosis and treatment according to weight status, race/ethnicity, socioeconomic background, and sex among college students. *International Journal of Eating Disorders*, *51*(6), 518–526. https://doi.org/10.1002/eat.22846

Stadterman, J., Karvay, Y. G., Feuerstahler, L., & Burke, N. L. (2022). Comparison of ad libitum snack consumption and acquisition between adolescents living with food security and food insecurity: A stage 1 registered report. *International Journal of Eating Disorders*, *55*(3), 406–414. https://doi.org/10.1002/eat.23693

Strother, E., Lemberg, R., Stanford, S. C., & Turberville, D. (2012). Eating disorders in men: Underdiagnosed, undertreated, and misunderstood. *Eating Disorders*, *20*(5), 346–355. https://doi.org/10.1080/10640266.2012.715512

Tanofsky-Kraff, M., Sbrocco, T., Theim, K. R., Cohen, L. A., Mackey, E. R., Stice, E., Henderson, J. L., McCreight, S. J., Bryant, E. J., & Stephens, M. B. (2013). Obesity and the U.S. military family. *Obesity* *21*(11), 2205–2220. https://doi.org/10.1002/oby.20566

Udo, T., & Grilo, C. M. (2018). Prevalence and correlates of DSM-5-defined eating disorders in a nationally representative sample of U.S. adults. *Biological Psychiatry*, *84*(5), 345–354. https://doi.org/10.1016/j.biopsych.2018.03.014

U.S. Department of Health and Human Services Office of Minority Health. (2016). *National standards for culturally and linguistically appropriate services in health care from the health and human services department's office of minority health*.

Voelker, D. K., Reel, J. J., & Greenleaf, C. (2015). Weight status and body image perceptions in adolescents: Current perspectives. *Adolescent Health, Medicine and Therapeutics*, *6*, 149–158. https://doi.org/10.2147/AHMT.S68344

Wilfred, S. A., & Lundgren, J. D. (2021). The Double Consciousness Body Image Scale: A body image assessment centering the experiences of Black women. *International Journal of Eating Disorders*, *54*(10), 1771–1781. https://doi.org/10.1002/eat.23581

CHAPTER 2

ETHICAL AND SOCIAL ISSUES IN THE TREATMENT OF EATING DISORDERS

Melinda Parisi Cummings

Managing ethical and social concerns are an inevitable part of clinical practice across disciplines. When and how to terminate treatment, how to manage risk, how to maximize access to care, how to preserve clients' autonomy, among many others, are questions treatment providers regularly face. While clear guidelines and prescriptions for conduct are available in many cases, at other times, choosing an appropriate course of action is anything but straightforward. Conflicting priorities coupled with limited available guidance substantially complicate decision-making. Navigating such matters can be considerably more challenging when applied to the treatment of eating disorders (EDs), owing to their complexity and profound consequences, which may be life-threatening. Very often, the stakes are high, and no course of action may prove entirely satisfying.

Each healthcare discipline's code of ethics is guided by core values that inform decision-making. For example, the American Psychological Association's (2017) *Ethical Principles of Psychologists and Code of Conduct* outlines five aspirational principles. The first, Beneficence and Nonmaleficence, is concerned with taking actions intended to provide benefit, avoid or minimize harm, and safeguard the welfare and rights of others. The second principle, Fidelity and Responsibility, centers on the importance

Counseling Individuals With Eating Disorders: An Intersectional Approach, pp. 25–40

of establishing trusting relationships and being aware of professional obligations both in one's immediate communities and more broadly (i.e., the larger society). The principle of Integrity speaks to being truthful in all professional activities, and the principle of Justice calls for fairness, avoiding bias, and promoting equal access to services. Lastly, the principle of Respect for People's Rights and Dignity calls for an appreciation of the worth of all people as well as their rights to autonomy, privacy, and confidentiality. Similar values are reflected in the ethics codes of other disciplines engaged in the treatment of EDs, such as those of the American Medical Association (2016), the Academy of Nutrition and Dietetics/Commission on Dietetic Registration (2018), the National Association of Social Workers (2017), and the American Counseling Association (2014) and they communicate a commitment to equity and social justice.

While the ethical principles are generally clear, they frequently conflict in the treatment of EDs. Treatment interventions aimed at reducing the potential for harm (such as hospitalization and imposed weight gain) are frequently at odds with patients' own goals; as such, patients may experience them as coercive, threatening their autonomy (Long, 2014). Patients may similarly experience interventions such as monitoring meals or bathroom visits as an invasion of privacy. Yet, there is a clear duty to protect the welfare of vulnerable patients. The principles of fidelity and justice may similarly conflict. The importance of using evidence-based practices is implied by the value of fidelity. However, much of the extant research on assessment and treatment for EDs has been conducted with White cisgender, female-identifying participants (Calzo et al., 2021; Mikhail & Klump, 2021; Murray et al., 2017). Consequently, important diversity and other contextual considerations may not be adequately addressed by current treatment models, especially with respect to intersectionality. Limitations in the present understanding of EDs pose a threat to justice if interventions are not similarly effective across members of diverse groups.

While ethical conflicts are not unique to the treatment of EDs, certain considerations make treatment of EDs especially ethically challenging. The symptoms associated with EDs are inherently dangerous and contribute to risk for multiple medical complications, premature mortality, and suicide (Chesney et al., 2014; Mehler & Andersen, 2022; Smith et al., 2018).

At the same time, individuals with EDs often have low motivation to change their behaviors, as the disorder's central features are often valued and perceived as adaptive (Denison-Day et al., 2018). Individuals with anorexia nervosa (AN), in particular, are typically ambivalent about change and may even be opposed to it; presentations often range from deliberate denial or refusal of self-disclosure (i.e., hiding symptoms), to unintentional lack of recognition of a problem resulting from distorted information processing or impaired self-awareness (a condition called anosognosia;

Vandereycken, 2006). Indeed, what makes EDs so ethically challenging is that they are often desired and vigorously defended by the individual, while obviously self-destructive and even deadly (Giordano, 2005). Given this quandary, how to honor the client's wishes (and thus respect autonomy) while providing benefit and avoiding harm is a common ethical challenge encountered by clinicians. A similar dilemma exists when the client expresses the desire to remain at a lower level of care than is clinically indicated.

Faced with such challenges, treatment professionals often experience their own distress, including anxiety, anger, helplessness, and hopelessness (Giordano, 2005). Such emotions may lead to a continuum of unproductive and likely harmful responses: at one end, unproductive power struggles or ultimatums with abrupt treatment endings (e.g., abandoning a "difficult" patient); at the other, an erosion of active treatment into one that lacks clear goals or indicators of progress (Parisi Cummings & Erckert, 2020). As effective and ethical decision-making may be hindered by clinicians' frustrations, practical strategies for managing clinician emotions are critical. Some of these may include:

- Reframing the challenge from one of managing a demanding patient to one of caring for an individual who has a difficult-to-treat illness.
- Avoiding isolation by working as part of a treatment team that communicates frequently and effectively, and by making use of professional consultation.
- Practicing one's own self-care, emotional regulation, and distress tolerance skills.
- Choosing one's battles wisely by allowing choices within the structure of a clear treatment plan.
- Recognizing and applauding even the smallest of changes.
- Embracing the complexity inherent to working in this specialty area.

CAPACITY, CONSENT, AND REJECTION OF TREATMENT

A key consideration in the discussion of patient autonomy is that of capacity. The right to voluntary agreement to treatment is protected in most jurisdictions and is a fundamental element of informed consent. As such, individuals have the right to refuse treatment, even if that may result in adverse outcomes (including death), *provided* they have the capacity to understand the consequences of those decisions (Giordano, 2005). An essential question, therefore, is whether or not the ED, given the nature of the illness itself, interferes with the individual's ability to understand the implications of their choices. In other words, does the distortion that is central to these disorders preclude the possibility of a truly autonomous choice? While a thorough analysis of the issues involved in this matter is beyond the scope of this chapter (see Giordano [2005] for a comprehensive discussion), Campbell and Aulisio (2012) argued that assuming incapacity for those with mental illness perpetuates both the stigma associated with mental illness and an untenable belief in mind-body dualism. As such, capacity in those with EDs should be presumed unless there are clear indicators to the contrary.

Nowhere is this dilemma more complicated than in considering the ability of those with EDs to reject life-saving treatment. In limited cases, individuals with EDs have been granted the right to refuse life-saving measures, typically with the agreement of their family members and institutions' ethics committees (Giordano, 2010; Goldner et al., 1997; Tan & Hope, 2008; Tan et al., 2003). Overall, however, the literature supports implementing coercive interventions when patients lack capacity and when those interventions are thought to be life-saving (Westmoreland et al., 2017).

The need to override a patient's autonomy in order to protect from harm is a situation that is not exclusive to the treatment of EDs, but the decision to do so should not be made lightly or out of anger (e.g., arising from a control battle). A paternalistic intervention is one that interferes with an individual's freedom of choice and is implemented to protect that individual's welfare (i.e., it is in the individual's best interest; Giordano, 2005). It prioritizes beneficence over autonomy. Paternalism is at the core of interventions such as involuntary commitment and is often ethically justified (Matusek & Wright, 2010).

Westmoreland and Mehler (2016) argued that because the best outcomes (including prevention of chronicity) are obtained with a full course of treatment that is initiated early in the course of illness, compulsory treatment may not only be life-saving but essential to recovery overall. This consideration is especially appropriate in the treatment of children and adolescents, for whom intensive treatment is often critical due to their developmental stage and initiated by parents or other caregivers. Additionally, children and adolescents may not yet have the experience and cognitive skills to make sound decisions on their own. Many adults may also benefit from coercive treatment, which does not need to be involuntary in a legal sense to be perceived as compulsory. Some patients have described feeling relieved that decisions were taken out of their hands as they struggled with guilt, shame, and ambivalence (Bohon & McCurdy, 2014). Watson and colleagues (2000) found similar rates of short-term weight gain in involuntarily and voluntarily admitted patients. Notably, they found that most of the patients who had been treated involuntarily later acknowledged that they had needed treatment despite their unwillingness, and were then more positively inclined toward treatment. In addition, the cognitive symptoms associated with EDs (especially AN), such as severe body image distortion, diminished cognitive flexibility, and lack of insight call into question patients' ability to fully appreciate the impact of their decision-making and therefore their capacity to refuse treatment (Geppert, 2015). Taken together, these considerations provide important context when assessing risks and benefits of compulsory treatment. Indeed, an overemphasis on autonomy at the expense of patient welfare can lead to adverse outcomes, including death and chronicity.

At the same time, enacting involuntary treatment is logistically difficult. Even when healthcare providers believe an adult lacks capacity, they may only override that individual's declared wishes upon a court's determination that the individual is incapacitated to make medical decisions (specific legal procedures and requirements vary by jurisdiction). While compulsory treatment may be needed, it risks rupturing the relationship between patients and their treatment providers and diminishing treatment engagement (Douzenis & Michopoulos, 2015). Furthermore, it is not in itself curative, nor does it always prove to be effective. For example, Westmoreland and Mehler (2016) found that while most patients involuntarily committed to a specialty ED program benefitted from their treatment, involuntary treatment did not appear to be helpful for 24% of them. In a systematic review of the impact of involuntary treatment for AN, Douzenis and Michopoulos (2015) concluded that results are controversial with a mix of benefits and adverse consequences; as such, consensus on the best course of action remains elusive. Overall, these authors recommend implementing coercive, life-saving treatment in the face of immediate risk of death, while recognizing that this may have long-term negative impacts. Ultimately, the decision to treat patients against their will must be carefully considered on a case-by-case basis and remain rooted in principles such as compassion and respect for dignity.

While most patients admitted for inpatient ED care do so voluntarily and of their own accord, perceived coercion is a common feature of more restrictive levels of care. This may occur through pressure from others (e.g., clinicians, family members, or employers) to accept voluntary admission (Schreyer et al., 2016) as well as standard invasive interventions such as bathroom observation, prescribed feeding, or restriction of movement to conserve energy (Bohon & McCurdy, 2014). While these are valuable practices that may well be beneficial to the patient (especially in the long term) and ethically justified under the principle of paternalism, it is important to remain mindful that these actions do represent a clear infringement on patients' autonomy. As such, their use must be carefully considered and weighed against the threat of harm to the patient and the benefits they are likely to provide. Ethical practice dictates choosing the least restrictive interventions that are appropriate to the individual patient's needs, and thoroughly and compassionately explaining the rationale for those interventions. Of course, the choice of interventions should be based on a thorough assessment of patient needs rather than for the convenience of clinicians or retribution for difficult behavior. Use of threats or deception should be considered only as a last resort and in very limited circumstances (Blumenthal-Barby et al., 2013).

USE OF HARM-REDUCING INTERVENTIONS

The collaborative approach inherent to a harm-reduction model may represent a viable alternative to coercive interventions for patients with long-standing EDs, such as those with severe and enduring AN (SE-AN; Russell et al., 2019; Westmoreland & Mehler, 2016; Yager, 2020). In this treatment paradigm, goals are collaboratively set, with improvements in quality of life prioritized over weight restoration in an attempt to maintain long-term treatment engagement. Individuals are helped to actively engage in life, amplify their strengths, and live purposefully in spite of persisting ED symptoms (Russell et al., 2019). It is important to note that this approach does not preclude the possibility of full recovery from the ED (including full weight restoration and other symptom resolution), nor does it represent "giving up" on the patient. Rather, it espouses a stance of professional humility, recognizing that patients have important information about what does and does not work for them that should be incorporated into treatment planning, which helps to avoid power struggles and validate patients' own valuable knowledge of themselves and their illness (Bamford & Mountford, 2012). Elwyn (2023) poignantly described the benefit of such an approach from the perspective of one with lived experience:

> Therapy was approached from a collaborative, trauma-informed, harm-reductive approach that affirmed my gender, sexuality and neurotype, and centered my strengths. Through this work, I have regained a sense of self-connection, meaning in life, and was able to continue university study, casual work, and to live independently. It was consistently predicted throughout my years of earlier treatment that I would be too debilitated by AN to engage in these life domains meaningfully. (p. 6)

While promising, support for this approach is largely conceptual rather than empirical. One randomized controlled trial (Touyz et al., 2013) did find that two treatment approaches prioritizing quality of life and harm reduction resulted in meaningful improvements in social adjustment and other life domains in addition to weight gain and decreases in ED symptoms in women with long-standing AN. Of note, treatment retention rates were high despite the typically high dropout rates found in this population. Additional empirical work in this area is needed to identify strategies for effectively engaging and retaining patients in treatment, improving quality of life, and reducing core symptoms.

BARRIERS TO ACCESSING CARE

Individual-level barriers to care, such as ambivalence and treatment-resistant illness, are well known to ED clinicians. However, addressing less obvious social impediments is essential for a more complete understanding of those with EDs, and to foster equal access to services (thus serving the ethical principle of Justice). Regrettably, even when they desire treatment, many patients with EDs face systemic barriers to accessing it, particularly in the United States and other countries where care is significantly funded by private insurers (Wonderlich et al., 2020). Many U.S.-based treatment settings offering higher levels of care (e.g., residential and partial hospitalization programs) do not accept public insurance for payment (Guarda et al., 2018), resulting in greatly diminished choices and access to specialty services. Similarly, many individual clinicians who provide specialized, evidence-based care do not participate in public insurance programs; many times they do not participate with any insurers. Patients with public insurance typically rely on academic medical centers or other nonprofit facilities, which may be located at large distances from them, offer treatment at an intensity not matched to their need, or lack providers with the appropriate specialty training. Owing to the accompanying disability, individuals with a chronic course of illness, such as those with SE-AN, are disproportionately covered by public insurance (Guarda et al., 2018; Wonderlich, 2020), as are those with limited economic resources. For patients with children, inadequate access to affordable and quality childcare places another undue burden on an already overtaxed individual. These considerations further complicate ethical decision-making and speak to the need for system-level advocacy and change.

A continued lack of recognition of EDs in certain populations poses additional barriers to accessing care. EDs have been stereotyped as a problem primarily afflicting females who are thin, White, and affluent, despite abundant data to the contrary (Solmi et al., 2016; Sonneville & Lipson, 2018; Udo & Grillo, 2018). Consequently, EDs are both underdiagnosed and undertreated in individuals who do not fit this profile. For example, race-related bias about EDs has been found to hamper recognition of disordered eating among people of color in multiple quantitative studies (e.g., Becker et al., 2003; Cachelin & Striegel-Moore 2006; Gordon et al., 2006). Using qualitative research methodology, Becker et al. (2010) found stereotypes about EDs to negatively impact care for some individuals; specifically, some African American study participants felt that their ED symptoms were disregarded by clinicians who did not expect them in African American patients. More recently, Sonneville and Lipson (2018) found that among undergraduate and graduate students reporting ED symptoms, White students were more likely to have received an ED diagnosis than students of color. Similar findings have been obtained when considering males with EDs, who are more likely than females to be misdiagnosed and less likely to receive an ED diagnosis even when describing identical symptoms (Murray et al., 2017). In a qualitative investigation, Whitney and colleagues (2023) found that mothers of sons with EDs reported that physicians often did not consider an ED diagnosis for their sons or were dismissive of their concerns about their sons' behavior.

Similarly, much of the research on the diagnosis and treatment of EDs focuses on patients who are young, White, and female (Mikhail & Klump, 2021; Murray et al., 2017), and often rely on clinical samples. Given known barriers to care, reliance on clinical samples in ED research helps to maintain outdated perceptions about who develops EDs and to perpetuate disparities in accessing treatment (Sonneville & Lipson, 2018). As such, there are critical gaps in our understanding of EDs in diverse populations, especially with respect to intersectionality. Recent advances have been made in developing culturally sensitive and effective diagnostic criteria, assessments, and interventions (Rodgers et al., 2018), though continued work in this area is essential. In particular, the cumulative effect of discrimination, prejudice, and harassment is an important area for further study. The impact of factors that may contribute to the development of EDs in diverse groups, such as sexual minority stress, acculturative stress, or race-based traumatic stress, needs to be incorporated into assessment, case conceptualization, and treatment planning.

A related issue is the failure to recognize EDs and disordered eating in those with higher-weight bodies. Per the *Diagnostic and Statistical Manual of Mental Disorders* (DSM-5-TR; American Psychiatric Association, 2022) while the diagnosis of AN requires an individual to be at a "significantly low weight," weight is not a requisite consideration for the diagnosis of bulimia nervosa (BN), avoidant/restrictive food intake disorder (ARFID), and binge eating disorder (BED). Furthermore, atypical AN, noted when all criteria for AN have been met by an individual who has lost significant weight but is not underweight, has been identified as an example of "other specified feeding and EDs" (OSFED). EDs clearly affect people of all sizes. It is essential to appreciate this fact, as significant physical and psychological complications can occur at all points along the spectrum of size and weight (Peebles et al., 2010; Sawyer et al., 2016).

There also is an erroneous belief that patients in larger bodies have BED verus other EDs (Spotts-De Lazzer & Muhlheim, 2019). These biases appear to be operating in both professionals and the general public. Using body mass index (BMI) to define weight status among a sample of college students reporting ED symptoms, Sonneville and Lipson (2018) found that students who were classified as underweight (BMI <18.5) were more likely than those classified as being at a healthy weight (BMI of 18.5–24.9) to perceive a need for treatment, have been diagnosed with an ED, and have received treatment. Furthermore, students classified as being overweight (BMI of 25.0–29.9) or obese (BMI ≥30) were less likely to have been diagnosed with an ED than those identified as being at a healthy weight. These results are particularly concerning in light of Forney and colleagues' (2017) finding that more than a quarter of adults with atypical AN would be categorized as overweight or obese using BMI as a marker. In a systematic review centered on atypical AN, Harrop and colleagues (2021) noted that while atypical AN is generally more prevalent than traditional AN, those with atypical AN are less likely to be referred to and receive specialized ED treatment. Of further concern, dieting/weight loss is a known risk factor for the development of EDs (Hilbert et al., 2014; Patton, et al., 1999). Given that dieting/weight loss is often advised for those in higher-weight bodies, it is probable that many individuals with atypical AN have not only been misdiagnosed or undiagnosed with an ED but are encouraged to pursue interventions that likely contribute to further harm. It is essential that screening and treatment for restrictive EDs occur across the weight continuum, not just in those individuals perceived to be at a low weight. Further attention to bias in the recognition of EDs is especially important when considering the intersection of weight, race, gender, and other contextual considerations.

TERMINAL ANOREXIA AND MEDICAL ASSISTANCE IN DYING

A particularly controversial issue that has recently emerged is the concept of terminal AN, defined to assist in considering a patient's decision to terminate active treatment, engage in palliative care, or even seek medical assistance in dying (MAiD). Discussion of terminal AN was initiated by Gaudiani and colleagues (2022) in a case report discussing the care of three patients, one of whom served as a posthumous co-author. They posited that, for a small subset of individuals with SE-AN who "simply cannot continue to fight" (p. 1), treatment may be both harmful and futile. As such, they proposed several criteria for defining terminal AN in order to begin to identify consensus criteria and a framework for making care decisions, so that patients with AN (provided they retain capacity) can be given the same considerations and rights as others with terminal illness, including the provision of MAiD where legal. Their proposed criteria include:

1. Having a diagnosis of AN
2. Being at least 30 years of age
3. Having received previous care that is multidisciplinary, of high quality, and focused on the treatment of the ED
4. Having decision-making capacity and

    a. consistently expressing the view that continued change-oriented ED treatment would be futile, and
    b. understanding that their death will result from stopping active treatment.

These authors justifiably highlight the ethical imperative to honor the autonomy of individuals who still want to work toward recovery by continuing to support active ED treatment for as long as they desire it, regardless of the length or severity of illness or the presence of treatment-interfering behaviors. Further, they explicitly exclude the application of a terminal diagnosis to a younger patient (i.e., under the age of 30).

Despite these caveats, there are substantial concerns regarding both the proposed criteria and the construct itself. As previously discussed, patients with EDs often prompt strong emotions in clinicians and, at times, counterproductive behaviors. It is not difficult to envision a scenario in which clinical decision-making, including labeling a patient's course of illness as "terminal," is inappropriately influenced by the clinician's own sense of anger, helplessness, or fatigue. Moreover, change-oriented ED treatment is not limited to interventions aimed primarily at resolving core symptoms; indeed, alternatives such as a harm-reduction approach or a focus on quality of life can result in meaningful progress (Russell et al., 2019; Touyz et al., 2013).

In a review of five published responses to the initial conceptualization of terminal anorexia, Crow (2023) identified several concerns including the current lack of standardization of high quality care, differential access to high-quality care, the complexity of determining capacity, and problems with the age criterion. Furthermore, he argued that, since the ability to predict outcomes is presently lacking, it is impossible to draw reliable conclusions about futility for a specific patient and that, as such, the construct should therefore not be used. Ultimately, while terminal AN is a potentially useful construct, an appreciation of its complexity and potential for harm must be recognized. Clearer definitions, more objective markers, and more robust predictors of futility need to be identified and agreed upon prior to more widespread adoption. While the work of Gaudiani and colleagues (2022) represents an important step in this discussion, the application of the construct is currently premature.

CONCLUSIONS

The treatment of EDs is frequently complicated by ethical dilemmas involving specific individuals and/or by social issues that exert a negative impact on a broader population. Ethical quandaries require careful consideration on a case-by-case basis and are best approached using a comprehensive decision-making model, beginning with identification of the conflicting ethical principles (Knapp et al., 2015). While such models can be applied to individuals facing systemic barriers, social issues require structural solutions and a commitment to fostering equal access to care.

Recommendations

1. External, social barriers to care should be considered in addition to internal barriers (such as ambivalence) when making decisions around treatment refusal.
2. Decision-making around treatment refusal and the use of coercive interventions need to be made on a case-by-case basis, using validated ethical decision-making models. Given multi-layered and complex individual differences, decisions are best approached in a tailored fashion rather than by using rigid policies and protocols.
3. For patients with long-standing EDs, a harm-reduction approach may be an appropriate alternative to coercive interventions and may help to retain patients in treatment.
4. Clinicians should include cultural, gender-related, and other important contextual considerations, including intersectionality, in case conceptualizations and treatment planning.
5. Researchers should make concerted efforts to diversify their samples, to include more people of color, people with diverse body sizes, males, sexual minorities, and gender minorities. In addition, these demographic characteristics should be reported when describing samples.
6. Clinicians should make efforts to become more aware of their biases and attend to them accordingly (e.g., through additional educa-

tion), to ensure inaccurate stereotypes do not cause harm by interfering with appropriate diagnosis and treatment planning.
7. Increased advocacy from ED clinicians, researchers, and other stakeholders is essential for developing structural solutions to challenges in accessing care.

DISCUSSION QUESTIONS

1. Which ethical principles are most likely to conflict in the treatment of those with eating disorders, and why?
2. What are some challenges that researchers are likely to encounter in attempting to diversify their samples?
3. What are some advocacy activities that can be taken to improve access to treatment?
4. How might clinicians work to both identify and challenge their biases?

REFERENCES

Academy of Nutrition and Dietetics and Commission on Dietetic Registration. (2018). *Code of ethics for the nutrition and dietetics profession*. https://www.cdrnet.org/vault/2459/web/CodeofEthicsHandout.pdf

American Counseling Association. (2014). *ACA code of ethics*. https://www.counseling.org/resources/aca-code-of-ethics.pdf

American Medical Association. (2016). *AMA principles of medical ethics*. https://www.ama-assn.org/delivering-care/ama-principles-medical-ethics

American Psychiatric Association. (2022). *Diagnostic and statistical manual of mental disorders* (5th ed., text rev.). https://doi.org/10.1176/appi.books.9780890425787

American Psychological Association. (2017). *Ethical principles of psychologists and code of conduct*. https://www.apa.org/ethics/code/ethics-code-2017.pdf

Bamford, B. H., & Mountford, V. A. (2012). Cognitive behavioural therapy for individuals with longstanding anorexia nervosa: Adaptations, clinician survival and system issues. *European Eating Disorders Review*, *20*, 49–59.

Becker, A. E., Franko, D. L., Speck, A., & Herzog, D. B. (2003). Ethnicity and differential access to care for eating disorder symptoms. *International Journal of Eating Disorders*, *33*(2), 205–212.

Becker, A. E., Hadley Arrindell, A., Perloe, A., Fay, K., & Striegel Moore, R. H. (2010). A qualitative study of perceived social barriers to care for eating disorders: Perspectives from ethnically diverse health care consumers. *International Journal of Eating Disorders*, *43*(7), 633–647.

Blumenthal-Barby, J. S., McCullough, L. B., Krieger, H., & Coverdale, J. (2013). Methods of influencing the decisions of psychiatric patients: An ethical analysis. *Harvard Review of Psychiatry, 21*(5), 275-279. https://doi.org/10.1097/HRP.0b013e3182a75d4f

Bohon, C., & McCurdy, D. (2014). Ethical considerations in the treatment of eating disorders. *Ethics Commentary, 12*(4), 409–413.

Cachelin, F. M., & Striegel-Moore, R. H. (2006). Help seeking and barriers to treatment in a community sample of Mexican American and European American women with eating disorders. *International Journal of Eating Disorders, 39*, 154–161.

Calzo, J. P., Lopez, E. E., Siverstein, S., Brown, T. A., & Blashill, A. J. (2020). Where is the evidence of evidence-based treatment for LGBTQIA+ individuals experiencing eating disorders? In Tortolani, C. C., Goldschmidt, A. B., & Le Grange, D. (Eds.), *Adapting evidence-based eating disorder treatments for novel populations and settings*. Routledge.

Campbell, A. T., & Aulisio, M. P. (2012). The stigma of "mental" illness: End stage anorexia and treatment refusal. *International Journal of Eating Disorders 45*(5), 627–634.

Chesney, E., Goodwin, G. M., & Fazel, S. (2014). Risks of all-cause and suicide mortality in mental disorders: A metareview. *World Psychiatry, 13*(2), 153–160.

Crow, S. (2023). Terminal anorexia nervosa cannot currently be identified. *International Journal of Eating Disorders, 56*(7), 1329–1334.

Denison-Day, J., Appleton, K. M., Newell, C., & Muir, S. (2018). Improving motivation to change amongst individuals with eating disorders: A systematic review. *International Journal of Eating Disorders, 51*(9) 1033–1050.

Douzenis, A., & Michopoulos, I. (2015). Involuntary admission: The case of anorexia nervosa. *International Journal of Law and Psychiatry, 39*, 31–35.

Elwyn, R. (2023). A lived experience response to the proposed diagnosis of terminal anorexia nervosa: Learning from iatrogenic harm, ambivalence and enduring hope. *Journal of Eating Disorders, 11*(2). https://doi.org/10.1186/s40337-022-00729-0

Forney, K. J., Brown, T. A., Holland-Carter, L. A., Kennedy, G. A., & Keel, P. K. (2017). Defining "significant weight loss" in atypical anorexia nervosa. *International Journal of Eating Disorders, 50*(8), 952–962. https://doi.org/10.1002/eat.22717

Gaudiani, J. L., Bogetz, A., & Yager, J. (2022). Terminal anorexia nervosa: three cases and proposed clinical characteristics. *Journal of Eating Disorders, 10*(23).

Geppert, C. M. A. (2015). Futility in chronic anorexia nervosa: A concept whose time has not yet come. *American Journal of Bioethics, 15*(7), 34–43. https://doi.org/10.1080/15265161.2015.1039720

Goldner, E. M., Birmingham, C. L., & Smye, V. (1997). Addressing treatment refusal in anorexia nervosa: Clinical, ethical, and legal considerations. In D. M. Garner & P. E. Garfinkel (Eds.), *Handbook of treatment for eating disorders* (pp. 450–461). Guilford Press.

Giordano, S. (2005). *Understanding eating disorders: Conceptual and ethical issues in the treatment of anorexia and bulimia nervosa*. Oxford.

Giordano, S. (2010). Anorexia and refusal of life-saving treatment: The moral place of competence, suffering, and the family. *Philosophy, Psychiatry, & Psychology, 17*, 143–154.

Gordon, K. H., Brattole, M. M. Wingate, L. R., & Joiner, T. E. (2006). The impact of client race on clinician detection of eating disorders. *Behavior Therapy, 37*(4), 319–325.

Guarda, A., Wonderlich, S., Kaye, W., & Attia, E. (2018). A path to defining excellence in intensive treatment for eating disorders. *International Journal of Eating Disorders, 51*(9) 1051–1055.

Harrop, E. N., Mensinger, J. L., Moore, M., & Lindhorst, T. (2021). Restrictive eating disorders in higher weight persons: A systematic review of atypical anorexia nervosa prevalence and consecutive admission literature. *International Journal of Eating Disorders, 54*(8), 1328–1357. https://doi.org/10.1002/eat.23519

Hilbert, A., Pike, K. M., Goldschmidt, A. B., Wilfley, D. E., Fairburn, C. G., Dohm, F. A., Walsh, B. T., & Striegel Weissman, R. (2014). Risk factors across the eating disorders. *Psychiatry Research, 220*(1–2). https://doi.org/10.1016/j.psychres.2014.05.054

Jones, R. M., & Simpson, A. I. F. (2018). Medical assistance in dying: Challenges for psychiatry. *Frontiers in Psychiatry, 9*(678).

Knapp, S. J., Gottlieb, M. C., & Handelsman, M. M. (2015). The ethical decision-making model. In S. J. Knapp, M. C. Gottlieb, & M. M. Handelsman, *Ethical dilemmas in psychotherapy: Positive approaches to decision making* (pp. 25–45). American Psychological Association. https://doi.org/10.1037/14670-003

Long, S. (2014). Potential ethical dilemmas in the treatment of eating disorders. *Psychotherapy Bulletin, 41*(1), 37–44.

Matusek, R., & Wright, M. (2010). Ethical dilemmas in treating eating disorders. *European Eating Disorders Review, 18*, 434–452.

Mehler, P. S., & Andersen, A. E. (Eds.). (2022). *Eating disorders: A comprehensive guide to medical care and complications* (4th ed.). Johns Hopkins University Press.

Mikhail, M. E., & Klump, K. (2021). A virtual issue highlighting eating disorders in people of Black/African and Indigenous heritage. *International Journal of Eating Disorders, 54*(3), 459–467.

Murray, S. B., Nagata, J. M., Griffiths, S., Calzo, J. P., Brown, T. A., Mitchison, D., Blashill, A. J., & Mond, J. M. (2017). The enigma of male eating disorders: A critical review and synthesis. *Clinical Psychology Review, 57*, 1–11.

National Association of Social Workers. (2017). *NASW code of ethics*. https://www.socialworkers.org/About/Ethics/Code-of-Ethics/Code-of-Ethics-English

Parisi Cummings, M., & Erckert, I. M. (2020, September 25). *Working with severe and enduring eating disorders: Managing treatment resistance and refusal* [Webinar]. International Association of Eating Disorders Professionals, Greater Philadelphia Chapter, Newtown, PA.

Patton, G. C., Selzer, R., Coffey, C., Carlin, J. B., & Wolfe, R. (1999). Onset of adolescent eating disorders: Population based cohort study over 3 years. *British Medical Journal, 318*(7186). https://doi.org/10.1136/bmj.318.7186.765

Peebles, R., Hardy, K. K., Wilson, J. L., & Lock, J. D. (2010). Are diagnostic criteria for eating disorders markers of medical severity? *Pediatrics, 125*(5), e1193–1201. https://doi.org/10.1542/peds.2008-1777

Rodgers, R. F., Berry, R., & Franko, D. L. (2018). Eating disorders in ethnic minorities: An update. *Current Psychiatry Reports, 20*(10), 90. https://doi.org/10.1007/s11920-018-0938-3

Russell, J., Mulvey, B., Bennett, H., Donnelly, B., & Frig, E. (2019). Harm minimization in severe and enduring anorexia nervosa. *International Review of Psychiatry, 31,* 391–402. https://doi.org/10.1080/09540261.2019.1601073

Sawyer, S. M., Whitelaw, M., Grange, D. L., Yeo, M., & Hughes, E. K. (2016). Physical and psychological morbidity in adolescents with atypical anorexia nervosa (report). *Pediatrics, 137*(4). e20154080. https://doi.org/10.1542/peds.2015-4080

Schreyer, C. C., Coughlin, J. W., Makhzoumi, S. H., Redgrave, G W., Hansen, J. L., & Guarda, A. S. (2016). Perceived coercion in inpatients with anorexia nervosa: Associations with illness severity and hospital course. *International Journal of Eating Disorders, 49*(4), 407–412. https://doi.org/10.1002/eat.22476

Solmi, F., Hotopf, M., Hatch, S. L., Treasure, J., & Micali, N. (2016). Eating disorders in a multi-ethnic inner-city UK sample: Prevalence, comorbidity and service use. *Social Psychiatry and Psychiatric Epidemiology, 51*(3), 369–381. https://doi.org/10.1007/s00127-015-1146-7

Sonneville, K. R., & Lipson, S. K. (2018). Disparities in eating disorder diagnosis and treatment according to weight status, race/ethnicity, socioeconomic background, and sex among college students. *International Journal of Eating Disorders, 51*(6), 518–526.

Smith, A. R., Zuromski, K. L., & Dodd, D. R. (2018). Eating disorders and suicidality: What we know, what we don't know, and suggestions for future research. *Current Opinion in Psychology, 22,* 63–67.

Spotts-De Lazzer, A., & Muhlheim, L. (2019). Could your higher weight patient have atypical anorexia? *Journal of Health Service Psychology, 45*(1), 3–10. https://doi.org/10.1007/BF03544674

Tan, J., & Hope, T. (2008). Treatment refusal in anorexia nervosa: a challenge to current concepts of capacity. In G. Widdershoven, J. McMillan, T. Hope, & L. van der Scheer (Eds.), *Empirical ethics in psychiatry* (pp. 187–210). OUP Oxford.

Tan, J., Hope, T., & Stewart, A. (2003). Competence to refuse treatment in anorexia nervosa. *International Journal of Law and Psychiatry, 26,* 697-707. doi:10.1016/j.ijlp.2003.09.010

Touyz, S., LeGrange, D., Lacey, H., Hay, P., Smith, R., Maguire, S., Bamford, B., Pike, K. M., & Crosby, R. D. (2013). Treating severe and enduring anorexia nervosa: A randomized controlled trial. *Psychological Medicine, 43,* 2501–2511.

Udo, T., & Grillo, C. M. (2018). Prevalence and correlates of DSM-5–defined eating disorders in a nationally representative sample of U.S. adults. *Biological Psychiatry, 84*(5), 345–354.

Vandereycken, W. (2006). Denial of illness in anorexia nervosa—a conceptual review: Part 1 diagnostic significance and assessment. *European Eating Disorders Review, 14*(5), 341–351. https://doi.org/10.1002/erv.721

Watson, T. L, Bowers, W. A., & Anderson, A. E. (2000). Involuntary treatment of eating disorders. *American Journal of Psychiatry, 157,* 1806–1810.

Westmoreland, P., Johnson, C., Stafford, M., Martinez, R., & Mehler, P. S. (2017). Involuntary treatment of patients with life-threatening anorexia nervosa. *Journal of the American Academy of Psychiatry and the Law, 45*(4), 419–425.

Westmoreland, P., & Mehler, P. S. (2016). Caring for patients with severe and enduring eating disorders (SEED): Certification, harm reduction, palliative care, and the question of futility. *Journal of Psychiatric Practice*, *22*(4), 313–320.

Whitney, J., Keitel, M, Parisi Cummings, M., Ponterotto, J. G., & Ott, E. (2023). Caring for sons with anorexia: The perspective of mothers. *Journal of Child and Family Studies*. https://doi.org/10.1007/s10826-022-02525-5

Wonderlich, S. A., Bulik, C. M., Schmidt, U., Steiger, H., & Hoek, H. W. (2020). Severe and enduring anorexia nervosa: Update and observations about the current clinical reality. *International Journal of Eating Disorders, 53*(8), 1303–1312.

Yager, J. (2020). Managing patients with severe and enduring anorexia nervosa: When is enough, enough? *Journal of Nervous and Mental Disease*, *208*(4), 277–282.

CHAPTER 3

AN INTERSECTIONAL APPROACH TO AVOIDANT RESTRICTIVE FOOD INTAKE DISORDER (ARFID)

Case Analysis of a Transgender Identifying Individual

Carly Pershyn, Maya Cottone, and Catherine Cook-Cottone

Avoidant/restrictive food intake disorder (ARFID) is characterized by a broad range of criteria associated with the consequences of prolonged and intense food restriction. It is marked by a disturbance in the feeding or eating behaviors that interfere with an individual's day-to-day life. Those diagnosed with ARFID often experience significant weight loss, nutritional deficiency, or dependence on external feeding (American Psychiatric Association [APA], 2022). Unlike some other eating disorder (ED) diagnoses included in the DSM-5-TR, diagnostic criteria for ARFID do not include shape and weight concerns or guidelines for weight ranges indicating levels of malnutrition; however, the diagnosis is characterized by a failure to meet appropriate energy and/or nutritional needs (Zickgraf et al., 2019). Empirically and clinically, *appropriate* is understood as a relative term, distinguished by an individual's current developmental and cultural context. It is essential for diagnosing clinicians to have familiarity with and an

Counseling Individuals With Eating Disorders: An Intersectional Approach, pp. 41–63

understanding of each patient's sociocultural factors and ethnic values relevant to their experience of eating behaviors (Katzman et al., 2019). For example, food restrictions and traditions based on religious views must be taken into account. For children, adolescents, and emerging adults, life experiences, comorbidities, and intersectionality can complicate an ARFID diagnosis. This chapter will review the ARFID diagnosis, nuances in expression of the disorder, prevalence, and comorbidities. Intersectionality will be explored and then illustrated through a focus on ARFID among transgender individuals. A case study is presented to facilitate discussion on etiology, assessment, diagnosis, and treatment of ARFID with an individual who identifies as transgender. Questions for discussion and implications for future directions are included.

The Three Expressions of ARFID

To receive an ARFID diagnosis, the eating disturbance cannot otherwise be due to lack of availability of food, a body-satisfaction-oriented ED, or other medical condition or mental disorder (APA, 2022). Due to its broad diagnostic scope, ARFID is not limited to one expression of food avoidance/restriction, as with other EDs. Instead, ARFID is characterized by three distinct profiles: *limited intake*, *limited variety*, and *fear-oriented*, which represent unique manifestations of both somatic and cognitive experiences (Katzman et al., 2019). Each profile is thought to reflect distinct experiences of comorbid psychiatric disorders and include concise criteria that often overlap in clinical presentation (Zickgraf et al., 2018).

The *limited intake* profile is appetite-oriented and includes individuals whose limited food intake results from a lack of interest in eating itself, or otherwise poor appetite (Norris et al., 2017). Individuals with this profile may describe feeling a lack of hunger at mealtimes, forgetting to eat, finding food less rewarding or feeling full quicker than others (Thomas et al., 2017). Behaviorally, research suggests individuals may endorse these feelings by prematurely finishing meals and/or skipping meals (Thomas & Eddy 2019; Kambanis et al., 2019; Norris et al., 2017). This profile represents a variety of heterogeneous experiences. For example, some research suggests comorbidities between a limited intake ARFID profile and major depressive disorder (MDD), which may involve disinterest in eating due to lack of associated pleasure (Zickgraf et al., 2019). Additional research suggests these individuals may not reflect longstanding or historic appetite disturbance; rather, their limited food intake is marked by the onset of a stressor, anxiety symptoms, and/or depressed mood (e.g., Zickgraf et al., 2018). These individuals may also experience appetite loss as a side effect of medication, such as in cases of stimulant medications used to treat attention deficit hyperactivity disorder (Zickgraf et al., 2018).

The *limited variety* profile is food-selection focused and is the least common of the three types (Norris et al., 2017). In this presentation, an individual's limited food intake is related to specific sensory characteristics associated with food or eating food (APA, 2022). These characteristics can include, but are not limited to, food's texture, color, smell, and appearance. As a result, these individuals endorse a distinctively narrow range of food preferences, which typically excludes specific meats, vegetables, and/or fruits (Thomas et al., 2017; Zickgraf et al., 2019). Additionally, these individuals are likely to describe excluded foods as intensely negative tasting. Sometimes, this profile may be outwardly described in conjunction with behavioral manifestations such as "choosy" or "picky" eaters (APA, 2022, p. 376). ARFID should be distinguished from picky eating behaviors that do not interfere with weight status, which are considered common across the lifespan (Zickgraf et al., 2016). Individuals with this profile of ARFID have additionally shown profound rigidity surrounding the act of eating (e.g., not allowing food to touch on a plate; Norris et al., 2017). Comorbidities commonly seen in this profile include neurodevelopmental disorders such as ADHD and autism (Kambanis et al., 2020; Smith et al., 2020).

The third and most prevalent profile of ARFID is *fear-oriented*, which occurs on a continuum of severity, and can be characterized by fear-related food avoidance (Kambanis et al., 2019; Nicely et al., 2014; Norris et al., 2017; Zickgraf et al., 2018). These individuals are typically motivated to avoid experiences such as choking, vomiting, difficulty swallowing, or some other gastrointestinal sensation (APA, 2022). Current research hypothesizes that this avoidance occurs as a result of food-related traumatic experiences (such as an allergic reaction) which give rise to a phobic response (Thomas et al., 2017). Remarkably, one study found anxiety disorders were comorbid among 77% of individuals with this ARFID profile (Kambanis et al., 2019). These experiences are not limited to events which happen to an individual, and may include those to which they were a witness. While it is common for individuals to experience an aversive food-related event across their lifespan, those with ARFID develop specific avoidances which interfere with normal feeding behaviors.

Differentiating ARFID and Anorexia Nervosa (AN)

ARFID's variability in presentation speaks to the heterogeneity of its diagnosable population. For example, in some individuals, ARFID manifests as a general lack of interest in eating or food. Importantly, experiences of each profile are not mutually exclusive; each can occur independently or in combination with another profile (Thomas et al., 2017). The reasons for individuals' eating disturbances are unique to them; however, none of them are motivated predominantly by a desire to appear thinner nor is dissatisfaction with their body shape and weight a primary driver of their behavior (APA, 2022). Thus, ARFID represents a feeding and eating-related disorder with cognitions that are distinct from AN in several ways (APA, 2022).

While ARFID's diagnostic population is more female-identifying than male-identifying, it has proportionally greater numbers of male-identifying individuals than in the AN population (Katzman et al., 2022). Those with ARFID are typically younger than those with AN and experience a longer period of illness evolution (Cañas et al., 2021). In a recent analysis differentiating psychiatric comorbidities for ARFID and AN, the average age of participants with ARFID was 16.61 (SD = 3.92, n = 51) while the average age of participants with AN was 19.59 (SD = 2.16, n = 40; Kambanis et al., 2022). Of note, current research has suggested clinically homogeneous presentations of AN may be attributable to diagnostic weight requirements and criteria. Since ARFID's diagnostic criteria remain comparably broad, it encompasses a vast array of clinical manifestations as evidenced by the profiles described earlier in this chapter.

Current research suggests ARFID typically co-occurs with other psychiatric disorders. More specifically, ARFID populations typically have greater rates of anxiety and neurodevelopmental disorders, such as obsessive-compulsive disorder (OCD), generalized anxiety disorder (GAD), attention-deficit/hyperactivity disorder (ADHD), and autism spectrum disorder (ASD) than those diagnosed with other EDs (Bourne et al., 2020; Cañas et al., 2021; Katzman et al., 2022). Conversely, other feeding and EDs are found to co-occur in greater rates with depressive and bipolar disorders. When compared to individuals with ARFID, research suggests those with AN have significantly greater depressive symptomatology. Research further suggests that those with ARFID are three times less likely than those with AN to experience suicidal ideation and suicide (Kambanis et al., 2022).

Differential diagnosis between ARFID and AN is outlined as particularly challenging in both empirical and clinical settings. This diagnostic difficulty relates to the reasons underlying individuals' eating behavior (Cañas et al., 2021). In both ARFID and AN, individuals engage in behaviors which prevent weight gain, and ultimately cause weight loss (APA, 2022). Furthermore, patients with both ARFID and AN display similar rates of malnutrition and weight loss (Katzman et al., 2019). Notably, however, AN is characterized by a fear of "becoming fat" or gaining weight and disturbed perceptions of how one experiences their own body, its weight, and its shape. These body-oriented motivations for weight loss which perpetuate AN are not present in individuals with ARFID (APA, 2022).

Prevalence of ARFID

Several behaviors connected to an ARFID diagnosis are highly associated with and influenced by both environmental and social factors. Due to the relatively new conceptualization of ARFID, research is still emerging regarding various populations, which may likely receive this diagnosis. Notably, ARFID is understood to manifest across broad spectrums of both age and weight (Hilbert et al., 2021). Diagnosis is currently understood as occurring slightly more frequently in individuals identifying as female than those identifying as male (Kennedy et al., 2022). Notably, in a retrospective chart review of limited variety (i.e., selective intake) ARFID cases, Zickgraf and colleagues (2019) found 81.8% of identified patients were reported male ($n = 18$, $N = 22$). To date, ARFID is thought to manifest more frequently within child and adolescent populations than adult populations (APA, 2022). Limited research suggests ARFID occurs at a rate of about 0.3% for individuals older than 15 years of age (APA, 2022). A recent publication estimates that between 0.5% and 5% of the general population of children and adults experience ARFID (Kennedy et al., 2022). Remarkably, the same study concluded that ARFID is likely prevalent within 1.5% to 64% of clinical ED populations.

While current research is generally limited with regard to large-scale analyses of prevalence rates of ARFID, the prevalence of characteristics relevant to each profile have been investigated in isolation. For example, Hilbert and colleagues (2021) summarized community-based studies and estimated that picky eating behaviors (limited variety profile) are found among 30–46% of adults. Further, another study found diagnosable ARFID in 22.5% (39 of 177) of patients referred for a day program ED treatment (Nicely et al., 2014). A systematic review of pediatric intakes for an obsessive-compulsive disorder and anxiety clinic reported 5.5% of 400 intakes represented cases with selective and/or avoidant ARFID (Zickgraf et al., 2019). Additional research focusing on pediatric presentations of ARFID estimates a prevalence rate of 5-14% within North American ED treatment programs (Katzman et al., 2019). Available research has been limited to assessment of ARFID with predominantly White samples (e.g., Kambanis et al., 2019, 2022; Zickgraf et al., 2019, 2022) or does not include race/ethnicity as part of analysis (e.g., Fisher et al., 2014; Norris et al., 2017; Zickgraf & Ellis, 2018). ARFID's novelty highlights a need for further research into its prevalence, especially within diverse populations.

Special Considerations: Gender Identity

Current ED research represents a disproportionate focus on cisgender female-identifying individuals (Brownstone et al., 2022; Coelho et al.,

2019; Cusack et al., 2022; Riddle & Safer, 2022). Emerging research suggests individuals who represent marginalized gender minorities (e.g., transgender, gender non-conforming) may be at a disproportionate risk for both disordered eating and body image challenges (Brownstone et al., 2022; Calzo et al., 2020). Transgender is a wide-scoping term used to describe individuals whose gender identity differs from their assigned gender at birth (National Center for Transgender Equality [NCTE], 2016). Transgender populations represent gender minorities and encompass a wide spectrum of individuals with diverse experiences of gender, gender identity, and gender expression (NCTE, 2016).

Remarkably, one survey of 300,000 college students discovered ED diagnoses present in 15.82% of transgender individuals compared to the 1.85% reported by cisgender heterosexual women (Diemer et al., 2015). Further, Ferrucci and colleagues' (2022) review of insurance claims from 10,415 transgender adults and youth found 2.43% of the sample reported having a diagnosed ED. These findings were notably lower than self-reported estimates of EDs within transgender populations. Importantly, this study was limited to transgender individuals who had received gender-affirming surgery and, as a result, excludes those identifying as nonbinary (Ferrucci et al., 2022). Further, these authors suggested that their results are representative of the empirically highlighted disproportionate barriers to care faced by transgender individuals as well as diagnostic bias.

Clinicians must be cognizant of their susceptibility to treatment bias when working with transgender clients with or at risk for ARFID. Current research suggests disordered eating behaviors of transgender individuals may be wrongfully attributed to their gender-related body dissatisfaction (Calzo et al., 2020; Cusack et al., 2022). Accordingly, clinicians have an obligation to address this attribution error to best serve transgender populations. First, clinicians must have a foundational understanding of terminology for sexual orientation and gender (Calzo et al., 2020) and be familiar with their client's experiences of gender dysphoria (i.e., experienced incongruence between an individual's assigned and experienced gender; APA, 2022). Gender dysphoria is distinct from yet may be experienced at the same time as body-related dissatisfaction (Calzo et al., 2020; Cusack et al., 2022; Kaplan et al., 2019). Importantly, clinicians must not assume gender dysphoria's correlation with EDs implies the existence of a causal relationship and should recognize each as distinct with potential overlap on a case-by-case basis (Calzo et al., 2020). A complete and comprehensive conceptualization of the client will consider sex and gender identity, as described above, as well as race, ethnicity, and age.

Evidenced-Based Treatments

ARFID is a complex and multidimensional condition. The first step in effective treatment planning is establishing a healthcare team trained to address the psychological, physiological, interpersonal, and cultural components that make up the disorder. Treatment for EDs is unlike treatment for other mental health disorders because of their physiological effects; in ARFID, these often include vitamin deficiencies and malnourishment due to a tendency to eat limited food groups and other behaviors resulting in reduced caloric intake. The team of health professionals includes a medical doctor, a nutritionist, and a psychotherapist, at minimum (Oliveira & Kaul, 2022). The treatment team may also include a speech-language pathologist, physical therapist, and/or occupational therapist. Each of them is responsible for assessing a different feature that may contribute to the presence of ARFID. Depending on the patient's unique symptomatology, speech-language pathologists may need to assess oral-motor functioning and swallowing behavior. Physical therapists can evaluate posture that affects oral-motor functioning, and occupational therapists may help evaluate fine-motor skills used for self-feeding and sensory processing issues around food texture (Brigham et al., 2018). As mentioned previously, individuals who have ARFID often have comorbid medical and psychiatric illnesses, which may require the help of a psychiatrist for medication management (Katzman et al., 2019). Other members of the treatment team may include a gastroenterologist who can consider any medical factors related to the gastrointestinal system, and/or an otolaryngologist who is responsible for assessing airway function that may contribute to swallowing. Depending on the individual's circumstances, adequate treatment may require assistance from other professionals, including school counselors and educators, and other specialists. Often the individual's primary care doctor or a counselor who specializes in EDs will be useful in identifying the necessary members of the treatment team.

Initial evaluation by a physician, usually a pediatrician, will include a careful review of the patient's history. A retrospective chart review may identify evidence of choosy eating throughout childhood or adolescence or history of a traumatic eating event (e.g., choking), and the individual's attitude towards their body image and weight should be assessed to rule out other body-image-based EDs (Brigham et al., 2018). Blood panels and bone x-rays may be requested to get a full picture of the individual's nutrient deficiencies and malnutrition. The physician will then identify whether additional specialists, such as a gastroenterologist, are necessary for effective treatment. Individuals with ARFID who have significant weight loss may require hospitalization (Białek-Dratwa et al., 2022). One study found that 16 out of 28 participants (57.1%) had spent time in inpatient treatment (Cooney et al., 2018).

Psychotherapy is provided in conjunction with medical treatment. Several therapeutic modalities have been effective in the treatment of ARFID. One of the most common approaches to ED treatment is family-based therapy (FBT). FBT is an established, evidence-based treatment that is effective in the treatment of EDs, particularly AN (Rosania & Lock, 2020; Spettigue et al., 2018). FBT is structured and based on an approach originally developed at Maudsley Hospital in London, as a caregiver-based follow-up treatment for inpatient rehabilitation (Le Grange, 2005). Research assessing the modality has since made it the gold standard of outpatient psychotherapy treatment for child/adolescent AN and BN (Rienecke & Le Grange, 2022).

The FBT model consists of three treatment phases designed to remove blame, educate, and empower family members to renourish their child from home (Davis & Stone, 2020). Phase one focuses on weight restoration, parental support, and externalizing the disorder to decrease feelings of guilt and blame. Phase two consists of establishing healthy eating behaviors (amount, time, nutrition), and begins once the child has increased food intake and begun sustaining weight gain. An important part of phase two is gradually returning control of food intake and eating to the child/adolescent. Phase three occurs once weight is restored and eating behavior has improved and moves to address psychosocial and emotional concerns (Bialek-Dratwa et al., 2022). Unlike other forms of talk therapy, FBT includes the family in the recovery process and aims to address ED symptoms first, then moves to psychosocial and emotional factors that may contribute to maintaining the disorder. Commonly used to treat AN, FBT begins with addressing weight gain. If ARFID has led to significant weight loss and/or malnourishment, the first aim of treatment will be nutritional rehabilitation and weight restoration. Trained professionals provide support for family members via weekly therapy sessions that vary in frequency depending on the patient's severity and need. Involving parents directly in the treatment of ARFID increases supervision of eating behaviors. This includes structured meal planning and systematic exposure to novel foods. Although research is limited, the development of an FBT-ARFID model requires some adaptations to the original structure, to account for unique symptomatology associated with varying ARFID profiles. With child populations, these adaptations focus on the acceptance of avoided food through play (Białek-Drawta et al., 2022; Lock, 2021). One approach aims to combine traditional methods of FBT with interoceptive awareness and exposure skills, tailoring the well-established approach to individuals with ARFID whose food aversion stems from internal sensation avoidance (Zucker et al., 2018). Lock and colleagues (2018) show promising results via a case study adapting FBT to fit each of the three ARFID profiles: *limited intake, limited variety,* and *fear-oriented.* These tailored approaches to treatment using FBT are expanded upon by Lock (2021), emphasizing the importance of using a developmental approach appropriate for age and profile. These relatively new adaptations to the original FBT treatment structure are promising, but require further research.

In the treatment of ARFID for pediatric populations, FBT is more effective in conjunction with additional modalities, such as cognitive behavioral therapy (CBT), dialectical behavioral therapy (DBT), or exposure therapy (Białek-Dratwa et al., 2022). Thomas and Eddy's (2019) treatment manual for the treatment of ARFID in younger populations integrates CBT into FBT as a singular intervention. A CBT approach focuses on identifying maladaptive cognitions and beliefs around the individual's eating behavior and works to establish healthier thought patterns. Typically used for the treatment of EDs in adults, current studies are exploring the efficacy of CBT among child and adolescent populations (Thomas et al., 2020).

The CBT conceptualization of ARFID considers biological predispositions, and potential food-related trauma, leading to "negative feelings and predictions about the consequences of eating" which leads to food restriction (Thomas et al., 2018, p. 428). CBT-AR (CBT for ARFID) consists of four phases of treatment. Phase one consists of psychoeducation on the ED and CBT approach, and encourages the patient to begin self-monitoring food intake. The patient is encouraged to establish a regular feeding schedule with a minor introduction to novel foods. Phase two consists of psychoeducation on nutrition, and the patient may select new nutritious foods to incorporate into their meal planning. Phase three, the most intensive phase of treatment, differs depending on the individual-specific ARFID profile. For example, individuals who fall under the *limited-variety* profile may be asked to consider foods that cause sensory discomfort. They begin by describing the food nonjudgmentally, and move to practice tasting. For individuals suffering from the *fear-oriented* profile, this phase may include psychoeducation around avoidance and anxiety and graduated exposure to feared food or eating situations. The fourth and final phase of CBT-AR consists of two sessions dedicated to relapse prevention during which the patient identifies strategies for maintenance and sets goals to continue remission (Thomas et al., 2020; Thomas et al., 2018). CBT-AR can be offered individually or with caregiver support, in which one or more caregivers actively participate in therapy sessions. Thomas and colleagues (2020) tested this model and found this intervention was associated with the successful and sustained incorporation of novel foods and increased weight gain. At the conclusion of the study, 70% of participants no longer met the criteria for ARFID (Thomas et al., 2020). Due to CBT's established efficacy in the treatment of generalized anxiety and other anxiety disorders, some research suggests it may be the most effective treatment for children suffering from ARFID with comorbid anxiety (Bialek-Drawta et al., 2022; Thomas et al., 2018).

DBT may be similarly effective in treating patients with ARFID who have psychiatric comorbidities. DBT is a skill-based approach focused on mindfulness, distress tolerance, emotion regulation, and interpersonal functioning. Individuals practicing DBT will be encouraged to sit with uncomfortable thoughts and feelings around the experience of eating. DBT may be particularly useful for targeting individuals who respond poorly to FBT (Reilly et al., 2020). DBT was originally designed for the treatment of borderline personality disorder (BPD) and focuses on emotion regulation and interpersonal functioning, which emphasizes validation and effective communication. This approach may be advantageous in combating challenges related to psychiatric comorbidities with high rates of depressive symptoms and/or interpersonal distress (Reilly et al., 2020). Like FBT and CBT, traditional components of DBT have been adapted to meet the needs of individuals with ARFID. Examples include the addition of food intake tracking on diary cards, and the addition of nutrition-education modules (Pennell et al., 2019). While DBT and CBT have been predominantly used in the treatment of EDs for adults, new research suggests they may be equally effective in adolescent populations, either on their own or in combination with FBT (Pennell et al., 2019).

Effective treatment of ARFID requires comprehensive care and a multifaceted approach from a team of healthcare providers. Each ARFID profile has a unique set of symptoms and contributing factors that must be addressed individually to achieve sustainable remission from the ED. Individuals with ARFID and their families should consult their doctor for information on who to involve in the treatment process, as well as which therapeutic approach is right for the individual's profile, developmental stage, and other cultural and social factors. As stands true for all EDs, early recognition and prevention is associated with better outcomes (Stice et al., 2013). As individuals with ARFID tend to be diagnosed earlier than those with other EDs, parental observation plays a significant role in early detection and reporting of symptoms (Zimmerman & Fisher, 2017).

Strategies for Prevention

The factors contributing to the development of ARFID are distinct from those that cause other EDs; primarily, they are unrelated to body-image concerns. Preventative treatment for other EDs often centers around education on sociocultural factors that contribute to body image concerns. Factors contributing to the development of ARFID stem from sensory avoidance and food-related fears. These elements tend to develop in tandem with feeding behavior established in childhood and progress through adolescence. Effective prevention strategies will therefore target feeding behavior in terms of exposure to a variety of foods and food textures, as well as appropriate and timely responses to traumatic feeding/eating events encountered in early life. ARFID is a relatively new diagnosis and so adequate data on ARFID prevention is lacking. Current and proposed research aims to investigate strategies for prevention that target these factors as well as to investigate factors that determine whether a child is at risk for developing ARFID (Stice et al., 2013; Zimmerman & Fisher, 2017). Some researchers suggest that parenting behaviors related to feeding in early childhood may play a role in the development of choosy eating - a unique feature of ARFID that is observed across profiles. For example, one study hypothesized that pressure from parents during early feeding stages may inhibit healthy eating habits (Ellis et al., 2016). Zimmerman and Fisher (2017) suggest seeking assistance from pediatricians at the initial stages of feeding if texture aversion or food-related trauma is present. Pediatricians can provide assessment tools to help parents determine whether their child is getting enough to eat. Pediatricians, dietitians, and/or nutritionists may be involved in the early stages of food aversion and can help with feeding schedules, food recommendations, and navigating sensory avoidance of particular foods starting in infancy (Zimmerman & Fisher, 2017). Parent-report-based screening tools for young preschool-aged children are currently being developed as early recognition has been shown to improve rates of remission. These tools are designed to identify food aversion due to texture sensitivity, disinterest, and fear-based experiences regarding the effects of eating, per DSM-5-TR criteria for ARFID as outlined previously. For example, a recent questionnaire developed in a sample of Japanese children between the ages of 4 and 7 includes items assessing criteria such as avoidance of intake, significant weight loss, significant nutritional deficiency, dependence on nutritional supplements, interference with psychosocial functioning, eating disturbance not due to body-image or weight concerns, and eating disturbance not due to another underlying medical condition (Dinkler et al., 2022). The same study found discrepancies between previously established ED screening tools, such as the Eating Disorder in Youth Questionnaire (EDY-Q; Hilbert & van Dyck, 2016) leading to underreporting of children who meet ARFID criteria, and under-researched parent-report-based questionnaires leading to over-reporting. Previously established screening tools may be insufficient for identifying the unique criteria of ARFID, and more research needs to be done on effective screening tools for early recognition of ARFID in children before the disease reaches a chronic stage.

CASE STUDY: SAGE

Sage is a 17-year-old biracial, trans male (pronouns he, him, his) diagnosed with ARFID. Sage was assigned the female sex at birth by his pediatrician and lived within the gender identity of a girl/woman for his first 16 years. Both parents identify as African American women, are cisgender female and identify as gay/lesbian. Sage was born via in vitro fertilization, the third pregnancy after two miscarriages. His grandparents include a White female married to an African American male and two African American females married to each other. From a young age Sage has preferred gender neutral or more traditionally male clothing. His interests include drawing, cross-country running, and poetry.

Overall, Sage currently presents as very anxious and generally does not like to eat when feeling anxious. In the past, Sage was described as a picky eater by his parents, something they have noticed since he began eating whole foods at 9 months of age. As a child, there were particular foods he did not like including tomatoes, kiwi, peaches, oatmeal, and other foods he described as "slimy." He currently strongly prefers carbohydrate-based foods above fruits, vegetables, and protein. His favorite foods include cereal (with no milk), muffins, bread or any bread-like food (English muffins, bagel, soft taco shells), pretzels, and cake. He will eat mashed potatoes, rice, French fries, and tater tots. He generally prefers a peanut butter and jam sandwich for all his meals, over fruit, vegetables, and meat.

When Sage was 10 years old, he lost two grandparents in a car accident. One of his mothers described the incident as "traumatizing for everyone." Sage refused to eat for almost two weeks and stayed home from school with a reported stomachache for 7 of the 10 school days within that 2-week period. Following the funeral and the family's return to routine, he slowly regained his previous eating patterns, still refusing fruits, vegetables, and meat. He was eating enough to maintain his weight; however, his weight was not increasing, as would be expected developmentally. At his yearly check-up shortly after his 11th birthday, Sage's weight was at 82% of the weight expected for his age and height. His pediatrician recommended nutrition counseling for the family. They did not follow through as they believed it was a phase.

Around this same time (his 11th and 12th years), Sage began expressing gender dysphoria. His parents reported that he began to report his desire to be a boy and that he felt like his female gender was an error. Sage believed that if his parents conducted a genetic test, they would see that he was meant to be a male, despite lacking the male genitalia. Sage insisted on wearing only masculine clothing and began using a lower-pitched voice in an attempt to sound more male. When he played video games, he always chose a male character. His poetry and drawings were filled with masculine content, including self-portraits of himself as a male and poems expressing his longing to be a male. His friends at school were generally male, with the exception of one female friend who was and remains a close confidant and a fellow, avid fantasy-based video game player. Sage has always refused to wear dresses and the dolls he was given in younger years were left in the box and/or abandoned in his closet.

Just short of his 13th birthday, Sage formally asked his parents if he could begin gender-affirming treatment. His parents told him that he was too young and therefore did not support treatment. They added that he should focus on gaining weight and school. He had remained visibly underweight and his grades had been gradually declining from As and Bs throughout elementary school to Bs and Cs in middle school. His mid-term reports insinuated that he was behind in homework submission and had uncharacteristically low test scores. Sage became extremely upset. He fell into what his mom described as "a hysterical rage" in which he said he hates his body because he was not female and his body was wrong. He said he could not go on like this and felt like he should end his life if this is the way his life was going to be. His parents reported that they did not know where to turn and that their mid-sized city did not have anyone who specialized in gender dysphoria and EDs.

At this point, his parents reached out to a local mental health counselor known to specialize in gender dysphoria. She refused to see him due to his weight and eating concerns, stating that she does not treat EDs. Several weeks later, the school psychologist called, stating that several of Sage's friends reported that they feared he was suicidal. After a psychiatric consultation, Sage spent 72 hours in an emergency inpatient setting, leaving with a prescription for antidepressant medication and diagnosed with AN, MDD, and GAD. He was also discharged to the outpatient care of an ED specialist since this was now his primary concern as his weight had now dropped to 79% of his expected weight.

For the past three and a half years, he has been seeing an ED specialist (a pediatrician), a nutritionist, and a mental health counselor who works in the ED clinic. His ED diagnosis was changed from AN to ARFID. The treatment goals included weight gain, increased variety in food eaten, increased food intake, and decreased body dissatisfaction. Despite weekly medical, nutritional, and mental health counseling appointments, Sage gained minimal weight and remained depressed and anxious, although the medication seemed to be helping reduce his suicidal ideation. His grades remained at Bs and Cs. He had gradually become less social and frequently refused to go to school, staying up late to play fantasy-based video games, a space in which he described feeling "safe and accepted."

Due to his extensive absenteeism (he missed 40 days in his senior year) and his parents' inability to get him to attend school, the school's attendance officer called child protective services and reported educational neglect. This action resulted in a family crisis and ultimately Sage was returned to inpatient care for suicidal ideation, stating, "I would rather die than go to school." After a full diagnostic workup, it became clear that Sage was depressed, anxious, underweight for his age and height, and experiencing gender dysphoria. After a comprehensive, multi-disciplinary assessment and review of his records, he and his family were referred to a psychologist in a city about an hour from them for counseling associated with his depression, mood, and gender dysphoria. He was to remain with his ED treatment team. He was classified as Other Health-Impaired at school, allowing the school to provide additional support for his school refusal and academic progress.

Medically, Sage was found to have deficits in vitamin B-12, iron and vitamin D, all related to his restrictive food intake. His weight was at 84% of expected weight for his height and age. His daily food intake was tracked for one week at home for a baseline. This revealed that Sage continued to prefer processed carbohydrates over fruit, vegetables, and protein and was still avoiding foods he described as "slimy."

The comprehensive psychological assessment found significant levels of depression, anxiety, and gender dysphoria (scores below). Sage was asked about race-based stress, and reported that his parents are heavily involved in the social justice movement. Sage denied race issues were related to his distress and stated that he is aligned with and proud of his mother's work. His score on the Beck Depression Inventory-II indicated moderate levels of depression (Beck et al., 1996; Osman et al., 2004). Notably, the items assessed weight loss, fatigue, and lack of interest in sex, items that overlap with his other concerns. He had elevations on the somatic symptoms, school avoidance, and general anxiety domains on the Screen for Child Anxiety Disorders (SCARED; Birmaher et al., 1999). Sage received a score of 20 on the Avoidant/Restrictive Food Intake Disorder Screen (NIAS; Zickgraf et al., 2018), indicating ARFID-related issues such as picky eating, disliking foods, having to push himself to eat, and having trouble eating large volumes of food. On the Eating Disorder Examination Questionnaire (EDE-Q; Fairburn & Beglin, 2008) his scores reflected difficulties with restraint and no elevations on eating concern, shape concern, or weight concern domains. On the Body Dysmorphic Symptoms Scale, Sage scored within the normal range, with scores showing an interest in body surgery (Wilhelm et al., 2016).

On the Utrecht Gender Dysphoria Scale- Gender Spectrum (McGuire et al., 2020), Sage indicated that he would prefer to behave and be treated like his affirmed gender, he feels hurt when he is treated like his assigned sex, his life in his affirmed gender is preferable, behaving like his assigned sex makes him unhappy, body functions of assigned sex are stressful (menstrual cycles, breast development), life would not be meaningful in his assigned sex, and he would rather die than live a life in his assigned sex. When asked about his feelings about his race and ethnicity, he reported that racial stress was less salient than gender stress.

The assessment process also included a series of family meetings in which his parents began to see the level of stress associated with gender dysphoria. Sage revealed in a family meeting that his discomfort with his body as female, the stress of trying to manage life without gender affirming treatment, and his struggle with menstruation and breast development were "making my eating stuff way worse." He disclosed to his parents and his therapist that he was sexually oriented toward females and felt like he could not date when he was not the gender he felt himself to be. He showed his parents how he bound his breasts with breast binding material that he wore and secretly washed. He explained that he felt his whole life was off track and that eating and living did not seem to matter anymore. His parents agreed to follow through with gender-affirming therapy so long as Sage agreed to commit to following the nutritionist recommendations and putting in the work at school.

Ultimately, Sage was treated using an integrative approach. His ED treatment team collaborated with the treatment team, offering gender affirming treatments. Treatment goals specific to ARFID, depressive, and anxious symptomatology included (1) Increased consumption of amount and variety of food consumed, (2) Increased weight, (3) Increased knowledge and use of tools to manage distress and cope while eating, (4) Decreased symptoms related to depression and anxiety, and (5) Increased, in person, social engagement with peers (Thomas et al., 2018). CBT was used to treat the ED symptoms and underlying anxiety and mood issues and was conducted by a mental health professional working with the ED treatment team. The CBT intervention included psychoeducation (on ARFID, depression, anxiety, and stress), emotion regulation skills development and practice, regular eating (increasing variety and amount of food intake), self-monitoring of food intake, stress management/relaxation training, distress tolerance, exposure and response prevention, and behavioral experiments (Thomas et al., 2018). Therapy also included work on social skills and scheduling pleasant events with peers. The psychologist coordinated with Sage's school psychologists to develop a plan for missed work, increased academic performance, and a strategy for consistent attendance to keep him on track to graduate. The nutritionist and physician specializing in EDs monitored weight and physiological wellbeing and helped coach Sage on nutrition.

Once weight and eating were stabilized at levels the team believed were medically safe, his primary psychological treatment shifted to gender-affirming- CBT (GA-CBT; Austin & Craig, 2019). This treatment protocol is a version of CBT that has been adapted to include an affirming stance toward gender diversity, recognition and acknowledgement of transgender-specific courses of stress and resilience, as well as delivery of the CBT content within the context of an affirming and trauma-informed framework (Austin & Craig, 2019). Sage began gender-affirming hormone therapy on his seventh visit and planned masculinizing chest surgery for the summer of his 19th year. He began weightlifting to build up his muscles and experienced an increase in appetite.

Sage was able to gain weight and increase muscle mass, likely related to enhanced nutrition and prescribed vitamin supplements. His depression scores normalized, and suicidal ideation resolved. Sage decided to take a gap year after working very hard to complete high school. His plans were to complete the masculinizing breast surgery and continue to work on his mental health, and to attend college for computer programming and gaming once he felt ready. His anxiety has remained at clinically significant levels and he continues to present with picky eating, still preferring processed carbohydrates. However, his work with the nutritionist shifted to include gender-affirming conversations, and he began to see the benefit in eating sufficient nutrients, including protein, as part of his body self-care. By his 20th year, he no longer met criteria for diagnosis with ARFID due to increases in weight, food intake, and variety of food consumed. He is enrolled in college in the same city that his gender-affirmation treatment center is located and now volunteers in their youth support group program.

FUTURE DIRECTIONS FOR TREATMENT, RESEARCH, THEORY AND POLICY

Due to ARFID's more recent emergence as a recognized disorder and its diagnostic novelty, there is a need for further research into its prevalence, especially within diverse populations, well-designed studies exploring prevention and treatment interventions, as well as intervention research that includes diverse populations. It is important to remember that available research has been limited to assessment of ARFID with predominantly White samples (e.g., Kambanis et al., 2019, 2022; Zickgraf et al., 2019, 2022). And research with more diverse samples does not include a complete and comprehensive discussion of race/ethnicity as part of analysis (e.g., Fisher et al., 2014; Norris et al., 2017; Zickgraf et al., 2018).

Going forward it will be important for researchers and journal editors to prioritize the reporting of demographic information that includes race, ethnicity, sex, gender assignment at birth, gender identification, sexual orientation, educational levels, weight and shape diversity, and socioeconomic status. For example, asking participants to describe their gender as an open-ended question or to provide expanded options is important. Many of the currently available studies collected data on gender as a binary, limiting the ability to explore experiences of those who would not identify on the binary (e.g., Fisher et al. 2014; Norris et al., 2021; Zickgraf et al., 2018). As another illustration of need, Zickgraf and colleagues (2019) suggest that future research should include broader weight criteria for inclusion, as research usually focuses on underweight people with little known about the experience of those who are at normal or higher weights. Some researchers call for more genomic research to address questions surrounding risk factors and early prevention strategies (Kennedy et al., 2022).

Currently, there is limited prevention and treatment research to draw on. Recent research on adaptations to CBT are promising; however, there are limitations such as lack of rich demographic information, small sample sizes, and focus on primarily White, heterosexual participants or participants for whom little is known about gender identity and sexual orientation. Additional research is needed to establish the efficacy of adaptations of CBT, FBT, and DBT for ARFID and the different presentations of ARFID. Further, research is needed on how these same interventions work or do not work given important multicultural/contextual considerations such as race, ethnicity, weight, body shape, gender identity, sexual orientation, socioeconomic status, and age. Finally, future research should include attention to experiences of stress and trauma that may be associated with bias, racism, and prejudice.

DISCUSSION QUESTIONS

1. What ARFID subtype best describes Sage's experience? Describe the symptoms that support your choice.
2. What assessments were used to help diagnose Sage and plan for his treatment? If you could design the assessment battery, which assessments would you choose? Why?
3. Do you agree with the treatment that Sage received? Why or why not? What treatment would you recommend and what specific adaptations do you think would be important to include?
4. What was missed in the discussion of Sage's assessment and treatment? Are there key pieces you think are missing? Explain what and why.
5. Discuss a new research study that would help to further inform Sage's case. Detail the rationale, suggest a design, and identify the measures you would use.

REFERENCES

American Psychiatric Association. (2022). *Diagnostic and statistical manual of mental disorders* (5th ed., text rev.). https://doi.org/10.1176/appi.books.9780890425787

Austin, A., & Craig, S. L. (2019). Transgender affirmative cognitive–behavioral therapy. In J. E. Pachankis, & S. A. Safren (Eds.), *Handbook of evidence-based mental health practice with sexual and gender minorities* (pp. 74–123). Oxford. https://doi.org/10.1093/med-psych/9780190669300.003.0004

Beck, A. T., Steer, R. A., & Brown, G. K. (1996). *Manual for the Beck Depression Inventory-II*. Psychological Corporation.

Białek-Dratwa, A., Szymańska, D., Grajek, M., Krupa-Kotara, K., Szczepańska, E., & Kowalski, O. (2022). ARFID—Strategies for dietary management in children. *Nutrients, 14*(9), 1739. https://doi.org/10.3390/nu14091739

Birmaher, B., Brent, D. A., Chiappetta, L., Bridge, J., Monga, S., & Baugher, M. (1999). Psychometric properties of the Screen for Child Anxiety Related Emotional Disorders (SCARED): A replication study. *Journal of the American Academy of Child and Adolescent Psychiatry, 38*(10), 1230–1236.

Bourne, L., Bryant-Waugh, R., Cook, J., & Mandy, W. (2020). Avoidant/restrictive food intake disorder: A systematic scoping review of the current literature. *Psychiatry Research, 288*, 1–21. https://doi.org/10.1016/j.psychres.2020.112961

Brigham, K. S., Manzo, L. D., Eddy, K. T., & Thomas, J. J. (2018). Evaluation and treatment of avoidant/restrictive food intake disorder (ARFID) in adolescents. *Current Pediatrics Reports, 6*(2), 107–113. https://doi.org/10.1007/s40124-018-0162-y

Brownstone, L. M., Kelly, D. A., Maloul, E. K., Dinneen, J. L., Palazzolo, L. A., Raque, T. L., & Greene, A. K. (2022). "It's just not comfortable to exist in a body": Transgender/gender nonbinary individuals' experiences of body and eating distress during the COVID-19 pandemic. *Psychology of Sexual Orientation and Gender Diversity, 9*(4), 434–445. https://doi.org/10.1037/sgd0000519

Calzo, J. P., Lopez, E. E., Siverstein, S., Brown, T. A., & Blashill, A. J. (2020). Where is the evidence of evidence-based treatment for LGBTQIA+ individuals experiencing eating disorders? In C. C. Tortolani, A. B. Goldschmidt, & D. Le Grange (Eds.), *Adapting evidence-based eating disorder treatments for novel populations and settings*. Routledge.

Cañas, L., Palma, C., Molano, A. M., Domene, L., Carulla-Roig, M., Cecilia-Costa, R., Dolz, M., & Serrano-Troncoso, E. (2021). Avoidant/restrictive food intake disorder: Psychopathological similarities and differences in comparison to anorexia nervosa and the general population. *European Eating Disorders Review: The Journal of the Eating Disorders Association, 29*(2), 245–256. https://doi.org/10.1002/erv.2815

Coelho, J. S., Suen, J., Clark, B. A., Marshall, S. K., Geller, J., & Lam, P. (2019). Eating disorder diagnoses and symptom presentation in transgender youth: A scoping review. *Current Psychiatry Reports, 21*(107), 106–107. https://doi.org/10.1007/s11920-019-1097-x

Cooney, M., Lieberman, M., Guimond, T., & Katzman, D. K. (2018). Clinical and psychological features of children and adolescents diagnosed with avoidant/restrictive food intake disorder in a pediatric tertiary care eating disorder program: A descriptive study. *Journal of Eating Disorders*, *6*(1). https://doi.org/10.1186/s40337-018-0193-3

Cusack, C. E., Iampieri, A. O., & Galupo, M. P. (2022). "I'm still not sure if the eating disorder is a result of gender dysphoria": Trans and nonbinary individuals' descriptions of their eating and body concerns in relation to their gender. *Psychology of Sexual Orientation and Gender Diversity*, *9*(4), 422–433. https://doi.org/10.1037/sgd0000515

Davis, E., & Stone, E. L. (2020). Avoidant restrictive food intake disorder—More than just picky eating: A case discussion and literature review. *The Journal for Nurse Practitioners*, *16*(10), 713–717. https://doi.org/10.1016/j.nurpra.2020.08.011

Diemer, E. W., Grant, J. D., Munn-Chernoff, M. A., Patterson, D. A., & Duncan, A. E. (2015). Gender identity, sexual orientation, and eating-related pathology in a national sample of college students. *Journal of Adolescent Health*, *57*(2), 144–149. https://doi.org/10.1016/j.jadohealth.2015.03.003

Dinkler, L., Yasumitsu-Lovell, K., Eitoku, M., Fujieda, M., Suganuma, N., Hatakenaka, Y., Hadjikhani, N., Bryant-Waugh, R., Råstam, M., & Gillberg, C. (2022). Development of a parent-reported screening tool for avoidant/restrictive food intake disorder (ARFID): Initial validation and prevalence in 4-7-year-old Japanese children. *Appetite*, *168*, 1–10. https://doi.org/10.1016/j.appet.2021.105735

Ellis, J. M., Galloway, A. T., Webb, R. M., Martz, D. M., & Farrow, C. V. (2016). Recollections of pressure to eat during childhood, but not picky eating, predict young adult eating behavior. *Appetite*, *97*, 58–63. https://doi.org/10.1016/j.appet.2015.11.020

Fairburn, C. G., & Beglin, S. (2008). Eating Disorder Examination Questionnaire (EDE-Q 6.0). In C. G. Fairburn (Ed.), *Cognitive behavior therapy and eating disorders* (pp. 309–313). Guilford Press.

Ferrucci, K. A., Lapane, K. L., & Jesdale, B. M. (2022). Prevalence of diagnosed eating disorders in US transgender adults and youth in insurance claims. *The International Journal of Eating Disorders*, *55*(6), 801–809. https://doi.org/10.1002/eat.23729

Fisher, M. M., Rosen, D. S., Ornstein, R. M., Mammel, K. A., Katzman, D. K., Rome, E. S., Callahan, S. T., Malizio, J., Kearney, S., & Walsh, B. T. (2014). Characteristics of avoidant/restrictive food intake disorder in children and adolescents: A "new disorder" in DSM-5. *The Journal of Adolescent Health*, *55*(1), 49–52. https://doi.org/10.1016/j.jadohealth.2013.11.013

Hilbert, A., & van Dyck, Z. (2016). *Eating Disorders in Youth-Questionnaire* (English version.) University of Leipzig: http://nbn-resolving.de/urn:nbn:de:bsz:15-qucosa-197246.

Hilbert, A., Zenger, M., Eichler, J., & Brähler, E. (2021). Psychometric evaluation of the Eating Disorders in Youth-Questionnaire when used in adults: Prevalence estimates for symptoms of avoidant/restrictive food intake disorder and population norms. *International Journal of Eating Disorders*, *54*(3), 399–408. https://doi.org/10.1002/eat.23424

Kambanis, P. E., Harshman, S. G., Kuhnle, M. C., Kahn, D. L., Dreier, M. J., Hauser, K., Slattery, M., Becker, K. R., Breithaupt, L., Misra, M., Micali, N., Lawson, E. A., Eddy, K. T., & Thomas, J. J. (2022). Differential comorbidity profiles in avoidant/restrictive food intake disorder and anorexia nervosa: Does age play a role?. *The International Journal of Eating Disorders*, *55*(10), 1397–1403. https://doi.org/10.1002/eat.23777

Kambanis, P. E., Kuhnle, M. C., Wons, O. B., Jo, J. H., Keshishian A. C., Hauser, K., Becker, K. R., Dranko, D. L., Misra, M., Micai, N., Lawson, E. A., & Thomas, J. J. (2019). Prevalence and correlates of psychiatric comorbidities in children and adolescents with full and subthreshold avoidant/restrictive food intake disorder. *International Journal of Eating Disorders, 53*(2), 256–265. https://doi.org/10.1002/eat.23191

Kaplan, S. C., Swee, M. B., & Heimberg, R. G. (2019). Social anxiety among transgender and gender nonconforming individuals: The role of gender-affirming medical interventions. *American Psychological Association*, *128*(1), 25–31. http://dx.doi.org/10.1037/abn0000399

Katzman, D. K., Guimond, T., Spettigue, W., Agostino, H., Couturier, J., & Norris, M. L. (2022). Classification of children and adolescents with avoidant/restrictive food intake disorder. *Pediatrics*, *150*(3), e2022057494. https://doi.org/10.1542/peds.2022-057494

Katzman, D. K., Norris, M. L., & Zucker, N. (2019). Avoidant restrictive food intake disorder. *Psychiatric Clinics of North America*, *42*(1), 45–57. https://doi.org/10.1016/j.psc.2018.10.003

Kambanis, P. E., Kuhnle, M. C., Wons, O. B., Jo, J. H., Keshishian, A. C., Hauser, K., Becker, K. R., Franko, D. L., Misra, M., Micali, N., Lawson, E. A., Eddy, K. T., & Thomas, J. J. (2020). Prevalence and correlates of psychiatric comorbidities in children and adolescents with full and subthreshold avoidant/restrictive food intake disorder. *International Journal of Eating Disorders*, *53*(2), 256–265. https://doi.org/10.1002/eat.23191

Kennedy, H. L., Dinkler, L., Kennedy, M. A., Bulik, C. M., & Jordan, J. (2022). How genetic analysis may contribute to the understanding of avoidant/restrictive food intake disorder (ARFID). *Journal of Eating Disorders, 10*(1), 53. https://doi.org/10.1186/s40337-022-00578-x

Le Grange D. (2005). The Maudsley family-based treatment for adolescent anorexia nervosa. *World Psychiatry*, *4*(3), 142–146.

Lock, J. D. (2021). Family-Based Treatment for Avoidant/Restrictive Food Intake Disorder (1st ed.). Routledge. https://doi.org/10.4324/9781003042020

Lock, J., Robinson, A., Sadeh Sharvit, S., Rosania, K., Osipov, L., Kirz, N., Derenne, J., & Utzinger, L. (2018). Applying family based treatment (FBT) to three clinical presentations of avoidant/restrictive food intake disorder: Similarities and differences from FBT for anorexia nervosa. *International Journal of Eating Disorders, 52*(4), 439–446. https://doi.org/10.1002/eat.22994

McGuire, J. K., Berg, D., Catalpa, J. M., Morrow, Q. J., Fish, J. N., Rider, G. N., Steensma, T., Cohen-Kettenis, P. T., & Spencer, K. (2020). Utrecht Gender Dysphoria Scale—Gender Spectrum (UGDS-GS): Construct validity among transgender, nonbinary, and LGBQ samples. *International Journal of Transgender Health*, *21*(2), 194–208. https://doi.org/10.1080/26895269.2020.1723460

National Center for Transgender Equality. (2016). *Understanding transgender people: The basics*. https://transequality.org/issues/resources/understanding-transgender-people-the-basics

Nicely, T. A., Lane-Loney, S., Masciulli, E., Hollenbeak, C. S., & Ornstein, R. M. (2014). Prevalence and characteristics of avoidant/restrictive food intake disorder in a cohort of young patients in day treatment for eating disorders. *Journal of Eating Disorders*, *2*(1). http://www.jeatdisord.com/content/2/1/21

Norris, M. L., Obeid, N., Santos, A., Valois, D. D., Isserlin, L., Feder, S., & Spettigue, W. (2021). Treatment needs and rates of mental health comorbidity in adolescent patients with ARFID. *Frontiers in Psychiatry*, *12*, 680298. https://doi.org/10.3389/fpsyt.2021.680298

Norris, M. L., Spettigue, W., Hammond, N. G., Katzman, D. K., Zucker, N., Yelle, K., Santos, A., Gray, M., & Obeid, N. (2017). Building evidence for the use of descriptive subtypes in youth with avoidant restrictive food intake disorder. *International Journal of Eating Disorders*, *51*(2), 170–173. https://doi.org/10.1002/eat.22814

Oliveira, S. B., & Kaul, A. (2022). Invited Commentary Re: Prevalence and characteristics of avoidant/ restrictive food intake disorder in pediatric neurogastroenterology patients. *Journal of Pediatric Gastroenterology & Nutrition*, *74*(5), 547–548. https://doi.org/10.1097/mpg.0000000000003431

Osman, A., Kopper, B. A., Barrios, F., Gutierrez, P. M., & Bagge, C. L. (2004). Reliability and validity of the Beck Depression Inventory-II with adolescent psychiatric inpatients. *Psychological Assessment*, *16*(2), 120–132. http://dx.doi.org/10.1037/1040-3590.16.2.120

Pennell, A., Webb, C., Agar, P., Federici, A., & Couturier, J. (2019). Implementation of dialectical behavior therapy in a day hospital setting for adolescents with eating disorders. *Journal of the Canadian Academy of Child and Adolescent Psychiatry*, *28*(1), 21–29.

Reilly, E. E., Orloff, N. C., Luo, T., Berner, L. A., Brown, T. A., Claudat, K., Kaye, W. H., & Anderson, L. K. (2020). Dialectical behavioral therapy for the treatment of adolescent eating disorders: a review of existing work and proposed future directions. *Eating Disorders*, *28*(2), 122–141. https://doi.org/10.1080/10640266.2020.1743098

Rienecke, R. D., & Le Grange, D. (2022). The five tenets of family-based treatment for adolescent eating disorders. *Journal of Eating Disorders*, *10*(1), 60. https://doi.org/10.1186/s40337-022-00585-y

Riddle, M. C. & Safer, J. D. (2022). Medical considerations in the care of transgender and gender diverse patients with eating disorders, *Journal of Eating Disorders, 10*(178) https://doi.org/10.1186/s40337-022-00699-3

Rosania, K., & Lock, J. (2020). Family-based treatment for a preadolescent with avoidant/restrictive food intake disorder with sensory sensitivity: A case report. *Frontiers in Psychiatry*, *11* https://doi.org/10.3389/fpsyt.2020.00350

Smith, B., Rogers, S. L., Blissett, J., & Ludlow, A. K. (2020). The relationship between sensory sensitivity, food fussiness and food preferences in children with neurodevelopmental disorders. *Appetite*, *150*, 104643. https://doi.org/10.1016/j.appet.2020.104643

Spettigue, W., Norris, M. L., Santos, A., & Obeid, N. (2018). Treatment of children and adolescents with avoidant/restrictive food intake disorder: a case series examining the feasibility of family therapy and adjunctive treatments. *Journal of Eating Disorders*, *6*(1). https://doi.org/10.1186/s40337-018-0205-3

Stice, E., Becker, C. B., & Yokum, S. (2013). Eating disorder prevention: Current evidence-base and future directions. *International Journal of Eating Disorders*, *46*(5), 478–485. https://doi.org/10.1002/eat.22105

Thomas, J. J., Becker, K. R., Kuhnle, M. C., Jo, J. H., Harshman, S. G., Wons, O. B., Keshishian, A. C., Hauser, K., Breithaupt, L., Liebman, R. E., Misra, M., Wilhelm, S., Lawson, E. A., & Eddy, K. T. (2020). Cognitive behavioral therapy for avoidant/restrictive food intake disorder: Feasibility, acceptability, and proof of concept for children and adolescents. *International Journal of Eating Disorders*, *53*(10), 1636–1646. https://doi.org/10.1002/eat.23355

Thomas, J. J., & Eddy, K. (2019). *Cognitive-behavioral therapy for avoidant/restrictive food intake disorder: Children, adolescents, and adults*. Cambridge University Press.

Thomas, J. J., Lawson, E. A., Micali, N., Misra, M., Deckersbach, T., & Eddy, K. T. (2017). Avoidant/restrictive food intake disorder: A three-dimensional model of neurobiology with implications for etiology and treatment. *Current Psychiatry Reports*, *19*(8), 1–9. https://doi.org/10.1007/s11920-017-0795-5

Thomas, J. J., Wons, O. B., & Eddy, K. T. (2018). Cognitive–behavioral treatment of avoidant/restrictive food intake disorder. *Current Opinion in Psychiatry*, *31*(6), 425–430. https://doi.org/10.1097/yco.0000000000000454

Wilhelm, S., Greenberg, J. L., Rosenfield, E., Kasarskis, I., & Blashill, A. J. (2016). The Body Dysmorphic Disorder Symptom Scale: Development and preliminary validation of a self-report scale of symptom specific dysfunction. *Body Image, 17*, 82–87.

Zickgraf, H. F., & Ellis J. M. (2018). Initial validation of the 9-Item Avoidant/Restrictive Food intake disorder screen (NIAS): A measure of three restrictive eating patterns. *Appetite*, *123*, 32–42.

Zickgraf, H. F., Franklin, M. E., & Rozin, P. (2016). Adult picky eaters with symptoms of avoidant/restrictive food intake disorder: Comparable distress and comorbidity but different eating behaviors compared to those with disordered eating symptoms. *Journal of Eating Disorders* *4*(26), 1–11. https://doi.org/10.1186/s40337-016-0110-6

Zickgraf, H. F., Lane-Loney, S., Essayli, J. H., & Ornstein, R. M. (2018). Further support for diagnostically meaningful ARFID symptom presentations in an adolescent medicine partial hospitalization program. *International Journal of Eating Disorders* *52*(4), 402–409. https://doi.org/10.1002/eat.23016

Zickgraf, H. F., Loftus, P., Gibbons, B., Cohen, L. C., & Hunt, M. G. (2022). "If I could survive without eating, it would be a huge relief": Development and initial validation of the Fear of Food Questionnaire. *Appetite*, *69*, 105808. https://doi.org/10.1016/j.appet.2021.105808

Zickgraf, H. F., Murray, H. B., Kratz, H. E., & Franklin, M. E. (2019). Characteristics of outpatients diagnosed with the selective/neophobic presentation of avoidant/restrictive food intake disorder. *International Journal of Eating Disorders*, *52*(4), 367–377.https://doi.org/10.1002/eat.23013.

Zimmerman, J., & Fisher, M. (2017). Avoidant/Restrictive Food Intake Disorder (ARFID). *Current Problems in Pediatric and Adolescent Health Care*, *47*(4), 95–103. https://doi.org/10.1016/j.cppeds.2017.02.005

Zucker, N. L., LaVia, M. C., Craske, M. G., Foukal, M., Harris, A. A., Datta, N., Savereide, E., & Maslow, G. R. (2018). Feeling and body investigators (FBI): ARFID division—An acceptance-based interoceptive exposure treatment for children with ARFID. *International Journal of Eating Disorders*, *52*(4), 466–472. https://doi.org/10.1002/eat.22996

CHAPTER 4

RECOGNIZING DIVERSITY AND EXPANDING TREATMENT PARADIGMS

Working With a Midlife Jewish Woman With Anorexia Nervosa

Melinda Parisi Cummings and Robbi K. Alexander

Anorexia nervosa (AN) is a debilitating illness characterized by significantly low body weight, intense fear of weight gain, and distortion in the way weight or shape is perceived (American Psychiatric Association [APA], 2013). Though frequently trivialized, glamorized, or misunderstood as a disorder of choice (Gordon, 2000; Walsh et al., 2020), the burden of this illness is extremely high. AN has one of the highest mortality rates of any mental disorder, second only to substance use disorders (Chesney et al., 2014), with premature deaths attributed to both medical complications and suicide. Comorbidity with other psychiatric disorders is common, especially for anxiety disorders, obsessive compulsive disorder, and depressive disorders (Bühren et al., 2014; Carrot et al., 2017, Levinson et al., 2018). AN also has a high rate of relapse, with estimates ranging from 6–57% depending on the length of follow-up and the application of targeted relapse prevention strategies (Berends et al., 2016).

Counseling Individuals With Eating Disorders: An Intersectional Approach, pp. 65–90

Despite a long-standing perception that EDs primarily affect "skinny, White, affluent girls" (the SWAG stereotype; Halbeisen et al., 2022), eating disorders (EDs) in general are increasingly being recognized as impacting people of any race, ethnicity, gender, age, and body type. As this is true of AN as well, the goal of this chapter is to discuss and expand current conceptualizations of AN. We will examine important multicultural/diversity characteristics, discuss evidence-based treatments, provide an overview of the severe and enduring subtype of AN (SE-AN), identify an alternative treatment paradigm for those with SE-AN, and discuss that paradigm in the context of a case, with attention to important contextual considerations.

EPIDEMIOLOGY

Much of what is currently known about EDs comes from research focused on patients who are young, White, and female (Mikhail & Klump, 2021; Murray, Nagata, et al., 2017); as discussed throughout this book, there is a shortage of literature that centers other populations. AN is most frequently diagnosed in young females, with a lifetime prevalence in women ranging from 2–4% and the highest prevalence found in Europe, North America, Australia and New Zealand (Wonderlich et al., 2020). However, findings from the U.S. National Comorbidity Replication Survey suggest that 25% of individuals with AN are male (Hudson et al., 2007). Further, this figure may well underestimate the prevalence of AN in males given "female-centric" diagnostic criteria and systematic underrepresentation of males in research (Murray, Nagata, et al., 2017).

A similar problem exists with respect to estimating the prevalence of AN in diverse racial/ethnic groups. Prevalence rates based on clinical samples may be misleading, given that members of diverse racial/ethnic groups tend to underutilize health services and that EDs are often overlooked in people of color (Cachelin et al., 2000; Dohm et al., 2009). For example, Gordon and colleagues (2006) found that race-based stereotypes may hamper clinicians' recognition of disordered eating symptoms: when provided with nearly identical case studies (the only difference being race—African American, White, or Hispanic) only 17% of clinicians identified the African American adolescent's behavior as problematic, while 11% identified the White adolescent's behavior and 41% identified the Hispanic adolescent's behavior as problematic. Cachelin and Striegel-Moore (2006) found that Mexican American (MA) women were less likely to seek ED treatment than European American (EA) women. While MA women were as likely as EA women to recognize they had a serious eating problem (73.7% and 73.9%, respectively) and want help for it (72.4% and 65.2%, respectively), only 27% of MA women had sought treatment, compared to 44.9% of EA women.

Furthermore, even when they did seek help, MA women (14.3%) were less likely to be diagnosed with an ED than EA women (51%) or be treated for it (23.8% vs. 61.3%, respectively).

Notwithstanding this caveat, findings from community samples in the United States, though somewhat inconsistent across racial/ethnic groups, suggest that Black individuals may be at lower risk for the development of AN than White individuals. Udo and Grillo (2018) found higher lifetime prevalence rates of AN in White adults (.96) compared to non-Hispanic Black (.19) and Hispanic (.46) adults. Kamody et al. (2019) found the likelihood of lifetime diagnosis of AN to be lower for non-Hispanic Black adults than non-Hispanic White adults (adjusted odds ratio = 0.25), though no significant differences in lifetime prevalence rates were found between Hispanic and non-Hispanic White or non-Hispanic Black adults. Conversely, other studies have reported similar prevalence rates for AN across racial/ethnic groups. Using a nationally representative adult sample, Marques and colleagues (2011) compared AN prevalence rates among non-Latino White, Latino, Asian American, and African American respondents and found no significant racial/ethnic group differences in either lifetime or 12-month prevalence estimates. Similarly, no significant racial/ethnic differences were found when comparing lifetime prevalence rates among Hispanic, non-Hispanic Black, non-Hispanic White, and "other" -identified adolescents (Swanson et al., 2011).

Both sexual minorities (people whose sexual orientation is not exclusively heterosexual) and gender minorities (people whose gender identity varies from their sex assigned at birth) have been found to have elevated rates of AN (Calzo et al., 2021). In a representative sample of U.S. adults, the lifetime prevalence of AN was found to be significantly higher for sexual minority individuals (1.7%) vs. heterosexual individuals (.77%; Kamody et al., 2019). Based on self-report of diagnosis by a healthcare provider, lifetime prevalence of AN is estimated to be 4.2% for transgender men and 4.1% for transgender women in the United States (Nagata et al., 2020).

One limitation of extant prevalence research is that most diagnostic tools for AN were developed based on work with White females, and may therefore not adequately reflect variability in presentation among members of diverse groups (Rodgers et al., 2018). In addition, potentially meaningful differences between subgroups of individuals are obscured in current research, likely due to insufficient power. For example, various racial/ethnic groups are not homogeneous (e.g., South Asians, East Asians) nor are sexual minorities (e.g., gay men, lesbian women, bisexual individuals). Intersectionality further complicates this picture, making a more nuanced discussion of prevalence difficult. Despite these caveats, it is clear that AN is increasingly being recognized as occurring across diverse groups and with varied clinical presentations. Identifying factors that impede or facilitate access to treatment as well as sensitive and effective interventions for members of diverse groups is needed; as of yet, this research is in the nascent stage (Rodgers et al., 2018).

TREATMENT OF AN

Empirically supported treatments for AN typically focus on weight restoration and elimination of additional eating-related psychopathology. In 2020, the Academy for Eating Disorders developed an international guide to evidence-based psychotherapies for eating disorders. Basing their recommendations on the integration of national treatment guidelines from several countries, they identified family-based treatment (FBT) as a first-line intervention for children and adolescents, and enhanced cognitive behavioral therapy (CBT-E), the Maudsley model of treatment for adults with AN (MANTRA), and specialist supportive clinical management (SSCM) as first-line treatments for adults. Each of these therapies are manualized and have been methodically evaluated in high-quality trials (Leonidas et al., 2019; Zeeck et al., 2018).

FBT was developed from multiple family therapy models and takes the overall perspective that the family is an essential resource in treating adolescents with AN (Lock & Le Grange, 2013; Lock & Nicholls, 2020). It is theoretically agnostic regarding etiology of the disorder and is delivered in three phases; in each phase, parents play a central role. Phase I targets weight restoration and normalization of eating as parents take up the task of refeeding their child. In Phase II, parents gradually turn over control of eating and related behaviors back to their child. Once the adolescent has resumed appropriate control of eating without relapsing, Phase III focuses on normalizing adolescent development and planning for the future.

CBT-E is an individual therapy developed for use across multiple eating disorders, and is thus considered a "transdiagnostic" treatment that targets core symptoms (Fairburn et al., 2013; Murphy et al., 2010). It consists of four stages, typically in 40 sessions over 40 weeks for those in need of weight gain. Stage 1 is intensive and aims to engage the individual in treatment, develop a CBT-informed case conceptualization and treatment plan, stabilize eating patterns, and address weight and shape concerns. Stage 2 is brief and focuses on reviewing progress, identifying barriers, and planning for Stage 3. The essence of treatment takes place in Stage 3, in which central processes that maintain the eating disorder psychopathology are targeted. Lastly, Stage 4 is future-oriented and focuses on strategies for maintaining therapeutic gains and preventing relapse.

MANTRA (Schmidt et al., 2013) is based on a cognitive interpersonal model of AN in which factors that maintain the illness are identified and more adaptive ways of coping are developed. Four factors are considered central to the maintenance of AN and are thus targeted: an inflexible and overly detail-oriented thinking style, social and emotional avoidance, believing that AN serves an adaptive role, and close others' responses to the illness. MANTRA is designed to unfold flexibly over 20 to 40 sessions, with a hierarchy of treatment procedures tailored to the individual's needs and preferences.

Lastly, SSCM integrates the clinical management of AN symptoms (e.g., monitoring symptoms and physical status, providing information) with supportive psychotherapy that seeks to promote change (Schmidt et al., 2013). First developed as a control condition for use in AN treatment trials, it has more recently been recognized as an active treatment in its own right (Jordan et al., 2020). Treatment is geared toward helping individuals recognize the link between their symptoms, weight, and abnormal eating behaviors and supporting them in normalizing their eating and restoring weight (Schmidt et al., 2013).

While each of these treatments have demonstrated empirical support, some important limitations must be noted. As previously discussed, much of the work on treatment for AN thus far focuses on White female patients, and may not adequately reflect the needs of diverse populations. In addition, full and sustained remission has been reported for only 35–45% of adolescents treated with FBT (Lavender, 2020). Furthermore, FBT is typically studied in adolescents with a short duration of illness, typically three years or less (e.g., Eisler et al., 2000). Indeed, in the first randomized controlled trial investigating an early form of FBT, adults and adolescents with AN who had been symptomatic for more than three years showed less improvement than did adolescents with a short (3 years or less) illness duration (Russell et al., 1987). This consideration is especially concerning given that as the illness progresses over time, symptoms tend to become more entrenched and less responsive to treatment (Treasure et al., 2015). Finally, the effectiveness of first-line treatments for adults is modest, with approximately equal efficacy across CBT-E, SSCM, and MANTRA; in the United States, no first-line treatment for adults with AN has been identified (Academy for Eating Disorders, 2020). High attrition rates in treatment studies of adults have especially hampered the identification of effective interventions (Lock & Le Grange, 2013).

The fundamental goal of these treatments, which are likely indicated for the majority of those with AN, involves symptom remission, including weight restoration (Bamford et al., 2015). However, these treatments may have limited efficacy for individuals who are past young adulthood. While the onset of AN is typically in adolescence or young adulthood (APA, 2013), it frequently extends well beyond this period. Empirically supported treatments, however, have typically been developed through research with adolescent and young adult participants (Murray, Nagata, et al., 2017). Similarly, outcome studies commonly employ individuals who have had a short course of illness, despite the reality that a sizeable percentage of those with AN experience a lengthy course of illness that becomes less responsive to treatment over time (Ciao et al., 2016; Treasure et al., 2015). As such, there is insufficient awareness of the needs of midlife and older individuals with AN (McCallum & Alaggia, 2021), especially those with a long course of illness.

AN in later adulthood may take multiple forms with different attendant treatment needs. For example, some individuals had AN earlier in their lives and recovered, with relapse occurring in midlife. Others experienced the initial onset of AN in midlife or later, though this presentation is infrequent (Gonidakis & Karapavlou, 2014). For the majority of adults with AN, however, early symptoms of the disorder such as a drive for thinness and body dissatisfaction were present in adolescence or earlier, even if they were not evident to them or others at that time, and they have had the disorder for a prolonged course (Russell et al., 2019). Approximately 20-25% of those with AN will develop this protracted form of illness (Ciao et al., 2016), a course that has been increasingly described as severe and enduring anorexia nervosa (SE-AN).

As previously discussed, current interventions for AN focus on its core symptoms, stressing weight gain as a key treatment outcome. These goals are essential for recovery as traditionally conceptualized and remain indicated for most individuals with AN. However, they may represent a mismatch for those with SE-AN (Bamford et al., 2015). Patients with a prolonged course of illness and entrenched symptoms, whose illness may have become a central feature of their identity, and who have been through multiple treatments without lasting benefit, may well require a different approach.

CHARACTERIZING SE-AN

Agreement on the essential features of SE-AN is presently lacking. In a systematic review of descriptions of SE-AN, Broomfield and colleagues (2017) found that most definitions include clinical severity, long duration of illness, and a history of treatment interventions that have not resulted in sustained improvement beyond temporary periods of weight restoration. They found that other criteria, less consistently applied, have included degree of underweight, entrenchment of thinking or behavior patterns, and impairment in quality of life. The lack of consensus on the essential features of SE-AN is further complicated by difficulty operationalizing the criteria once established. For example, the minimum duration of illness to be considered "chronic" or "enduring" has been specified to be as few as 3 years (e.g., Dalton et al., 2020), and as much as 10 or more (e.g., Bamford & Mountford, 2012; Robinson, 2009), though the modal duration is 7 years (Broomfield et al., 2017). Developmental factors also warrant attention: assuming a consistent and appropriate length of illness can be reliably established, it is likely that the clinical presentation and treatment needs of a 40-year-old patient with a long duration of AN are quite different from that of a 22-year-old patient who has a similar duration of illness. An additional concern is the definition of failed treatment interventions. For example, what is considered to be an adequate attempt at treatment? Should this include any treatment of any quality, or a particular type of treatment (e.g., one that is empirically supported)? Given these difficulties, it is perhaps unsurprising that empirical evidence for a chronic subtype of AN has not been established (Wildes et al., 2017); calls have therefore been made for the establishment of clearly-defined criteria that can be empirically validated (Wonderlich et al., 2020). Hay and Touyz (2018) proposed the following testable criteria:

1. Impairment in functioning and persistent AN symptoms that include restriction of food intake, maintenance of an underweight state, and overvaluing of weight and shape.
2. Illness length of at least three years.
3. Having been treated with at least two appropriate, evidence-based interventions, including a diagnostic assessment/case formulation that evaluates the individual's health literacy and stage of change.

Despite the complexity of establishing a consistent definition of SE-AN, the burden of illness for this population is known to be especially high. Compared to adolescents, the prevalence of comorbid psychiatric disorders and suicidal ideation are higher for adults with AN (Bühren et al., 2014). Furthermore, as in individuals with other chronic illnesses, those with SE-AN commonly experience diminished quality of life and impairment in multiple areas of functioning such as work, social relationships, degree of independence, and physical and psychological health (Arkell & Robinson, 2008; Ciao et al., 2016). They may be depressed and stigmatized and feel burdensome to their loved ones (Westmoreland & Mehler, 2016). Their experience of multiple previous treatment failures may result in internalizing a sense of failure that can result in rejection of necessary treatment in the future (Conti et al., 2016), hopelessness (Robinson et al., 2015), and increased risk for suicide (Smith et al., 2018). Westmoreland and Mehler (2016) observed that some patients with SE-AN contemplate a "compassionate death" (p. 313) versus continued successive treatments with little to no time in recovery. Of particular note, the overall likelihood of long-term full recovery decreases with increased duration of illness (Fichter et al., 2006; Robinson, 2014).

As patients with SE-AN are less responsive to treatment than are those at earlier stages of the illness they present complex clinical challenges. Treasure et al. (2015) suggested that this diminished treatment responsivity is at least partially due to neuroprogression caused by chronic malnutrition. For example, they cited evidence for reduced brain size and dysfunctional signaling in the brain's reward circuit in those with SE-AN. These authors also posited that as the illness progresses, psychosocial functioning declines, typical life milestones are often missed, brain functioning is further impacted; as a result, symptoms become even more entrenched. The ambivalence and entrenched psychopathology experienced by those with SE-AN may not pair well with the active stance of traditional treatments, causing both patients and treatment providers to feel stuck, hopeless, or even adversarial (Bamford et al., 2015).

TREATMENT OF SE-AN

In response to these realities, there has been increasing awareness that effective treatment of patients with SE-AN may require a different approach than traditional methods that prioritize complete resolution of symptoms, including full weight restoration and return to a pre-illness level of functioning. This shift has been informed by the "recovery model," which acknowledges that those with severe mental illness can have fulfilling lives despite the continued presence of psychiatric symptoms (Dawson et al., 2014; Pike & Olmstead, 2016). For example, Touyz and colleagues (2013) advocated for the widening of treatment goals in SE-AN to include a focus on harm reduction, retention in treatment, and improvement in quality of life and psychosocial functioning. Similarly, Russell et al. (2019) called for an expanded definition of recovery, one that emphasizes restoring hope, autonomy, meaning, a sense of purpose, and positive self-image rather than focusing unrealistically on full resolution of symptoms. In these paradigms, a more collaborative and less directive therapeutic stance, while still maintaining clear safety parameters, is advised.

It is essential to note, however, that the evidence base for the treatment of SE-AN is limited. As individuals with SE-AN have largely been excluded from treatment studies to date (Ciao et al., 2016; Pike & Olmstead, 2016), much more is known about effectiveness of treatment at earlier stages of AN. High-quality outcome studies examining treatment approaches tailored to SE-AN are scant, and treatment recommendations are largely theoretical rather than empirically supported (Kotilahti et al., 2020; Wildes et al., 2017). To date, there has been only one randomized controlled trial

(RCT) that focuses on psychosocial treatments for SE-AN. Touyz and colleagues (2013) compared the efficacy of cognitive behavioral therapy for AN (CBT-AN) with specialist supportive clinical management (SSCM-AN) in 63 women with SE-AN, defined by at least 7 years of active illness. Both approaches consisted of 30 outpatient sessions delivered over an eight-month period, and both were adapted for SE-AN by prioritizing quality of life and harm reduction over weight restoration and symptom reduction (these were considered secondary goals). After treatment and at 12-month follow-up, both treatment groups showed improvements on primary outcome measures, which included quality of life and social adjustment. Furthermore, both groups also showed improvement in eating symptoms and weight gain while treatment dropout, typically high in this population, was low. A secondary analysis of data (Bamford et al., 2015) revealed that weight gain and improvement in other symptoms were linked to increased quality of life, both at the end of treatment and at follow-up. Taken together, these results suggest a reciprocal relationship between symptoms and quality of life, such that improvement in one area may generate improvement in the other. The authors concluded that balancing symptom-focused and quality of life goals may help to engage patients in areas that are important to them, retain them in treatment, and enhance quality of life while nonetheless reducing core symptoms.

Somatic therapies, such as pharmacological agents and brain stimulation studies may ultimately be of value in the treatment of SE-AN. Novel medications such as ketamine, dronabinol, and oxytocin have been identified as promising candidates for reducing symptoms (Wonderlich et al., 2020), though only dronabinol, an appetite-enhancing cannabinoid agonist, has been specifically trialed in those with SE-AN. In one RCT with 25 women who had AN for at least 5 years, adjunctive use of dronabinol was associated with slightly greater (.73 kg) weight gain; furthermore, the medication was well-tolerated (Andries et al., 2014). Dalton and colleagues (2018) conducted a feasibility trial of real versus sham repetitive transcranial magnetic stimulation (rTMS) in which 34 patients with SE-AN (including illness duration of 3 or more years) were randomized into two groups. They found moderate to large treatment effect sizes favoring rTMS (vs. sham) for quality of life and mood, but small effect sizes (also favoring rTMS over sham) for body mass index and ED symptoms. Follow-up 18 months later revealed that initial improvements in mood were essentially retained. Encouragingly, 5 of 12 patients in the real rTMS group were weight restored, while only 1 of 12 in the sham group was similarly weight restored, indicating that BMI and ED symptom improvements may need more time to emerge. Taken together, the results of these studies suggest additional viable treatment options, though larger scale investigations are needed.

An essential proviso in any discussion of SE-AN is that it is possible for full recovery to be achieved despite protracted illness. For example, Noordenbos et al. (2002) found that while most of the patients in their sample had not recovered, a small percentage (8%) described themselves as "fully recovered" and another 25% described themselves as "nearly recovered," despite having been ill for at least 10 years. Eddy et al. (2017) similarly found recovery from AN to be possible over the long term, with half of their cohort of patients with AN who had not recovered after 9 years progressing to recovery at 22-year follow-up. While the likelihood of recovery does decrease with increasing length of illness, it never reaches zero, suggesting the prospect of recovery at any point (Robinson, 2014). In addition, it is imperative to differentiate treatments that prioritize quality of life and harm reduction from a palliative approach to care; these approaches do not preclude the possibility of recovery, which can become a focal goal at any time. Indeed, as discussed, improvements in quality of life may provide increased motivation for further recovery. At no time is treatment conceptualized as "futile."

While treatments targeted to the unique needs of those with SE-AN are still in the early stages of development, some recommendations can be made based on the existing literature. First, goals should be widened to include an explicit focus on improving quality of life and psychosocial functioning. While this does not prevent attention to symptom reduction, including weight gain, prioritizing outcomes that are especially meaningful to the patient are likely to help retain them in treatment, minimize failure experience, and improve motivation.

In addition, it is important for the provider's therapeutic stance to be tailored to the distinctive experience of those with SE-AN. Given their varied previous treatment experiences, patients have considerable knowledge and their own unique perspectives on treatment, and a decidedly collaborative (rather than prescriptive) approach is critical to help avoid power struggles (Bamford & Mountford, 2012; Cummings et al., 2023). This may include expression of appreciation for patients' lived experience of chronic illness and acknowledgement of their strength and resiliency. At the same time, maintaining safety is key. Physical health should be consistently monitored and medical interventions implemented when needed (with clear communication of their rationale to the patient) to avoid further declines in health status (Touyz & Strober, 2016). Overall, a more collaborative and less direct approach is expected to result in greater engagement and retention in treatment, improved motivation, and hope that may ultimately result in improved weight restoration and symptom reduction in the long run.

CASE EXAMPLE

Sarah is a 37-year-old single Jewish woman with a 22-year history of restricting AN. She is the oldest of two siblings and was raised by both parents in the midwestern United States. She is a college graduate and former high school and college gymnast who lives alone in her own apartment, which her parents, who live locally, help subsidize. She has minimal contact with her older brother, who experienced depression as an older teen and is now a married father and successful financial advisor who lives with his wife and 8-year-old daughter in a town about 45 minutes away. Sarah notes that her parents are her biggest support; she is concerned for their health as they age, and states that they live in fear of her being re-hospitalized or succumbing to AN. Despite their unconditional support, Sarah believes that her parents are disappointed in her for several reasons, including lack of attainment in her teaching career, missed opportunities for her success as an athlete, and her distancing from her faith.

Sarah says that she always felt like an outsider. She attributes this, in part, to growing up in a Reform Jewish household in the Midwest, an area that she notes is home to fewer Jewish individuals than other parts of the United States. She never felt as capable as her more outgoing older brother. She describes herself as always having been "shy and sensitive," even as a child, though she did have a few close friends while growing up through her participation on sports teams and acknowledged an intense drive to perform well and please her coaches.

Sarah first became symptomatic at age 15 and while there have been periods where her symptoms were less severe, she has not been without some symptoms of AN since its onset. At age 16, Sarah was diagnosed with AN and began seeing a therapist. After about two years without significant behavior change, she was hospitalized at a very low body weight. Since then, she has received treatment in multiple levels of care, including five hospitalizations, two longer-term residential stays, partial hospitalization, and traditional outpatient treatment. Though she has partially weighted-restored on several occasions, Sarah has not maintained her discharge weight for any length of time, typically relapsing within several weeks of leaving structured treatment settings. She has remained at about 95–99 pounds since her pre-teen years.

At age 20, Sarah had to leave the university that she had attended for two years after high school; she lost her athletic scholarship and continued her studies at a local college part-time. Over several years, Sarah completed a bachelor's degree in education with a 3.8 GPA, despite having to interrupt her studies several times to seek treatment. After graduation, Sarah began work as an elementary school teacher. In her first year of employment, however, she had difficulty completing job-related tasks in an appropriate time frame, often spending hours at work after the school day ended meticulously re-working projects and tasks. Lack of confidence in her teaching and organizational abilities led her to leave her job before the end of her first year. Since that experience (which she internalized as a failure) Sarah has worked intermittently at a bookstore to obtain health benefits; as of late, she feels less competent and connected at work. She also has recently begun to avoid one of her few social outlets, reading to children at her community library. Sarah's parents help to subsidize her living expenses so that she can maintain a degree of independence, which she finds both desirable and shameful. She has never been in a serious intimate relationship and has not casually dated for many years; however, she would like to be in a committed relationship and to have children of her own in the future. Sarah stated, "Packing lunches for my children someday is not off the table in terms of my hopes."

Most recently, Sarah sought treatment from a therapist because she was feeling anxious, isolated, and depressed, and wanted to improve her mood. She may have experienced some recent weight loss; she currently weighs 94 pounds, which at a height of 63 inches places her at a BMI of 16.6, which her PCP estimates to be approximately 80% of her ideal body weight. She would like to feel better, but she is fearful about changing current dietary habits (citing inability to stray from routine) and the potential for weight gain. She is very ambivalent about making changes, especially in regard to food. She stated, "I just want the normal things in life that everyone has – to enjoy my family, have a job and friends. I just don't know how to get there."

Theoretical Underpinnings of Treatment

Therapeutic Stance

A review of the theoretical literature suggests that a harm-reduction approach may have value to the treatment of SE-AN and could potentially limit the devastating physical and mental consequences it often causes (Russell et al., 2019; Touyz et al., 2013). In this approach, goals for treatment are collaboratively set with the patient. Quality of life and the maintenance of physical and psychological safety are prioritized over planned, formulaic weight restoration. Developing a wider set of goals beyond ED symptom management is encouraged; complete eradication of the disorder is not the treatment focus. The patient is considered the expert on their illness and life goals, while the therapist's expertise is applied to implement treatment strategies and interventions to help patients successfully continue in treatment and realize goals.

Translating the theoretical literature on SE-AN to actual practice, a comprehensive treatment plan would include components such as:

- engaging the patient in treatment and prospect of change
- strengths based assessment of positive adaptation and protective factors
- validation of the patients' experience and intimate knowledge of the illness
- ongoing assessment of medical and psychological safety
- collaborative goal setting that is aligned with patients' stage of change and values
- use of evidence-based techniques and tools that promote wellness and help patients to attain goals they have identified for treatment
- CBT interventions to explore and address central cognitions/core beliefs/maladaptive schemas and avoidance
- a harm reduction approach that does not preclude hope for recovery

Prior efforts at recovery are framed in terms of hope theory (Snyder, 2000), the reciprocal process of renewing motivation/agency/goal setting and finding pathways to goals, to lessen the internalized sense of failure. Combined with a motivational interviewing approach, this is a collaborative endeavor. Treatment strategies are not rigidly adhered to or applied in a stepwise manner; how and at what point in treatment interventions are utilized is highly individualized to each patient and are decided upon in an ongoing process of collaborative goal setting (including review and revision as needed) between therapist and patient.

Culture and Culture Care Theory

Culture and religion transmit knowledge, beliefs, practices, and ideas in the service of navigating and finding meaning in life (Masten, 2014). Culture is transmitted across generations and can promote positive adaptation and resilience (Masten, 2014; Ungar, 2012). Leininger's (2006a) culture care theory may be useful in supporting patients' values clarification work, to validate their lived experiences (cultural values, care meanings, and action) and to improve overall quality of life. The theory postulates that human care is what gives dignity to humans and inspires people to get well; there is no cure without caring, but caring can exist without curing. Care is essential for human growth and survival, necessary in the face of illness and disability, and embedded in culture. Culturally congruent care is necessary for care to be meaningful, explicit and beneficial, and must be understood and actualized in diverse and specific cultural contexts. "Care has cultural and symbolic meanings such as care as protection, care as respect, and care as presence" (Leininger, 2006a, p.12).

Leininger (2006b) identified several central values held by Orthodox, Conservative, and Reform Jewish-Americans as well as acts that facilitate the expression of those values. Exploration of these themes could be useful in Sarah's therapy. Some values include maintaining respect for Jewish religious beliefs and practices, supporting education and intellectual achievements, prioritizing family relationships, and valuing the arts and religious rituals. Some actions include expressing emotions honestly, nurturing and protecting others, teaching Jewish values, and helping others in need as social justice (*tsdokeh*).

Early Treatment: Assessment and Collaborative Case Formulation

Assessment

When therapy began, Sarah and her therapist discussed aspects of treatment that were non-negotiable and the importance of maintaining physical and psychological safety. They discussed, described, and outlined factors related to the development of her AN and associated symptoms:

- Predisposing factors: Sarah and her therapist identified the following factors as playing a role in the development of her ED: personality characteristics that include fear of negative appraisals/criticism of others and resultant perfectionism and risk-avoidance; membership in an underrepresented minority religious group; athleticism and overvaluation of shape and weight.
- Precipitating factors: Sarah listed a number of internalized failures/stressors related to underachievement in the work and sports worlds, and this current episode of low mood and urges to restrict intake was preceded by an acceptable but mediocre performance appraisal at her current job. Since that time, Sarah has noted a vicious cycle of restricting food and strict adherence to food rituals, needing to reduce work hours, staying at home, and avoiding calls from friends.
- Perpetuating factors: Continued risk aversion, perfectionism, isolation, overvaluation of appearance/athletic physique, and food restriction/rituals are some of the most notable factors that Sarah

and her therapist identified as serving to maintain her low mood and AN. They identified that living apart from her values was a continued source of distress and also noted that she had not lived at a weight above 99 pounds since childhood.

- Protective Factors: Sarah acknowledged that the support of her family was essential to her existence, and it provides motivation to continue to seek treatment. With some hesitation, she acknowledged that the physical consequences of malnutrition/SE-AN are reversible and she has hope for future happiness and a more fulfilling existence.

Sarah and the therapist also explored the nature and impact of her ED:

- Periods of recovery: Sarah talked about the origins and trajectory of her illness, including times that she was doing better, and how that compares to her life currently.
- Consequences of SE-AN: Sarah demonstrated an awareness of the many ways SE-AN has negatively impacted her, including limited attainment of her personal and professional goals, missed developmental milestones, and social isolation. At the same time, she explored ways the illness "worked" for her, including helping her to avoid difficult emotions and perceived risks, and to elicit care from others.
- Past history of treatment: It was important to tap into Sarah's extensive knowledge of what did and did not work for her in treatment. She identified partnering with therapists and dietitians to be especially helpful, and that prescriptive goal setting often led her to become more avoidant and leave treatment prematurely.

Summary of Sarah's Case Formulation: Problems, Goals and Treatment Plan

Problem List. Jointly established between Sarah and her therapist, Sarah's problems were listed in order of importance, with number one being the most distressing.

1. Depression/anxiety/low mood
2. Isolation
3. Irregular menses and osteopenia
4. Low body weight

Treatment Priorities. This list was also jointly established with Sarah, and she named her goals in order of importance, with number one being the most important:

1. Mood improvement, including decreased fear and anxiety
2. Improved/enhanced work and social life
3. Medical and psychological stability/health

While Sarah listed stability/health last, maintaining safety was discussed as a non-negotiable treatment target. All goals set for ED symptom management were set collaboratively and in the service of medical and psychological safety and overall improvement of her quality of life.

Treatment Plan. Sarah and her therapist agreed to the following:

- **Ongoing assessment of the nature and severity of illness.** As medical and psychological safety were non-negotiable, Sarah agreed to ongoing medical monitoring with her PCP and referral to a psychiatrist (with the possibility of starting psychotropic medications if needed); consultation with a gynecologist or endocrinologist remained open for discussion as therapy progressed.
- **Values exploration and clarification.** Sarah was encouraged to explore and evaluate her current behaviors and situation in light of her ideals and values, using a values exploration and clarification exercise developed by Swedish acceptance and commitment therapy (ACT) therapist Tobias Lundgren (Lundgren et al. 2012). She concluded that that there was a moderate to great deal of discrepancy between her current lifestyle and behaviors and her ideal in all four life domains: work/education, leisure activities, personal growth/ health, and relationships. There was no aspect of life that she could label as living fully by her values.
- **Quality of life goals.** Sarah, with her therapist, identified the following:
    - Develop more genuine/authentic relationships with her parents, brother, and other family members (and begin to have a place in her niece's life)
    - Increase time with coworkers and reconnect with friends
    - Connect with Jewish family members and community to explore her heritage and spiritual and sustaining values
    - Join a local sports team and coach children's sports for fun and socialization
    - Evaluate her career goals/path

Traditional CBT and Cognitive Behavioral Case Conceptualization

Sarah and her brother were raised in the Jewish faith by professional parents; her father is an attorney, and her mother is a high school principal. Both parents were supportive, neither were critical nor were they particularly emotionally demonstrative. They had high expectations of themselves and their children, strongly encouraging them to be the best they could be academically, athletically, and socially. Intellectual pursuits, community contribution, and support of the fine arts were important to this family. Sarah's parents placed high value on the positive regard of their family by their community, in which they were deeply involved.

Sarah described herself as having an "anxious temperament" from an early age and believed that she needed to meet or exceed expectations to be valued by her family, despite their consistent care and support. Sarah tended to compare herself to her older brother, who seemed to make her parents proud and appeared to be more capable, socially adept, and confident than she believed she was. Sarah developed a core belief that she was average at best, and as such, less deserving of care from her family and others, which reinforced her need to be as perfect as she could possibly be. Perfectionism served to both lessen the risk of negative appraisal by others and meet her parents' expectations and ensure their care. Sarah, over time, developed compensatory strategies that included being overly agreeable, setting rigid rules and expectations for herself, and striving for perfection in all aspects of her life.

A precipitating event to Sarah's current mood and increase in ED symptoms was that she received a mediocre performance appraisal by her work supervisor. Since that meeting, she has had the following automatic thoughts: "I can't even function in a bookstore! How could I ever be a teacher? I'm generally incapable of good performance and overall incompetent at adulthood/life." Emotionally she feels anxious, ashamed and sad, and her behavior is to call out from work and avoid any situations that could be stressful or result in negative evaluation by others. She is feeling that her incompetence overflows into her social life and that she has nothing to offer a friend; the automatic thoughts she has around this are, "I am surrounded by attractive family and friends who are successful in their careers and their adult life who must feel that they have outgrown me," and, "I have nothing to offer my family or friends; I am not important." Sarah also suspects her parents are disappointed in her lack of success (although they have not voiced this), and an automatic thought she has in this regard is "I have not been able to function on my own or contribute to our family or community; I've dashed their hopes."

Therapy sessions targeted:

- Identifying and testing maladaptive thoughts/behaviors to help Sarah develop more realistic and effective ones
- Improving coping skills, especially in the areas of distress tolerance, problem-solving, interpersonal communication, emotion regulation, and self-soothing
- Increasing Sarah's sense of self-efficacy, resilience, and flexibility
- Addressing key maintaining (perpetuating) factors of the disorder through exploration of her values and culture
- Assisting Sarah to examine early maladaptive schemas (including defectiveness and shame), and challenge core beliefs and enduring patterns of behavior
- Increasing Sarah's motivation to engage in ongoing exposure to negative affect
- Implementing behavioral experiments/exposures (such as joining outings with coworkers) to challenge Sarah's avoidance and increase her self-efficacy
- Continued work on motivation and hope; a continual process of renewing motivation and developing pathways to goals
- Active CBT work to avoid disengagement and maintain flexibility

Measuring Progress/Outcomes

Despite Sarah's history of premature termination, Sarah remained in treatment and continued to collaborate in her care. She consistently completed her CBT assignments. She demonstrated improved cognitive flexibility; for example, she could consider alternative explanations for others' behavior that she had previously seen as devaluing and directed toward herself. By exploring her cultural beliefs and connecting with her values she became more mindful of what was important to her; as a result, she became more willing to take some interpersonal risks and more actively engage with family and coworkers. In particular, she began spending regular time with her niece. She also began to attend synagogue services to find meaning and a sense of connection in that community. She continues to work on increasing her socialization, with longer-term goals of finding more meaningful work, coaching sports, and eventually having a family of her own.

Without an intensive focus on her weight and eating behavior, Sarah nonetheless made changes in this area and experienced more intrinsic motivation to do so as she became more engaged. She increased her food intake, expanded her food choices beyond "safe" foods, and attained and maintained a weight of 102–104 pounds for several months. This was especially meaningful as she had not weighed over 100 pounds since the onset of her ED, nor had she maintained a weight over 80% of her ideal for any period. She maintained regular appointments with her PCP to ensure that she remained physically stable. She also worked in therapy to identify relapse triggers and warning signs, and more adaptive ways of coping with them.

Improved Quality of Life

The limited extant research suggests that there may be a reciprocal relationship between ED symptoms and quality of life, such that improvement in one area may generate improvement in the other. Balancing focus on symptom-focused and quality of life goals may help to engage and retain patients in treatment, and enhance quality of life while reducing core ED symptoms.

FUTURE DIRECTIONS

While there is increasing awareness that AN affects individuals with diverse identities, a more nuanced understanding of contextual factors and the complexities of identity is essential. Future research with large, representative, and community-based samples is needed to get a more accurate understanding of the prevalence of AN across diverse groups. Similarly, increasing the diversity of participants in treatment studies—including attention to gender, race/ethnicity, age, and length of illness—may represent one step toward improving evidence-based and culturally sensitive interventions for AN. Attention to the lived experiences of those with AN, including their preferences and perspectives, can further inform the development and refinement of treatment approaches. In addition, there remains a crucial need to identify and eliminate barriers to treatment-seeking, accurate diagnosis, and access to care.

With respect to SE-AN specifically, additional research attention to the identification of SE-AN is also critical, including empirical examination of its operationally-defined characteristics. Furthermore, while CBT-AN and SSCM-AN have shown to be of benefit, more work needs to be done to establish these or other approaches as first-line psychosocial treatments. Similarly, with additional study somatic treatments such as rTMS may ultimately provide viable treatment additions or alternatives.

Opportunities exist at the policy level as well. It is essential to ensure access to care, especially for underrepresented groups. In the U.S., individuals of lower socioeconomic status, those with SE-AN (who are often receiving disability benefits), and many others may not have private health insurance; however, many treatment providers and programs do not accept public insurance (Guarda et al., 2018; Wonderlich et al., 2020). Inability to access effective care further burdens individuals with AN and is likely a factor in the illness becoming protracted.

Funding is another critical issue. While the burden of EDs in general, and AN in particular, remain high, ED research has historically been under-funded relative to other disorders (Murray, Pila, et al., 2017). In the absence of increased financial support for research and treatment efforts, evidence-based, nuanced treatments that take into account the whole person and complexity of the disorder may remain elusive.

DISCUSSION AND REFLECTION QUESTIONS

1. How might we increase access to care for people of diverse groups?
2. What is your reaction to the idea of different treatment for different stage of disorder? What questions or concerns might you have about treatment that prioritizes quality of life over symptom resolution?
3. How would you go about working with Sarah?
4. What do you think is the role of values clarification in meaning making and work with EDs?
5. What changes might you make in your practice after reading this chapter?

REFERENCES

Academy for Eating Disorders (2020). *A guide to selecting evidence-based psychological therapies for eating disorders.* https://higherlogicdownload.s3.amazonaws.com/AEDWEB/27a3b69a-8aae-45b2-a04c2a078d02145d/UploadedImages/Publications_Slider/FINAL_AED_Psycholohgical_book.pdf

American Psychiatric Association [APA]. (2013). *Diagnostic and statistical manual of mental disorders* (5th ed.). American Psychiatric Publishers.

Andries, A., Frystyk, J., Flyvbjerg, A., & Støving, R. K. (2014). Dronabinol in severe, enduring anorexia nervosa: A randomized controlled trial. *International Journal of Eating Disorders, 47*(1), 18–23. https://doi.org/10.1002/eat.22173

Arkell, J., & Robinson, P. (2008). A pilot case series using qualitative and quantitative methods: Biological, psychological, and social outcome in severe and enduring eating disorder (anorexia nervosa). *International Journal of Eating Disorders, 41*(7), 650–656. https://doi.org/10.1002/eat.20546

Bamford, B. H., Barras, C., Sly, R., Stiles-Shields, C., Touyz, S., Le Grange, D., Hay, P., Crosby, R., & Lacey, H. (2015). Eating disorder symptoms and quality of life: Where should clinicians place their focus in severe and enduring anorexia nervosa? *International Journal of Eating Disorders, 48*(1), 133–138. https://doi.org/10.1002/eat.22327

Bamford, B. H., & Mountford, V. A. (2012). Cognitive behavioural therapy for individuals with longstanding anorexia nervosa: Adaptations, clinician survival and system issues. *European Eating Disorders Review, 20*(1), 49–59. https://doi.org/10.1002/erv.1080

Berends, T., van Meijel, B., Nugteren, W., Deen, M., Danner, U. N., Hoek, H. W., & van Elburg, A. (2016). Rate, timing, and predictors of relapse in patients with anorexia nervosa following a relapse prevention program: A cohort study. *BMC Psychiatry, 16*, 316. https://doi.org/10.1186/s12888-016-1019-y

Broomfield, C., Stedal, K., Touyz, S., & Rhodes, P. (2017). Labeling and defining severe and enduring anorexia nervosa: A systematic review and critical analysis. *International Journal of Eating Disorders, 50*(6), 611–623. https://doi.org/10.1002/eat.22715

Bühren, K., Schwarte, R., Fluck, F., Timmesfeld, N., Krei, M., Egberts, K., Pfeiffer, E., Fleischhaker, C., Wewetzer, C., & Herpertz-Dahlmann, B. (2014). Comorbid psychiatric disorders in female adolescents with first-onset anorexia nervosa. *European Eating Disorders Review, 22*(1), 39–44. https://doi.org/10.1002/erv.2254

Cachelin, F. M., & Striegel-Moore, R. H. (2006). Help seeking and barriers to treatment in a community sample of Mexican American and European American women with eating disorders. *International Journal of Eating Disorders, 39*(2), 154–161. https://doi.org/10.1002/eat.20213

Cachelin, F. M., Veisel, C., Barzegarnazari, E., & Striegel-Moore R. H. (2000). Disordered eating, acculturation, and treatment-seeking in a community sample of Hispanic, Asian, Black, and White women. *Psychology of Women Quarterly, 24*(3), 244–253. https://doi.org/10.1111/j.1471-6402.2000.tb00206.x

Calzo, J. P., Lopez, E. E., Silverstein, S., Brown, T. A., & Blashill, A. J. (2021). Where is the evidence of evidence-based treatment for LGBTQIA+ individuals experiencing eating disorders? In C. C. Tortolani, A. B. Goldschmidt, & D. Le Grange (Eds.), *Adapting evidence-based eating disorder treatments for novel populations and settings: A practical guide* (pp. 50–73). Routledge/Taylor & Francis Group. https://doi.org/10.4324/9780429031106-3

Carrot, B., Radon, L., Hubert, T., Vibert, S., Duclos, J., Curt, F., & Godart, N. (2017). Are lifetime affective disorders predictive of longterm outcome in severe adolescent anorexia nervosa? *European Child and Adolescent Psychiatry, 26*(8), 969–978. https://doi.org/10.1007/s00787-017-0963-5

Chesney, E., Goodwin, G. M., & Fazel, S. (2014). Risks of all-cause and suicide mortality in mental disorders: A metareview. *World Psychiatry, 13*(2), 153–160. https://doi.org/10.1002/wps.20128

Ciao, A. C., Accurso, E. C., & Wonderlich, S. A. (2016). What do we know about severe and enduring anorexia nervosa? In S. Touyz, D. Le Grange, J. H. Lacey, & P. Hay (Eds.), *Managing severe and enduring anorexia nervosa: A clinician's guide* (pp. 1–12). Routledge/Taylor & Francis Group.

Conti, J., Rhodes, P., & Adams, H. (2016). Listening in the dark: Why we need stories of people living with severe and enduring anorexia nervosa. *Journal of Eating Disorders, 4*(1), 1–7. https://doi.org/10.1186/s40337-016-0117-z

Cummings, M. P., Alexander, R. K., & Boswell, R. G. (2023). "Ordinary days would be extraordinary": The lived experiences of severe and enduring anorexia nervosa. *International Journal of Eating Disorders*, 1–10. https://doi.org/10.1002/eat.24058

Dalton, B., Bartholdy, S., McClelland, J., Kekic, M., Rennals, S. J., Werthmann, J., Carter B., O'Day, O. G., Campbell, I. C., David, A. S., Glennon, D., Kern, N., & Schmidt, U. (2018). Randomised controlled feasibility trial of real versus sham repetitive transcranial magnetic stimulation treatment in adults with severe and enduring anorexia nervosa: The TIARA study. *BMJ Open, 8*(7), e021531. https://doi.org/10.1136/bmjopen-2018-021531

Dalton, B., Lewis, Y. D., Bartholdy, S., Kekic, M., McClelland, J., Campbell, I. C., & Schmidt, U. (2020). Repetitive transcranial magnetic stimulation treatment in severe, enduring anorexia nervosa: An open longer-term follow-up. *European Eating Disorders Review, 28*(6), 773–781. https://doi.org/10.1002/erv.2766

Dawson, L., Rhodes, P., & Touyz, S. (2014). The recovery model and anorexia nervosa. *Australia and New Zealand Journal of Psychiatry, 48*(11), 1009–1016. https://doi.org/10.1177/0004867414539398

Dohm, F., Brown, M., Cachelin, F. M., & Striegel-Moore, R. H. (2009). Ethnicity, disordered eating, and body image. In H. E. Landrine & N. F. Russo (Eds.), *Handbook of diversity in feminist psychology* (pp. 285–309). Springer Publishing Company.

Eddy, K. T., Tabri, N., Thomas, J. J., Murray, H. B., Keshaviah, A., Hastings, E., Edkins, K., Krishna, M., Herzog, D. B., Keel, P. K., & Franko, D. L. (2017). Recovery from anorexia nervosa and bulimia nervosa at 22-year follow-up. *Journal of Clinical Psychiatry, 78*(2), 184–189. https://doi.org/10.4088/JCP.15m10393

Eisler, I., Dare, C., Hodes, M., Russell, G. F. M., Dodge, E., & Le Grange, D. (2000). Family therapy for adolescent anorexia nervosa: The results of a controlled comparison of two family interventions. *Journal of Child Psychology and Psychiatry, 41*(6), 727–736.

Fairburn, C., G., Cooper, Z., Doll, H. A., O'Connor, M. E., Palmer, R. L., & Dalle Grave, R. (2013). Enhanced cognitive behavior therapy for adults with anorexia nervosa: A UK-Italy study. *Behaviour Research and Therapy, 51*(1), R2–R8. https://doi.org/10.1016/j.brat.2012.09.010

Fichter, M. M., Quadflieg, N., & Hedlund, S. (2006). Twelve-year course and outcome predictors of anorexia nervosa. *International Journal of Eating Disorders, 39*(2), 87–100. https://doi.org/10.1002/eat.20215

Gonidakis, F., & Karapavlou, D. (2014). Eating disorders in late life: Implications for clinicians. *Psychiatric Times, 31*(11).

Gordon, K. H., Brattole, M. M. Wingate, L. R., & Joiner, T. E. (2006). The impact of client race on clinician detection of eating disorders. *Behavior Therapy, 37*(4), 319–325. https://doi.org/10.1016/j.beth.2005.12.002

Gordon, R. A. (2000). *Eating disorders: Anatomy of a social epidemic* (2nd ed.). Blackwell.

Guarda, A., Wonderlich, S., Kaye, W., & Attia, E. (2018). A path to defining excellence in intensive treatment for eating disorders. *International Journal of Eating Disorders, 51*(9) 1051–1055. https://doi.org/10.1002/eat.22899

Hay, P., & Touyz, S. (2018). Classification challenges in the field of eating disorders: can severe and enduring anorexia nervosa be better defined? *Journal of Eating Disorders, 6*, 41. https://doi.org/10.1186/s40337-018-0229-8

Halbeisen, G., Brandt, G., & Paslakis, G. (2022). A plea for diversity in eating disorders research. *Frontiers in Psychiatry, 13*, 820043. https://doi.org/10.3389/fpsyt.2022.820043

Hudson, J. I., Hiripi, E., Pope, H. G., Jr, & Kessler, R. C. (2007). The prevalence and correlates of eating disorders in the National Comorbidity Survey Replication. *Biological Psychiatry, 61*(3), 348–358. https://doi.org/10.1016/j.biopsych.2006.03.040

Jordan, J., McIntosh, V. V. W., & Bulik, C. M. (2020). Specialist supportive clinical management for anorexia nervosa: What it is (and what it is not). *Australasian Psychiatry, 28*(2), 156–159. https://doi.org/10.1177/1039856219875024

Kamody, R. C., Grilo, C. M., & Udo, T. (2019). Disparities in DSM-5 defined EDs by sexual orientation among U.S. adults. International Journal of EDs, *53*(2), 278–287. https://doi.org/10.1002/eat.23193

Kotilahti, E., West, M., Isomaa, R., Karhunen, L., Rocks, T., & Ruusunen, A. (2020). Treatment interventions for severe and enduring eating disorders: Systematic review. *International Journal of Eating Disorders, 53*(8), 1280–1302. https://doi.org/10.1002/eat.23322

Lavender K. R. (2020). Rebooting "failed" family-based treatment. *Frontiers in Psychiatry, 11*, 68. https://doi.org/10.3389/fpsyt.2020.00068

Leininger, M. M. (2006a). Culture care diversity and universality theory and evolution of the ethnonursing method. In M. M. Leininger & M. R. McFarland (Eds.), *Culture care diversity and universality* (2nd ed., pp 1–42). Jones and Bartlett Publishers.

Leininger, M. M. (2006b). Selected culture care findings of diverse cultures using culture care theory and ethnomethods. In M. M. Leininger & M. R. McFarland (Eds.), *Culture care diversity and universality* (2nd ed., pp. 281–306). Jones and Bartlett Publishers.

Leonidas, C., Nazar, B. P., Munguía, L., & Santos, M. A. (2019). How do we target the factors that maintain anorexia nervosa? A behaviour change taxonomical analysis. *International Review of Psychiatry, 31*(4), 403–410. https://doi.org/10.1080/09540261.2019.1624509

Levinson, C. A., Zerwas, S. C., Brosof, L. C., Thornton, L. M., Strober, M., Pivarunas, B., Crowley, J. J. Yilmaz, Z., Berrettini, W. H., Brandt, H., Crawford, S., Fichter, M. M., Halmi, K. A., Johnson, C., Kaplan, A. S., La Via, M., Mitchell, J., Rotondo, A., Woodside, D. B., … W. H., & Bulik, C. M. (2018). Associations between dimensions of anorexia nervosa and obsessive–compulsive disorder: An examination of personality and psychological factors in patients with anorexia nervosa. *European Eating Disorders Review, 27*(2), 161–172. https://doi.org/10.1002/erv.2635

Lock, J., & Le Grange, D. (2013). *Treatment manual for anorexia nervosa: A family-based approach* (2nd ed.). Guilford Press.

Lock, J., & Nicholls, D. (2020). Toward a greater understanding of the ways family-based treatment addresses the full range of psychopathology of adolescent anorexia nervosa. *Frontiers in Psychiatry, 10*, 968. https://doi.org/10.3389/fpsyt.2019.00968

Lundgren, T., Luoma, J. B., Dahl, J., Strosahl, K., & Melin, L. (2012). The bull's-eye values survey: A psychometric evaluation. *Cognitive & Behavioral Practice*, *9*(4), 518–526. https://doi.org/10.1016/j. cbpra.2012.01.004

Marques, L., Alegria, M., Becker, A. E., Chen, C., Fang, A., Chosak, A., & Diniz, J. B. (2011). Comparative prevalence, correlates of impairment, and service utilization for eating disorders across US ethnic groups: Implications for reducing ethnic disparities in health care access for eating disorders. *International Journal of Eating Disorders*, *44*(5), 412–420. https://doi.org/10.1002/eat.20787

Masten, A. S. (2014). *Ordinary magic: Resilience in development.* Guilford Press.

McCallum, L. A., & Alaggia, R. (2021). Achieving recovery through resilience: Insights from adults in midlife living with anorexia nervosa. *Qualitative Health Research*, *31*(4), 619–630. https://doi.org/10.1177/1049732320978202

Mikhail, M. E., & Klump, K. (2021). A virtual issue highlighting eating disorders in people of Black/African and Indigenous heritage. *International Journal of Eating Disorders*, *54*(3), 459–467. https://doi.org/10.1002/eat.23402

Murphy, R., Straebler, S., Cooper, Z., & Fairburn, C. G. (2010). Cognitive behavioral therapy for eating disorders. *Psychiatry Clinics of North America*, *33*(3), 611–627. https://doi.org/10.1016/j.psc.2010.04.004

Murray, S. B., Nagata, J. M., Griffiths, S., Calzo, J. P., Brown, T. A., Mitchison, D., Blashill, A. J., & Mond, J. M. (2017). The enigma of male eating disorders: A critical review and synthesis. *Clinical Psychology Review*, *57*, 1–11. https://doi.org/10.1016/j.cpr.2017.08.001

Murray, S. B., Pila, E., Griffiths, S., & Le Grange, D. (2017). When illness severity and research dollars do not align: Are we overlooking eating disorders? *World Psychiatry*, *16*(3), 321. https://doi.org/10.1002/wps.20465

Nagata, J. M., Ganson, K. T., & Austin, S. B. (2020). Emerging trends in eating disorders among sexual and gender minorities. *Current opinion in psychiatry*, *33*(6), 562–567. https://doi.org/10.1097/YCO.0000000000000645

Noordenbos, G., Oldenhave, A., Muschter, J., & Terpstra, N. (2002). Characteristics and treatment of patients with chronic eating disorders. *Eating Disorders*, *10*(1), 15–29. https://doi.org/10.1080/106402602753573531

Pike, K. M., & Olmsted, M. P. (2016). Cognitive behavioral therapy for severe and enduring anorexia nervosa. In S. Touyz, D. Le Grange, J. H. Lacey, & P. Hay (Eds.), *Managing severe and enduring anorexia nervosa: A clinician's guide* (pp. 128–145). Routledge/Taylor & Francis Group.

Robinson, P. (2009). *Severe and enduring eating disorder (SEED): Management of complex presentations of anorexia and bulimia nervosa*. Wiley.

Robinson, P. (2014). Severe and enduring eating disorders: Recognition and management. *Advances in Psychiatric Treatment, 20*(6), 392–401. https://doi.org/10.1192/apt.bp.113.011841

Robinson, P., Kukucska, R., Guidetti, G., & Leavey, G. (2015). Severe and enduring anorexia nervosa (SEED-AN): A qualitative study of patients with 20+ years of anorexia nervosa. *European Eating Disorders Review, 23*(4), 318–326. https://doi.org/10.1002/erv.2367

Rodgers, R. F., Berry, R., & Franko, D. L. (2018). Eating disorders in ethnic minorities: An update. *Current Psychiatry Reports, 20*(10), 90. https://doi.org/10.1007/s11920-018-0938-3

Russell, G. M. F., Szmukler, G. I., Dare, C., & Eisler, I. (1987). An evaluation of family therapy in anorexia nervosa and bulimia nervosa. *Archives of General Psychiatry, 44*(12), 1047–1056. https://doi.org/10.1001/archpsyc.1987.01800240021004

Russell, J., Mulvey, B., Bennett, H., Donnelly, B., & Frig, E. (2019). Harm minimization in severe and enduring anorexia nervosa. *International Review of Psychiatry, 31*(4), 391–402, https://doi.org/10.1080/09540261.2019.1601073

Schmidt, U., Renwick, B., Lose, A., Kenyon, M., DeJong, H., Broadbent, H., Loomes, R., Watson, C., Ghelani, S., Serpell, L., Richards, L., Johnson-Sabine, E., Boughton, N., Whitehead, L., Beecham, J., Treasure, J., & Landou, S. (2013). The MOSAIC study-comparison of the Maudsley Model of Treatment for Adults with Anorexia Nervosa (MANTRA) with Specialist Supportive Clinical Management (SSCM) in outpatients with anorexia nervosa or eating disorder not otherwise specified, anorexia nervosa type: Study protocol for a randomized controlled trial. *Trials, 14*, 160. https://doi.org/10.1186/1745-6215-14-160

Smith, A. R., Ortiz, S. N., Forrest, L. N., Velkoff, E. A. & Dodd, D. R. (2018). Which comes first? An examination of associations and shared risk factors for eating disorders and suicidality. *Current Psychiatry Reports, 20*(9), 77. https://doi.org/10.1007/s11920018-0931-x

Snyder, C.R. (Ed.). (2000). *Handbook of hope: Theory, measures and applications.* Academic Press.

Swanson, S. A., Crow, S. J., Le Grange, D., Swendsen, J., Merikangas, K. R. (2011). Prevalence and correlates of eating disorders in adolescents: Results from the national comorbidity survey replication adolescent supplement. *Archives of General Psychiatry, 68*(7), 714–723. https://doi.org/10.1001/archgenpsychiatry.2011.22

Touyz, S., Le Grange, D., Lacey, J. H., & Hay, P., Smith, R., Maguire, S., Bamford, B., Pike, K. M., & Crosby, R. D. (2013). Treating severe and enduring anorexia nervosa: A randomized controlled trial. *Psychological Medicine, 43*(12), 2501–2511. https://doi.org/10.1017/S0033291713000949

Touyz, S., & Strober, M. (2016). Managing the patient with severe and enduring anorexia nervosa. In S. Touyz, D. Le Grange, J. H. Lacey, & P. Hay (Eds.), *Managing severe and enduring anorexia nervosa: A clinician's guide* (pp. 95–111). Routledge.

Treasure, J., Cardi, V., Leppanen, J., & Turton, R. (2015). New treatment approaches for severe and enduring eating disorders. *Physiology and Behavior, 152*, 456–465. https://doi.org/10.1016/j.physbeh.2015.06.007

Udo, T., & Grillo, C. M. (2018). Prevalence and correlates of DSM-5–defined eating disorders in a nationally representative sample of U.S. adults. *Biological Psychiatry, 84*(5), 345–354. https://doi.org/10.1016/j.biopsych.2018.03.014

Ungar, M. (Ed.). (2012). *The social ecology of resilience: A handbook of theory and practice.* Springer.

Walsh, B. T., Attia, E., & Glasofer, D. R. (2020). *Eating disorders: What everyone needs to know.* Oxford University Press.

Westmoreland, P., & Mehler, P. S. (2016). Caring for patients with severe and enduring eating disorders (SEED): Certification, harm reduction, palliative care, and the question of futility. *Journal of Psychiatric Practice, 22*(4), 313–320. https://doi.org/10.1097/PRA.0000000000000160

Wildes, J. E., Forbush, K. T., Hagan, K. E., Marcus, M. D., Attia, E., Gianini, L. M., & Wu, W. (2017). Characterizing severe and enduring anorexia nervosa: An empirical approach. *International Journal of Eating Disorders, 50*(4), 389–397. https://doi.org/10.1002/eat.22651

Wonderlich, S. A., Bulik, C. M., Schmidt, U., Steiger, H., & Hoek, H. W. (2020). Severe and enduring anorexia nervosa: Update and observations about the current clinical reality. *International Journal of Eating Disorders, 53*(8), 1303–1312. https://doi.org/10.1002/eat.23283

Zeeck, A., Herpertz-Dahlmann, B., Friederich, H.-C., Brockmeyer, T., Resmark, G., Hagenah, U., Ehrlich, S., Cuntz, U., Zipfel, S., & Hartmann, A. (2018). Psychotherapeutic treatment for anorexia nervosa: A systematic review and network meta-analysis. *Frontiers in Psychiatry, 9*, 158. https://doi.org/10.3389/fpsyt.2018.00158

CHAPTER 5

THE PSYCHOSOCIAL EXPERIENCES OF PARENT CAREGIVERS

Caring for a Son With Anorexia

Erin E. Ott, Jessica Lennon Whitney, Melinda Parisi Cummings, and Merle A. Keitel

Anorexia nervosa (AN) is a chronic and potentially life-threatening eating disorder (ED) that has a profound impact on both the patient and their family. AN can be protracted, intractable, and has one of the highest mortality rates of any psychiatric disorder (Arcelus et al., 2011; Smink et al., 2012; Thornton et al., 2016). Many adolescents with AN require acute medical hospitalization to address the medical sequalae of progressive malnutrition (Kapphahn et al., 2017). Serious consequences of AN also include functional impairment and psychiatric comorbidity (Mehler & Brown, 2015). Some of the very features that characterize AN (e.g., fear of gaining weight, excessive exercise) often impede recovery and risk of relapse is high (Berends et al., 2018). Given the complex psychiatric, medical, and cognitive features of this illness, parent caregivers and adolescents with AN have described the illness as "taking over" or "consuming" the ill child (Blondin et al., 2019; Sibeoni et al., 2017), resulting in significant distress for both the diagnosed child or teen and their parents.

Counseling Individuals With Eating Disorders: An Intersectional Approach, pp. 91–115

In the face of a potentially fatal illness, issues with food, weight, and excessive exercise not only dominate the ill child's thoughts and behaviors but also profoundly impact the family system (e.g., Anastasiadou et al., 2014; Doba et al., 2014; Fox et al., 2017; Marchetti & Sawrikar, 2023). Phrases reported by parent caregivers such as, "our world blew up," "life turned upside down," and "everything was uprooted" capture the magnitude of the influence of AN symptoms on family life (Ott, 2020; Whitney et al., 2022; Williams et al., 2020). Since the typical onset of AN is during adolescence (Swanson et al., 2011) and parental involvement is linked to positive recovery outcomes (Ellison et al., 2012; Le Grange et al., 2010), parents of a child with AN play a central role in the recognition, treatment, and recovery of their child's illness. Consequently, parents are placed in an essential yet precarious position—they are a crucial resource for their child's recovery, yet can face substantial challenges to their effectiveness in that endeavor. Therefore, understanding parent experiences of caring for a child or adolescent with AN is necessary for clinicians as they attend to the ill child, the parents, and the family system throughout treatment.

Parent Caregiver Distress

Caring for a child with a chronic and life-threatening disorder is psychologically taxing and can even be traumatic for parents (Timko et al., 2022). Parents of a child with AN consistently report high levels of emotional and psychological distress as they navigate the psychological and medical needs of their ill child (e.g., Anastasiadou et al., 2014; Blondin et al., 2019; Coelho et al., 2021; Oketah et al., 2023; Williams et al., 2020). Further, post-traumatic stress symptoms have been endorsed by parents of an adolescent hospitalized for medical stabilization due to AN (Timko et al., 2022). Caregiver burden, understood as caregivers' perceptions of physical, emotional, and social problems associated with caregiving, is consistently identified in parents of a child with AN (e.g., Padierna et al., 2013), even exceeding that of caregivers of individuals with depression and schizophrenia (Martín et al., 2015). Costly treatment and time away from work outside the home increases financial strain on families and adds to parents' distress (e.g., Keitel et al., 2010; Marchetti & Sawrikar, 2023; Stuhldreher et al., 2012), a dynamic which may be heightened in single-parent families (e.g., Scarborough, 2018).

Distress in parents is exacerbated by misconceptions about the etiology of AN. Historically, parents, and most often mothers, have been blamed for contributing to the development of their child's AN by both healthcare communities and popular culture (Le Grange et al., 2010). The Academy of

Eating Disorders has stated that family influences are not the exclusive or primary cause of AN, but rather, parents should be considered an essential element in the treatment and recovery of their child with AN (Lock, 2019). Yet, studies consistently reveal that parents feel blamed and stigmatized by treatment providers (e.g., Keitel et al., 2010; Williams et al., 2020) and struggle with self-imposed blame and guilt related to not recognizing their child's AN earlier and believing that they "caused" their child's ED (Oketah et al., 2023). Further, parents report personalizing their child's progress in recovery, describing self-blame and guilt when the child does not achieve or maintain target weight gain during treatment (Coelho et al., 2021; Marchetti & Sawrikar, 2023; Oketah et al., 2023). As outdated and unsupported theories implicating parents may persist in the consciousness of both treatment providers and parents, researchers and clinicians should explore their personal biases as they consider how to empower parents as an essential treatment resource.

Parent Caregiving Demands

The process of assisting a child through a prolonged and often grueling course of AN is intensely demanding for parents. The recommended treatment for pediatric AN is family-based, requiring a high level of parental involvement to foster the child's physical, nutritional, and emotional health (Lock, 2019). Parents report that while caregiving, their lives are "put on hold" and have likened caregiving tasks to a full-time job (Oketah et al., 2023), requiring between 21 and 31 hours per week, with a majority of this time involving encouragement to eat and supervision of food intake (Raenker et al., 2013).

In outpatient family-based treatment (FBT)—the first line treatment for children and adolescents with AN—parents are directed to assume complete responsibility of their ill child's eating-related tasks (e.g., meal planning, preparation, supervision of mealtimes) and interruption of symptoms (e.g., exercise, purging) until weight is restored (Le Grange et al., 2010; Scarborough, 2018). Parents face a steep learning curve as they take responsibility for their child's nutritional rehabilitation and are often unprepared for the level of engagement required in their child's treatment (Blondin et al., 2019; Oketah et al., 2023). Compounding this distress is the adolescent's developmental desire for autonomy and treatment-interfering symptoms (e.g., fear of gaining weight; excessive exercise; lack of insight into the illness).

Consequently, parents have described mealtimes as "battles," as their efforts to provide practical support (e.g., meal supervision) are often met with anger and resistance from the ill adolescent, who wants to maintain independence while simultaneously experiencing extreme distress around food and eating (Scarborough, 2018; Whitney et al., 2022). With tension and hostility around the dinner table, mealtimes can take several hours; reintroduction of a challenging food item is noted as particularly difficult and emotionally taxing for parents (Scarborough, 2018). During these efforts to support their child's recovery, parents commonly report frustration, hopelessness, and powerlessness, especially during the initial stages of treatment (Fox et al., 2017; McCormack & McCann, 2015).

Despite the fact that treatment success is largely contingent upon caregivers' effectiveness in facilitating nutritional rehabilitation (Lock & Le Grange, 2013), parent caregivers consistently report unmet practical needs and lack of support from treatment providers (Coelho et al., 2021; Oketah et al., 2023; Raenker et al., 2013). With the responsibility to refeed their ill child, yet inadequate clinical supervision to do so, parents struggle with successful and consistent implementation of at-home treatment interventions (Scarborough, 2018). These parental caregiving challenges are of concern for the health of both the ill child and the parents, as early intervention can prevent more chronic psychological and medical consequences of AN (Robinson et al., 2013) and ineffective strategies to manage a child's AN has been linked to caregiver burden (Goddard et al., 2013).

When parents of a child with AN feel more empowered and confident in their caregiving ability, the impact may be profound. Indeed, parental self-efficacy has been linked to reduction of adolescent AN symptoms (Robinson et al., 2013) and improved patient weight (Byrne et al., 2015) at the end of FBT. Additionally, parents have reported increased confidence and skills in treatment implementation at later stages of their child's illness (e.g., Coelho et al., 2021), often due to seeking peer support from parent-specific networks (Oketah et al., 2023). Collaboration between parents and treatment professionals, especially during the early stages of the child's AN, is essential for both the recovery of the ill child and the wellness of the parent caregiver.

Impact of Caregiving on Relationships

As family members respond to this serious and potentially life-threatening illness, their lives may begin to revolve around AN (Fox et al., 2017; Whitney & Eisler, 2005). As such, AN takes a central position within family life and can have a pervasive impact on the family structure (Whitney & Eisler, 2005). Families affected by AN report more impairment in family functioning compared to community samples (Doba et al., 2014) and non-psychiatric controls (Emanuelli et al., 2004). Compared to other chronic illnesses, mothers of daughters with AN report greater family conflict (Sim et al., 2009). Parents, and notably mothers (Whitney et al., 2022), have felt targeted by their ill child's anger and described a previously close relationship as now conflict-ridden (Sibeoni et al., 2017; Williams et al., 2020). With substantial parental focus on the ill child, less attention is allocated to the well siblings (Fox et al., 2017) and consequent resentment between well and ill siblings is common (Scarborough, 2018).

A child's AN and treatment demands can place enormous stress on the spousal unit, with more severe ED pathology linked to lower marital satisfaction (Rienecke, 2018). Differences in perceived illness severity and disagreement in how to approach mealtimes have been linked to marital conflict and increased arguments in parents of a child with AN (McCormack & McCann, 2015; Scarborough, 2018). As treatment programs are geographically dispersed, one parent is often forced to relocate to be close to their ill child. Separation for lengthy periods of time has been identified by parent caregivers as contributing to marital strain (Ott, 2020). Importantly, marital strengths can co-occur alongside marital strain. For example, caregiving challenges can engender positive outcomes in the marital relationship, as some parents have voiced that collaboratively navigating the child's AN strengthened marital solidarity, communication, and cooperation (e.g., Ott, 2020; Williams et al., 2020).

Outside the home, maintaining relationships with friends and extended family members can be overshadowed by illness severity and caregiving demands. Further, feeling stigmatized by community members is commonly reported by parents (Griffiths et al., 2015; Whitney et al., 2022), as well-intended friends and family often do not understand the illness. Because of the protracted course of AN, parents have also reported a decline in social supports outside the immediate family as the illness progresses (e.g., Raenker et al., 2013). A lack of social support and stigma may be especially challenging for single-parent families who are tasked with managing their child's AN without an immediate partner.

PARENTS CARING FOR A SON WITH ANOREXIA

While EDs are thought to be one of the most gendered psychiatric disorders (Murray et al., 2017) and research on AN has primarily focused on females (Griffiths et al., 2015), the recent decade has brought more attention to males with EDs (e.g., Nagata et al., 2021). Boys and men may represent up to 25% of lifetime diagnoses of AN (Murray et al., 2017), with actual incidence rates potentially higher, due to diagnostic bias and gender-based stigma (Murray et al., 2017; Nagata et al., 2020). EDs in general and AN in particular can no longer be viewed as uncommon in males, and the male experience as an ED patient can no longer be dismissed or minimized (Murray et al., 2017; Nagata et al., 2021).

Despite increased awareness of boys and men with EDs, caregiving research remains predominantly focused on parents of female children with EDs. The Parent Caregiver research team led by Dr. Merle Keitel at Fordham University's Counseling Psychology Department has conducted a number of qualitative studies on parent caregiving experiences, examining both maternal and paternal experiences of caring for boys and girls with AN. The following section, including interview quotes, summarizes qualitative studies focused exclusively on parenting a son with AN (Ott, 2020; Whitney et al., 2022). Collectively, these studies reflect results from 22 parent interviews and the themes of delayed diagnosis, treatment challenges, stigma and lack of social support, and emotional impact are discussed.

Delayed Diagnosis

Parents highlighted healthcare professionals' lack of training in ED presentations in male patients as contributing to delays in accurate diagnosis. A majority of parents reported that front-line providers who physically examined their sons (e.g., pediatricians, psychiatrists, emergency room practitioners) either dismissed or minimized their son's AN symptoms, including weight loss, restrictive eating, compulsive exercise, and low heart rate.

One father, whose son was on a cross-country team, worried about his son's intense running: "We brought our concerns to the pediatrician who said, 'Well, it's very rare for a boy to have anorexia and it's very unlikely'. [Pediatrician] kinda led us away from trying to do any kind of counseling or therapy" (Ott, 2020). A mother reported her concerns over her son's restrictive eating were dismissed by a doctor on the basis of her son's gender: "I felt like there was that undertone of, 'Well he's a boy and his BMI (body mass index) is okay and I can see some muscle definition so he probably isn't that bad' " (Ott, 2020). Another mother, whose son lost about 60 pounds, was told she was "just interfering" by calling attention to her son's weight: "The pediatrician got out the BMI chart and said to my son, 'You could lose 20 more pounds and still be safe.' And said to me 'You need to stay out of this … to not talk to him about meals … to let him eat what he wants" (Whitney et al., 2022). While parents of girls with AN have also reported that providers' dismissal of their concerns and delayed diagnosis are significant stressors (e.g., Coelho et al., 2021; Keitel et al., 2010), these findings illuminate the healthcare barriers that may be exacerbated for boys with AN.

The removal of amenorrhea from the DSM-5 diagnostic criteria for AN indicates progress in gender-aware ED diagnosis, yet, the most widely utilized ED symptomology and severity assessments were developed and validated on female samples, so they lack sensitivity for male presentations of AN (Murray et al. 2017; Nagata et al., 2020). Evidence suggests that body image disturbances in males orient toward the goal of muscularity, compared to the goal of thinness, seen in females (Murray & Touyz, 2013; Murray et al., 2017). Assessments normed on girls and women do not capture the muscularity-oriented eating patterns and body image disturbances seen in males, which may result in males scoring lower on measurements of ED symptom severity (Darcy & Lin, 2012).

In addition, BMI is an inadequate assessment of illness severity (Nagata et al., 2020). Males with restrictive EDs are likely to have had a larger premorbid body size (Gueguen et al., 2012); as such, they may present with "normal" BMIs, but with clinical signs evidencing significant malnourishment (Vo et al., 2016). A male participant in a study investigating men's experiences with ED services further illustrates this point: "Needing a low BMI to be diagnosed with AN is like needing to be terminally ill to be diagnosed with cancer" (Dearden & Mulgrew, 2013, p. 598).

Without a gender-sensitive nosological framework for conceptualizing and diagnosing AN in males, parents' concerns about their son's compulsive exercise and desire for a "six-pack," for example, will likely continue to be dismissed by even the most well-intended practitioners. Consequently, boys with AN, their parents, *and* healthcare professionals may be less likely to recognize eating disordered behavior as being symptomatic of a mental health problem (Murray et al., 2017). Parents' abilities to intervene in their son's illness in a timely manner are stymied when boys' ED symptoms are overlooked (Murray et al., 2017) and they are misdiagnosed or underdiagnosed (Murray & Touyz, 2013). By the time parents obtain an accurate diagnosis and seek treatment for their son, symptoms are more entrenched and challenging to address, thus the ill child is at more acute risk, more medically compromised, and more in need of immediate weight restoration (Nagata et al., 2020; Vo et al., 2016).

One mother highlighted the serious consequences of delayed diagnosis: "We lost so much time trying to get [son] diagnosed. By the time we were looking for an inpatient program, it was life or death. He was 56 pounds at 4'11"" (Whitney et al., 2022). Another parent shared that emergency room doctors at a children's hospital discharged her son with a prescription for an antidepressant, while two days later her son was admitted to another hospital with a resting heart rate of 36 (Whitney et al., 2022). These reports align with a study indicating that more than 50% of adolescent males with retrospective diagnoses of AN who presented to an outpatient clinic met criteria for urgent inpatient admissions (Vo et al., 2016). Together, these findings underscore the direct and detrimental impact of the existing female-centric diagnostic system for EDs, which reasonably intensifies parents' distress trying to help their son with AN.

Treatment Challenges

Parents noted a paucity of informational resources targeted toward males with EDs, and AN in particular. One father summed it up, "The biggest challenge was finding anything that dealt specifically with male anorexia ... it's all female-centric" (Ott, 2020). One mother shared her challenges determining her son's caloric needs, since most published resources were based on caloric needs for girls and women. Another father noted, "All the articles were written from a female perspective ... it didn't relate to my son" (Ott, 2020). This perception of rarity may contribute to feelings of marginalization among men and boys with AN. In a recent review of men's perceptions of ED informational resources, study participants noted sparse male-oriented resources at treatment centers (Richardson & Paslakis, 2020).

Almost all parents of sons reported difficulty accessing treatment due to limited ED programs that accept boys, with few to no local options available. A father summarized, "We couldn't find any [programs] that would accept males.... That was a big challenge and very stressful" (Ott, 2020). Importantly, several parents noted that they were told that their son was the first male patient at their respective treatment center and reported that treatment paradigms and interventions were female-focused. Men participating in ED treatment programs have voiced feeling unwanted in ED treatment environments and that the physical space prioritizes women's preferences (Richardson & Paslakis, 2020; Robinson et al., 2012). Moreover, the lack of any male-specific best practice guidelines for treating EDs (e.g., Murray et al., 2017; Robinson et al., 2012) can reasonably and substantially exacerbate the stress parents already feel as they seek help for their sons.

Given the relative scarcity of ED treatment programs that accept males, many parents reported that their only treatment options were far from home, sometimes forcing families to be separated for lengthy periods. A father described how he and his wife managed to be with their son during his treatment: "We didn't think it was right for [son] to go through [treatment] alone—and so that's why we basically said, "We'll take turns driving back and forth—about three and a half hours each way—and staying in a hotel while he's in the treatment program" (Ott, 2020). This geographic separation from their sons was reported as distressing, as were the long stretches of separation from spouses who accompanied their sons to treatment. Needing to travel long distances for their son's treatment has broader financial and family implications. Financial strain due to high treatment costs (e.g., Keitel et al., 2010) and less attention allocated to the ill child's siblings (Scarborough, 2018) has been reported by parents of girls with AN. Yet, the geographic-related treatment challenges reported by parents of boys suggest that financial and family disruption may be exacerbated by additional travel costs and parents' limited time to be physically present for their other children while away at treatment with their ill son.

Parents also expressed feeling insufficiently supported by mental health and/or medical providers at some point in the treatment process (e.g., lack of clinical supervision for at-home intervention), which has been documented in prior research (e.g., Fox et al., 2017; Marchetti & Sawrikar, 2023) and is of concern given that family involvement is crucial for good outcomes of AN treatment (Le Grange at al., 2010). Although parents' unmet needs reported in these studies align with research on parents of daughters with AN (e.g., Keitel et al., 2010), the lack of gender-specific parent informational resources and support may further compromise these parents' ability to care for their son. Notably, parents who participated in the study by Whitney and colleagues (2022) reported feeling satisfied with ED specialists, highlighting the need for timely and accurate diagnosis by front line providers, since early intervention can mitigate more protracted psychological and medical consequences of AN (Robinson et al., 2013).

Stigma and Lack of Social Support

Parents voiced that their son's illness challenged gender norms for themselves, friends, family, and/or community members. A mother summarized, "People said, 'I didn't know that boys could get an eating disorder' and I didn't either, so I get that. You just don't look for it in boys." Similarly, upon parents' disclosure of their son's illness, responses such as "That's a girl thing, isn't it?" and "That's not a boy problem" were common and encapsulate the pervasive social misconception that AN afflicts only girls and women. Concern about the impact of stigma on their son and family was reported by some parents. A father reflected, "How do you tell people something like that because of the stigma that's going to come with it. And it's bad enough if you're a girl, but it's not something that boys are supposed to get" (Ott, 2020).

Misconceptions about the etiology of AN compounded stigma experienced by parents. Some parents perceived friends and family as implicating them in the cause of their son's AN. A mother described this stigma and blame from an extended family she previously used as a support network: "They don't understand anorexia and I have a son and no one hears of boys with [AN] ... the isolation was really hard ... we had some family members that said, 'What have you done to this child to cause this? You must have done something.' Just like it's genetic ... that isolation sort of was really hard" (Ott, 2020). Relatedly, a mother expressed frustration about her friends' intrusive curiosity and questions: "They always assumed that there was a trigger event, that he was molested, he was gay, he was abused ... I would get so frustrated with the questioning ... I started to sort of isolate" (Whitney et al., 2022).

Unsurprisingly, stigma adversely impacted parents' social supports, with a majority of parents noting a decline of support from friends and extended family, which is consistent with literature on parents of girls with AN (e.g., Raenker et al., 2013). Several parents felt that they were not supported the way they might have been if their son were diagnosed with a non-psychiatric illness. A mother reflected: "If he had cancer or a surgery, my friends would have called...would have sent a card or checked on him. There's a stigma, a sense that kids chose it or families cause it. It was very lonely" (Whitney et al., 2022). Because caregivers' perceptions about the social stigma of EDs has been shown to be a predictor of caregiver distress (Whitney et al., 2007), bolstering the supports of parents caring for a son with AN is critical.

Emotional Impact

Emotional distress was described by all parents, with shock, fear, and isolation most commonly cited. It is important to note that parents reported a range of emotional reactions during their caregiving journey. One father summarized, "Initially it was a relief that we figured out what was wrong with him ... [then] frustration that it took that long to figure it out.... And then doubt and sadness because we're sending our son away to treatment for three months" (Ott, 2020). Some positive outcomes, such as post-traumatic growth, were also reported.

Shock

Parents expressed feeling "shocked" by the diagnosis itself and related this emotional experience to the fact that their son was diagnosed with a severe and the highly gendered disorder. A father shared, "I was completely unaware ... never even crossed my mind that my son had an eating disorder even though he wasn't eating. I just never thought about it—just because of, I guess [the] stereotype that only women have eating disorders, which isn't right." A mother summarized her surprise at the severity of the diagnosis: "I had no idea how serious ... that his brain was so malnourished ... for educated people, we were just absolutely clueless" (Whitney et al.,

2022). Men have similarly reported being unaware that their behaviors and struggles are characteristic of an ED (Robinson et al., 2012). The shock of both parent caregivers and men with AN can certainly be connected to the historical marginalization of boys and men in ED research literature and resultant lack of health literacy surrounding boys and men with EDs.

Fear and Anxiety

The life-threatening nature of AN and enduring course of illness elicited fear in parent caregivers. To summarize this, one father shared, "I think the hardest thing is learning it [AN] is the one psychiatric illness that is the highest resulting in death. That's a little tough to swallow" (Ott, 2020). The mother of a son who relapsed with AN four times shared, "There's such a fear that it'll [AN] come back. You're still afraid, you know? Don't lose sight of it [AN] too much because you're so fricken frightened that it's gonna come back" (Ott, 2020). Specific psychiatric issues implicated with AN, including self-harm and suicidal ideation, were also noted to exacerbate parents' fear and anxiety.

It is important to situate parents' fear within the research specific to AN in males. Studies of males with AN indicate greater mortality in boys compared to girls (Gueguen et al., 2012) and higher mortality compared to males with other EDs (Quadflieg et al., 2019). Moreover, when compared to girls, boys have more rapid weight loss before receiving treatment (e.g., Nagata et al., 2020), higher rates of comorbid conditions (Weltzin et al., 2012), and greater unremitting compulsive exercise behaviors linked to risk of relapse (Murray et al., 2014). These disconcerting data, combined with parents' difficulties identifying gender-inclusive treatment for their sons, suggest that fear and anxiety in this subset of parent caregivers may be reasonably higher than that of other parent caregivers. Not only is this of great concern for the psychological well-being of these parents, but also for the ill son, as linkages between parent caregiver fear and lower parental self-efficacy has been documented (Stillar et al., 2016).

Isolation and Shame

AN was characterized as a "long, lonely journey" by one parent, with others sharing the isolation ("Nobody really gets it, you're the only one in it") and loneliness ("You can't explain it to anyone unless they've been through it") of the experience. One parent noted, "We have friends that we lost during the time when [son] came home [from treatment]—we didn't leave him on Saturday nights by himself. We were constantly with him to get him through it. So the isolation piece is really challenging" (Ott, 2020).

Shame and embarrassment co-occurred and/or perpetuated isolation. A father detailed how he and his wife felt shame when their son first returned from treatment. "We hid from it. We wouldn't tell others where he went, when he returned from school, what he was away for.... And then there was a self-realization that, 'Oh wow, I do have this shame that my son has an eating disorder'" (Ott, 2020). Although studies on parents of girls have also documented isolation (e.g., Oketah et al., 2023), stigma surrounding AN in males, treatment-related challenges, and limited social supports may situate parents of boys with AN at greater risk for isolation compared to other caregivers.

Post-Traumatic Growth

While the circumstances of caring for a child with AN are undisputedly stressful, attention to parents' strength and resilience in the face of this complex, protracted, and potentially life-threatening illness is of value. Cook-Darzens et al. (2005) asserted that a "family in crisis" is not necessarily a "dysfunctional family," noting that exclusive focus on "family deficits" in families of a child with AN may prevent clinicians from utilizing a more resource-oriented approach to leverage family members' strengths. More than half of the parents in our studies voiced that they found meaning through the ongoing stress and challenge of caregiving, describing positive interpersonal changes and individual growth, such as greater self-awareness and reflection. Overall, these findings suggest a need to more fully understand the totality of the parent caregiver experience, which includes both emotional distress and post-traumatic growth.

CASE STUDY

Julia and Mark, cisgender, White individuals, both age 41, have been married for 18 years and have two children: Rebecca, age 17 and Aiden, age 15. Julia is a high school science teacher at the local public school and Mark works for the county as a firefighter. Mark also has a side business detailing vehicles, which he started 5 years ago. Julia and Mark were high school sweethearts and live in the town in which they grew up. Mark's parents are deceased; Julia's mother and stepfather live in town and helped with childcare when the children were younger.

When Aiden was 13, early in 8th grade, he went through puberty and subsequently grew four inches and gained 20 pounds in the course of 4 months. At the beginning of 9th grade, Aiden joined the cross-country team. While never much of an athlete as a child, he found he loved the sport and became very committed to his team. During the fall season, Aiden continued to grow in height, but began losing weight. It was not until Julia saw him without his shirt on, while changing clothes, that she could see his ribs pulling at his skin. Julia wasn't worried—she recalled the "up and out" growth spurts of adolescence that Rebecca experienced, and also knew Aiden's daily running was causing him to "lean out."

Julia and Mark discussed Aiden's weight loss with one another, but decided not to raise it with their son, as they had read about body shaming and didn't want Aiden to feel self-conscious. As the cross-country season progressed, though, Julia became concerned. She noticed that since Aiden started running, he'd become extremely focused on eating "healthy"—he talked about getting "lean" and "cut;" he no longer ate dessert, and he sometimes skipped breakfast. Rebecca, who was 16 at the time, decided to become a vegetarian after watching a documentary about climate change. As Mark's job required 24-hour shifts, he wasn't as involved in the day-to-day feeding and care of the children. Julia initially welcomed the children's emphasis on eating healthier, though she was becoming stressed at meeting the needs of both of her teens, who once enjoyed fast food dinners she picked up on the way home from work, but who were now requesting "cleaner" food and showing her TikTok videos about the dangers of sugar.

At Aiden's 14th well visit with the pediatrician, Julia raised his weight with Aiden's doctor, a friend and classmate from high school, who had seen Aiden since birth. The pediatrician commended Aiden for his commitment to cross-country and told Julia that skipping breakfast occasionally and not having dessert was no cause for concern. At 5'9", 125 pounds, and 14 years of age, Aiden's BMI was considered "healthy" according to typical pediatric assessments. The pediatrician instructed Aiden to "have a cheeseburger and a milkshake from time to time!" and encouraged Julia not to worry.

When the cross-country season ended in the winter of 9th grade, Aiden continued running, stating he wanted to train for both next year's season and for a marathon in the summer. Julia had been reassured by the pediatrician's dismissal of her concerns and felt that Aiden was healthy and strong. Aiden continued to grow in height, though there were no major changes in his weight or health for months.

Now 15 and in 10th grade, Aiden is once again entrenched in the cross-country team, running 5–6 miles every day. He no longer eats any sugar, carbohydrates, or dairy, and will only eat food he prepares in their own home. Julia continues to worry about his weight, but Mark and Aiden both echo the pediatrician's feedback and tell her she is being controlling, that she needs to back off, and that Aiden is fine. Julia's concerns about Aiden have increasingly been causing conflict in her marriage to Mark, who she feels is "checked out" about the reality of Aiden's health. Julia confides her concerns to her mother, who also expressed worry about her grandson's eating habits. Mark feels stressed about Julia's worries, but doesn't know what's wrong with Aiden or how to help him. To cope, he begins taking on more shifts at work.

Mark and Julia both attended Aiden's third meet of the season to cheer him on. At the conclusion of the race, after coming in second place, Aiden collapsed and fell unconscious. Mark felt equipped to care for his needs as a firefighter with paramedic training, but the school athletics protocol was to call an ambulance, given that Aiden hit his head on a bench when he passed out. At the emergency department, Aiden's BMI was determined to be 17.9, at 5'11" tall and 128 pounds. His resting heart rate was 52 beats per minute, well below the normal range for his age. The emergency room physicians were concerned by the results of his bloodwork, his blood pressure, and his physical presentation, though no one mentioned the possibility of an eating disorder. At discharge, they recommended that Aiden see both a gastroenterologist and an endocrinologist for evaluation. Julia asked the treating physician about whether his symptoms could relate to not eating enough; the physician said that was possible, though unlikely, "since Aiden didn't report a longingness to be thin, like we see in anorexia."

Julia took Aiden to see a pediatric gastroenterologist in a larger town 70 miles from their home. After a thorough clinical assessment, the GI doctor told Julia she was concerned about Aiden's disordered eating habits and physical presentation and that they needed to consider whether they were dealing with a mental health issue; she provided a referral for a psychotherapist, an eating disorder specialist, 30 miles from Aiden's home.

Three weeks later, Aiden collapsed at school. He was unconscious for an extended period and was once again rushed to the hospital. Upon evaluation, emergency department physicians decide to admit Aiden, who is kept in the hospital for 7 days. Mark and Julia learn that his weight is dangerously low and gain much more information about how little he has been eating. Aiden is formally diagnosed with AN and the hospital team determines that he needs a nasogastric (NG) feeding tube to medically stabilize him. Julia takes time off of work while Aiden is hospitalized. She and Mark don't know what to tell friends and family, so they lie and say Aiden is dealing with an immune system issue. They are both confused and somewhat embarrassed by his diagnosis, which they thought impacted only girls. The treating physicians recommend that Mark and Julia find an eating disorder inpatient or residential treatment for Aiden immediately upon discharge.

As Julia begins researching programs, she realizes they don't all admit males and that their insurance will not pay for much of the treatment cost. Julia struggles to find time to research programs, call their insurance provider repeatedly, monitor Aiden, who is now home from the hospital and doing remote learning, and parent Rebecca. Mark and Julia do a virtual visit with one program that is 300 miles away but have concerns about the program. Mark is becoming increasingly reluctant about inpatient treatment, noting that they can't afford it and that Aiden will miss too much of "real life" if he goes away for treatment. Mark and Julia are arguing regularly in the weeks since Aiden was diagnosed. Julia is worried about Rebecca, who is in her senior year of high school and has been relatively on her own during the past weeks and months, because of Aiden's health needs.

Mark and Julia determine that they cannot afford to send Aiden to one of the inpatient treatment programs that specialize in boys, which are all more than 1,000 miles from their home. After consulting with the ED specialist referred by the gastroenterologist, they decide to embark on FBT with Aiden. Julia is extremely nervous, knowing she is not an "expert" on helping Aiden, and worried because she must take a temporary unpaid leave of absence from her teaching job to manage Aiden's home treatment.

CASE CONCEPTUALIZATION: INTERSECTIONALITY AND CONTEXTUAL ISSUES

Several factors are important to consider when conceptualizing the issues Aiden presented with and planning his treatment, including his gender, age, and the socioeconomic status of the family. As an adolescent male with a highly gendered illness, both Aiden and his parents may experience stigma (e.g., the perception that AN is a "girls' illness") and frustration with the length of time it took to get a diagnosis and appropriate treatment (and, consequently, the severity of his illness). It is important for treatment providers to validate their feelings about challenges more specific to boys and men with EDs. The family's financial status must be considered given the substantial costs associated with ED diagnosis and treatment (Stuhldreher et al., 2012). For example, although Aiden's family had health insurance, their policy had a high deductible and coinsurance rate that would result in significant out-of-pocket costs. In addition, Aiden's family would need to pay for lodging and other expenses associated with an extensive stay away from home, including travel to and from treatment. Time and distance considerations would be compounded by the presence of a sibling and the overall interference with family life. In addition to the cost, prolonged treatment in a residential treatment center can be disruptive to normal adolescent development (e.g., schooling, peer and family relationships). Intensive treatment is especially important for Aiden, given his age and the need to restore him to a normal developmental trajectory, in terms of both physical (body and brain development) and psychosocial issues. FBT would provide an intensive treatment experience delivered in the home setting. It would also closely involve Aiden's parents in treatment, a critical consideration for adolescents (Lock, 2019).

FBT, also known as the Maudsley method, is recommended as a first-line treatment for adolescent AN across several national treatment guidelines (Academy for Eating Disorders, 2020). Unlike traditional family therapy that tends to implicate families in the etiology of eating disorders, FBT empowers parents to manage the symptoms and behaviors of AN and places families at the center of the refeeding process (Lock & Le Grange, 2005, 2013). Delivered over three phases, parents are guided to (a) refeed their child, (b) return control of eating back to their child (as appropriate to the child's age and developmental level) as weight is restored and eating is normalized, and (c) address relevant developmental issues.

During Phase I, Aiden and his family were provided with psychoeducation that emphasized both the seriousness of AN and that neither Aiden nor his parents, Julia and Mark, are to blame for it. Aiden's parents were assigned the task of weight restoration, and Aiden was described as "overtaken" by AN, to help externalize the illness and to help mobilize Aiden's parents toward the task of refeeding him. They even came up with a name for it (after an antagonist in the "Harry Potter" series), which helped Aiden to see his parents and the therapist as allied with him against the illness rather than fighting against Aiden himself. In the second session, they participated in a family meal, which helped the therapist further understand the family's mealtime behaviors and gave Julia and Mark an opportunity to experience some early success (e.g., helping Aiden to eat at least "one bite more" than he had intended to). Phase I sessions focused on supporting Mark and Julia's efforts to promote weight restoration by identifying and reinforcing effective strategies, helping them to work as a team, underscoring that they are in charge, and minimizing blame and criticism.

Phase I was very difficult. Aiden was initially very angry and exhibited behaviors that were extremely upsetting to his parents, including crying, screaming, throwing objects, and self-inflicting pain (e.g., scratching and pinching his skin or slapping himself). He frequently yelled that he "would rather die than gain weight," which was especially upsetting to Mark, who often became angry or overwhelmed by the possibility of losing his son. Mark also became angry about the way Aiden treated Julia, especially during mealtimes, and frequently yelled at Aiden to "get it together." Rebecca coped by going out with friends as much as possible to avoid being at home, hiding her distress to keep from further burdening her parents.

The treatment team provided a great deal of encouragement and education in this phase, emphasizing that Aiden's behavior was not unusual ("it usually gets worse before it gets better") while reinforcing that it was not their fault and that they were helping rather than hurting Aiden. The therapist helped Julia and Mark to tolerate Aiden's anger and remain calm while setting appropriate limits and monitoring his behavior, including his safety. Julia and Mark were also encouraged to maintain consistency and to disagree privately rather than in front of Aiden. Julia, who remained on leave from her teaching job and prepared and supervised most of Aiden's meals, began to lean on Mark when she was exhausted, helping her to maintain a non-critical stance toward Aiden. Mark, in turn, reduced his work shifts and made himself available for meals whenever possible to provide relief for Julia. While this was financially quite difficult for them, they found that it brought them closer together. It also allowed them to spend more time with Rebecca, who had verbalized her own struggles with conflicting emotions—sadness because she felt "left on her own" much of the time, and guilt because she recognized the severity of Aiden's illness and thought her feelings were selfish. During this time, Rebecca (Aiden's sister) became a significant source of support for Aiden by listening and providing comfort when he expressed anger and fear, especially after meals. Mark and Julia were also provided with additional resources, such as parent websites, online forums, and support groups, where they connected with other parents, including parents of boys. The therapist also made herself available in between sessions to offer consultation and encouragement to Aiden's parents. Together, these activities helped to bolster their sense of self-efficacy; in time, Aiden's disruptive behavior decreased, and he steadily gained weight.

During Phase II, parents gradually return control of eating and related behaviors to their child; a return to normal adolescent development, which has been interrupted by the ED, is also fostered. Julia was initially more comfortable than Mark in this phase, and treatment remained focused on ensuring that they were making decisions together and that they agreed. Navigating Aiden's full-time return to school was a significant step. While Aiden's parents worried that his symptoms might increase upon returning to school and having less parental supervision, they agreed that it was important for his psychosocial development to do so as soon as was feasible. During Phase I, Aiden had taken a leave from school, and then returned for mornings only, so that he could eat all his meals at home with Julia. In Phase II, after Aiden began eating his morning snack on his own, he began attending school full time, at first eating lunch with the school nurse. As he continued to gain weight despite increased activity and decreased parental supervision, he began to eat in the cafeteria with his peers. During this time, Aiden was also encouraged to increase the variety of foods in his diet, including foods prepared by others. Aiden also began socializing with his peers again, especially his cross-country teammates; though he was not participating in practices or races, he attended the meets to support the team. Notably, as Aiden increased his activity level, he needed to increase his food intake.

As the focus is no longer on symptomatic behavior, treatment during Phase III focuses on related developmental issues and future plans. It begins when the child is fully weight restored and maintaining appropriate eating and exercise behaviors without parental supervision or relapse. For Aiden and his family, treatment in Phase III involved navigating more typical adolescent-parent relationship conflicts. For example, Aiden was having difficulty with time management, especially in the morning, which caused him to occasionally be late for school (and consequently, for Julia to be late for work). In addition, as Aiden spent more time with his teammates, he frequently neglected his chores at home and spent less time with his family. Interventions during this phase included normalizing the more typical conflict that occurs between adolescents and parents; the therapist once remarked (with a smile), "As stressful as this is, isn't it so much better to be talking about Aiden spending time with friends and not doing his chores than about the possibility of needing to be hospitalized?" The therapist encouraged collaborative problem-solving, and the family negotiated an agreement that supported Aiden's desire to strengthen peer relationships, including more flexible timeframes for chores and appropriate consequences for being late to school. In addition, Aiden's renewed interest in activities outside the home was reframed as an opportunity for Julia and Mark to re-focus on their relationship as a couple, which they did. This phase of treatment was brief, and treatment concluded when the family's interaction no longer needed to be centered on the ED.

RECOMMENDED INTERVENTIONS TO SUPPORT PARENT CAREGIVERS

Upon working with parents of a child with AN, healthcare providers should take care to address the high levels of psychological distress experienced by parent caregivers. Especially for parents of boys, parents may arrive at their child's treatment feeling stigmatized by their child's highly gendered illness and that prior concerns were minimized by previous healthcare providers. Acknowledgement and validation of parents' persistence in obtaining treatment for their son and recognition and validation of parents' concerns for their child's health is imperative. Practitioners should take care not to blame parents for their child's AN and recognize potential self-blame and misattribution of causes for their child's illness. When clinicians acknowledge the challenges faced by parent caregivers, relationships with treatment team members are strengthened, which better equips parents as they navigate their child's long-term recovery (Oketah et al., 2023).

Accurso et al. (2019) recently noted that other *parents'* perspectives on caregiving and their child's treatment may be the best resource of meaningful and realistic recommendations for parent caregivers. When participants in the Ott (2020) study were asked to offer advice to other parent caregivers, seeking emotional and practical support from other parents with a child with AN was noted as "invaluable" and strongly recommended, which is consistent with studies on parents of girls with EDs (Engman-Bredvik et al., 2016). Specifically, several parents recommended F.E.A.S.T—an online network established specifically for parent caregivers. Parents have highlighted that connecting with other ED parent caregivers has helped them gain a better understanding of the illness, helped navigate treatment services, and provided hope for the future (Mitrofan et al., 2019). Parents supporting parents may be particularly important for parents of sons with AN given the specific treatment-related challenges and stigma associated with caring for a child with a highly gendered disorder.

Parent groups focused on caregiving skill development have been identified as valuable in increasing self-efficacy in implementation of at-home treatment (e.g., FBT; Williams et al., 2020). Focused on management of the child's ED behaviors, interpersonal effectiveness, and adaptive coping, these groups offer parents opportunities to acquire or strengthen crucial skills and have been shown to decrease caregiver distress (Macdonald et al., 2011). To best equip parents as early as possible, caregivers recommend participation in these groups in the early stages of the loved one's illness (Macdonald et al., 2011).

Finally, increasing awareness of male AN and eating disorders through training, continuing education, and connecting to parent resources is a crucial task for all medical and mental health professionals. As awareness and understanding of the occurrence and presentation of EDs in males improves, parents, boys with AN, and front-line providers may be more likely to recognize AN symptoms and intervene to provide gender sensitive assessment and referrals. In research, mental health, and medical communities, deconstructing the current prevailing thinness-oriented conceptualizations of AN is urgently needed to accommodate for male presentations of AN, male-specific diagnostic assessment resources, and gender sensitive treatment options. Improving mental health literacy of EDs in boys and men is a public health imperative and supports the APA recommendation that, "psychologists strive to build and promote gender-sensitive psychological services" (American Psychological Association, Boys and Men Guidelines Group, 2018, p. 17).

DISCUSSION QUESTIONS

1. What are the most prevalent stressors for parents who have a child with AN?

2. What misconceptions have compromised treatment for males with AN and also negatively impacted parents' social and emotional well-being?
3. What are the unique stressors for parents of boys with AN with regard to diagnosis and treatment?
4. What can medical professionals, counselors, and psychotherapists do to empower parents and increase their self-efficacy in responding to their child and the illness?
5. What can professionals do to increase awareness of AN and other eating disorders in males?

REFERENCES

Academy for Eating Disorders (2020). A guide to selecting evidence-based psychological therapies for eating disorders. https://higherlogicdownload.s3.amazonaws.com/AEDWEB/27a3b69a-8aae-45b2-a04c-2a078d02145d/UploadedImages/Publications_Slider/FINAL_AED_Psycholohgical_book.pdf

Accurso, E. C., Sim, E., Muhlheim, L., & Lebow, J. (2019). Parents know best: Caregiver perspectives on eating disorder recovery. *International Journal of Eating Disorders*. Advance online publication. https://doi.org/10.1002/eat.23200

American Psychological Association, Boys and Men Guidelines Group (2018). *APA guidelines for psychological practice with boys and men*. http://www.apa.org/about/policy/psychological-practice-boys-men-guidelines.pdf

Anastasiadou, D., Medina-Pradas, C., Sepulveda, A. R., & Treasure, J. (2014). A systematic review of family caregiving in eating disorders. *Eating Behaviors, 15*(3), 464–477. https://doi.org/10.1016/j.eatbeh.2014.06.001

Arcelus, J., Mitchell, A. J., Wales, J., & Nielsen, S. (2011). Mortality rates in patients with anorexia nervosa and other eating disorders. *Archives of General Psychiatry, 68*(7), 724–731. https://doi.org/10.1001/archgenpsychiatry.2011.74

Berends, T., Boonstra, N., & van Elburg, A. (2018). Relapse in anorexia nervosa: A systematic review and meta-analysis. *Eating Disorders: The Journal of Treatment and Prevention, 31*(6), 445–455. https://doi.org/10.1097/YCO.0000000000000453

Blondin, S., Meilleur, D., Taddeo, D., & Frappier, J. (2019). Caregiving experience and expressed emotion among parents of adolescents suffering from anorexia nervosa following illness onset. *Eating Disorders, 27*(5), 453–470. https://doi.org/10.1080/10640266.2018.1553431

Byrne, C. E., Accurso, E. C., Arnow, K. D., Lock, J., & Le Grange, D. (2015). An exploratory examination of patient and parental self-efficacy as predictors of weight gain in adolescents with anorexia nervosa. *International Journal of Eating Disorders, 48*(7), 883–888. https://doi.org/10.1002/eat.22376

Coelho, J. S., Suen, J., Marshall, S. Burns, A., Lam, P., & Geller, J. (2021). Parental experiences with their child's eating disorder treatment journey. *Journal of Eating Disorders, 9*(1), 92. https://doi.org/10.1186/s40337-021-00449-x

Cook-Darzens, S., Doyen, C., Falissard, B., & Mouren, M. C. (2005). Self-perceived family functioning in 40 French families of anorexic adolescents: Implications for therapy. *European Eating Disorders Review, 13*(4), 223–236. https://doi.org/10.1002/erv.628

Darcy, A., & Lin, I. H. (2012). Are we asking the right questions? A review of assessment of males with eating disorders. *Eating Disorders: The Journal of Treatment and Prevention, 20*(5), 416–426. https://doi.org/10.1080/10640266.2012.715521

Dearden, A., & Mulgrew, K. E. (2013). Service provision for men with eating issues in Australia: An analysis of organizations', practitioners', and men's experiences. *Australian Social Work, 66*(4), 590–606. https://doi.org/10.1080/0312407X.2013.778306

Doba, K., Nandrino, J. L., Dodin, V., & Antoine, P. (2014). Is there a family profile of addictive behaviors? Family functioning in anorexia nervosa and drug dependence disorder. *Journal of Clinical Psychology, 70*(1), 107–117. https://doi.org/10.1002/jclp.21977

Ellison, R., Rhodes, P., Madden, S., Miskovic, J., Wallis, A., Ballie, A., Kohn, M., & Touyz, S. (2012). Do the components of manualized family-based treatment for anorexia nervosa predict weight gain? *International Journal of Eating Disorders, 45*(4), 609–614. https://doi.org/10.1002/eat.22000

Emanuelli, F., Ostuzzi, R., Cuzzolaro, M., Baggio, F., Lask, B., & Waller, G. (2004). Family functioning in adolescent anorexia nervosa: A comparison of family members' perceptions. *Eating & Weight Disorders, 9*(1), 1–6. https://doi.org/10.1007/BF03325038

Engman-Bredvik, S., Suarez, N. C., Levi, R., & Nilsson, K. (2016). Multi-family therapy in anorexia nervosa: A qualitative study of parental experiences. *Eating Disorders: The Journal of Treatment and Prevention, 24*(2), 186–197. https://doi.org/10.1080/10640266.2015.1034053

Fox, J. R., Dean, M., & Whittlesea, A. (2017). The experience of caring for or living with an individual with an eating disorder: A meta-synthesis of qualitative studies. *Clinical Psychology and Psychotherapy, 24*(1), 103–125. https://doi.org/10.1002/cpp.1984

Goddard, E., Salerno, L., Hibbs, R., Raenker, S., Naumann, U., Arcelus, J. Ayton, A., Boughton, N., Connan, F., Goss, K., Lacey, H., Laszlo, B., Morgan, J., Moore, K., Robertson, D., Schreiber-Kouine, C., Sharma, S., Whitehead, L., Shmidt, U., & Treasure, J. (2013). Empirical examination of the interpersonal maintenance model of anorexia nervosa. *International Journal of Eating Disorders, 46*(8), 867–874. https://doi.org/10.1002/eat.22172

Griffiths, S. G., Mond, J. M., Li, Z., Gunatilake, S., Murray, S. B., Sheffield, J., & Touyz, S. W. (2015). Self-stigma of seeking treatment and being male predict an increased likelihood of having an undiagnosed eating disorder. *International Journal of Eating Disorders, 48*(6), 775–778. https://doi.org/10.1002/eat.22413

Gueguen, J., Godart, N., Chambry, J., Brun-Eberentz, A., Foulon, C., Divac, S. N., Guelfi, J., Rouillon, F., Falissard. B., & Huas, C. (2012). Severe anorexia nervosa in men: Comparison with severe AN in women and analysis of mortality. *International Journal of Eating Disorders, 45*(4), 537–545. https://doi.org/10.1002/eat.20987

Kapphahn, C. J., Graham, D. A., Woods, E. R., Hehn, R., Mammel, K. A., Forman, S. F., Fisher, M., Robinson, K. A., Ellen, S. R., Hergenroeder, A., & Golden, N. H. (2017). Effect of hospitalization on percent median body mass index at one year, in underweight youth with restrictive eating disorders. *Journal of Adolescent Health, 61*(10), 310–316. https://doi.org/10.1016/j.jadohealth.2017.03.020

Keitel, M. A., Parisi, M., Whitney, J. L., & Stack, L. F. (2010). Salient stressors for mothers of children and adolescents with anorexia nervosa. *Eating Disorders: The Journal of Treatment & Prevention, 18(5)*, 435–443. https://doi.org/10.1080/10640266.2010.511937

Le Grange, D., Lock, J., Loeb, K., & Nicholls, D. (2010). Academy for Eating Disorders position paper: The role of the family in eating disorders. *International Journal of Eating Disorders, 43*(1), 1–5. https://doi.org/10.1002/eat.20751

Lock, J. (2019). Updates on treatments for adolescent anorexia nervosa. *Child and Adolescent Psychiatric Clinics of North America, 28*(4), 523–535. https://doi.org/10.1016/j.chc.2019.05.001

Lock, J. & Le Grange, D. (2005). *Help your teenager beat an eating disorder*. Guilford Press.

Lock, J., & Le Grange, D. (2013). *Treatment manual for anorexia nervosa: A family-based approach* (2nd ed.). Guilford Press.

Macdonald, P., Murray, J., Goddard, E., & Treasure, J. (2011). Carers' experience and perceived effects of a skills based training programme for families of people with eating disorders: A qualitative study. *European Eating Disorders Review, 19*(6), 475–486. https://doi.org/10.1002/erv.1065

Marchetti, D., & Sawrikar, V. (2023). Parents' illness representations of their child with anorexia nervosa: A systematic review of qualitative studies using the common-sense model. *International Journal of Eating Disorders*, 1–20. https://doi.org/10.1002/eat.24081

Martín, J., Padierna, A., van Wijngaarden, B., Aguirre, U., Anton, A., & Muñoz, P. (2015). Caregivers consequences of care among patients with eating disorders, depression, or schizophrenia. *BioMed Central, 15*, 124–134. https://dx.doi.org/10.1186%2Fs12888-015-0507-9

McCormack, C., & McCann, E. (2015). Caring for an adolescent with anorexia nervosa: Parent's views and experiences. *Archives of Psychiatric Nursing, 29*(3), 143–147. https://doi.org/10.1016/j.apnu.2015.01.003

Mehler, P. S., & Brown, C. (2015). Anorexia nervosa: Medical complications. *Journal of Eating Disorders, 3*, 11–19. https://doi.org/10.1186/s40337-015-0040-8

Mitrofan, O., Petkova, H., Janssens, A., Kelly, J., Edwards, E., Nicholls, D., et al. (2019). Care experiences of young people with eating disorders and their parents: Qualitative study. *BJ Psych Open, 5*(1). https://doi.org/10.1192/bjo.2018.78

Murray, S. B., Griffiths, S., Rieger, E., & Touyz, S. (2014). A comparison of compulsive exercise in male and female presentations of anorexia nervosa: What is the difference? *Advances in Eating Disorders, 2*(1), 65–70. https://doi.org/10.1080/ 21662630.2013.839189

Murray, S. B., Nagata, J. M., Griffiths, S., Calzo, J. P., Brown, T. A., Mitchison, D., Blashill, A. J., & Mond, J. M. (2017). The enigma of male eating disorders: A critical review and synthesis. *Clinical Psychology Review, 57*, 1–11. https://doi.org/10.1016/j.cpr.2017.08.001

Murray, S. B. & Touyz, S. W. (2013). How do clinicians in the field conceptualize muscle dysmorphia? *Advances in Eating Disorders: Theory, Research, and Practice, 1*(3), 207–212. https://doi.org/10.1080/21662630.2013.794517

Nagata, J. M., Brown, T. A., Lavender, J. M., & Murray, S. B. (2021). *Eating disorders in boys and men*. Springer.

Nagata, J. M., Ganson, K. T., & Murray, S. B. (2020). Eating disorders in adolescent boys and young men: An update. *Current Opinion in Pediatrics, 32*(4), 478–881. https://doi.org/10.1097/MOP.0000000000000911

Oketah, N. O., Hur, J. O., Talebloo, J., Cheng, C. M., & Nagata, J. M (2023). Parents' perspectives of anorexia nervosa treatment in adolescents: A systematic review and metasynthesis of qualitative data. *Journal of Eating Disorders, 11*(1), 193. https://doi.org/10.1186/s40337-023-00910-z

Ott, E. (2020). Parents caring for a son with anorexia: Stress, coping, and the marital relationship [Unpublished doctoral dissertation]. Fordham University.

Padierna, A., Martín, J., Aguirre, U., Gonzalez, N., & Quintana, J. M. (2013). Burden of caregiving amongst family caregivers with eating disorders. *Social Psychiatry and Psychiatric Epidemiology, 48*, 151–161. https://doi.org/10.1007/ s00127-012-0525-6

Quadflieg, N., Strobel., C., Naab, S., Voderholzer, U., & Fichter, M. M. (2019). Mortality in males for an eating disorder: A large prospective study. *International Journal of Eating Disorders, 52*(12), 1365–1369. https://doi.org/10.1002/ eat.23135

Raenker, S., Hibbs, R., Goddard, E., Naumann, U., Arcelus, J., Ayton, A., Bamford, B., Boughton, N., Connan, F., Goss, K., Lazlo, B., Morgan, J., Moore, K., Robertson, D., Schreiber-Kounine, C., Sharma, S., Whitehead, L., Beecham, J., Schmidt, U., & Treasure, J. (2013). Caregiving and coping in carers of people with anorexia nervosa admitted for intensive hospital care. *International Journal of Eating Disorders, 46*(4), 346–354. https://doi.org/10.1002/ eat.22068

Richardson, C., & Paslakis, G. (2020). Men's experiences of eating disorder treatment: A qualitative systematic review of men-only studies. *Journal of Psychiatric and Mental Health Nursing, 28*(2), 237–250. https://doi.org/10.1111/ jpm.12670

Rienecke, R. D. (2018). Parental marital satisfaction in a family-based partial hospitalization program. *Eating Disorders: The Journal of Treatment and Prevention, 26*(2), 143–148. https://doi.org/10.1080/10640266.2017.1330320

Robinson, K. J., Mountford, V. A., & Sperlinger, D. J. (2012). Being men with eating disorders: Perspectives of male eating disorder service-users. *Journal of Health Psychology, 18*(2), 176–186. https://doi.org/10.1177/1359105312440298

Robinson, A. L., Strahan, E., Girz, L., Wilson, A., & Boachie, A. (2013). "I know I can help you": Parental self-efficacy predicts adolescent outcomes in family-based therapy for eating disorders. *European Eating Disorders Review, 21*(2), 108–114. https://doi.org/10.1002/erv.2180

Scarborough, J. (2018). Family-based therapy for pediatric anorexia nervosa: Highlighting the implementation challenges. *The Family Journal: Counseling and Therapy for Couples and Families, 26*(1), 90–98. https://doi.org/10.1177/1066480717754280

Sibeoni, J., Orri, M., Colin, S., Valentin, M., Pradere, J., & Revah-Levy (2017). The lived experience of anorexia nervosa in adolescence, comparison of the points of view of adolescents, parents, and professionals: A metasynthesis. *International Journal of Nursing, 65*, 25–34. https://doi.org/10.1016/j.ijnurstu.2016.10.006

Sim, L. A., Homme, J. H., Lteif, A. N., Vande Voort, J. L., Schak, K. M., & Ellingson, J. (2009). Family functioning and maternal distress in adolescent girls with anorexia nervosa. *International Journal of Eating Disorders, 42*(6), 531–539. https://doi.org/10.1002/eat.20654

Smink, F. R., van Hoeken, D., & Hoek, H. W. (2012). Epidemiology of eating disorders: Incidence, prevalence and mortality rates. *Current Psychiatric Reports, 14*(4), 406–414. https://doi.org/10.1007/s11920-012-0282-y

Stillar, A., Strahan, E., Nash, P., Files, N., Scarborough, J., Mayman, S., Henderson, K., Gusella, J., Connors, L., Orr, E. S., Marchand, P., Dolhanty, J., & Robinson, A. L. (2016). The influence of carer fear and self-blame when supporting a loved one with an eating disorder. *Eating Disorders: The Journal of Treatment and Prevention, 24*(2), 173–185. https://doi.org/10.1080/10640266.2015.1133210

Stuhldreher, N., Konnopka, A., Wild, B., Herzog, W., Zipfel, S., Löwe, B., & König, H. (2012). Cost-of-illness studies and cost-effectiveness analyses in eating disorders: A systematic review. *International Journal of Eating Disorders, 45*(4), 476–49. https://doi.org/10.1002/eat.20977

Swanson, S. A., Crow, S. J., Le Grange, D., Swendsen, J., & Merikangas, K. R. (2011). Prevalence and correlates of eating disorders in adolescents. *Archives of General Psychiatry, 68*(7), 714–723. https://doi.org/10.1001/archgenpsychiatry.2011.22

Timko, C. A, Dennis, N. J., Mears, C., Rodriguez, D., Fitzpatrick., K. K., & Peebles, R. (2022). Post-traumatic stress symptoms in parents of adolescents hospitalized with anorexia nervosa. *Eating Disorders: The Journal of Treatment and Prevention, 31*(3), 212–224. https://doi.org/10.1080/10640266.2022.2099604

Thornton, L. M., Welch, E., Munn-Chernoff, M. A., Lichtenstein, P., & Bulik, C. M. (2016). Anorexia nervosa, major depression, and suicide attempts: Shared genetic factors. *Suicide and Life-Threatening Behavior, 46*(5), 525–534. https://doi.org/10.1111/sltb.12235

Vo, M., Lau, J., & Rubinstein, M. (2016). Eating disorders in adolescent and young adult males: Presenting characteristics. *Journal of Adolescent Health, 59*(4), 397–400. https://doi.org/10.1016/j.jadohealth.2016.04.005

Weltzin, T. E., Cornella-Carson, T., Fitzpatrick, M. E., Kennington, B., Bean, P., & Jefferies, C. (2012). Treatment issues and outcomes for males with eating disorders. *Eating Disorders: The Journal of Treatment and Prevention, 20*(5), 444–459. https://doi.org/10.1080/10640266.2012.715527

Whitney, J., & Eisler, I. (2005). Theoretical and empirical models around caring for someone with an eating disorder: The reorganization of family life and inter-personal maintenance factors. *Journal of Mental Health, 14*(6), 575–585. https://doi.org/10.1080/09638230500347889

Whitney, J., Haigh, R., Weinman, J., & Treasure, J. (2007). Caring for people with eating disorders: Factors associated with psychological distress and negative caregiving appraisals in carers of people with eating disorders. *British Journal of Clinical Psychology, 46,* 413–428. https://doi.org/10.1348/014466507X173781

Whitney, J. L., Keitel, M. A., Cummings, M. P., Ponterotto, J. G., & Ott, E. (2022). Caring for sons with anorexia: The perspective of mothers. *Journal of Child and Family Studies, 32*(4), 2637–265. https://doi.org/10.1007/s10826-022-02525-5

Williams, E. P., Russell-Mayhew, S., Moules, N. J., & Dimitropoulous, G. (2020). "My whole world fell apart": Parents discovering their child has anorexia nervosa. *Qualitative Health Research, 30*(12), 1821–1832. https://doi.org/10.1177/1049732320939508

CHAPTER 6

ASSESSMENT AND TREATMENT OF BULIMIA NERVOSA

Case Examination of a Bisexual, Nonbinary Hispanic Individual

Francesca Gomez and Marisol Perez

This chapter provides a brief overview of the prevalence rates of bulimia nervosa (BN) within the United States population in general, and across gender, race, ethnicity, sexual orientation, and age. Using the American Psychological Association Division 12's guidelines for empirically-supported treatments, cognitive behavioral therapy, interpersonal therapy, and family therapy for bulimia nervosa are discussed. The empirical literature on treatment adaptation due to social identities is reviewed, although it is sparse. A case study of a patient with intersecting social identities, including Hispanic, bisexual, and nonbinary, is presented and discussed in terms of assessment and treatment.

BN is an eating disorder associated with serious medical and psychological issues. Medical complications from BN include, but are not limited to, dental issues, gastro-intestinal problems, and nutritional abnormalities (Mehler, 2011). Further, BN has been associated with depression, anxiety, post-traumatic stress, and substance use disorders (Udo & Grilo, 2019) as

Counseling Individuals With Eating Disorders: An Intersectional Approach, pp. 117–138

well as suicidal ideation, attempts, and completion (Bodell et al., 2013). BN can lead to significant disability and impairment (Udo & Grilo, 2019). The prevention and treatment of BN is an important societal issue, as total economic costs associated with eating disorders in the U.S. were estimated to be $59.9 billion in 2018-2019 alone (Deloitte Access Economics, 2020).

According to the American Psychiatric Association (2022), BN is characterized by a pattern of recurrent episodes of binge eating followed by the use of compensatory behaviors to prevent weight gain (i.e., vomiting, laxatives, diuretics, medication, fasting, or excessive exercise). Binge eating is defined as eating a large amount of food within a meal time frame given the situation and circumstance. The binge eating episode is accompanied by a feeling that one cannot stop or control the eating (i.e., loss of control over eating). According to diagnostic criteria of the DSM 5-TR, binge eating and compensatory behaviors occur on average once a week for at least 3 months, are influenced by overvaluation of shape and weight concerns, and are distinct from episodes of anorexia nervosa (American Psychiatric Association, 2022). Importantly, severity of the disorder is characterized by frequency of compensatory behaviors during a week: Mild: 1–3 episodes, Moderate: 4–7 episodes, Severe: 8–13 episodes, Extreme: 14 or more episodes (American Psychiatric Association, 2022).

PREVALENCE OF BULIMIA NERVOSA

In the most recent national epidemiological study in the United States, Udo and Grilo (2018) found that the lifetime prevalence estimate for BN was 0.28% and the 12-month prevalence estimate was 0.14% using diagnostic interviews to determine diagnosis. These prevalence rates were lower than previously documented prevalence rates with diagnostic interviews. Hudson and colleagues (2007) found a 1.0% lifetime prevalence and 0.30% 12-month prevalence rate; however, this was with the DSM-IV.

It is important to note that although BN can occur across race/ethnicity, gender, sexual orientation, and age, current prevalence studies of BN may underestimate the burden of the disease (U.S. Preventive Services Task Force, 2022). There are several factors that can contribute to the underreporting of BN including secrecy related to eating disorder pathology, stereotypes of eating disorders that can influence detection and diagnosis, and screener items that may systematically exclude ethnic minorities because they fail to capture the symptom presentation of diverse individuals (Hernández et al., 2022; Marques et al., 2011; Udo & Grilo, 2018). Importantly, emerging evidence suggests that populations who identify with multiple marginalized social identities have a greater risk of eating disorder pathology (Burke et al., 2020; Calzo et al., 2017). The field needs future epidemiological research on prevalence rates to include and examine intersectional identities as well as expand prevalence rates within other vulnerable groups including, but not limited to socioeconomic status/class, country of origin, acculturation/acculturative stress, immigration status, and ability (Burke et al., 2020).

Although there is a paucity of research on prevalence rates across underrepresented individuals, the following subsections will review the existing epidemiological literature across gender, sexual orientation, age, and race/ethnicity.

Gender

Lifetime prevalence rates of BN across individuals who identify as men or women are 0.08% and 0.46% respectively, while 12-month prevalence rates are 0.05% in men and 0.22% in women (Udo & Grilo, 2018). Currently, there is a paucity of national data on the prevalence of eating disorders, including BN, within gender diverse individuals (i.e., those whose sex assigned at birth does not align with their gender identity or who have diverse gender expressions) in the U.S. (Grammer et al., 2021). Within a study that examined the prevalence of eating disorders in a sample of commercially insured individuals who identified as transgender (N = 10,418), 0.36% met criteria for BN (Ferrucci et al., 2022). This is smaller than past prevalence studies which found that 7.4% of a transgender sample had been diagnosed with anorexia nervosa or BN across a sample of 452 (Diemer et al., 2018), and that 2.9% of transgender women and 3.2% of transgender men had diagnoses of BN across a sample of 484 individuals (Nagata et al., 2020). Further, in a large national sample of college students, Grammer and colleagues (2021) found that across sexual orientations, gender diverse students (i.e., transgender and other diverse gender expressions) and cisgender female students reported significantly higher odds of eating disorder diagnosis, including BN, compared to cisgender male students. According to a study by Nagata and colleagues (2020), transgender men reported the following clinical symptoms: binge eating (6.4%), self-induced vomiting (1.0%), laxative misuse (0.3%), and excessive exercising (1.0%) in the past 28 days. Transgender women in this study reported binge eating (4.7%), self-induced vomiting (1.2%), laxative misuse (0.6%), and excessive exercising (1.7%). Representation of gender diverse individuals in epidemiological research is emerging, and greatly needed.

Sexual Orientation

Results from a nationally representative study found that compared to cisgender heterosexual adults, sexual minority adults (i.e., any individual who does not identify as heterosexual) had between 2 to 4 times greater odds of an eating disorder diagnosis (Kamody et al., 2020). In fact, overall lifetime prevalence for BN was 1.3%, which is higher than for cisgender heterosexual adults. Von Schell and colleagues (2018) reported the following statistics: Studies demonstrate that among women who have sex with only women, 15% report binge eating, 2.5%, laxative misuse, and 5% report excessive exercising at frequencies that meet clinical criteria. Among women who have sex with either men or women, 11.9% report binge eating, 1.9% report self-induced vomiting, 1.3% report laxative misuse, and 17.5% report excessive exercising at clinical levels. Men who have sex with men reported the following clinical symptoms: binge eating (6.2%), self-induced vomiting (3.1%), and excessive exercising (13.8%), but no laxative misuse. Among men who have sex with either men or women, symptom level rates are binge eating (29.5%), self-induced vomiting (2.1%), and excessive exercising (14.6%), but no laxative misuse. Current research suggests that sexual minority subgroups may have increased risk for eating disorder pathology; however, more research is needed to understand the prevalence of BN diagnosis across sexual minority subgroups (Kamody et al., 2020).

Race/Ethnicity

According to Udo and Grilo (2018), the lifetime prevalence rate of BN is 0.31% within non-Hispanic Whites, 0.2% in non-Hispanic Blacks, 0.24% in Hispanics, and 0.17% in individuals who identify with a different race/ethnicity. The 12-month prevalence rate of BN is 0.15% in Non-Hispanic Whites, 0.09% Non-Hispanic Blacks, 0.14% Hispanics, and 0.11% in individuals who identified with a different race/ethnicity. In a nationally representative sample that compared prevalence of eating disorders across all major ethnic minority groups, the lifetime prevalence rates of BN were significantly greater in Latinos and African Americans compared to White and Asian Americans, with Latinos having the highest rates of BN (Marques et al., 2011). The predominant literature with majority cisgender White women finds that overvaluation of weight and shape and dietary restraint are key symptoms to target within eating disorder populations. However, among racial and ethnic minority women, purging behaviors emerge as key symptoms to potentially target within treatment (Perez et al., 2021). Research is lacking that documents the prevalence of BN in other race/ethnicities in the United States, including, but not limited to, Asian, American Indian/Alaskan Natives, Native Hawaiian and Other Pacific Islanders.

Age

Overall, the lifetime and 12-month prevalence of BN in adult cohorts tends to decrease with age with the highest prevalence rates in 18–29 and 30 to 44-year-olds and the lowest in adults over 60 years of age (Udo & Grilo, 2018). Further, in a large representative study of U.S. inner city youth aged 11 to16 years old, the 3-month BN prevalence was higher in girls (5.1%) than in boys (2.3%) (Ruchkin et al., 2021).

TREATMENT OF BULIMIA NERVOSA

The American Psychological Association discusses how evidence-based practice consists of clinicians using the best and most recent research evidence in treatment decision-making (APA Presidential Task Force on Evidence-Based Practice, 2006). APA's Society of Clinical Psychology maintains a list of research-supported treatments, with support considered "strong" if there is evidence of a treatment's efficacy from multiple independent high-quality studies, and support considered "modest" if there is evidence from at least two adequately designed studies.

Currently, there are three empirically supported treatments for individuals with BN: cognitive behavioral therapy (CBT) with strong research support (Fairburn, 2008; Walsh et al., 2004), family-based treatment (FBT) with modest research support (Le Grange & Lock, 2007; Schmidt et al., 2007), and interpersonal therapy (ITP) with strong research support (Fairburn et al., 2015; Stuart & Robertson, 2012). However, since the last update of the research-supported treatments by APA, new empirical work has emerged supporting dialectical behavior therapy (DBT; Safer et al., 2001) as well as acceptance and commitment therapy (ACT) as potentially efficacious for treating individuals with BN.

Although empirically supported treatments exist, the eating disorder field has been criticized for not addressing the role of culture, intersectionality, and personal identification with marginalized groups within current treatment (i.e., sexuality, gender, ethnicity/race, socioeconomic status; Acle et al., 2021). Summaries of the latest research on adaptations to empirically supported treatments for underrepresented groups are presented in the following sections.

Cognitive Behavioral Therapy

Cognitive behavioral therapy (CBT) for eating disorders has the most empirical support for binge spectrum eating disorders (Fairburn et al., 1993; Fairburn, 2008), and is an effective treatment for BN (Waller et al., 2014). CBT treatments for eating disorders are characterized by modifying eating habits, weight control behaviors, and concerns about eating, shape and weight through the use of behavioral and cognitive strategies within 20 sessions. Strategies include identification and restructuring of unhelpful thinking patterns, behavioral experiments, exposure and approach techniques, as well as psychoeducation to encourage reduction of compensatory behaviors and regular eating patterns of a broad range of foods (Fairburn, 2008). Across CBT treatments, research has shown that CBT leads to a reduction in core eating disorder psychopathology and maintenance of gains at the 15-month followup (Atwood & Friedman, 2020). Further, specific to symptoms of BN, CBT has aided in the reduction of binge eating and purging behaviors (Fairburn et al., 2008; Linardon & Wade, 2018; Linardon et al., 2017; Shafran et al., 2009). Studies have also shown that 30–50% of participants experienced remission of the disorder following treatment as well as increases in mood, eating habits, and self-esteem (Lampard & Sharbanee, 2015; Linardon & Wade, 2018; Waller et al., 2014; Glasofer & Devlin, 2013). Although a highly empirically supported treatment, CBT has been criticized for its lack of strategy or skills that address maintenance factors of BN, specifically, negative affect secondary to shape/weight concerns (Lampe et al., 2021). This is concerning as these factors have been correlated with poorer treatment outcomes in BN (Lampe et al., 2021; Linardon, 2018).

Emerging literature describes cultural adaptations to CBT. In an adaptation of CBT for a Latina patient with BN symptoms, modifications were made in conceptualizing the binge/purge cycle and understanding how familial settings normalized overeating, which led to drives in dieting behavior (Patmore et al., 2019). Other guidelines included incorporating values of family connectedness, ethnic identity, and desires surrounding dependence/independence (Patmore et al., 2019). In a preliminary controlled treatment trial for Latinas engaging in binge eating (BE), cultural adaptations included role playing to practice assertiveness strategies, using a food guide with normal portions with culturally appropriate foods, and ongoing training of therapists in cultural worldviews, life expectations, and sociocultural contexts (Cachelin et al., 2019).

There are no empirical studies on adaptations of CBT for individuals who identify as LGBTQIA+. Guidelines for adapting CBT recommend examining client's beliefs about whether sexual orientation has an effect on the presenting problem, addressing potential harassment or abuse due to sexuality, examining presence of internalized homophobia, and understanding social support (Minaiy et al., 2017). This information should be used while exploring and challenging core beliefs and attitudes surrounding weight, shape, and food concerns (Minaiy et al., 2017).

Interpersonal Therapy for Bulimia Nervosa

Interpersonal therapy (IPT) was originally a treatment for depression, but has been used in a wide variety of psychological disorders, including the treatment of BN (Hagan & Walsh, 2021). The IPT model suggests that negative affect and low self-esteem are secondary to interpersonal difficulties, which lead to disordered eating behaviors that maintain interpersonal difficulties (Karam et al., 2019). IPT is a 6–20 session treatment aimed at strengthening social support and interpersonal skills while decreasing emotional distress secondary to social and interaction difficulties and ultimately reducing eating disorder symptoms (Lipsitz & Markowitz, 2013). Research supports the use of IPT for the treatment of eating disorders. Past research has found that 6% of participants reached abstinence from eating disorder behaviors at end of treatment (Agras et al., 2000), and found no statistically significant difference in eating disorder behaviors between those who received IPT vs CBT at 1 year follow up (Fairburn et al., 1993; Agras et al., 2000). Importantly, IPT for BN primarily focuses on interpersonal problems instead of bulimic symptoms (Hagan & Walsh, 2021).

Although IPT-BN has not been adapted to under-represented populations, IPT for depression has been adapted significantly for implementation in international settings as well as specific cultural populations in the United States (Ravitz & Watson, 2014). Within the cultural adaptation of IPT for Hispanic patients, the IPT approach remained unchanged, however, emphasis was given to helping patients find indirect and less confrontational ways of confronting family problems, familial interpersonal relationships, understanding conflicts due to migration and acculturation, recognizing gender roles, appealing to resiliency, and spirituality (Markowitz et al., 2009). Research focused on producing intersectional guidelines for adapting IPT specific to BN and other eating disordered behavior is needed.

Family-Based Therapy for Children and Adolescents

According to Le Grange and Lock (2007), family-based treatment for BN (FBT-BN) is a 6-month treatment. FBT-BN uses parental empowerment and control to manage eating disordered behaviors, normalize eating patterns, and, ultimately, facilitate a return to adolescent development without focusing on changing pathological thinking related to shape and weight (Le Grange & Locke, 2009). Past research has found that about 40% of adolescent individuals in FBT-BN clinically reduced binge eating and purging following treatment (Schmidt et al., 2007). Further, FBT-BN has been shown to lead to sustained rates of abstinence from binge eating and purging up to 12-months post treatment and to significantly less hospitalization (Le Grange et al., 2015).

There is a paucity of research on the adaptation of FBT-BN for those with intersectional identities; however, a case study utilized a culturally adapted brief family therapy for a Mexican American adolescent with BN (Binkley & Koslofsky, 2017). Cultural adaptation within the treatment included the use of the client's preferred language, consideration of factors like privilege, marginalization, and discrimination, use of culturally appropriate metaphors, integrating the family's values and experiences of familismo, respeto, and personalismo, and reframing acculturative stress in the family as cultural conflicts (Binkley & Koslofsky, 2017). The use of these cultural adaptations within the brief family-based therapy were effective according to Binkley and Koslofsky (2017). This case study highlights the importance of providing better treatments for individuals that occupy marginalized social identities and address all aspects of the multiple social identities the individual may occupy.

Emerging Treatments for Bulimia Nervosa—Dialectical Behavior Therapy

Created by Marsha Linehan and originally designed for suicidality, dialectical behavior therapy (DBT) is a skills-based treatment based on the biosocial theory which posits that biological vulnerability and invalidating environment result in emotion dysregulation (Linehan, 1993), a trigger for disordered eating behavior (Lavender et al., 2015). DBT for BN is a structured treatment in which patients enhance skills in interpersonal effectiveness, distress tolerance, emotion regulation, and mindfulness to reduce emotion dysregulation and subsequently eating disorder behaviors (Safer et al., 2001). There is preliminary evidence suggesting improvement of disordered eating symptoms from the use of DBT-BN in randomized control trials (Hill et al., 2011; Safer et al., 2001). Although a systematic review of literature found improvement (post-DBT) in emotion regulation, overall well-being, and BMI as well as reductions in psychopathology, future research is needed to determine effectiveness in contrast to well known ED therapies like CBT and IPT (Rozakou-Soumalia et al., 2021). Overall, research suggests the use of DBT for BN is promising (Hagan & Walsh, 2021).

There is emerging research in the cultural adaptation of DBT for disordered eating. For example, DBT for disordered eating was adapted for a Chinese international student, in which attention was given to the client-therapist relationship (Cheng & Merrick, 2017). Considerations included being aware of cultural differences and the individual's unique expression of emotion, as well as discussion pertaining to obligation to family, child-parent relationship, and independence from social-cultural framework (Cheng & Merrick, 2017). These adjustments led to a culturally informed sense of understanding the client's eating disordered symptoms and guided structure of goals within the DBT framework. Importantly, one study adapted an adolescent DBT skills group for emotional overeating behavior to address race/ethnicity, socioeconomic class, developmental age, and gender (Kamody et al., 2020). The considerations began with the selection of the theoretical model: DBT was chosen given the focus on affect regulation and its potential responsiveness to racial minority populations. Further, group format was chosen to increase adolescent validation of stigmatizing behaviors, while curriculum was condensed to 10 weeks and taught in 1-hour sessions during flexible meeting times to be responsive to working parent schedules and barriers to transportation. Further, the curriculum included visual images and cultural references that reflected the racial and ethnic backgrounds of individuals in the group. Finally, the order of curriculum was altered to address the needs of the adolescents, specifically using distress tolerance skills to increase crisis skills and resistance to emotional overeating urges. However, overall, there is a paucity of research addressing multiple aspects of one's identity in treatment. Kamody and colleagues (2020) provided a thorough explanation of culturally relevant adaptations to a DBT treatment.

Guidelines for Adapting Treatments

Although there are evidence-based treatments currently available, barriers to treatment are a problem for individuals with marginalized social identities. Barriers can include cost of treatment, eating disorder stigma, and shame surrounding disordered eating and mental health (Hernandez et al., 2022; Neyland & Bardone-Cone, 2019). Importantly, research in culturally sensitive interventions for eating disorders suggests that treatment providers for individuals with BN and other eating disorders address patients' barriers to treatment, understand patients within their cultural context, explore the impact of culturally contextual factors, understand cultural nuances that impact clinical presentations, explore and utilize family and social supports, provide psychoeducation, explore ethnic identity, acculturation, and acculturative stress, become educated about working with racial and ethnic minorities, and use culturally flexible diagnostic models (Acle et al., 2021). Further, in a study which sought to adapt ED treatments for African Americans, suggestions included: addressing cultural deviation from the "thin ideal," skepticism of weight standards, and addressing motivation to change (Scott et al., 2019).

Current State of Research and Treatment of Bulimia Nervosa

Historically, empirically supported treatments have been studied in young, affluent, White populations causing (a) empirically supported treatments to be inaccessible to those who occupy marginalized identities and (b) an overall lack of guidance for how to adapt treatments for individuals with marginalized identities. Although guidance for adaptation of treatments has been briefly reviewed, it is important to identify current marginalized populations that remain understudied in the research of BN as well as other gaps in the literature. Current research has identified multiple understudied populations with increased prevalence of BN: individuals living with food insecurity (Hazzard et al., 2022), military and veteran populations who experienced trauma, military sexual trauma, or intimate partner violence (Bartlett et al., 2018), racial/ethnic minority individuals (Egbert et al., 2022), gender and sexual minorities (Ferrucci et al., 2022), and individuals with disabilities (Burke et al., 2020), among others. Further, it is important to understand comorbidities of BN to help guide treatment. Current research suggests that major depressive disorder and substance use disorder are commonly comorbid with BN (Keshishan et al., 2021). Past research suggests that substance use disorders may be a maintaining factor of eating disorder symptoms among individuals with BN by promoting mood dysregulation and interpersonal problems, which reinforce BN symptoms (Keshishian et al., 2021). More research is needed to understand this association and improve treatment outcomes.

CASE STUDY

Sam is a 23-year-old Hispanic individual who identifies as bisexual and nonbinary. Sam was assigned as male at birth. Currently, Sam uses they/them pronouns. They self-referred for outpatient therapy, wanting to address social anxiety and loneliness. Sam also reported being referred to therapy by their medical provider due to poor sleep.

Assessment

Sam completed a clinical interview and brief assessment measures to obtain information about the presenting concerns. The clinical interview was guided by the traditional guidelines for a scientific informed case conceptualization, in which presenting problem, client strengths, and overall quality of life as well as causal, maintaining, and historical factors (e.g., developmental history, medical history, history of trauma/abuse, and family psychiatric history) pertaining to the presenting problem were identified (Christon et al., 2015; Nezu et al., 2004). Through the course of the clinical interview, it became apparent that Sam suffered from body image issues, fear of negative evaluation, and loss of control over eating. As such, the Eating Disorder Examination (EDE) interview was used to evaluate eating disorder psychopathology over the last 28 days (Fairburn et al., 2014). Specifically, the EDE assesses binge eating episodes, overeating episodes, dietary restraint, as well as eating, shape, and weight concerns (Fairburn et al., 2014). Through the EDE, Sam reported subjective and objective binge eating about 3 to 4 times per week, compulsive exercising almost daily, use of laxatives averaging twice per week, and occasional vomiting. Sam reported no fear of fat, but a drive for muscularity. Sam also reported strong beliefs that muscularity would increase quality of life, attractiveness, and the ability to secure a lifelong partner.

In order to address cultural concerns, the Cultural Formulation Interview (American Psychiatric Association, 2022) was used to elicit information about cultural identity as it relates to the presenting problem, coping skills, and help to seek perceptions. Sam reported the importance of family and lived at home with parents and younger siblings, but also noted family was not a source of emotional support. Sam explained that their parents were accepting of their gender and sexual identities, but did not understand or were fully supportive. For example, in an expression of acceptance, the parents would say, “You are our son, will always be our son, and nothing will change that.” Sam reported appreciating the sentiment, but that their parents could not seem to think in nonbinary terms. In addition, they became hopeful when Sam dated a woman and appeared disappointed when dating a man. Through the cultural interview, rigid social and cultural rules related to food, eating and family meals were raised by Sam. The family ate most dinner-time meals together during the week and had an extended family lunch on Sundays. Sam reported getting consistently praised for overeating by their mother and older maternal caregivers of the extended family during family meals.

Throughout the intake and assessment sessions, a person-centered approach was used to guide all clinical interviews to ensure that focus was placed on the person as a whole versus diagnostic symptoms or group level demographic indicators alone. The person-centered approach recognizes the possibility of intersecting identities within each client and, in turn, tries to understand salient cultural and contextual factors of the individual's presenting problem including: values, cultural strengths, stressors, experiences with discrimination, immigration stress, prior experiences with mental health, and overall help-seeking attitudes unique to the individual (Sanchez et al., 2022). To increase client buy-in, rationale and methods for the assessment were discussed with Sam prior to administration (Cofresí & Gorman, 2004).

Treatment

Sam agreed to engage in an adaptation of CBT that included 25 individual CBT sessions, 3 nutritional sessions with a dietician, and 6 family sessions. Individual sessions focused on establishing a regular eating pattern to reduce and ultimately stop the binge eating and weight control behaviors. Family sessions included psychoeducation about eating disorders, increasing communication, problem solving on eating disorder-specific topics such as interactions during the family meal, and identification of patterns that triggered Sam's eating disordered thoughts and behaviors consistent with the existing literature (Reyes-Rodriguez et al., 2021).

In the first phase of treatment, the main goal was identifying and stopping the binge eating and purging cycle. Sam was asked to track their eating, weight control behaviors, and sleep patterns. Sam identified that negative thoughts related to their body shape (specifically lack of muscularity) led to their purging behaviors (e.g., excessive exercising, laxative use) which in turn, created excessive hunger cues, eventually leading to binge eating during family dinners. Sam's mother unintentionally reinforced the binge eating by communicating to Sam that she views their eating as an expression of love for her and a compliment for a well-cooked meal. After binge eating, Sam reported feeling guilt, shame, and anger, and would engage in more excessive exercising or laxative use. Sam identified the triggers for their body-related negative thoughts. In addition, through tracking the negative thoughts, Sam recognized that feelings of guilt, shame, and anger in response to family interactions also triggered them to excessively exercise.

A regular eating pattern was implemented with Sam. The meal plan incorporated cultural foods. Sam's mother was invited to attend a portion of one nutritional session to discuss the family dinner meals. In addition, Sam's sleep hygiene was discussed and they worked on establishing a more consistent sleep schedule. Sam was more reluctant to decrease exercise and laxative use.

In phase two of treatment, the goal was to maintain the successes of phase one of treatment while identifying triggers of the binge eating and purging cycle. Through the daily eating tracking, Sam found that negative interactions with family members and body dissatisfaction thoughts were the most frequent triggers of the exercising. Culture-specific social gatherings were the most frequent triggers of binge eating. Cognitive restructuring and reframing were used to challenge negative thoughts related to the self and the body. Coping skills and emotion regulation strategies were taught to assist Sam with coping with negative affect. Social problem solving was used to assist Sam in setting boundaries and changing negative interactions and maladaptive interpersonal patterns that occurred during family meals. In addition, family sessions supplemented the individual sessions and focused on changing the meanings ascribed to meals to reduce the binge eating and stop the exacerbation of eating disorder thoughts and behaviors. The family developed a list of ways that Sam could show respect and love for their mother and convey the deliciousness of the food without overeating or binge eating.

After making substantial progress in coping skills and emotion regulation, as well as changing interaction patterns with the family, Sam became more willing to reduce the excessive exercise and laxative use. Sam collaborated with their therapist on developing a healthy exercise regimen. A behavioral reinforcement schedule was used where Sam found ways to replace exercising with other rewarding or pleasurable activities and rewarded themselves for meeting weekly goals.

During this time, Sam expressed a readiness to focus on feelings of inadequacy, disappointment, and shame related to their non-binary gender identity and sexual orientation. Sam expressed interest in using social problem solving to address interactions with their parents related to gender and sexual orientation based on previous treatment success with this technique. Cognitive restructuring and reframing were also used to combat the negative automatic thoughts that elicited the feelings of inadequacy and shame.

The last phase of treatment focused on relapse prevention and the things that could occur in the future that might lead Sam to binge and purge again. Sam compiled a folder of all the worksheets, techniques, and tools that they found most helpful, and identified future events, interactions, and triggers that might cause a lapse. In addition, strategies for handling each of these situations were developed. During this time, attention was shifted to increasing social support and decreasing loneliness. Sam worked on increasing their social support network by joining a LGBTQIA+ community center and participating in several support groups. Behavioral experiments were conducted to assist Sam with reducing social anxiety and being more present in the moment. Organically, Sam raised future environmental discrimination as potential negative events that could trigger a recurrence of binge eating or purging. Strategies for coping and handling these situations were developed. Treatment concluded with Sam thinking about how life would be different with the ending of treatment and worked on transitioning to a life without psychological treatment.

Treatment progress was monitored using several objective assessments. The Eating Disorders Examination Questionnaire (Smith et al., 2017) was used to track progress in eating disorder specific symptoms. In addition, the Outcome Questionnaire-45 (OQ-45; Lambert et al., 1996) was used to assess changes in symptomatic distress, interpersonal relations, and distress in social relations throughout treatment (Lambert et al., 2005). The OQ-45 was administered before every session.

Treatment was successful both in eliminating the binge eating and over eating episodes, instituting a regular and healthy eating and physical activity pattern, and reducing negative cognitive thoughts related to body dissatisfaction. Treatment also increased Sam's coping and emotion regulation skills. Further, treatment increased overall quality of life and life satisfaction via increased social support and improving familial relationships. It is important to note that treatment was informed by American Psychological Association's *Guidelines for Psychological Practice with Transgender and Gender Nonconforming People* (APA, 2015) and provided in alignment with Acle's and colleagues' recommendations for the treatment of eating disorders among racial/ethnic minorities (Acle et al., 2021). Given the adaptations made to the CBT treatment, close monitoring of treatment progress using objective assessments was relied upon heavily. In addition, cultural humility was a foundational value of the therapist administering the treatment (Fisher-Borne et al., 2015); that is, a stance of self-reflection of bias and power, of unconditional acceptance of their identity and culture, a recognition that culture can be fluid, and giving Sam complete control in discussing identity and culture in treatment.

CONCLUSIONS

The field of eating disorders is in dire need of empirical studies that address prevalence rates, clinical presentation, and effective treatments for BN from an intersectional framework. Currently, clinicians have little to no empirical research to guide their treatment decision making and are required to adapt evidence-based interventions to the intersectional identities that might be influencing the treatment target goals. According to Morales and Norcross (2010), when clinicians face dilemmas where there is a lack of research to inform treatment, they have three options: to either adopt, adapt or abandon a treatment, with benefits and drawbacks to each decision. Of all three options, adoption of a treatment is the most ideal, but only when the treatment is supported with research specifically on the target problem and when the clinician is appropriately trained in that treatment. Although this is the "safest" course of action in that research demonstrates the treatment's effectiveness, this approach does not consider cultural context and may ignore issues that are culturally driven (Morales & Norcross, 2010). An ideal context for treatment adaptation is when the original treatment is empirically supported for the target problem, and the clinician is highly experienced in both the treatment and the client's culture. In these instances, treatment adaptations may be the best choice for tailoring treatment to a client's individual needs. However, if treatment failure occurs, it will be unknown if this is due to the treatment, the adaptations, or the clinician (Morales & Norcross, 2010). Clinicians may consider abandoning an evidence-based treatment altogether when the treatment has not shown positive outcomes with their client, or when the clinician has reason to believe that the client's cultural context or other factors may inhibit the generalizability of the treatment. From a social justice lens, the lack of empirical studies on BN across intersectional identities creates a treatment disparity among these under-represented individuals. The effective treatment of all individuals with BN will require a concerted effort to address this gap in the literature.

DISCUSSION QUESTIONS

1. Emerging evidence suggests that populations who identify with multiple marginalized social identities have a greater risk for eating disorders; why might that be?
2. What assessments could be developed to assist clinicians in understanding the extent to which identity characteristics may be influencing psychopathology?
3. What are the pros and cons of adapting evidence-based treatments for BN?
4. What might be a situation where a clinician might decide to adopt, adapt, or abandon an evidence-based treatment, such as CBT?

REFERENCES

Acle, A., Cook, B. J., Siegfried, N., & Beasley, T. (2021). Cultural considerations in the treatment of eating disorders among racial/ethnic minorities: A systematic review. *Journal of Cross-Cultural Psychology, 52*(5), 468–488. https://doi.org/10.1177/00220221211017664

Agras, W. S., Walsh, T., Fairburn, C. G., Wilson, G. T., & Kraemer, H. C. (2000). A multicenter comparison of cognitive-behavioral therapy and interpersonal psychotherapy for bulimia nervosa. *Archives of General Psychiatry, 57*(5), 459–466. https://doi.org/10.1001/archpsyc.57.5.459

American Psychiatric Association. (2022). Feeding and eating disorders and cultural formulation interview. In Diagnostic and statistical manual of mental disorders (5th ed., text rev.). https://doi-org.ezproxy1.lib.asu.edu/10.1176/appi.books.9780890425787

American Psychological Association, Presidential Task Force on Evidence-Based Practice. (2006). Evidence-based practice in psychology. *American Psychologist, 61*(4), 271–285. https://doi.org/10.1037/0003-066X.61.4.271

American Psychological Association (2015). Guidelines for psychological practice with transgender and gender nonconforming people. *The American Psychologist, 70*(9), 832–864. https://doi.org/10.1037/a0039906

Atwood, M. E., & Friedman, A. (2020). A systematic review of enhanced cognitive behavioral therapy (CBT-E) for eating disorders. *International Journal of Eating Disorders, 53*(3), 311–330. https://doi.org/10.1002/eat.23206

Bartlett, B. A., Iverson, K. M., & Mitchell, K. S. (2018). Intimate partner violence and disordered eating among male and female veterans. *Psychiatry Research, 260*, 98–104. https://doi.org/10.1016/j.psychres.2017.11.056

Binkley, J., & Koslofsky, S. (2017). Una Familia Unida: Cultural Adaptation of Family-Based Therapy for Bulimia with a Depressed Latina Adolescent. *Clinical Case Studies, 16*(1), 25–41. https://doi.org/10.1177/1534650116668268

Bodell, L. P., Joiner, T. E., & Keel, P. K. (2013). Comorbidity-independent risk for suicidality increases with bulimia nervosa but not with anorexia nervosa. *Journal of Psychiatric Research, 47*(5), 617–621. https://doi.org/10.1016/j.jpsychires.2013.01.005

Burke, N. L., Schaefer, L. M., Hazzard, V. M., & Rodgers, R. F. (2020). Where identities converge: The importance of intersectionality in eating disorders research. *International Journal of Eating Disorders, 53*(10), 1605–1609. https://10.1002/eat.23371

Cachelin, F. M., Gil-Rivas, V., Palmer, B., Vela, A., Phimphasone, P., de Hernandez, B. U., & Tapp, H. (2019). Randomized controlled trial of a culturally-adapted program for Latinas with binge eating. *Psychological Services, 16*(3), 504. https://doi.org/10.1037/ser0000182

Calzo, J. P., Blashill, A. J., Brown, T. A., & Argenal, R. L. (2017). Eating disorders and disordered weight and shape control behaviors in sexual minority populations. *Current Psychiatry Reports, 19*(8), 49. https://doi.org/10.1007/s11920-017-0801-y

Cheng, P. H., & Merrick, E. (2017). Cultural adaptation of dialectical behavior therapy for a Chinese international student with eating disorder and depression. *Clinical Case Studies, 16*(1), 42–57. https://doi.org/10.1177/1534650116668269

Christon, L. M., McLeod, B. D., & Jensen-Doss, A. (2015). Evidence-based assessment meets evidence-based treatment: An approach to science-informed case conceptualization. *Cognitive and Behavioral Practice, 22*(1), 36–48. https://doi.org/10.1016/j.cbpra.2013.12.004

Cofresí, N. I., & Gorman, A. A. (2004). Testing and assessment issues with Spanish-English bilingual Latinos. *Journal of Counseling & Development, 82*(1), 99–106. https://doi.org/10.1002/j.1556-6678.2004.tb00290.x

Deloitte Access Economics. (2020, June). *The social and economic cost of eating disorders in the United States of America: A report for the Strategic Training Initiative for the Prevention of Eating Disorders and the Academy for Eating Disorders*. Harvard T.H. Chan School of Public Health. https://www.hsph.harvard.edu/striped/report-economic-costs-of-eating-disorders/.

Diemer, E. W., White Hughto, J. M., Gordon, A. R., Guss, C., Austin, S. B., & Reisner, S. L. (2018). Beyond the binary: Differences in eating disorder prevalence by gender identity in a transgender sample. *Transgender Health, 3*(1), 17–23. https://doi.org/10.1089/trgh.2017.0043

Egbert, A. H., Hunt, R. A., Williams, K. L., Burke, N. L., & Mathis, K. J. (2022). Reporting racial and ethnic diversity in eating disorder research over the past 20 years. *International Journal of Eating Disorders, 55*(4), 455–462. https://doi.org/10.1002/eat.23666

Fairburn, C. G. (2008). *Cognitive behavior therapy and eating disorders*. Guildford Press.

Fairburn, C. G., Bailey-Straebler, S., Basden, S., Doll, H. A., Jones, R., Murphy, R., O'Connor, M. E., & Cooper, Z. (2015). A transdiagnostic comparison of enhanced cognitive behaviour therapy (CBT-E) and interpersonal psychotherapy in the treatment of eating disorders. *Behavior Research and Therapy, 70*, 64–71.

Fairburn, C. G., Cooper, Z., & O'Connor, M. (2014, April). *The eating disorder examination 17.0D*. https://www.cbte.co/site/download/ede-17-0d/?wpdmdl=615&masterkey=5c644ef9b6149

Fairburn, C. G., Jones, R., Peveler, R. C., Hope, R. A., & O'Connor, M. (1993). Psychotherapy and bulimia nervosa. Longer-term effects of interpersonal psychotherapy, behavior therapy, and cognitive behavior therapy. *Archives of General Psychiatry, 50*(6), 419–428. https://doi.org/10.1001/archpsyc.1993.01820180009001

Ferrucci, K. A., Lapane, K. L., & Jesdale, B. M. (2022). Prevalence of diagnosed eating disorders in US transgender adults and youth in insurance claims. *International Journal of Eating Disorders, 55*(6), 801–809. https://doi.org/10.1002/eat.23729

Fisher-Borne, M., Cain, J. M., & Martin, S. L. (2015). From mastery to accountability: Cultural humility as an alternative to cultural competence. *Social Work Education, 34*(2), 165–181. https://doi.org/10.1080/02615479.2014.977244

Glasofer, D. R., & Devlin, M. J. (2013). Cognitive behavioral therapy for bulimia nervosa. *Psychotherapy, 50*(4), 537–542. https://doi.org/10.1037/a0031939

Grammer, A. C., Vázquez, M. M., Fitzsimmons-Craft, E. E., Fowler, L. A., Rackoff, G. N., Schvey, N. A., Lipson, S. K., Newman, M. G., Eisenberg, D., Taylor, C. B., & Wilfley, D. E. (2021). Characterizing eating disorder diagnosis and related outcomes by sexual orientation and gender identity in a national sample of college students. *Eating Behaviors, 42*, 101528. https://doi.org/10.1016/j.eatbeh.2021.101528

Hagan, K. E., & Walsh, B. T. (2021). State of the art: The therapeutic approaches to bulimia nervosa. *Clinical Therapeutics, 43*(1), 40–49. https://doi.org/10.1016/j.clinthera.2020.10.012

Hazzard, V. M., Barry, M. R., Leung, C. W., Sonneville, K. R., Wonderlich, S. A., & Crosby, R. D. (2022). Food insecurity and its associations with bulimic-spectrum eating disorders, mood disorders, and anxiety disorders in a nationally representative sample of US adults. *Social Psychiatry and Psychiatric Epidemiology, 57*(7), 1483–1490. https://doi.org/10.1007/s00127-021-02126-5

Hernández, J. C., Perez, M., & Hoek, H. W. (2022). Update on the epidemiology and treatment of eating disorders among Hispanic/Latinx Americans in the United States. *Current Opinion in Psychiatry, 35*(6), 379–384. https://doi.org/10.1097/YCO.0000000000000819

Hill, D. M., Craighead, L. W., & Safer, D. L. (2011). Appetite-focused dialectical behavior therapy for the treatment of binge eating with purging: A preliminary trial. *The International Journal of Eating Disorders, 44*(3), 249–261. https://doi.org/10.1002/eat.20812

Hudson, J. I., Hiripi, E., Pope, H. G., Jr, & Kessler, R. C. (2007). The prevalence and correlates of eating disorders in the National Comorbidity Survey Replication. *Biological Psychiatry, 61*(3), 348–358. https://doi.org/10.1016/j.biopsych.2006.03.040

Kamody, R. C, Grilo, C. M., & Udo, T. (2020). Disparities in DSM-5 defined eating disorders by sexual orientation among U.S. adults. *International Journal of Eating Disorders, 53*(2), 278–287. https://doi.org/10.1002/eat.23193

Kamody, R. C., Thurston, I. B., & Burton, E. T. (2020). Acceptance-based skill acquisition and cognitive reappraisal in a culturally responsive treatment for binge eating in adolescence. *Eating Disorders, 28*(2), 184–201. https://doi.org/10.1080/10640266.2020.1731055

Karam, A. M., Fitzsimmons-Craft, E. E., Tanofsky-Kraff, M., & Wilfley, D. E. (2019). Interpersonal psychotherapy and the treatment of eating disorders. *Psychiatric Clinics of North America, 42*(2), 205–218. https://doi.org/10.1016/j.psc.2019.01.003

Keshishian, A. C., Tabri, N., Becker, K. R., Franko, D. L., Herzog, D. B., Thomas, J. J., & Eddy, K. T. (2021). Comorbid depression and substance use prospectively predict eating disorder persistence among women with anorexia nervosa and bulimia nervosa. *Journal of Behavioral and Cognitive Therapy, 31*(4), 309–315. https://doi.org/10.1016/j.jbct.2021.09.003

Lampard, A. M., & Sharbanee, J. M. (2015). The cognitive-behavioural theory and treatment of bulimia nervosa: An examination of treatment mechanisms and future directions. *Australian Psychologist, 50*(1), 6–13. https://doi.org/10.1111/ap.12078

Lambert, M. J. (1996). *Administration and scoring manual for the Outcome Questionnaire.* American Professional Credentialing Services.

Lambert, M. J., Harmon, C., Slade, K., Whipple, J. L., & Hawkins, E. J. (2005). Providing feedback to psychotherapists on their patients' progress: Clinical results and practice suggestions. *Journal of Clinical Psychology, 61*(2), 164–174. https://doi.org/10.1002/jclp.20113

Lampe, E. W., Forman, E. M., Juarascio, A. S., & Manasse, S. M. (2021). Feasibility, acceptability, and preliminary target engagement of a healthy physical activity promotion intervention for bulimia nervosa: Development and evaluation via case series design. *Cognitive and Behavioral Practice, 29*(3), 598–613. https://doi.org/10.1016/j.cbpra.2021.05.006

Lavender, J. M., Wonderlich, S. A., Engel, S. G., Gordon, K. H., Kaye, W. H., & Mitchell, J. E. (2015). Dimensions of emotion dysregulation in anorexia nervosa and bulimia nervosa: A conceptual review of the empirical literature. *Clinical Psychology Review, 40*, 111–122. https://doi.org/10.1016/j.cpr.2015.05.010

Le Grange, D., & Lock J. D. (2007). *Treating bulimia in adolescents: A family-based approach.* Guilford Press.

Le Grange, D., & Lock, J. D. (2009). *Treating bulimia nervosa in adolescents: A family-based approach.* Guilford Press.

Le Grange, D., Lock, J. D., Agras, W. S., Bryson, S. W., & Jo, B. (2015). Randomized clinical trial of family-based treatment and cognitive-behavioral therapy for adolescent bulimia nervosa. *Journal of the American Academy of Child & Adolescent Psychiatry, 54*(11), 886–894. https://doi.org/10.1016/j.jaac.2015.08.008

Linardon, J. (2018). Meta-analysis of the effects of cognitive-behavioral therapy on the core eating disorder maintaining mechanisms: Implications for mechanisms of therapeutic change. *Cognitive Behaviour Therapy, 47*(2), 107–125. https://doi.org/10.1080/16506073.2018.1427785

Linardon, J., & Wade, T. D. (2018). How many individuals achieve symptom abstinence following psychological treatments for bulimia nervosa? A meta-analytic review. *International Journal of Eating Disorders, 51*(4), 287–294. https://doi.org/10.1002/eat.22838

Linardon, J., Wade, T. D., De la Piedad Garcia, X., & Brennan, L. (2017). The efficacy of cognitive-behavioral therapy for eating disorders: A systematic review and meta-analysis. *Journal of Consulting and Clinical Psychology, 85*(11), 1080–1094. https://doi.org/10.1037/ccp0000245

Linehan, M. M. (1993). *Cognitive-behavioral treatment of borderline personality disorder.* Guilford Press.

Lipsitz, J. D., & Markowitz, J. C. (2013). Mechanisms of change in interpersonal therapy (IPT). *Clinical Psychology Review, 33*(8), 1134–1147. https://doi.org/10.1016/j.cpr.2013.09.002

Markowitz, J. C., Patel, S. R., Balan, I. C., Bell, M. A., Blanco, C., Brave Heart, M. Y. H., Sosa, S. B., & Lewis-Fernandez, R. (2009). Toward an adaptation of interpersonal psychotherapy for Hispanic patients with DSM-IV major depressive disorder. *Journal of Clinical Psychiatry, 70*(2), 214–222. https://doi.org/10.4088/jcp.08m04100

Marques, L., Alegria, M., Becker, A. E., Chen, C., Fang. A., Chosak, A., & Diniz, J. B. (2011). Comparative prevalence, correlates of impairment, and service utilization for eating disorders across US ethnic groups: Implications for reducing ethnic disparities in health care access for eating disorders. *International Journal of Eating Disorders, 44*(5), 412–420. https://doi.org/10.1002/eat.20787

Mehler, P. S. (2011). Medical complications of bulimia nervosa and their treatments. *International Journal of Eating Disorders, 44*(2), 95–104. https://doi.org/10.1002/eat.20825

Minaiy, C., Johnson, N., Ciochon, T., & Perkins, D. (2017). Adaptability of family therapy modalities in the treatment of lesbian and gay clients with bulimia nervosa. *Contemporary Family Therapy: An International Journal, 39*(2), 121–131. https://doi.org/10.1007/s10591-017-9410-5

Morales, E., & Norcross, J. C. (2010). Evidence-based practices with ethnic minorities: Strange bedfellows no more. *Journal of Clinical Psychology, 66*(8), 821–829. https://doi.org/10.1002/jclp.20712

Nagata, J. M., Murray, S. B., Compte, E. J., Pak, E. H., Schauer, R., Flentje, A., Capriotti, M. R., Lubensky, M. E., Lunn, M. R., & Obedin-Maliver, J. (2020). Community norms for the Eating Disorder Examination Questionnaire (EDE-Q) among transgender men and women. *Eating Behaviors, 37*, 101381. https://doi.org/10.1016/j.eatbeh.2020.101381

Neyland, M. K. H., & Bardone-Cone, A. M. (2019). Treatment experiences of Latinas with current or past binge eating disorder and/or bulimia nervosa. *Eating Disorders, 27*(2), 253–265. https://doi.org/10.1080/10640266.2019.1591827

Nezu, A. M., Nezu, C. M., Peacock, M. A., & Girdwood, C. P. (2004). Case formulation in cognitive-behavior therapy. In M. Hersen (Series Ed.) & S. N. Haynes & E. M. Heiby (Vol. Eds.), *Comprehensive handbook of psychological assessment: Vol. 3* (pp. 402–426). Wiley.

Patmore, J., Meddaoui, B., & Feldman, H. (2019). Cultural considerations for treating Hispanic patients with eating disorders: A case study illustrating the effectiveness of CBT in reducing bulimia nervosa symptoms in a Latina patient. *Journal of Clinical Psychology, 75*(11), 2006–2021. https://doi.org/10.1002/jclp.22860

Perez, M., Perko, V., Yu, K., Hernández, J. C., Ohrt, T. K., & Stadheim, J. (2021). Identifying central symptoms of eating disorders among ethnic and racial minority women. *Journal of Abnormal Psychology, 130*(7), 748–760. https://doi.org/10.1037/abn0000695

Ravitz, P., & Watson, P. (2014). Interpersonal psychotherapy: Healing with a relational focus. *Focus, 12*(3), 275–284. https://doi.org/10.1176/appi.focus.12.3.275

Reyes-Rodríguez, M. L., Watson, H. J., Smith, T. W., Baucom, D. H., & Bulik, C. M. (2021). Promoviendo una Alimentación Saludable (PAS) results: Engaging Latino families in eating disorder treatment. *Eating Behaviors, 42*, 101534. https://doi.org/10.1016/j.eatbeh.2021.101534

Rozakou-Soumalia, N., Dârvariu, Ş., & Sjögren, J. M. (2021). Dialectical behaviour therapy improves emotion dysregulation mainly in binge eating disorder and bulimia nervosa: A systematic review and meta-analysis. *Journal of Personalized Medicine, 11*(9), 931. https://doi.org/10.3390/jpm11090931

Ruchkin, V., Isaksson, J., Schwab-Stone, M., & Stickley, A. (2021). Prevalence and early risk factors for bulimia nervosa symptoms in inner-city youth: Gender and ethnicity perspectives. *Journal of Eating Disorders, 9*(1), 1–13. https://doi.org/10.1186/s40337-021-00479-5

Safer, D. L, Telch, C., & Agras, W. S. (2001). Dialectical behavior therapy for bulimia nervosa. *American Journal of Psychiatry, 158*(4), 632–634. https://doi.org/10.1176/appi.ajp.158.4.632

Sanchez, A. L., Jent, J., Aggarwal, N. K., Chavira, D., Coxe, S., Garcia, D., La Roche, M., & Comer, J. S. (2022). Person-centered cultural assessment can improve child mental health service engagement and outcomes. *Journal of Clinical Child & Adolescent Psychology, 51*(1), 1–22. https://doi.org/10.1080/15374416.2021.1981340

Schmidt, U., Lee, S., Beecham, J., Perkins, S., Treasure, J., Yi, I., Winn, S., Robinson, P., Murphy, R., Keville, S., Johnson-Sabine, E., Jenkins, M., Frost, S., Dodge, L., Berelowitz, M., & Eisler, I. (2007). A randomized controlled trial of family therapy and cognitive behavior therapy guided self-care for adolescents with bulimia nervosa and related disorders. *American Journal of Psychiatry, 164*(4), 591–598. https://doi.org/10.1176/ajp.2007.164.4.591

Scott, T. N., Gil-Rivas, V., & Cachelin, F. M. (2019). The need for cultural adaptations to health interventions for African American women: A qualitative analysis. *Cultural Diversity and Ethnic Minority Psychology, 25*(3), 331–341. https://doi.org/10.1037/cdp0000228

Shafran, R., Clark, D. M., Fairburn, C. G., Arntz, A., Barlow, D. H., Ehlers, A., Freeston, M., Garety, P. A., Hollon, S. D., Ost, L. G., & Salkovskis, P. M. (2009). Mind the gap: Improving the dissemination of CBT. *Behaviour Research and Therapy, 47*(11), 902–909. https://doi.org/10.1016/j.brat.2009.07.003

Smith, K. E., Mason, T. B., Murray, S. B., Griffiths, S., Leonard, R. C., Wetterneck, C. T., Smith, B. E. R., Farrell, N. R., Riemann, B. C., & Lavender, J. M. (2017). Male clinical norms and sex differences on the Eating Disorder Inventory (EDI) and Eating Disorder Examination Questionnaire (EDE-Q). *International Journal of Eating Disorders, 50*(7), 769-775. https://doi.org/10.1002/eat.22716

Society of Clinical Psychology. (n.d.). *Psychological treatments*. Retrieved November 15, 2023, from https://div12.org/psychological-treatments/

Stuart, S., & Robertson, M. (2012). *Interpersonal psychotherapy 2E a clinician's guide*. CRC Press.

Udo, T., & Grilo, C. M. (2018). Prevalence and correlates of DSM-5–defined eating disorders in a nationally representative sample of US adults. *Biological Psychiatry, 84*(5), 345–354. https://doi.org/10.1016/j.biopsych.2018.03.014

Udo, T., & Grilo, C. M. (2019). Psychiatric and medical correlates of DSM-5 eating disorders in a nationally representative sample of adults in the United States. *International Journal of Eating Disorders, 52*(1), 42–50. https://doi.org/10.1002/eat.23004

U.S. Preventive Services Task Force. (2022, March 15). *Eating Disorders in Adolescents and Adults: Screening*. https://www.uspreventiveservicestaskforce.org/uspstf/recommendation/screening-eating-disorders-adolescentsadults#:~:text=What%20does%20the%20USPSTF%20recommend,nervosa)%20in%20adolescents%20and%20adults.

Von Schell, A., Ohrt, T. K., Bruening, A. B., & Perez, M. (2018). Rates of disordered eating behaviors across sexual minority undergraduate men and women. *Psychology of Sexual Orientation and Gender Diversity, 5*(3), 352–359. https://doi.org/10.1037/sgd0000278

Waller, G., Gray, E., Hinrichsen, H., Mountford, V., Lawson, R., & Patient, E. (2014). Cognitive-behavioral therapy for bulimia nervosa and atypical bulimia nervosa: Effectiveness in clinical settings. *International Journal of Eating Disorders, 47*(1), 13–17. https://doi.org/10.1002/eat.22181

Walsh, B. T., Fairburn, C .G., Mickley, D., Sysko, R., & Parides, M.K. (2004). Treatment of bulimia nervosa in a primary care setting. *American Journal of Psychiatry, 161*, 556–561. https://doi.org/10.1176/appi.ajp.161.3.556

CHAPTER 7

BINGE EATING DISORDER THROUGH AN INTERSECTIONAL LENS

Working With a Black Female Veteran

Kate Terranova, Allegra Borghese, and Tamique Ridgard

Binge eating disorder (BED) is considered the most prevalent eating disorder (ED) worldwide (Davis et al., 2020; Lindvall Dahlgren et al., 2017). Systematic reviews of epidemiological data for BED have estimated that global prevalence rates for BED are 0.9% (Erskine & Whiteford, 2018). In the U.S., prevalence rates for BED range from 0.85 to 2.6% (Davis et al., 2020; Micali et al., 2017; Udo & Grilo, 2018). BED and binge eating behaviors (e.g., eating an objectively large amount of food) have been well documented and studied. Key discrepancies, however, exist between diagnostic criteria for BED in the United States and internationally. Furthermore, across varying multicultural and social identity groups, notable differences in prevalence rates, clinical presentations/manifestations, and treatment considerations are present. Given these differences, this chapter will present research documenting binge eating behaviors and BED across diverse populations and then focus on a case of a Black, cisgender, heterosexual female veteran who was treated for BED.

Counseling Individuals With Eating Disorders: An Intersectional Approach, pp. 139–165

BINGE EATING DISORDER

According to the Diagnostic and Statistical Manual 5 (DSM-5), BED is characterized by engagement in recurrent episodes of eating an amount of food larger than what most people would consume under similar circumstances (American Psychiatric Association [APA], 2013). These episodes of overeating are accompanied by loss of control during which the individual feels they cannot stop or regulate how much they consume (APA, 2013). Behavioral manifestations include eating more quickly than normal, eating until uncomfortable, and eating a large amount of food when not hungry (APA, 2013). Psychological effects of binge episodes are often feelings of disgust, embarrassment, depression, and guilt (APA, 2013). The consumption of an objectively large amount of food and loss of control need to be present at minimum once per week for 3 months to establish a BED diagnosis.

The latest revision to the International Classification of Diseases (ICD) included the recognition and addition of BED. In contrast to the DSM-5, the ICD-11 shifts focus away from the quantity of food an individual consumes in a discrete period and instead defines binge eating by the experience of loss of control (LOC; Berner et al., 2020). As long as LOC is present, individuals can engage in binge eating episodes that are objectively large (e.g., the amount of food eaten is larger than what most people would eat under similar circumstances) or subjectively large (e.g., the amount of food consumed is considered being typical of what others would eat in similar situations, but individuals view the amount as large). In either case, individuals would be diagnosed with BED (Berner at al., 2020; Reed et al., 2019). Thus, a discrepancy exists between how BED is diagnosed in the United States and around the world. The DSM-5 and ICD-11 do agree, however, that BED remains untreated longer than is true for other EDs (67.4 months for BED vs. 53 months for BN and 29.9 months for AN; Austin et al., 2021), pointing to a need to enhance understanding of this highly prevalent disorder.

Psychiatric and Medical Comorbidities

BED is a serious illness that is associated with psychiatric and physical risks, as well as social and interpersonal limitations (Sheehan & Herman, 2015). Psychiatric comorbidities include lifetime major depression, increased rates of anxiety and stress, high correlations with trauma and substance use, self-harm behavior, and suicide in young adulthood (APA, 2013). Hypertension, type 2 diabetes, heart disease, metabolic syndrome, and non-alcoholic fatty liver disease are among the medical conditions commonly linked to BED (Hudson et al., 2010; World Health Organization,

2016). Interpersonal challenges include weight stigma, weight-based discrimination and/or abuse, lack of belonging, social role adjustment problems, and negative self-evaluation (Puhl & Heuer, 2010).

PREVALENCE AND MANIFESTATIONS OF BED: INTERSECTIONAL CONSIDERATIONS

Gender Identity

Globally, cisgender women (1.1–1.7%) have higher prevalence rates of BED than cisgender men (0.3–.6%; Erskine & Whiteford, 2018). In the U.S., lifetime prevalence rates for BED are estimated to be 2.8% for women and 1.0% for men (Davis et al., 2020; Galmiche et al., 2019). More specifically, U.S. women have a 2 to 3 times greater risk than men (Udo & Grilo, 2018). Among adults who seek treatment for BED, differences exist in the age of onset and in clinical presentation. Lydecker and Grilo (2018) found that men seem to develop BED more rapidly than women once they start dieting, while women start dieting and binge eating earlier than men and experience a longer duration of subthreshold BE symptoms. Additionally, they found that women exhibit more severe BED and depressive symptoms, which is believed, in part, to be related to a longer duration of eating pathology.

Transgender individuals engage in high rates of disordered eating (Parker & Harriger, 2020; Watson et al., 2017), but there is no evidence that they have higher rates of BED. Most studies report that compared to cisgender adults, transgender and gender non-conforming adults have higher rates of EDs (Diemer et al., 2015; Parker & Harriger, 2020; Simone et al., 2020). A range of ED behaviors, including restricting, binging, and purging, have been identified in these populations (Feder et al., 2017; Guss et al., 2017; Watson et al., 2017). Typically, studies have included transgender and gender-nonconforming individuals in one category (Parker & Harriger, 2020) and thus further research is needed to clarify the prevalence of particular ED diagnoses within each population.

Race

Most clinical knowledge abouts EDs has been garnered from studies of White females and poorly reflects the variety in ED presentations among diverse racial groups (Rodgers et al., 2018). Of note, Cachelin and colleagues (2001) found that racially diverse women desire treatment (85.2%), but only 8% of the respondents received care. The most common treatment barriers documented were finances and lack of insurance. Together, these studies point to systemic factors inhibiting equal participation in ED treatment. BED research has also focused primarily on White women and has contributed to reduced detection of BE in other racial and ethnic groups (Davis et al., 2020).

Binge eating rates in Black, Caribbean, and African American adults are comparable to other racial and ethnic groups, including White Americans (Goode, Cowell, et al., 2020; Taylor et al., 2007), but the lifetime prevalence of binge eating is higher in Black and African American individuals than among White individuals. It is important to note that Black and African American individuals are underrepresented in clinical trials, which has limited our understanding of BED prevalence, course, and treatment outcomes in this population (Goode, Cowell, et al., 2020). EDs, in general, are more common in Black and African American adult women than Black and African American adult men (Taylor et al., 2007). In a recent meta-analysis examining BE and BED in Black and African American women, Goode, Cowell, and colleagues (2020) found that there are few racial differences in symptom presentation between Black and African American women and White women. Notably, Black and African American women were significantly less likely than White women to seek out, or be referred for, treatment; to engage in treatment; or to remain in treatment for the duration of the treatment program (Goode, Cowell, et al., 2020). These differences in access to treatment speak to the need for culturally responsive treatment programs that are tailored to the unique needs of Black women.

Treatment programs designed to treat BE and BED in Black and African American women should consider how differences in socialization and cultural norms may impact the development and maintenance of their BE and BED (Goode, Cowell, et al., 2020; Goode, Kalarchian, et al., 2020). In a recent qualitative study, Black women with BED who participated in an appetite awareness treatment program identified several cultural values that influenced their eating behaviors, including the need to eat all the food on one's plate to not waste food; making food a central part of social and celebratory events; and seeing food as a means for survival, which was attributed to the legacy of slavery (Goode, Kalarchian, et al., 2020). Moreover, some studies reported an earlier age of onset of BE and BED for Black and African American women compared to White women (Goode, Cowell, et al., 2020). Relatedly, Black adolescents, in comparison to White adolescents, made more attempts to gain weight and reported eating behavior focused on promoting muscularity, including taking supplements, and eating more to gain muscle weight (Nagata et al., 2019). Nagata and colleagues (2019) emphasized that body satisfaction is evaluated differently across racial groups, which points to a need to focus on a variety of concerns instead of only a desire for thinness (Mikhail & Klump, 2021). For example,

Parker and colleagues (2022) found that skin color satisfaction was negatively associated with risk of BED and BE behaviors in Black adolescent girls; lower levels of skin color satisfaction were related to increased risk of BED and BE behaviors. This risk was mediated by body image satisfaction (Parker et al., 2022). Finally, the experience of race and racism seems to impact the development and maintenance of BED in Black and African American individuals; specifically, perceived discrimination has been associated with overeating among African American men (Kelly et al., 2018) and with emotional eating and binge eating in African American women (Durso et al., 2012; Harrington et al., 2006; Johnson et al., 2012). Also, ethnic identity has been associated with binge eating behaviors in Black and African American women (Goode, Cowell, et al., 2020). These findings underscore the need to identify variables that may differentially impact a Black individual's risk for BED.

BED is the most prevalent ED among Hispanic and Latinx populations. Latinx individuals have higher rates of lifetime BED than other racial groups and appear to struggle with weight regulation and binge eating at rates equal to or higher than White women (Perez et al., 2016; Rodgers et al., 2018). For example, in a diverse sample of first-year college students, a higher proportion of Latinas engaged in binge episodes compared to White, Asian, and African American females (Barrack et al., 2019). Research is mixed regarding whether higher rates of lifetime binge eating exist in Western countries than in Latin America (Kolar et al., 2016; Perez et al., 2016). Associations have been found between emotional eating and acculturative stress (feeling overwhelmed due to conflicting cultural practices), language difficulties, and self-consciousness as a result of adjustment to a dominant culture in Latino adolescents (Simmons & Limbers, 2019). While Latinx adolescents and other racial/ethnic groups reported similar engagement in emotional eating, acculturative stress was associated with more emotional eating in Latinx adolescents (Simmons & Limbers, 2019).

BED prevalence rates vary for Asian Americans. Some studies report similar rates of binge eating for Asian Americans compared to other racial groups, while other studies report that Asian Americans binge eat less than individuals from other racial groups (Davis et al., 2020; Yu et al., 2019). In contrast, in studies examining disordered eating generally, Asian identifying individuals have been found to engage in more disordered eating and weight control behaviors than other racial groups (Berry et al., 1986; Rodgers et al., 2017). Asian female adolescents had the highest rates of disordered eating behaviors compared to Black, Hispanic, and White female adolescents (Rodgers et al., 2018; Rodgers et al., 2017). Asian adolescent boys endorsed the highest rates of overeating, as well as other disordered eating behaviors, compared to other racial groups (Rodgers et al., 2018). Asian American males may be at a higher risk for ED symptoms than other racial groups. Kelly and colleagues (2015) further substantiated that Asian-American men reported higher rates of binge eating as well as other disordered eating behaviors.

Limited research exists examining EDs in Native Americans. In one of the few studies conducted to increase understanding of EDs in Native American/Alaska Native women and men, Striegel-Moore and colleagues (2011) found that Native women engaged in more binge eating and feared losing control over their eating more than White women. Australian researchers found that a greater proportion of indigenous Australians engaged in disordered eating compared to the general Australian population (Burt et al., 2020).

Racial and Ethnic Groups Not Well Represented in Research

In general, ED and BED research has focused on understanding differences in White, Black/African American, Asian, and Hispanic/Latinx populations with the exclusion of those who self-identify as multiracial, biracial, or other. While some studies have included a "more than one race" and "other" racial category, typically sample size is small for these groups, which restricts between-group comparisons to examine differences in ED symptom presentation.

Age

Binge eating disorder has two peak onset periods. One peak occurs in late adolescence and the other occurs in early adulthood (Bohon, 2019). Though onset is most typical in adolescence and early adulthood, a growing number of younger people are struggling with binge eating. BED seems to be as prevalent in children and adolescents as anorexia nervosa (AN) and bulimia nervosa (BN) (Kjeldbjerg & Clausen, 2021). Weight and shape concern, a predictor of eating disorder pathology among children and adolescents, develops from peer comparison, advertisements, social media, and parental attitudes about weight and eating (Allen et al., 2014). Further, during the COVID-19 pandemic, the lack of in-person services and structured programming for children and adolescents has increased social media use and mental health disorders, including BED (Couturier et al., 2021). A recent study showed that each additional hour that children spent on social media was associated with a 62% higher risk of BED one year later, and each extra hour spent watching or streaming television or movies was linked with a 39% higher risk of BED one year later (Nagata et al., 2021). In addition to the aforementioned onset periods, BED is one of the most common full-threshold ED diagnoses in individuals over 40 (Davis et al., 2020; Micali et al., 2017).

Socioeconomic Status

A recent meta-analysis by Huryk et al. (2021) found no consistent relationship between socioeconomic status (SES) and ED diagnosis; ED diagnoses were present at all SES levels. In low SES populations, connections between inconsistent access to food and BED have been observed (Huryk et al., 2021; Rasmusson et al., 2019). High SES groups are more likely to seek treatment for an ED (Huryk et al., 2021; Sonneville & Lipson, 2018), in part due to the greater likelihood of private health insurance coverage. Treatment costs and poor access serve as barriers to care for lower SES groups (Ali et al., 2017; Ali et al., 2020).

Sexual Orientation

In the U.S., sexual minority adults have been found to have higher rates of EDs than their heterosexual counterparts (Kamody et al., 2020). Lifetime prevalence of BED is 2.17% in sexual minority individuals compared to 0.81% in heterosexual individuals (Grunewald et al., 2021). Another study conducted by Kamody et al. (2020) identified similar prevalence rates of BED (2.2%) in sexual minority adults. In sexual minority men, BED is more prevalent than other EDs. In a study of undergraduates, more sexual minority men (38.1%) than heterosexual men (24.0%) reported one or more episodes of objective binge eating in the past month (Von Schell et al., 2018). Gay and bisexual male children and adolescents engaged in monthly binge eating at higher rates than heterosexual males (Austin et al., 2009). Among sexual minorities, research has substantiated that the development of and engagement in disordered eating behaviors are influenced by minority stress and discrimination (Nagata et al., 2020).

Veterans

Among service members and veterans, binge eating symptoms are prevalent (Bartlett & Mitchell, 2015; Davis et al., 2020). A study of veterans documented high rates of binge eating and found that 82% of veterans who needed to gain weight during their service reported binge eating episodes (Masheb et al., 2019). Further, a large proportion of the sample (57.9%)

continued to endorse binge eating episodes following their service (Masheb et al., 2019).

Unique institutional and environmental factors increase susceptibility to disordered eating for service members and veterans (Davis et al., 2020). The culture of maintaining physical fitness and "making weight" is linked to binge eating and disordered eating later in life (Masheb et al., 2019). In addition, fluctuations in eating patterns due to changes in job requirements, deployments, and exposure to combat also influence binge eating behaviors (Bartlett & Mitchell, 2015). Finally, veterans with PTSD or depression symptoms binge eat at significantly higher rates (26.4%) than veterans without psychological comorbidities (14.6%) (Hoerster et al., 2015).

RISK AND PROTECTIVE FACTORS FOR BED

Risk Factors

Race-based stress (e.g., perceived discrimination, stigma, prejudice) increases one's allostatic load and contributes to adverse health effects and maladaptive ways of coping among ethnic and racial minorities (English et al., 2018). Among immigrants, acculturative stress (Berry et al., 1987) has been linked to elevated rates of eating pathology across multiple ethnic groups who are adjusting to new cultural mores (Warren & Akoury, 2020). More acculturated individuals (increased orientation to Anglo American culture) have an increased likelihood of engaging in disordered eating. Among eating disordered individuals, less acculturated individuals face more barriers to treatment (Cachelin et al., 2006). Discrimination in the form of racial teasing has been linked to the development of body image concerns and disordered eating among Asian Americans (Levine & Smolak, 2010; Menzel et al., 2010). In three studies of South or East Asian women conducted from 2003 to 2014, significant relationships existed between racial teasing and disordered eating and/or maladaptive eating attitudes, after controlling for variables such as BMI, self-esteem, and perceived racial discrimination (Cheng, 2014; Reddy & Crowther, 2007). Among Latinas and Black women, relationships between perceived discrimination and binge eating have been identified (Borghese, 2020; Terranova, 2021); specifically, high levels of perceived discrimination and general life stressors are significantly associated with increased emotional eating (Durso et al., 2012; Johnson et al., 2012) and binge eating behaviors (Durso et al., 2012; Harrington et al., 2006).

Low SES is also a risk factor due to food insecurity and limited access to nutritious, fresh, and healthy food either due to geographical restrictions (i.e., food deserts) or affordability concerns (Firth, 2012). The stress of worrying about meeting daily needs for survival acts similarly to race-based stress, increasing allostatic load (Evans & Kim, 2012). Studies indicate that households with the most food insecurity (adults who reported having hungry children in the household) also experienced the highest rates of ED pathology, including BED (Becker et al., 2017). Low educational attainment is also a predictor of ED symptomatology (Maxwell et al., 2011) and studies show that low education attainment negatively impacts treatment outcomes for eating disorders (Thompson-Brenner et al., 2013).

Protective Factors

Psychological protective factors have been identified and can be strengthened within individuals who are at risk for BED. While self-criticism and low self-compassion are implicated in the development and maintenance of binge eating, self-acceptance and high self-compassion are associated with better food-related self-regulation (Serpell at al., 2020). In addition, resilience has been found to be an important factor in the relationship between stress and binge eating pathology, where higher resilience is associated with lower rates of binge eating behavior (Thurston et al., 2018). Self-acceptance, which has consistently emerged as a protective factor relative to all negative body image and ED behavior indices, is particularly important to cultivate (Romano, 2021). Mindfulness may be a worthwhile intervention to regulate impulsive food behaviors and may also serve as a protective factor, as it has been shown to disrupt the pathway between anxiety and impulsivity in maladaptive eating behaviors (Wilson et al., 2021).

Another important psychological protective factor is attachment style. Individuals who experience secure attachment and strong feelings of connectedness are well prepared to cope with life's stressors; they exhibit more effective emotion regulation than those who experienced insecure attachment. Those that are insecurely attached are more likely to develop maladaptive ways of regulating emotion, such as binge eating (Han & Pistole, 2014). Both mother-child and father-child connectedness in adolescence have been linked to lower odds of binge eating-related behaviors among adolescent girls (Hazzard, 2020).

Factors related to an individual's social system can help to curb maladaptive eating behaviors as well. A study that explored patterns of disordered eating among transgender youth found that protective factors such as family connectedness, school connectedness, caring friends, and social support were linked to lower endorsement of past year disordered eating (Watson et al., 2017). School achievement has also been associated with lower eating disorder symptoms (Croll et al., 2002), as has regular family meals (Hazzard, 2020) and maintaining an active lifestyle (Cook et al.,

2011). Finally, feminist perspectives have been cited as a possible protective factor against disordered eating attitudes and behaviors among African American women (Wolff, 2022).

EMPIRICALLY SUPPORTED PSYCHOSOCIAL TREATMENTS

Children and Adolescents

While the onset of BED is typically in late adolescence or early adulthood, a growing number of younger people struggle with binge eating. BED seems to be as prevalent in children and adolescents as anorexia nervosa (AN) and bulimia nervosa (BN); thus, treatment of BED in younger populations should be prioritized as much as AN and BN (Kjeldbjerg & Clausen, 2021). Weight and shape concern, a predictor of eating disorder pathology among children and adolescents, develops from peer comparison, advertisements, social media, and parental attitudes about weight and eating (Allen et al., 2014). Further, during the COVID-19 pandemic, the lack of in-person services and structured programming for children and adolescents has increased social media use and mental health disorders, including BED (Couturier et al., 2021). As stated earlier, time spent on social media is positively associated with higher risk of BED (Nagata et al., 2021).

Interpersonal psychotherapy (IPT) is an effective intervention for BED among adolescents (Burke et al., 2020). This approach proposes that difficulties in interpersonal relationships prompt mood-induced eating that promotes BED and weight gain (Tanofsky-Kraff et al., 2007). IPT is a 12-week treatment that focuses on (a) psychoeducation, (b) categorization of various interpersonal experiences (e.g., interpersonal role disputes, interpersonal role transitions, interpersonal deficits, and grief, or interpersonal loss), (c) the building of communication skills (i.e., making "I" statements, being specific, perspective taking, having patience, striking while the iron is cold, and compromising), (d) role-play, (e) confrontation, and (f) problem-solving (Burke et al., 2020). Individuals learn to track how their relationships impact their mood, as well as learn skills to engage in conversations to promote change in the outcomes that have historically led to negative moods and binge eating.

Adults

Multiple theoretical approaches have been shown to address BED among adults. In addition to IPT, cognitive behavioral therapy (CBT) has a large support base and has proven effective in decreasing the frequency of weekly binges, in improving overall attitudes toward body image and food, and in lowering BMI (Wilfley et al., 2002). CBT is based on the restraint model of binge eating (that restraint behavior leads to overwhelming hunger and binging) and it addresses both cognitive and behavioral factors involved in the development and maintenance of BED. Cognitive factors targeted in treatment include negative body image, self-evaluation, beliefs about self-worth, and overthinking one's weight and body shape. Behavioral treatment focuses on behaviors of restraint, restriction, binge eating, body avoidance, and body checking. Techniques employed include cognitive restructuring (challenging one's thinking processes to create a healthier perspective), developing coping strategies for negative thoughts and urges, and relapse prevention. CBT commonly utilizes homework assignments to make use of its time-limited approach and incorporates nutritional counseling when appropriate. Overall, the treatment aims to modify dysfunctional thoughts and behaviors related to one's body shape and weight, which is shown to reduce eating disorder pathology (da Luz et al., 2021).

Several approaches to BED treatment have taken the principles of CBT and incorporated aspects of other models to best help individuals struggling with binge eating. For example, guided self-help cognitive behavior therapy (CBTgsh) is another time-limited, effective treatment for BED for individuals who are reluctant to initiate therapy. In CBTgsh, a client works through a self-help workbook or computer course with the support of a therapist who is trained in CBT. Between sessions, the client is guided to read materials and complete assignments, such as mood diaries, which are then reviewed with the provider. It can be convenient for individuals who have time constraints, family, or work commitments, or who want a therapy that is anonymous (Striegel-Moore et al., 2011). CBTgsh is a first-line treatment option for most clients with BED (Glisenti et al., 2018).

Originally stemming from the work of mindfulness-based stress reduction (MBSR), mindfulness-based cognitive therapy (MBCT) combines the principles of cognitive therapy with meditative practices, which allows for shifts in attitudes based on the cultivation of mindfulness (Segal et al., 2002). A client is helped to become better acquainted with the modes of mind that often characterize psychopathology, while learning to develop a new relationship with them. Techniques include body scanning exercises, mindfulness movement, practicing non-judgment, and cultivating awareness of the present moment. MBCT is offered in an 8-week group format with a weekly 2-hour course and one day-long class after the fifth week (Segal et al., 2002). Studies that have examined the efficacy of using MBCT to treat individuals with BED showed improvements in binge eating symptoms and increased levels of mindfulness posttreatment and six months later (Baer et al., 2005).

Emotion-focused therapy (EFT) is an experiential approach to therapy informed by humanistic–phenomenological theories of therapy, emotion and cognition theory, affective neuroscience, and dynamic and family systems theory (Greenberg, 2017). EFT for BED is based upon the affect regulation theory of binge eating (that binge eating is an attempt to alter distressing emotional states), and therefore focuses on addressing emotion regulation difficulties in individuals with BED, rather than specific thoughts or behaviors. It is easily integrated into both cognitive-behavioral and psychodynamic approaches to therapy. The main goals of EFT are to help people understand emotion as a means of communication about core needs, goals, and values, as well as to help people identify actions and attitudes linked to meeting or better understanding such needs, goals, and values. EFT has been shown to result in (a) a decrease in binge eating frequency, (b) clinically significant improvements in binge eating psychopathology, (c) changes in eating disorder attitudes relating to eating, weight, and shape concern, and (d) better emotion and mood regulation (Glisenti et al., 2018).

According to the EFT model, emotion organizes experience through emotion schemes, or memories of lived emotional experience. EFT works to transform negative feelings that arise when these schemes are activated. This requires acceptance of the negative feeling plus feeling it (Greenberg, 2017). Six interventions are offered as a means to help transform negative feelings (Angus & Greenberg, 2011). First, *empathic attunement* from the provider is crucial for the client to access challenging feelings, where the client feels empathically heard, understood, supported, and safe. Second, *vivid re-entry* into a situation can expand the client's narrative when the client experiences a problematic reaction, especially when it feels sudden or unexpected. *Experiential focusing* is a third technique, which guides clients to experience sensations in the body as they discuss what they were feeling in distressing or confusing memories. This helps improve emotional intelligence by developing access to immediate experience and self-reflecting on internal experience. Fourth, a *two-chair task for self-critical split* helps a client to understand the function of self-criticism and become more aware of its impact on other parts of self. A *two-chair task for self-interruptive split* is another technique to transform negative feelings, which addresses the tendency for some clients to be limited in their expression of feelings. Intentionally heightening emotions that tend to be self-interrupted can protect against situations where attempts to suppress emotion led to a rebound effect of emotional flooding and impulsive behavior, such as binge eating. Finally, *empty chair work* can help address unresolved situations by mentalizing the 'other' in interpersonal confrontations. It allows the client who has experienced emotional injury to undertake an experiential entry into the perspective of the significant other with whom they have experienced problems to foster compassion and work towards understanding (Glisenti et al., 2018).

CASE EXAMPLE: TREATING BED WITH EFT

Janine, a 39-year-old Black, cisgender, and heterosexual female veteran, grew up in the Southeastern United States and enlisted in the Army Reserves at 18 years old. Throughout her 20 years of service, which included two tours overseas, she faced repeated acts of discrimination based on her racial and gender identities. Racial discrimination (Stewart, 2021) and sexual harassment (Stander & Thomsen, 2016) are well documented among U.S. service members and veterans. Upon returning to civilian life, Janine began to work in sales, where she faced difficulties interacting with her coworkers and developed maladaptive eating habits. She would come home from work and eat large portions of food rapidly, which elicited feelings of shame. After a year of trying to manage her symptoms on her own, a doctor diagnosed her with BED.

Having spent significant time in the military, where she adopted the Army's hierarchical leadership style, Janine was perceived as aggressive by civilian employees. She viewed the people she worked with as inferior due to their lack of military training, and she had a hard time collaborating. It is also important to recognize that her colleagues may have stereotyped her as "an angry Black woman," responded to her according to that stereotype, and a destructive cycle began. Janine reported that her colleagues responded to her with mocking insults to get under her skin, and that she would "lose it" by yelling, slamming doors, cursing, or ignoring people. On several occasions, Janine's boss had written her up for unprofessional behavior, and she was being threatened with suspension if she did not learn to appropriately cope with her reactions. Janine tried to solve the situation by suppressing her feelings and avoiding interactions at work; however, she would come home from the office and find herself overeating. This pattern of excessive eating and LOC, occurred almost daily, and led to weight gain and emotional distress.

Several factors inhibited Janine from seeking treatment for her binge eating. Internalized messages from the military led her to believe that she needed to toughen up and soldier on. Many individuals who have served in the military develop myths about those who seek help for mental health, such as equating help-seeking to inherent weakness or not being deserving of care because others "had it worse" (Patel, 2021). Black women are also less likely to seek treatment for BED than their White counterparts, perhaps due to distrust of White mental health providers and predominantly White-run mental health establishments. In addition to experiencing difficulties in accessing care, Black individuals can be made to feel that seeking professional treatment is a betrayal of faith, spirituality, and group culture (Dennis, 2015). Seeking mental health help can even be considered a form of excessive assimilation into Whiteness (Dennis, 2015). It is often the case that bigger bodies are celebrated among Black women and thus there may be fewer symptoms of distress with the weight gain that accompanies binge eating (Nagata et al., 2019). Further, Janine did not want to address her experiences of discrimination in her military career and was avoiding the likelihood that these events were contributing to her binge eating.

Nonetheless, at the encouragement of her primary care doctor, Janine agreed to seek treatment to improve her work experience and emotional life. She told her psychotherapist that she wanted to reduce her tendency to lose control while eating and was less concerned about her weight gain. Assessments revealed that Janine's military training was at odds with her workplace culture and was contributing to interpersonal stress and binging, and that she had experienced several traumatic events during her military career. A treatment was chosen that could help Janine to process her military experience, regulate her emotions, and accommodate her preference to focus on LOC instead of dietary behaviors.

Janine participated in a 12-week EFT program to increase access to her emotional experience, regulate and transform maladaptive emotions, and develop more positive identity narratives. EFT posits that addressing emotions can modify behavior and influence one's thoughts (Greenberg, 2017). Further, it is a treatment that has shown to effectively address complex trauma (Holowaty & Paivio, 2012; Paivio & Pascual-Leone, 2010), including acts of racism (Nightingale et al., 2019) and assault (Pascual-Leone et al., 2011).

Phase 1 of treatment focused on promoting awareness of Janine's emotions, welcoming and accepting them, and putting them into words. Evocative unfolding (vividly re-entering a situation to expand the client's narrative) and imaginal exposure exercises helped to elicit Janine's feelings of anger, helplessness, and anxiety. She was guided to allow herself to become upset, sit with, observe, and describe the experience. Over time, she was better able to (a) accept that she felt rage, helplessness, and anxiety based on her experience, (b) conceive that her emotions were there to help her understand something, and (c) examine boundaries and underlying feelings of violation. Phase 1 thus helped Janine widen her window of tolerance to her anger, helplessness, and anxiety and differentiate her anger from feelings of violation.

Phase 2 worked to evaluate the adaptive and maladaptive functions of her primary emotions (anger, helplessness, and anxiety), identify destructive emotion schemes, access other adaptive emotions and needs, and transform maladaptive emotion schemes. Experiential focusing (guiding a client to approach the embodied aspects of their experience with attention and a willingness to put words to their bodily felt sense) helped Janine revisit her military training, where she was bullied with racial and sexist insults by superiors. She had been humiliated and had felt both powerless and angry during these instances but trained herself to suppress these feelings because to show her emotions to the sergeants would be seen as disobedient and result in expulsion from the Army. The schema of "it is not safe to express myself" solidified during her service. In therapy, patterns of emotional suppression with authority figures were explored. Janine came to see how suppressing her emotions contributed to her tendency to explode at her coworkers and she gradually learned ways to express herself that decreased her tendency to bottle up her emotions.

Janine knew that to be vulnerable in combat—whether in training or in the field—could cause death or expose her to danger. Likewise, to allow herself to be close enough to the enemy could be met with demise. Janine ignoring or yelling at her coworkers was an adaptive attempt to keep people at a distance, because her beliefs were "I cannot let anyone close to me" and, "If I do not assert dominance, I will be victimized and die." By keeping emotional distance between herself and her coworkers, she attempted to control feeling victimized; however, this prevented her from being able to access her feelings and limited her awareness of her needs and informing her of her needs. Her habit of directing her attention away from feelings of vulnerability toward suppression of feeling or displays of anger was adaptive in the military, but was no longer necessary. Through split-chair work that brought forward latent feelings of violation—and without the expected life-threatening consequences—Janine learned to access and tolerate vulnerability and identify her core need for safety. Transformation came when Janine acknowledged her anger, helplessness, and anxiety as a sign of feeling hurt and learned that accepting her hurt did not mean she was "weak" or "a target." Phase 2 helped Janine accept her pain without judgment and develop ways to choose how to respond to her pain.

Further, Janine's workplace culture contained racial banter that compounded feelings of disrespect and provoked her to react aggressively. The schema, "If I do not fight, I allow disrespect," derived from peer harassment in the military that left Janine feeling like she was always at battle and on the attack. Feelings of violation brought on by interpersonal closeness were amplified by microaggressions that were part of her everyday experience. Over time, the identification of schemas of violation helped Janine to tolerate her vulnerability as well as recognize that her desire to be respected was driving her to confront her coworkers. Empty chair work helped Janine role play with ways she might confront her coworkers productively.

Through therapy, Janine built internal resources to understand her experience, cultivated a voice to communicate a more authentic self, and developed ways to imagine the feelings of others.

Janine's ability to learn skills and improve her emotion regulation helped her to develop self-efficacy and self-esteem that served to protect her from self-defeating behaviors like overeating. EFT helped Janine to better identify and address feelings as they arose instead of suppressing them or reacting defensively via verbal attack. She learned to validate her emotions and offer a nurturing and attuned inner dialogue so she could hear and meet her emotional needs. She was better able to differentiate challenges to her opinions in the workplace from memories of threatening confrontations in the Army. Janine learned that to show vulnerability did not make her susceptible to assault and instead made her available to connection and understanding. The more Janine was able to sit with and process her schemas related to victimization, anger, helplessness, and anxiety, the less focused she was on lashing out or overeating to soothe herself. Through EFT, Janine decreased her binge eating episodes by consistently attending to her emotional experience.

CONCLUSION: DIRECTIONS FOR TREATMENT, RESEARCH, THEORY AND POLICY

Treatment for individuals with BED needs to better address intersectional identities. While marginalized aspects of one's identity have been understood to have adverse effects in the development of BED, questions remain regarding how identities such as race may also serve as protective factors against the development and maintenance of BED (Lydecker et al., 2019). Deeper analysis into identity factors such as SES, psychiatric and/or medical comorbidity, acculturation status, and aspects of one's ability or sexual identity are needed to best treat BED. Cultural considerations in ED treatment are also essential, given the high proportion of racial/ethnic minorities diagnosed with EDs. A systematic review of clinical recommendations for ED treatment with racially and ethnically diverse individuals indicated that empirical research in this area is sparse and the literature addressing culture in ED treatment is not sufficient to make enhancements to existing protocols or develop new treatments (Acle et al., 2021). Furthermore, as EDs have been proven to affect racial/ethnic minorities at near equal, if not higher, rates than White women, attention should be given to training and recruiting providers from diverse backgrounds in order to improve the delivery of culturally competent care. In a recent global study assessing ED provider diversity, the overwhelming majority of providers identified as heterosexual, White, women (Jennings Mathis et al., 2020).

This lack of diversity may discourage people of color from seeking out treatment or from feeling that they can connect with their providers.

Research should aim to contribute to theoretical and empirical knowledge by improving understanding of the factors thought to maintain binge eating behavior among diverse populations. This would be the first step to improving evidence-based treatments for BED. Further, a focus on intersecting identities in ED research would enhance understanding of the ways intersectionality serves as an ED risk as well as a protective factor (Burke et al., 2020). Internet-based interventions, that are less costly than traditional ED treatments and have the potential to increase access, show promise for the reduction of BED symptoms, and should be investigated as well (Munsch et al., 2019; Pruessner et al., 2022).

Theory must better address internalized weight bias among individuals with EDs, especially when it is often reinforced by the weightiest views of clinicians. Training for clinicians should address internalized weight stigma that may interfere with best practices (Puhl et al., 2014). Theories that encompass these iterative and dynamic processes between therapists and their clients are likely to best serve individuals with BED. Feminist and critical approaches have been proposed as inclusive theoretical frameworks for conceptualizing intersectionality in ED development, maintenance, and recovery (Burke et al., 2020).

Policies must be enacted that address the global health burden and costs associated with EDs. From 2018 to 2019, EDs cost the U.S. an estimated 64.7 billion dollars with BED accounting for 30% of the economic cost (Streatfeild et al., 2021). In addition to the public cost of EDs, on an individual level, the cost to access ED treatment is high, which limits accessibility and effective treatment of EDs (Whiteford & Weissman, 2017). Without government intervention, EDs are currently creating an economic burden on the community due to increased disability and premature death among this population (Whiteford & Weissman, 2017). Furthermore, policy and legislation aimed at creating changes to the food environment and food industry can serve to mitigate disordered eating risk. For example, regulations regarding the production of processed foods could reduce binge eating symptomatology in larger segments of the population, as highly processed foods have been linked to LOC while eating (Rodgers & Sonneville, 2018).

DISCUSSION QUESTIONS

1. How can we decrease barriers to treatment for racial and ethnic minorities?
2. Discuss why you think certain components of BED are more or less salient among individuals of different backgrounds?

3. While the onset of BED is typically in one's teens or 20s, why do you think Janine did not start to develop BED symptoms until her late 30s?
4. What do you think are the most important predictors of treatment efficacy? (e.g., role of education, community resources, social support, body image ideals, self-compassion?)
5. How would you address Janine's intersectional identities (e.g., Black, female, veteran) in treatment?

REFERENCES

Acle, A., Cook, B. J., Siegfried, N., & Beasley, T. (2021). Cultural considerations in the treatment of eating disorders among racial/ethnic minorities: A systematic review. *Journal of Cross-Cultural Psychology*, *52*(5), 468–488. https://doi.org/10.1177/00220221211017664

Ali, K., Farrer, L., Fassnacht, D. B., Gulliver, A., Bauer, S., & Griffiths, K. M. (2017). Perceived barriers and facilitators towards help-seeking for eating disorders: A systematic review. *International Journal of Eating Disorders*, *50*(1), 9–21. https://doi.org/10.1002/eat.22598

Ali, K., Fassnacht, D. B., Farrer, L., Rieger, E., Feldhege, J., Moessner, M., Griffiths, S.B., & Bauer, S. (2020). What prevents young adults from seeking help? Barriers toward help-seeking for eating disorder symptomatology. *International Journal of Eating Disorders*, *53*(6), 894–906. https://doi.org/10.1002/eat.23266

Allen, K. L., Byrne, S. M., Oddy, W. H., Schmidt, U., & Crosby, R. D. (2014). Risk factors for binge eating and purging eating disorders: Differences based on age of onset. *International Journal of Eating Disorders*, *47*(7), 802–812. https://doi.org/10.1002/eat.22299

American Psychiatric Association [APA]. (2013). *Diagnostic and statistical manual of mental disorders* (5th ed.). https://doi.org/10.1176/appi.books.9780890425596

Angus, L. E., & Greenberg, L. S. (2011). *Working with narrative in emotion-focused therapy: Changing stories, healing lives*. American Psychological Association.

Austin, A., Flynn, M., Richards, K., Hodsoll, J., Duarte, T. A., Robinson, P., Kelly, J., & Schmidt, U. (2021). Duration of untreated eating disorder and relationship to outcomes: A systematic review of the literature. *European Eating Disorders Review*, *29*(3), 329–345. https://doi.org/10.1002/erv.2745

Austin, S. B., Ziyadeh, N. J., Corliss, H. L., Rosario, M., Wypij, D., Haines, J., Camargo, C. A., Jr., & Field, A. E. (2009). Sexual orientation disparities in purging and binge eating from early to late adolescence. *The Journal of Adolescent Health*, *45*(3), 238–245. https://doi.org/10.1016/j.jadohealth.2009.02.001

Baer, R. A., Fischer, S., & Huss, D. B. (2005). Mindfulness-based cognitive therapy applied to binge eating: A case study. *Cognitive and Behavioral Practice*, *12*(3), 351–358. https://doi.org/10.1016/S1077-7229(05)80057-4

Barrack, M. T., West, J., Christopher, M., & Pham-Vera, A. M. (2019). Disordered eating among a diverse sample of first-year college students. *Journal of the American College of Nutrition, 38*(2), 141–148. https://doi.org/10.1080/07315724.2018.1487345

Bartlett, B. A., & Mitchell, K. S. (2015). Eating disorders in military and veteran men and women: A systematic review. *International Journal of Eating Disorders, 48*(8), 1057–1069. https://doi.org/10.1002/eat.22454

Becker, C. B., Middlemass, K., Taylor, B., Johnson, C., & Gomez, F. (2017). Food insecurity and eating disorder pathology. *International Journal of Eating Disorders, 50*(9), 1031–1040. https://doi.org/10.1002/eat.22735

Berner, L. A., Sysko, R., Rebello, T. J., Roberto, C. A., & Pike, K. M. (2020). Patient descriptions of loss of control and eating episode size interact to influence expert diagnosis of ICD-11 binge-eating disorder. *Journal of Eating Disorders, 8*, 71–80. https://doi.org/10.1186/s40337-020-00342-z

Berry, J. W., Kim, U., Minde, T., & Mok, D. (1987). Comparative studies of acculturative stress. *International Migration Review, 21*(3), 491–511. https://doi.org/10.1177/019791838702100303

Berry, J. W., Trimble, J. E., & Olmedo, E. L. (1986). Assessment of acculturation. In W. J. Lonner & J. W. Berry (Eds.), *Field methods in cross-cultural research* (pp. 291–324). SAGE.

Bohon, C. (2019). Binge eating disorder in children and adolescents. *Child and Adolescent Psychiatric Clinics, 28*(4), 549–555. https://doi.org/10.1016/j.chc.2019.05.003

Borghese, A. E. (2020). *Acculturative stress, discrimination, ethnic identity, and binge eating among Latina college students.* [Doctoral dissertation, Fordham University]. ETD Collection for Fordham University. https://research.library.fordham.edu/dissertations/AAI27999803

Burke, N. L., Neyland, M. H., Young, J. F., Wilfley, D. E., & Tanofsky-Kraff, M. (2020). Interpersonal psychotherapy for the prevention of binge eating disorder and adult obesity in an African American adolescent military dependent boy. *Eating Behaviors, 38*, 1–6. https://doi.org/10.1016/j.eatbeh.2020.101408

Burt, A., Mannan, H., Touyz, S., & Hay, P. (2020). Prevalence of DSM-5 diagnostic threshold eating disorders and features amongst Aboriginal and Torres Strait islander peoples (First Australians). *BMC Psychiatry, 20*(1), 1–8. https://doi.org/10.1186/s12888-020-02852-1

Cachelin, F. M., Phinney, J. S., Schug, R. A., & Striegel-Moore, R. H. (2006). Acculturation and eating disorders in a Mexican American community sample. *Psychology of Women Quarterly, 30*(4), 340–347. https://doi.org/10.1111/j.1471-6402.2006.00309.x

Cachelin, F. M., Rebeck, R., Veisel, C., & Striegel-Moore, R. H. (2001). Barriers to treatment for eating disorders among ethnically diverse women. *International Journal of Eating Disorders, 30*(3), 269–278. https://doi.org/10.1002/eat.1084

Cheng, H. L. (2014). Disordered eating among Asian/Asian American women: Racial and cultural factors as correlates. *The Counseling Psychologist, 42*(6), 821–851. https://doi.org/10.1177/0011000014535472

Cook, B., Hausenblas, H., Tuccitto, D., & Giacobbi Jr, P. R. (2011). Eating disorders and exercise: A structural equation modeling analysis of a conceptual model. *European Eating Disorders Review, 19*(3), 216–225. https://doi.org/10.1002/erv.1111

Couturier, J., Pellegrini, D., Miller, C., Bhatnagar, N., Boachie, A., Bourret, K., Brouwers, M., Coelho, J. S., Dimitropoulos, G., Findlay, S., Ford, C., Geller, J., Grewal, S., Gusella, J., Isserlin, L., Jericho, M., Johnson, N., Katzman, D. K., Kimber, M., Lafrance, A., ... & Webb, C. (2021). The COVID-19 pandemic and eating disorders in children, adolescents, and emerging adults: Virtual care recommendations from the Canadian consensus panel during COVID-19 and beyond. *Journal of Eating Disorders, 9*(1), 1–40. https://doi.org/10.1186/s40337-021-00394-9

Croll, J., Neumark-Sztainer, D., Story, M., & Ireland, M. (2002). Prevalence and risk and protective factors related to disordered eating behaviors among adolescents: Relationship to gender and ethnicity. *Journal of Adolescent Health, 31*(2), 166–175. https://doi-org.avoserv2.library.fordham.edu/10.1016/S1054-139X(02)00368-3

da Luz, F. Q., Hay, P., Wisniewski, L., Cordás, T., & Sainsbury, A. (2021). The treatment of binge eating disorder with cognitive behavior therapy and other therapies: An overview and clinical considerations. *Obesity Reviews, 22*(5), 1–12. https://doi.org/10.1111/obr.13180

Davis, H. A., Graham, A. K., & Wildes, J. E. (2020). Overview of binge eating disorder. *Current Cardiovascular Risk Reports, 14*(12), 1–10. https://doi.org/10.1007/s12170-020-00664-2

Dennis, K. N. (2015, March 27). *Debunking myths about mental illness among Blacks.* Scholars. https://scholars.org/contribution/debunking-myths-about-mental-illness-among-blacks

Diemer, E.W., Grant, J. D., Munn-Chernoff, M. A., Patterson, D. A., & Duncan, A. E. (2015). Gender identity, sexual orientation, and eating-related pathology in a national sample of college students. *Journal of Adolescent Health, 57*(2), 144–199. https://doi.org/10.1016/j.jadohealth.2015.03.003

Durso, L. E., Latner, J. D., & Hayashi, K. (2012). Perceived discrimination is associated with binge eating in a community sample of non-overweight, overweight, and obese adults. *Obesity Facts, 5*(6), 869–880. https://doi.org/10.1159/000345931

English, D., Rendina, H. J., & Parsons, J. T. (2018). The effects of intersecting stigma: A longitudinal examination of minority stress, mental health, and substance use among Black, Latino, and multiracial gay and bisexual men. *Psychology of Violence, 8*(6), 669–679. https://doi.org/10.1037/vio0000218

Erskine, H. E., & Whiteford, H. A. (2018). Epidemiology of binge eating disorder. *Current Opinion in Psychiatry, 31*(6), 462–470. https://doi.org/10.1097/YCO.0000000000000449

Evans, G. W., & Kim, P. (2012). Child poverty, chronic stress, self-regulation, and coping. *Child Development Perspectives,* 7(1), 43–48. https://doi.org/10.1111/cdep.12013

Feder, S., Isserlin, L., Seale, E., Hammond, N., & Norris, M. L. (2017). Exploring the association between eating disorders and gender dysphoria in youth. *Eating Disorders, 25*(4), 310–317. https://doi.org/10.1080/10640266.2017.1297112

Firth, J. (2012). Healthy choices and heavy burdens: Race, citizenship and gender in the 'obesity epidemic'. *Journal of International Women's Studies, 13*(2), 33–50. https://vc.bridgew.edu/jiws/vol13/iss2/4

Galmiche, M., Déchelotte, P., Lambert, G., & Tavolacci, M. P. (2019). Prevalence of eating disorders over the 2000-2018 period: A systematic literature review. *American Journal of Clinical Nutrition, 109*(5), 1402–1413. https://doi.org/10.1093/ajcn/nqy342

Glisenti, K., Strodl, E., & King, R. (2018). Emotion focused therapy for binge eating disorder: A review of six cases. *Clinical Psychology & Psychotherapy, 25*(6), 842–855. https://doi.org/10.1002/cpp.2319

Goode, R. W., Cowell, M. M., Mazzeo, S. E., Cooper-Lewter, C., Forte, A., Olayia, O. I., & Bulik, C. M. (2020). Binge eating and binge-eating disorder in Black women: A systematic review. *The International Journal of Eating Disorders, 53*(4), 491–507. https://doi.org/10.1002/eat.23217

Goode, R. W., Kalarchian, M. A., Craighead, L., Conroy, M. B., Gary-Webb, T., Bennett, E., Cowell, M. M., & Burke, L. E. (2020). Perceptions and experiences of appetite awareness training among African-American women who binge eat. *Eating and Weight Disorders-Studies on Anorexia, Bulimia and Obesity, 25*(2), 275–281.

Greenberg, L. S. (2017). Introduction. In L. S. Greenberg, *Emotion-focused therapy* (pp. 3–11). American Psychological Association. https://doi.org/10.1037/15971-001

Grunewald, W., Convertino, A. D., Safren, S. A., Mimiaga, M. J., O'Cleirigh, C., Mayer, K. H., & Blashill, A. J. (2021). Appearance discrimination and binge eating among sexual minority men. *Appetite, 156*, 104819. https://doi.org/10.1016/j.appet.2020.104819

Guss, C. E., Williams, D. N., Reisner, S. L., Austin, S. B., & Katz-Wise, S. L. (2017). Disordered weight management behaviors, nonprescription steroid use, and weight perception in transgender youth. *Journal of Adolescent Health, 60*(1), 17–22. https://doi.org/10.1016/j.jadohealth.2016.08.027

Han, S., & Pistole, M.C. (2014). College student binge eating: Insecure attachment and emotion regulation. *Journal of College Student Development 55*(1), 16–29. https://doi.org/10.1353/csd.2014.0004

Harrington, E. F., Crowther, J. H., Henrickson, H. C., & Mickelson, K. D. (2006). The relationships among trauma, stress, ethnicity, and binge eating. *Cultural Diversity and Ethnic Minority Psychology, 12*(2), 212–229. https://doi.org/10.1037/1099-9809.12.2.212

Hazzard, V. M. (2020). Family risk and protective factors for binge eating-related concerns in a nationally representative sample of young adults in the United States [ProQuest Information & Learning]. In *Dissertation Abstracts International: Section B: The Sciences and Engineering* (Vol. 81, Issue 5–B). https://hdl.handle.net/2027.42/149973

Hoerster, K. D., Jakupcak, M., Hanson, R., McFall, M., Reiber, G., Hall, K. S., & Nelson, K. M. (2015). PTSD and depression symptoms are associated with binge eating among U.S. Iraq and Afghanistan veterans. *Eating Behaviors, 17*, 115–118. https://doi.org/10.1016/j.eatbeh.2015.01.005

Holowaty, K. A. M., & Paivio, S. C. (2012). Characteristics of client-identified helpful events in emotion-focused therapy for child abuse trauma. *Psychotherapy Research, 22*(1), 56–66. https://doi.org/10.1080/10503307.2011.622727

Hudson, J. I., Lalonde, J. K., Coit, C. E., Tsuang, M. T., McElroy, S. L., Crow, S. J., Bulik, C. M., Hudson, M. S., Yanovski, J. A., Rosenthal, N. R., & Pope, H. G. (2010). Longitudinal study of the diagnosis of components of the metabolic syndrome in individuals with binge-eating disorder. *The American Journal of Clinical Nutrition, 91*(6), 1568–1573. https://doi.org/10.3945/ajcn.2010.29203

Huryk, K. M., Drury, C. R., & Loeb, K. L. (2021). Diseases of affluence? A systematic review of the literature on socioeconomic diversity in eating disorders. *Eating Behaviors, 43*, 1–16. https://doi.org/10.1016/j.eatbeh.2021.101548

Jennings Mathis, K., Anaya, C., Rambur, B., Bodell, L. P., Graham, A. K., Forney, K. J., Anam, S., & Wildes, J. E. (2020). Workforce diversity in eating disorders: A multi-methods study. *Western Journal of Nursing Research, 42*(12), 1068–1077. https://doi.org/10.1177/0193945920912396

Johnson, P., Risica, P. M., Gans, K. M., Kirtania, U., & Kumanyika, S. K. (2012). Association of perceived racial discrimination with eating behaviors and obesity among participants of the SisterTalk study. *Journal of the National Black Nurses Association, 23*(1), 34–40.

Kamody, R. C., Grilo, C. M., & Udo, T. (2020). Disparities in DSM-5 defined eating disorders by sexual orientation among U.S. adults. *International Journal of Eating Disorders, 53*(2), 278–287. https://doi.org/10.1002/eat.23193

Kelly, N. R., Cotter, E. W., Tanofsky-Kraff, M., & Mazzeo, S. E. (2015). Racial variations in binge eating, body image concerns, and compulsive exercise among men. *Psychology of Men & Masculinity, 16*(3), 326–336. https://doi.org/10.1037/a0037585

Kelly, N. R., Smith, T. M., Hall, G., Guidinger, C., Williamson, G., Budd, E. L., & Giuliani, N. R. (2018). Perceptions of general and postpresidential election discrimination are associated with loss of control eating among racially/ethnically diverse young men. *The International Journal of Eating Disorders, 51*(1), 28–38. https://doi.org/10.1002/eat.22803

Kjeldbjerg, M. L., & Clausen, L. (2021). Prevalence of binge-eating disorder among children and adolescents: A systematic review and meta-analysis. *European Child & Adolescent Psychiatry, 32*(4), 549–574. https://doi.org/10.1007/s00787-021-01850-2

Kolar, D. R., Mejía Rodriguez, D. M., Mebarak Chams, M., & Hoek, H. W. (2016). Epidemiology of eating disorders in Latin America: A systematic review and meta-analysis. *Current Opinion in Psychiatry, 29*(6), 363–371. https://doi.org/10.1097/YCO.0000000000000279

Levine, M. P., & Smolak, L. (2010). Cultural influences on body image and the eating disorders. In W. S. Agras (Ed.), *The Oxford handbook of eating disorders* (pp. 223–246). Oxford University Press. https://doi.org/10.1093/oxfordhb/9780195373622.013.0013

Lindvall Dahlgren, C., Wisting, L., Rø, Ø. (2017). Feeding and eating disorders in the DSM-5 era: A systematic review of prevalence rates in non-clinical male and female samples. *Journal of Eating Disorders*, *5*(56), 1–10. https://doi.org/10.1186/s40337-017-0186-7

Lydecker, J. A., & Grilo, C. M. (2018). Comparing men and women with binge-eating disorder and co-morbid obesity. *International Journal of Eating Disorders*, *51*(5), 411–417. https://doi.org/10.1002/eat.22847

Lydecker, J. A., Gueorguieva, R., Masheb, R., White, M. A., & Grilo, C. M. (2019). Examining race as a predictor and moderator of treatment outcomes for binge-eating disorder: Analysis of aggregated randomized controlled trials. *Journal of Consulting and Clinical Psychology*, *87*(6), 530–540. https://doi.org/10.1037/ccp0000404

Perez, M., Ohrt, T. K., & Hoek, H. W. (2016). Prevalence and treatment of eating disorders among Hispanics/Latino Americans in the United States. *Current Opinion in Psychiatry*, *29*(6), 378–382. https://doi.org/10.1097/YCO.0000000000000277

Masheb, R. M., Kutz, A. M., Marsh, A. G., Min, K. M., Ruser, C. B., & Dorflinger, L. M. (2019). "Making weight" during military service is related to binge eating and eating pathology for veterans later in life. *Eating and Weight Disorders*, *24*(6), 1063–1070. https://doi.org/10.1007/s40519-019-00766-w

Maxwell, M., Thornton, L. M., Root, T. L., Pinheiro, A. P., Strober, M., Brandt, H., Crawford, S., Crow, S., Fichter, M. M., Halmi, K. A., Johnson, C., Kaplan, A. S., Keel, P., Klump, K. L., LaVia, M., Mitchell, J. E., Plotnicov, K., Rotondo, A., Woodside, D. B., … Bulik, C. M. (2011). Life beyond the eating disorder: Education, relationships, and reproduction. *The International Journal of Eating Disorders*, *44*(3), 225–232. https://doi.org/10.1002/eat.20804

Menzel, J. E., Schaefer, L. M., Burke, N. L., Mayhew, L. L., Brannick, M. T., & Thompson, J. K. (2010). Appearance-related teasing, body dissatisfaction, and disordered eating: A meta-analysis. *Body Image*, 7(4), 261–270. https://doi.org/10.1016/j.bodyim.2010.05.004

Micali, N., Martini, M. G., Thomas, J. J., Eddy, K. T., Kothari, R., Russell, E., Bulik, C. M., & Treasure, J. (2017). Lifetime and 12-month prevalence of eating disorders amongst women in mid-life: A population-based study of diagnoses and risk factors. *BMC Medicine*, *15*(12), 1–10. https://doi.org/10.1186/s12916-016-0766-4

Mikhail, M. E., & Klump, K. L. (2021). A virtual issue highlighting eating disorders in people of black/African and Indigenous heritage. *International Journal of Eating Disorders*, *54*(3), 459–467. https://doi.org/10.1002/eat.23402

Munsch, S., Wyssen, A., Vanhulst, P., Lalanne, D., Steinemann, S. T., & Tuch, A. (2019). Binge-eating disorder treatment goes online–feasibility, usability, and treatment outcome of an internet-based treatment for binge-eating disorder: Study protocol for a three-arm randomized controlled trial including an immediate treatment, a waitlist, and a placebo control group. *Trials*, *20*(128) 1–11. https://doi.org/10.1186/s13063-019-3192-z

Nagata, J. M., Ganson, K. T., & Austin, S. B. (2020). Emerging trends in eating disorders among sexual and gender minorities. *Current Opinion in Psychiatry*, *33*(6), 562–567. https://doi.org/10.1097/YCO.0000000000000645

Nagata, J. M., Iyer, P., Chu, J., Baker, F. C., Pettee Gabriel, K., Garber, A. K., Murray, S. B., Bibbins-Domingo, K., & Ganson, K. T. (2021). Contemporary screen time modalities among children 9-10 years old and binge eating disorder at one year follow up: A prospective cohort study. *International Journal of Eating Disorders, 54*(5), 887–892. https://doi.org/10.1002/eat.23489

Nagata, J. M., Murray, S. B., Bibbins-Domingo, K., Garber, A. K., Mitchison, D., & Griffiths, S. (2019). Predictors of muscularity-oriented disordered eating behaviors in U.S. young adults: A prospective cohort study. *The International Journal of Eating Disorders, 52*(12), 1380–1388. https://doi.org/10.1002/eat.23094

Nagata, J. M., Murray, S. B., Compte E. J., Pak, E. H., Schauer, R., Frlentje, A., Capriotti, M. R., Lubensky, M. E., Lunn, M. R., & Obedin-Maliver, J. (2020). Community norms for the Eating Disorder Examination Questionnaire (EDE-Q) among transgender men and women. *Eating Behaviors, 37*, 1–8. https://doi.org/10.1016/j.eatbeh.2020.101381

Nightingale, M., Awosan, C. I., & Stavrianopoulos, K. (2019). Emotionally focused therapy: A culturally sensitive approach for African American heterosexual couples. *Journal of Family Psychotherapy, 30*(3), 221–244. https://doi.org/10.1080/08975353.2019.1666497

Paivio, S. C., & Pascual-Leone, A. (2010). Experiencing. *Emotion-focused therapy for complex trauma: An integrative approach*. American Psychological Association. Washington, D.C. https://doi.org/10.1037/12077-004

Parker, J. E., Enders, C. K., Mujahid, M. S., Laraia, B. A., Epel, E. S., & Tomiyama, A. J. (2022). Prospective relationships between skin color satisfaction, body satisfaction, and binge eating in Black girls. *Body Image, 41*, 342–353.

Parker, L. L., & Harriger, J. A. (2020). Eating disorders and disordered eating behaviors in the LGBT population: A review of the literature. *Journal of Eating Disorders, 8*(51), 1–20. https://doi.org/10.1186/s40337-020-00327-y

Pascual-Leone, A., Bierman, R., Arnold, R., & Stasiak, E. (2011). Emotion-focused therapy for incarcerated offenders of intimate partner violence: A 3-year outcome using a new whole-sample matching method. *Psychotherapy Research, 21*(3), 331–347. https://doi.org/10.1080/10503307.2011.572092

Patel, S. (2021, August 23). *Veterans' mental health myths that should be dispelled.* National Alliance on Mental Illness (NAMI). https://www.nami.org/Blogs/NAMI-Blog/August-2021/Veterans-Mental-Health-Myths-That-Should-Be-Dispelled

Pruessner, L., Hartmann, S., Rubel, J. A., Lalk, C., Barnow, S., Timm, C. (2022). Integrating a web-based intervention into routine care of binge-eating disorder: Study protocol for a randomized controlled trial. *Internet Interventions, 28*, 1–10. https://doi.org/10.1016/j.invent.2022.100514

Puhl, R. M., & Heuer, C. A. (2010). Obesity stigma: Important considerations for public health. *American Journal of Public Health, 100*(6), 1019–1028. https://doi.org/10.2105/AJPH.2009.159491

Puhl, R. M., Latner, J. D., King, K. M., & Luedicke, J. (2014). Weight bias among professionals treating eating disorders: Attitudes about treatment and perceived patient outcomes. *International Journal of Eating Disorders, 47*(1), 65–75. https://doi.org/10.1002/eat.22186

Rasmusson, G., Lydecker, J. A., Coffino, J. A., White, M. A., & Grilo, C. M. (2019). Household food insecurity is associated with binge-eating disorder and obesity. *International Journal of Eating Disorders*, *52*(1), 28–35. https://doi.org/10.1002/eat.22990

Reddy, S. D., & Crowther, J. H. (2007). Teasing, acculturation, and cultural conflict: Psychosocial correlates of body image and eating attitudes among South Asian women. *Cultural Diversity and Ethnic Minority Psychology*, *13*(1), 45. https://doi.org/10.1037/1099-9809.13.1.45

Reed, G. M., First, M. B., Kogan, C. S., Hyman, S. E., Gureje, O., Gaebel, W., Maj, M., Stein, D. J., Maercker, A., Tyrer, P., Claudino, A., Garralda, E., Salvador-Carulla, L., Ray, R., Saunders, J. B., Dua, T., Poznyak, V., Medina-Mora, M. E., Pike, K. M., … Saxena S. (2019). Innovations and changes in the ICD-11 classification of mental, behavioural, and neurodevelopmental disorders. *World Psychiatry*, *18*(1), 3–19. https://doi.org/10.1002/wps.20611

Rodgers, R. F., Berry, R., & Franko, D. L. (2018). Eating disorders in ethnic minorities: An update. *Current Psychiatry Reports*, *20*(90), 1–11. https://doi.org/10.1007/s11920-018-0938-3

Rodgers, R., & Sonneville, K. (2018). Research for leveraging food policy in universal eating disorder prevention. *International Journal of Eating Disorders*, *51*(6), 503–506. https://doi.org/10.1002/eat.22877

Rodgers, R. F., Watts, A. W., Austin, S. B., Haines, J., & Neumark-Sztainer, D. (2017). Disordered eating in ethnic minority adolescents with overweight. *International Journal of Eating Disorders*, *50*(6), 665–671. https://doi.org/10.1002/eat.22652

Romano, K. (2021). Associations among weight suppression, self-acceptance, negative body image, and eating disorder behaviors among women with eating disorder symptoms. *Women and Health*, 61(8), 791–799. https://doi-org.avoserv2.library.fordham.edu/https://doi.org/10.1080/03630242.2021.1970082

Segal, Z. V., Williams, M., & Teasdale, J. (2002). *Mindfulness-based cognitive therapy for depression: A new approach to preventing relapse*. Guilford.

Serpell, L., Amey, R., & Kamboj, S. K. (2020). The role of self-compassion and self-criticism in binge eating behavior. *Appetite*, *144*. https://doi-org.avoserv2.library.fordham.edu/10.1016/j.appet.2019.104470

Sheehan, D. V., & Herman, B. K. (2015). The psychological and medical factors associated with untreated binge eating disorder. *The Primary Care Companion for CNS Disorders*, *17*(2). https://doi.org/10.4088/PCC.14r01732

Simmons, S., & Limbers, C. A. (2019). Acculturative stress and emotional eating in Latino adolescents. *Eating and Weight Disorders-Studies on Anorexia, Bulimia and Obesity*, *24*(5), 905–914. https://doi.org/10.1007/s40519-018-0602-2

Simone, M., Aske, A., Lust, K., Eisenberg, M. E., Pisetsky, E. M. (2020). Disparities in self-reported eating disorders and academic impairment in sexual and gender minority college students relative to their heterosexual and cisgender peers. *International Journal of Eating Disorders*, *53*(4), 513–524. https://doi.org/10.1002/eat233266

Sonneville, K. R., & Lipson, S. K. (2018). Disparities in eating disorder diagnosis and treatment according to weight status, race/ethnicity, socioeconomic background, and sex among college students. *International Journal of Eating Disorders*, *51*(6), 518–526. https://doi.org/10.1002/eat.22846

Stander, V.A. & Thomsen, C.J. (2016). Sexual harassment and assault in the U.S. military: A review of policy and research trends. *Military Medicine*, *181*(Suppl_1). https://doi.org/10.7205/MILMED-D-15-00336

Stewart, P. (2021, January 14). Exclusive: Long-withheld Pentagon survey shows widespread racial discrimination, harassment. *Reuters*. https://www.reuters.com/article/idUSKBN29J1N1

Streatfeild, J., Hickson, J., Austin, S. B., Hutcheson, R., Kandel, J. S., Lampert, J. G., Myers, E. M., Richmond, T. K., Samnaliev, M., Velasquez, K., Weissman, R. S., & Pezzullo, L. (2021). Social and economic cost of eating disorders in the United States: Evidence to inform policy action. *International Journal of Eating Disorders*, *54*(5), 851–868. https://doi.org/10.1002/eat.23486

Striegel-Moore, R. H., Rosselli, F., Holtzman, N., Dierker, L., Becker, A. E., & Swaney, G. (2011). Behavioral symptoms of eating disorders in Native Americans: Results from the add health survey wave III. *International Journal of Eating Disorders*, *44*(6), 561–566. https://doi.org/10.1002/eat.20894

Tanofsky-Kraff, M., Wilfley, D. E., Young, J. F., Mufson, L., Yanovski, S. Z., Glasofer, D. R., & Salaita, C. G. (2007). Preventing excessive weight gain in adolescents: Interpersonal psychotherapy for binge eating. *Obesity, 15*(6), 1345–1355. https://doi.org/10.1038/oby.2007.162

Taylor, J. Y., Caldwell, C. H., Baser, R. E., Faison, N., & Jackson, J. S. (2007). Prevalence of eating disorders among Blacks in the National Survey of American Life. *International Journal of Eating Disorders*, *40*(S3), S10–S14. https://doi.org/10.1002/eat.20451

Terranova, K. E. (2021). *Racism-related stress, social support, attachment, and binge eating in young adult Black women* [Doctoral dissertation, Fordham University]. ETD Collection for Fordham University. https://research.library.fordham.edu/dissertations/AAI28650835

Thompson-Brenner, H., Franko, D. L., Thompson, D. R., Grilo, C. M., Boisseau, C. L., Roehrig, J. P., Richards, L. K., Bryson, S. W., Bulik, C. M., Crow, S. J., Devlin, M. J., Gorin, A. A., Kristeller, J. L., Masheb, R., Mitchell, J. E., Peterson, C. B., Safer, D. L., Striegel, R. H., Wilfley, D. E., & Wilson, G. T. (2013). Race/ethnicity, education, and treatment parameters as moderators and predictors of outcome in binge eating disorder. *Journal of Consulting and Clinical Psychology, 81*(4), 710–721. https://doi.org/10.1037/a0032946

Thurston, I. B., Hardin, R., Kamody, R. C., Herbozo, S., & Kaufman, C. (2018). The moderating role of resilience on the relationship between perceived stress and binge eating symptoms among young adult women. *Eating Behaviors*, *29*, 114–119. https://doi-org.avoserv2.library.fordham.edu/10.1016/j.eatbeh.2018.03.009

Udo, T., & Grilo, C. M. (2018). Prevalence and correlates of DSM-5-defined eating disorders in a nationally representative sample of U.S. adults. *Biological Psychiatry*, *84*(5), 345–354. https://doi.org/10.1016/j.biopsych.2018.03.014

Von Schell, A., Ohrt, T. K., Bruening, A. B., & Perez, M. (2018). Rates of disordered eating behaviors across sexual minority undergraduate men and women. *Psychology of Sexual Orientation and Gender Diversity*, *5*(3), 352–359. https://doi.org/10.1037/sgd0000278

Warren, C. S., & Akoury, L. M. (2020). Emphasizing the "cultural" in sociocultural: A systematic review of research on thin-ideal internalization, acculturation, and eating pathology in U.S. ethnic minorities. *Psychology Research and Behavior Management*, *2020*(13), 319–330. https://doi.org/10.2147/PRBM.S204274

Watson, R. J., Veale, J. F., & Saewyc, E. M. (2017). Disordered eating behaviors among transgender youth: Probability profiles from risk and protective factors. *The International Journal of Eating Disorders*, *50*(5), 515–522. https://doi.org/10.1002/eat.22627

Whiteford, H., & Weissman, R. S. (2017). Key factors that influence government policies and decision making about healthcare priorities: Lessons for the field of eating disorders. *International Journal of Eating Disorders*, *50*(3), 315–319. https://doi.org/10.1002/eat.22688

Wilfley, D. E., Welch, R. R., Stein, R. I., Spurrell, E. B., Cohen, L. R., Saelens, B. E., Zoler Dounchis, J., Frank, M. A., Wiseman, C. V., & Matt, G. E. (2002). A randomized comparison of group cognitive-behavioral therapy and group interpersonal psychotherapy for the treatment of overweight individuals with binge-eating disorder. *Archives of General Psychiatry*, *59*(8), 713–721. https://doi.org/10.1001/archpsyc.59.8.713

Wilson, D. R., Loxton, N. J., Joynt, T., & O'Donovan, A. (2021). There is no such thing as a mindful binge: How mindfulness disrupts the pathway between anxiety and impulsivity on maladaptive eating behaviours. *Personality and Individual Differences*, *168*. https://doi-org.avoserv2.library.fordham.edu/10.1016/j.paid.2020.110393

Wolff, M. (2022). Feminist perspectives and eating disorder pathology in White and African American women in the United States [ProQuest Information & Learning]. In *Dissertation Abstracts International: Section B: The Sciences and Engineering* (Vol. 83, Issue 4–B). https://www.proquest.com/openview/88fe7d0d26cb1ecd5d1f1e08e0140080/1?pq-origsite=gscholar&cbl=18750&diss=y

World Health Organization. (2016). *Global report on diabetes*. https://apps.who.int/iris/bitstream/handle/10665/204871/9789241565257_eng.pdf;jsessio nid=713F15C4864B977199789420E237EFC3?sequence=1

Yu, K. Y., Pope, S. C., & Perez, M. (2019). Clinical treatment and practice recommendations for disordered eating in Asian Americans. *Professional Psychology: Research and Practice*, *50*(5), 279–287. https://doi.org/10.1037/pro0000244

CHAPTER 8

WORKING AT THE INTERSECTION OF EATING DISORDERS AND BODY IMAGE IN TRANSGENDER AND GENDER DIVERSE POPULATIONS

Heidi Dalzell

An emerging trend in eating disorder (ED) care involves increased recognition that EDs are unique and affect diverse people—that is, EDs are *not* just a White, middle-class disorder. The importance of considering these intersectional identities is quite evident when working with transgender and gender diverse (TGD) individuals. While this chapter will attempt to provide some guidance on working with gender diverse people as a whole, acknowledging and understanding that gender diverse people also have other intersectional identities is important. Some of the other identities we consider in our work include the intersection of gender identity and race, ethnicity, age, ability status, body size, sexual orientation, health conditions, and a host of others. For example, working with a person who identifies as gender diverse and Black will differ from working with a person who identifies as nonbinary, Christian, and affluent, or a person that is cisgender, White, and disabled.

Counseling Individuals With Eating Disorders: An Intersectional Approach, pp. 167–190

The terms associated with gender identity may already be familiar, and if they are not, it would be helpful to refer to a comprehensive glossary, several of which can easily be accessed online. Using appropriate language to locate self and others on the LGBTQ umbrella is one factor in providing a safe therapy space, and quickly signals to clients that they are working with someone who is knowledgeable about gender identity and who is openly affirming. Language includes our verbal language, as well as the language in intake forms and materials. *Affirming* environments promote respect and appreciation for many aspects of identity, including gender identity. Affirmation allows for openness, trust, and safety where all attitudes, beliefs, values, and behaviors can be freely explored and discussed.

Gender diversity (sometimes called gender expansiveness or gender non-conformity) refers to the extent to which a person's gender identity, gender role, or gender expression varies from the cultural norms prescribed for people of a particular sex. Gender diverse identities are varied and unique—that is, gender diversity encompasses a spectrum of identities.

Binary identities include persons who identify as "male" or "female" and include cisgender and transgender people who identify as male or female. In this context, gender is not about biology or natal sex (i.e., their sex assigned at birth), but is instead more about social and cultural expectations. *Nonbinary* gender identities do not fall within the strict categories of "male" or "female"; some people may not feel that any gender category fits them (such as genderqueer, nonbinary, or agender identities). The term *cisgender* signifies that a person's gender identity is the same as their sex assigned at birth. *Gender expression* involves the way in which people externally communicate gender to others, such as by the clothing they wear or their hairstyle. The term *sex assigned at birth* is used to denote the label ("boy"/"girl," "male"/"female" given to a child at birth and which is based most often on external genitalia.

Another area of clarification for clinicians newer to these ideas is the difference between the terms "gender diversity" and "gender dysphoria." They are *not* synonymous terms. In much the same way that other queer identities have been pathologized, people who identified as gender diverse were historically diagnosed with "gender identity disorder." This has changed with publication of the fifth edition of the *Diagnostic and Statistical Manual of Mental Disorders* (DSM-5; American Psychiatric Association, 2013). Diverse gender identity is *not* a disorder. Instead, the diagnosis *gender dysphoria* refers to the distress caused by the discrepancy between gender identity and sex assigned at birth and involves a desire to change primary and/or secondary sex characteristics. Not all TGD people experience such distress, or want to change their bodies, but many do at some point in their lifetimes. The DSM-5 estimates that gender dysphoria for assigned males has prevalence rates from 0.005% to 0.014%, and for assigned females from 0.002% to 0.003%. These statistics are likely underreported (American Psychiatric Association, 2013). While gender diversity is one factor in the etiology of EDs, it is not the only factor.

An introduction to working with gender diversity would not be complete without a mention of minority stress and resilience. Minority stress refers to experiences of stigma and marginalization that many minorities, including TGD persons, experience due to their identities. Research shows that minority stress leads to negative physical and mental health outcomes, including eating disorders (Meyer, 2003). Minority stress is a form of trauma. Minority stress theories also discuss resilience factors. These include pride regarding TGD identity and community connectedness.

Prevalence of EDs in TGD Populations

EDs are serious, potentially deadly illnesses. While EDs were once thought to affect only a small subset of individuals—primarily White, cisgender, affluent girls and women—there is increasing recognition that EDs affect people across a range of cultural groups, with a significant number of LGBT persons diagnosed with clinical and subclinical EDs.

LGBT communities are diverse and much of the research has focused on sexual minority individuals. Data from a nationally representative sample of U.S. adults indicates that sexual minority individuals have higher lifetime prevalence rates of EDs than heterosexual individuals do. Specifically, sexual minorities were found to have a higher lifetime prevalence rate of anorexia nervosa (AN; 1.71% vs. 0.77%), bulimia nervosa (BN; 1.25% vs. 0.24%), and binge ED (BED; 2.17% vs. 0.81%) when compared with heterosexual persons (Kamody et al., 2019).

Many studies have looked at the connections between EDs and sexual minority stress. Grunewald et al. (2021), for example, looked at appearance discrimination and binge eating in a small group of gay men. In study participants that reported binge eating, physical appearance-based discrimination was the most common form of discrimination, followed closely by bias based on income factors and homophobia. Meneguzzo et al. (2018) conducted a meta-analysis of studies examining EDs among sexual minority women. The researchers concluded that a higher number of ED diagnoses were found in sexual minority women as compared with controls, as well as a higher occurrence of binge eating and purging. More negative body image/body dissatisfaction and greater drive for thinness also were found in sexual minority women compared with controls.

Research specific to TGD persons is in the early stages with comparatively few studies. One of the difficulties in extrapolating from many of the published studies is that they combine gender minority *and* sexual minority groups in their samples, often have small samples, or use case studies. Many studies that are specific to TGD persons do not delineate binary and nonbinary identities. TGD people are *not* a homogeneous group, another research confound.

While these factors make it difficult to ascertain prevalence rates, research has clarified some of the dynamics of EDs and body image difficulties (Guss et al., 2017). Eating pathology is not uncommon among TGD people (Nagata et al., 2020). TGD people report higher incidences of general disordered eating behaviors such as fasting, use of laxative and diet pills, as well as higher incidence of restrictive eating, and binging and purging as compared to cisgender peers (Ålgars et al., 2012). Studies also point to higher rates of abuse of anabolic steroids (Diemer et al., 2015).

One large-scale study from 2014 surveyed approximately 300,000 college students at risk for AN and BN (Diemer et al., 2015). The results showed that transgender students had a risk of developing these disorders that was four times greater than their cisgender peers. Use of diet pills and compensatory behaviors was higher among transgender students as compared to cisgender peers. The researchers concluded that given the wide range of gender identities and life experiences of TGD persons, future research should examine potential distinctions in rates of eating-related pathology between subgroups of transgender populations (i.e., male-to-female, female-to-male, and genderqueer transgender persons), as well as the impact of an individual's coming out on ED symptomology.

Diemer et al. (2015) conducted a second study, using data from Project VOICE, a cross-sectional study of stress and health among 452 transgender adults (ages 18–75 years). The prevalence of self-reported EDs (AN and BN) in this sample was 7.4% (Diemer et al., 2015). Diemer and colleagues also compared the prevalence of self-reported lifetime EDs among transgender males, transgender females and nonbinary persons. Their results indicated that transgender males have heightened lifetime ED risk relative to transgender females and that collapsing TGD identities masks significant differences between subgroups.

Watson et al. (2017) also found high rates of ED symptomology among a sample of 1000 transgender youth (ages 14–25). They noted significant rates of binge eating, restrictive eating, and compensatory behaviors, including diet pill use, laxative use, and purging. Gender minority stress, including higher rates of harassment and discrimination, was linked to higher incidence of binge eating and fasting and vomiting. Protective factors, including family connectedness, school connectedness, having caring friends, and social support, were linked to lower odds of past year disordered eating. Youth who had experienced the highest levels of stigma and no protective factors had the highest probabilities of ED behaviors.

While published studies do not provide comprehensive prevalence data, they point to two helpful themes: (a) eating pathology is connected to negative body image, and may be used to help reduce gender dysphoria, and (b) minority stress has a negative impact and engaging in eating pathology may represent one effort to mitigate trauma reactions.

Body Image and TGD Persons

Body image is a complex construct. Thomas Cash, an expert in the field, states that body image has many facets, including the psychological experience of being "embodied" (Cash, 2011). Body image also encompasses one's body-related self-perceptions and self-attitudes, including thoughts, beliefs, feelings, and behaviors, all of which are unique to identity (Cash, 2011; Hosseini & Padhy, 2021). It is a component of self-esteem and self-concept, mood, and competence and affects social and occupational functioning. Body image concerns are common in both clinical and nonclinical settings.

In cisgender populations, negative body image is a key factor in the development and maintenance of clinical and subclinical EDs, as well as low self-esteem and mental health problems, including depression and substance abuse (Stice & Shaw, 2002). *Body dissatisfaction* is the difference between an individual's actual body and the person's ideal body size and shape. *Body image distortion* refers to a misperception of one or more features of the body. For example, a person with anorexia may see their hips as wider than they really are. Body image distortion may also result in smaller than actual assessments, such as a man who sees himself as "puny," despite being muscular. Body image falls on a continuum from healthy body image (body acceptance/ownership) to unhealthy body image (body preoccupation, disturbance, hatred). Some appearance concerns are normal, while others are more problematic.

A number of factors play a role in the development and maintenance of body image. These include messages from significant people, such as parents or peers, social pressures and acceptance, media and social media, as well as other factors, including chronic illnesses (Hosseini & Padhy, 2021). In TGD persons, we also include gender dysphoria, the discomfort or distress caused by the discrepancy between gender identity and sex assigned at birth, as a factor in body image (Dalzell & Protos, 2020). Racial and cultural values can also impact beliefs about body ideals, adding to complexity and nuance.

Negative body image appears to be a significant concern for TGD individuals in particular (Bandini et al., 2013; Bell et al., 2019) and LGBTQ persons in general (Conner et al., 2004). Themes common to cisgender and gender diverse people include body dissatisfaction (seeking a thin ideal), perfectionism/low self-esteem, and the use of ED symptoms as a form of control and a general way to cope (Hernando et al., 2019). TGD persons also experience many body-image challenges specific to identity such as drive to decrease or accentuate gendered body parts, binary beauty standards, thin ideal/muscular/ideal, internalized transphobia, coping with rejection, traditional conceptualizations of "masculinity" and "femininity", and rejection or marginalization of TGD bodies (Dalzell & Protos, 2020).

Several researchers have looked at body dissatisfaction and discomfort in TGD communities. For example, Rabito-Alcon and Rodríguez Molina (2015) studied the connections between body image, body size, and masculinity/femininity (those qualities or attributes regarded as characteristic of men or women). These researchers found that changes in body size are often equated with masculinity or femininity (such as the belief that women are smaller/thinner and men larger/thicker). They concluded that ED symptoms may be used to accentuate or decrease gendered features.

TGD people with gender and body dysphoria can develop a range of EDs, including AN, BN, BED, and orthorexic symptoms (an overfocus on food "purity" and healthy eating). Thus, we see a range of potential symptoms, such as restrictive eating, focusing on body size, engaging in food rituals, binge eating, use of compensatory mechanisms, body checking, obsessive weighing, and shame around symptom use. As with cisgender people, it is common that such disorders are rarely diagnostically "pure"; for example, we often see the same binge/purge/restrict cycle we see in cisgender individuals with EDs.

While these research studies are helpful, to fully understand the numerous pathways to and functions of ED symptoms, consideration of some additional aspects of gender diversity as an identity is needed. First, gender diversity involves an inner or "felt" sense of self. For many (but again not all) TGD people, the physical body differs from their inner sense of who they are. The body, and/or others' reactions to it, are a reminder that the physical body is different from their inner gender identity. This can create significant body discomfort. For example, some transgender males—especially adolescents who may already feel less of a sense of control over their changing bodies—become more dysphoric during their monthly menses. They often express that the monthly menstrual period is a reminder "I am not a male" or "I will never be the male I want to be" (Dalzell & Protos, 2020).

ED behaviors can be used to manage gender dysphoria. Restrictive eating, for example, can prevent puberty or delay further pubertal development (McClain & Peebles, 2016). As such, medically affirmative interventions, such as hormonal contraceptives to stop menses, puberty blockers, hormone therapies, and surgery, can often support more positive body image (Testa et al., 2017). In assessing EDs in gender diverse clients, then, body dissatisfaction may be less a function of feeling "fat," as in some cisgender people, and more a function of dissatisfaction regarding gendered body parts (e.g., breasts, hips). Of course, gender diverse people can also feel body dissatisfaction due to weight, so it is helpful to more fully unpack the nuances of clients' body image concerns to understand them more fully.

Trauma and Gender Minority Stress

Another significant theme emerging from the research are the connections between gender minority stressors, trauma, and ED symptomology. *Gender minority stressors* are those experiences that commonly occur in TGD populations. Minority stress theory proposes that minority health disparities can be explained in large part by stressors induced by a hostile, transphobic culture, which results in harassment, maltreatment, discrimination, and victimization (Meyer, 2003). Grant et al. (2011) studied a sample of 6,450 transgender and gender non-conforming study participants, and participants indicated that discrimination was pervasive. Many TGD persons describe repeated experiences of discrimination, marginalization, and trauma. It can be challenging to find a TGD person that has not experienced one or more of these stressors, and many report repeated incidents (Dalzell & Protos, 2020). A list of some common minority stressors includes bullying, physical/verbal/sexual assault, misgendering, rejection and expectations of rejection, poverty, homelessness, discrimination and microaggressions across multiple settings, concealment, and internalized transphobia (Dalzell & Protos, 2020).

A number of stressors confront persons that identify as TGD. *Misgendering* is the intentional or unintentional use of the person's incorrect pronoun, or the use of language that does not align with affirmed gender. Another stressor concerns hiding one's authentic self to be more "acceptable" (Grant et al., 2011) or trying to manage internalized transphobia (Bockting et al., 2020). Grant et al. (2011) found that most of their sample attempted to avoid discrimination by hiding their gender or gender transition (71%) or delaying their gender transition (57%). Such concealment may be a suicide risk factor (Narang et al., 2018). Many older people who identify under the TGD umbrella, such as the client described in the upcoming case study, report hopelessness that they could ever live an authentic life.

While TGD people are seeking therapeutic support in increasing numbers, this is often a risk that requires internal deliberation, and many TGD people hesitate to seek help. This may in part be due to their past negative experiences within therapeutic and healthcare settings. Study participants have reported serious hurdles in accessing healthcare; in one sample, 19% were refused care due to the TGD identity, 28% experienced harassment and violence in healthcare settings, and 50% reported significant gaps in provider knowledge of transgender care (Grant et al., 2011). Many TGD individuals experience repeated incidents of this nature (Bockting et al., 2020). These factors decrease the likelihood of seeking help (Dalzell & Protos, 2020).

In addition to the traumas connected to identity, many TGD persons also have other acute or chronic traumas in their backgrounds, including childhood abuse and neglect (Dalzell & Protos, 2020). Craig et al. (2020) studied frequencies and patterns of adverse childhood events (ACEs) among LGBT youth. While the sample included various sexual identities, they delineated among gender identity classifications (40% identified as female, 38% as non-conforming, 15% as male, and 17% as transgender). Participants in the study reported multiple ACEs including emotional neglect, emotional abuse, and living with a mentally ill family member as the most prevalent traumas. Over 40% of participants experienced four or more ACEs, considered being a high level of trauma exposure.

The connections between EDs and trauma has been well documented (Monteleone et al., 2021). There are several reasons for the close connection between EDs and trauma. ED symptoms can be adaptive responses to trauma; they can numb trauma symptoms, provide comfort and nurturance, help people attain power and control, discharge anger, provide self-esteem, and protect from further traumas such as by creating a larger or smaller body. Trauma symptoms may also be projected on the body, and such projections managed through eating food or restricting. While symptoms may be a form of control, they may also be a way to punish the self or to self-harm (Hodge & Baker, 2021).

Resiliency Factors and Prevention

Resilience factors are those protective elements that buffer psychological distress, especially in traumatic situations. Understanding these factors can help inform interventions.

Several factors seem to support resilience in TGD persons. These include family support, identity pride, employment, peer support, transgender community connectedness, and access to care (Bockting et al., 2016). Singh et al. (2011) conducted interviews and focus groups with transgender participants to determine additional resiliency factors. Several additional themes emerged during the research, including identity affirmation, awareness of oppression, hope and future outlook, social activism, and being a positive role model for others. Similar factors are seen to be supportive of ED prevention and recovery (Wacker & Dolbin-MacNab, 2020).

Project Affirm, a collaboration of several large university systems, is currently studying the application of such resiliency factors to TGD persons. These include promoting family acceptance, empowerment skills, peer mentors/support groups, policy changes, transition-related care, and provider training (Bockting et al., 2016).

Working With Gender Diverse People With EDs: An Integrated Model

In developing a guide to conceptualize and work with TGD people with EDs, this author and colleagues conducted a thorough review of the available research combined with clinical observation and many years of treating TGD persons. An additional source of direction includes the APA's *Guidelines for Psychological Practice with Transgender and Gender Nonconforming People* (American Psychological Association, 2015). These guidelines call for clinicians to educate themselves on TGD health, advocacy, and terminology and be affirming and compassionate towards TGD clients. The World Professional Association for Transgender Health (WPATH) also publishes standards on how to treat TGD persons from a mental health and medical standpoint (Coleman et al., 2012). These guidelines share several tenets, most notably that positive change and healthy coping can only occur through the creation of a safe, affirming, and collaborative therapeutic experience.

Research and clinical observation confirm that several pathways often work in tandem to set the stage for EDs (Dalzell & Protos, 2020; Dalzell et al., 2022). TGD persons are at increased risk of developing EDs due to the many factors outlined previously: the impacts of gender minority stressors and other traumas, as well as gender dysphoria/body discomfort. As such, assessment of TGD persons with EDs must include an exploration of the impact of gender dysphoria/body discomfort as well as identity-based trauma(s). Exposure to gender minority stressors and body dissatisfaction can place people at higher risk for EDs. TGD persons frequently describe a combination of these factors as central to the development of their EDs. By appreciating the complexity of each of these phenomena independently and concurrently, it is possible to meet the unique needs of the TGD with an ED (Dalzell et al., 2022).

Gender Affirming Social and Medical Interventions

In considering the connections between gender dysphoria and EDs, an important clinician competency is the understanding of gender affirming social and medical interventions (sometimes called social or medical transition). *Gender affirmation* is an interpersonal, interactive process whereby TGD persons receive social recognition and support for gender identity and expression (Bockting & Coleman, 2007). Social and medical affirmation can also support more positive body image (Connolly et al., 2016; Dalzell & Protos, 2020).

There are many ways to reduce gender dysphoria among TGD persons with EDs. What helps varies from person to person. *Social affirmation* (or social transition) is the process by which TGD people adopt the name, pronouns, and gender expression, such as clothing and haircuts, that match their gender identity. *Medical affirmation* options include surgeries that help the body more closely match gender identity. Such procedures include hormone therapy and/or surgeries, such as top surgery, bottom surgery, and facial feminization surgery. Younger clients who have not yet reached puberty may be provided puberty blockers to delay onset.

There has also been a shift away from a *gatekeeper* model where treatment providers are required to provide an evaluation as a prerequisite to affirming medical procedures (Coleman et al., 2022). For adult clients, many clinicians adopt an "informed consent model," where understanding of the risks and benefits of the procedure negates the need to assess the "legitimacy" of their identity.

Prerequisites to Conceptualization and Treatment: Cultural Humility

Our model for treating EDs (Dalzell & Protos, 2020; Dalzell et al., 2022) has evolved since its initial conceptualization, further reflecting the importance of a cultural humility lens rather than a cultural competence lens. Cultural humility is a process, rather than an endpoint (Hook et al., 2013). *Cultural humility* is defined as a lifelong process of self-reflection, self-critique, continual assessment of power imbalances, and developing mutually respectful relationships and partnerships (Tervalon & Murray-Garcia, 1998). Such mutually respectful relationships are key to working effectively with TGD populations.

According to SAMHSA (2019) and Testa et al. (2017), some facets to consider are:

1. Awareness of transgender/gender affirming treatment models, as well as professional standards, competencies, and guidelines for mental health practices.
2. Engaging in critical self-examination and self-awareness, including the identification of privilege. *Privilege* refers to the advantages, benefits, and respect that a person has by belonging to a majority group.
3. Facilitating a safe space in which clinicians can develop rapport and build a strong alliance through the use of appropriate language and pronouns.
4. Working from a trauma-informed lens, which acknowledges the impact of trauma, especially identity-based traumas and microaggressions. While marginalized groups experience oppression, they also experience resilience. With TGD populations, clinicians should act as advocates and models of resilience.
5. Navigating differences connected to the therapist/client dyad, including identity and value differences.

Case Vignette

Phil (pronouns, they/them) is a 64-year-old recently retired public school administrator. They are articulate and insightful, as well as creative. Phil has been journaling for many years, often about their gender journey, and continues to use this medium as an emotional outlet, coping skill, and therapeutic tool. Phil enjoys being in nature and walks daily. While not a "joiner," Phil does enjoy listening to church services online.

Phil initially presented with a masculine gender expression and has only recently begun to discuss what they describe as a lifelong search to feel comfortable and confident in their body. Phil is currently using they/them pronouns as a way to continue acknowledging their masculine side, while not invalidating their feminine side. Phil does not identify with any labels under the trans umbrella, describing their gender as closest to fluid, but leaning more towards feminine. Phil most often presents as masculine, primarily due to fears that they will be rejected as a female. "I could never pass," they state. This creates hopelessness, and the wish that they could have had the transition options "that younger people have."

Phil has always known that there was something "different" about them. As a child, they enjoyed playing with female peers and their sisters. Growing up in a large Italian Catholic family, there were distinct gender norms. Phil's father would become irate and was often physical when he noticed Phil playing with their sisters. Phil's mother was very passive and would not intervene to stop the emotional/physical abuse, although she would attempt to comfort Phil afterwards. As a child, Phil's primary advocate was their maternal grandmother, who lived with them. Phil's grandmother would try to stop Phil's father from hurting them, and while she was rarely successful, Phil felt loved. Phil's grandmother often comforted them by baking cookies and other treats, and Phil recalls this fondly. Phil's grandmother died suddenly when Phil was 7, and Phil still tears up when discussing her.

Phil describes a memory that occurred at about age 8, in which they borrowed their sister's doll and baby carriage and walked around the block with it. Phil remembers feeling "so proud"—until Phil's father heard about it from a neighbor. This resulted in a beating in which Phil's father threw Phil against a wall, breaking their arm, all the while telling Phil that he would toughen [them] up. He stated derisively, "I won't have a homo sissy boy. I'll make you a man."

Phil always tried hard to please their father, and usually wound up feeling like they were a "failure." They describe a constant cycle of bullying by their father about their sensitive nature, creativity, or anything he deemed as a "weakness." Phil struggled with self-esteem since childhood and also feels that the abuse was a part of why they could never allow their feminine side to emerge, and they attempted to bury it for years. Phil has had bouts of severe depression and thoughts of suicide.

In college, Phil made some efforts to explore their identity. At that time, Phil wondered if they may be gay. Phil had an affair with an older gay man. After engaging in this physical relationship, Phil realized that while he felt comforted by his partner's gentle nature, Phil did not actually identify as gay. Phil met their wife in college, and while there was no real attraction, marriage felt like a necessary step. Phil describes their marriage as "loveless," with no physical relationship. Phil describes their wife as "distant" and "unsupportive." When Phil has attempted to share their gender questioning with their wife, she has responded with anger and derisive comments. This reminds Phil of their father. While the marriage has been distant, Phil still feels a sense of loyalty towards their wife.

Phil has three grown children, all of whom are distant. Phil's daughter, in particular is very religious, and Phil does not believe she would accept Phil as a woman. Phil's siblings are distant, and their brother-in-law often comments negatively on Phil's mannerisms and hair. Phil is isolated, with few friends and social supports. They no longer connect with Catholicism, due to fears of rejection, but they do enjoy listening to Unitarian Universalist services online through The Church of the Larger Fellowship, and find these supportive.

With regard to ED symptoms, Phil describes daily discrete periods of binge eating, which they use to "numb" and "comfort." Phil's daily binging has contributed to a weight gain of about 30 lbs. since retirement. Phil's overall self-care is poor. They describe not showering for days (especially when they are feeling depressed). They are also not attuned to body cues, including hunger, fullness, and fatigue. Sleep is often poor, as is body image. They describe an internal mirror in which they see a petite and curvaceous yet slender body, which is very feminine in presentation. Phil does recognize that this is not the body they see in the mirror, which is larger and stockier, which Phil "hates." Phil views weight gain from the binging as positive: "it gives me boobs," although they are aware that it has been hard on their body, increasing knee and back pain. Phil notes that their body image is more positive when they wear more androgynous or feminine clothing or when they can sit or walk in a more feminine way. They would like to consider hormones, but do not think this would be acceptable to their wife, children, or friends.

Recently, Phil had an online relationship with a man in which they presented as a woman. They felt an "awakening—fully alive for the first time." Phil eventually broke ties with this man, knowing that things could never proceed as Phil is married, and they did not want to "lead him on." They mourn the loss of this friendship, describing this as their most significant loss, and stating "I grieve my inability to be the woman I was then." The depression resulting from this loss was one of the impetuses for seeking therapy.

Prior to seeking outpatient treatment, Phil attempted to be admitted to an inpatient ED program. The person conducting the intake kept using Phil's legal name and asking intrusive questions about Phil's gender identity. The intake left Phil with the sense that they were too complex to be admitted to this program. Phil admits that this experience nearly dissuaded them from seeking any subsequent therapeutic support. Phil's goal for therapy is to learn to "live a truer life." They report disabling depression, daily binge eating, and recurrent thoughts that things could be easier if they were dead. After a thorough suicide risk assessment, it was determined that Phil could be safely treated at an outpatient setting.

Treatment Approach

Our treatment approach (Dalzell & Protos, 2020; Dalzell et al., 2022) looks at how social identities and gender interact with traumas, mood disorders, and gender dysphoria to increase a client risk of EDs and negative body image. Using this lens, we also identify those areas that enable recovery. An overview of these intersecting components is shown in Figure 8.1. The left side of Figure 8.1 illustrates the many areas with which our clients struggle. Gender diverse clients with EDs are complex, and often have a combination of gender dysphoria or negative gender-based feelings about the body, clinical or subclinical ED symptoms, minority stressors, and

Figure 8.1

Model for Treating Eating Disorders in TGD Populations. The Issues on Left and Right Sides Are Factors to Assess and Address Clinically. The Center Circle Reflects Overall Therapeutic Tasks Regardless of Diagnoses or Contributing Factors

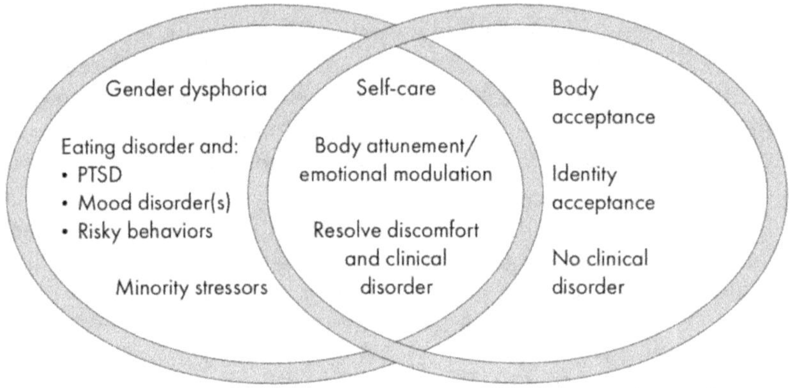

Reprinted with permission.

other traumas. Many of our clients also have other mental health symptoms such as anxiety, and/or engage in risky behaviors. The right side of Figure 8.1 shows the goals of therapy: body/identity acceptance. To achieve this, the client sometimes incorporates affirmative procedures (social, medical transition).

The intersection of the two sides—and the work of therapy—is a combination of self-care, body attunement, and emotional modulation. These factors support clients in decreasing or resolving ED symptoms. When clients begin to value themselves and to care for themselves differently, they are able to embrace their identities. For many clients, it is also important to work on other reasons that they are struggling, such as past situations and experiences that may be related to the ED. This treatment approach is eclectic and client-centered, and grounded in several models, including feminist treatment approaches, narrative approaches, and dialectical approaches. Most importantly, this model is a trauma focused approach.

Creating Rapport and Safety

It is essential to foster an environment in which clients feel respected in the uniqueness of their gender identities. Developing safety can occur from the first client contact. It is important that our language, intake, and other processes communicate an understanding of gender diversity. Suggestions include using the appropriate name and pronouns (these often differ from legal name and pronouns), a setting that supports diverse bodies (larger, comfortable furniture), and artwork that is free of gendered bodies. TGD clients may be quite verbal or more guarded. It is important to go at the client's pace and use containment methods to increase a sense of safety. Entering treatment takes courage—and this was very true for Phil, who was older, hopeless that they could ever be their authentic self, and had experienced discrimination within the mental health system.

The assessment is a chance to dive deeply into gender identity, ED(s), other symptoms, and traumas/minority stressors. Assessment begins with asking about symptoms, what maintains them (e.g., their function), and what strengths are present or need to be built for sustained recovery. Assessment guides treatment (Dalzell & Protos, 2020). A sample assessment is shown in Table 8.1.

Table 8.1

Case Study. This Chart Summarizes Case Study Data From the Assessment and Ongoing Treatment

Components Associated With Gender Dysphoria	
Gender Identity	No formal label, closest to fluid, but leaning towards feminine
	Strong gender role socialization; severe consequences for showing feminine traits
ED and Body Image Factors	
ED Symptoms	Daily binge eating to "numb" and "comfort"
	Binging has resulted in less masculine body presentation ("boobs")
Body Image	Has never felt comfortable/confident in body; contributes to low self-esteem
	Desire to "pass" as female; hopelessness that this could occur
	Some social transition—wearing more feminine clothing
	Feels good about kinesthetic aspects of body image
Minority Stressors	
Openness vs secrecy	Secrecy from family and friends esp. due to fears of rejection
Support system	Marital relationship distant; lack of acceptance regarding gender identity
	Loss of relationship where feminine side was acceptable
Trauma	Severe beatings, being called a "homo, sissy boy"
Invalidations	Invalidation by family members; ED program; feared rejection by Catholic church

(Table continued on next page)

Table 8.1 (Continued)

Other Trauma(s)	
ACEs	Severe childhood verbal, emotional and physical abuse
Other	Emotional/verbal abuse; bullying brother-in-law; grandmother's sudden death
Other Mental Health Concerns	
Other Symptoms/ Diagnoses	Significant depression, passive suicidal ideation
Risk Taking	
Risky behavior(s)	Extramarital affair
Resiliencies	
Traits	Articulate, insightful, creative, connected to nature
Tools and resources	Use of journaling and art as expression, therapy tool and coping strategy, spirituality, online church attendance, enjoys being outdoors in nature

In intake sessions, Phil demonstrated several strengths and resiliencies. Phil was persistent, articulate, insightful, and creative. They also actively journaled, something that they used to gain further insight and to express feelings. While Phil has a complicated relationship with religion, they are spiritual and enjoy listening to spiritual services online.

Phil had also taken some steps towards social transition and ED recovery. They were using a less gendered variation of their name, adopting they/them pronouns, and were dressing more androgynously. These steps resulted in a slight decrease in binging from about 10 times weekly to binging most days (which Phil had not realized until their intake). Phil expressed mixed feelings about these gains, due to their viewing the ED as something comforting and which increased curves. At the end of the initial session, they reported more hopefulness.

The initial stages of treatment focused on past and present experiences that contributed to Phil's distress and to the use of the ED symptoms. Phil acknowledged the pain they felt and how the binging helped them to tolerate emotional pain. Phil also used the binging to cope with feelings of hopelessness and gender dysphoria.

Phil has a significant history of trauma, and while Phil has never been "out," much of the trauma was identity based. Phil's father berated and beat Phil when they attempted to show any femininity. Phil described such childhood conditioning as one of the major blocks to fully accepting their identity, as was the anger Phil's wife expressed anytime they broached any gender questioning. Their marriage was complicated, and Phil did not feel ready to end the relationship. Another major block was Phil's hopelessness about transitioning, due to lack of support from others, and a sense that they would never look externally the way they envision themselves internally. The recent extramarital affair also felt like a significant trauma.

In the initial stages of treatment, establishing a sense of safety was key. Phil had never experienced safety. Their current home environment feels unsafe, and there are minimal supports. One important factor was stating that what Phil had experienced during the ED program intake was demoralizing and transphobic. Rather than reframing this experience, minimizing it, or universalizing it, we explored the discriminatory treatment, acknowledged barriers, and validated how such transphobic actions felt. This validation significantly reduced Phil's initial guardedness.

As Phil felt safer and rapport developed, we were able to further explore their gender story. This is an important part of the work, and the challenging piece is for the clinician to meet clients where they are, with no outcome in mind. Phil responded well to journaling prompts that allowed this exploration and began to understand that the traumas they had experienced, as a child and in their adult relationships, were a significant source of their hopelessness about possible transition. Phil recognized the connections between such hopelessness and binge eating. As Phil's narrative emerged, we began to simultaneously focus on coping, self-care, and body attunement.

Coping, Self-Care, and Body Attunement

As with many clients with EDs, Phil had a strong connection to the ED as their go-to coping strategy, and it worked, but only to a point. Phil acknowledged that binging was not always effective for numbing and that they were concerned about the health aspects of the binging, especially as they continued to get older. Phil resonated with the idea of dialectics; that something could be helpful and unhelpful simultaneously. Drawing from dialectical behavior therapy (DBT), we also focused on affecting modulation and distress tolerance strategies, including sitting with emotions in a non-judgmental way and self-soothing to decrease emotional intensity. The self-soothing skills were also helpful ways to connect with the senses and required a degree of embodiment that Phil had not engaged in previously.

As Phil connected more with body and self, they began to engage in more self-care. This was, at first, very difficult because of the depth of Phil's body hatred. We started to frame this care as a kind of re-parenting, and Phil ultimately could relax the most critical of the internal self/body talk and engage in more neutral self-statements at times.

As Phil embraced body neutrality, we began to focus on the importance of nourishing oneself consistently. Phil was open to working with a dietician who had worked with other TGD clients. They began to identify hunger cues prior to eating and fullness cues afterwards. Phil gained increasing awareness of the body sensations associated with various emotions, and could disrupt binge cycles sometimes. Phil also began to connect to their hunger and fullness. While Phil's overall body image varied, Phil could express more hope that they could develop a consistently neutral self-image. Phil began to allow their hair to grow long enough to put in a ponytail. This further reinforced the connection to their body.

One of the important discoveries Phil made was that when they were misgendered or devalued in terms of gender exploration, self-care always suffered and Phil was more prone to emotional eating. Understanding the ways in which minority stress intersected with self-care and binge eating was extremely helpful. We further supported insight into the interconnection between minority stress/trauma, emotional/physiological dysregulation, and binge eating. Phil began to identify fears of rejection and trauma-related core beliefs (e.g., "I'm damaged, I'm a disappointment, I can't trust my judgment, and I'm powerless.")

Trauma Work

Phil was now more actively using self-soothing and distress tolerance strategies. They were aware that there were times when they would "mindfully choose" to binge eat. As we further explored Phil's gender identity, the barriers to symptom resolution appeared to be connected to identity trauma. Phil was ready and willing to tackle these difficult traumas.

The modalities for our trauma work included journaling, talk therapy, and eye movement desensitization and reprocessing therapy (EMDR). The targets included the incident with the baby carriage, other incidences of physical abuse (and maternal passivity), and situations involving comments from others, including their brother-in-law, wife, and the intake team at the ED program. We also allowed space for Phil to grieve the loss of their extra-marital relationship, validating how difficult that was to be "seen" as their truer self. As the trauma work continued, Phil began to experiment more with dressing femininely at times, and journaling about the experience. Phil continues to work on a more positive body image. Binging incidences are rare.

Prevention and Best Practices

The case study demonstrated some of the best practices in working with TGD clients with EDs. Those and additional recommendations are given below. This list can be adapted to environments, including schools, agencies, workplaces, and outpatient mental health practices.

- **Foster an environment in which clients feel respected in the uniqueness of their gender identities.** Such identity factors include many intersections, including binary and nonbinary gender identities, race and ethnicity, religion, age, among others.
- **Value body diversity and expression.** It is helpful to adopt a body neutral stance that is positive about the diversity of body types. If there are bodies represented in your setting, consider whether these are diverse and include trans bodies.
- **Communicate understanding of gender diversity through use of language; own your mistakes.** Language supports safety and feeling understood.
- **Recognize that there are numerous social and cultural barriers to safety for TGD persons.** TGD persons face numerous barriers and safety concerns. Settings should actively work to dismantle these barriers, reducing traumatic impacts.
- **Create a safe space in which clients can explore and inhabit their own gender identities.** Create safety through language, forms, staff training, and other strategies. Recognize the inner connections between traumas and EDs. Provide clients with space and reassurance to take their own gender journey, without an outcome in mind.
- **Work with the entire family system; provide TGD spaces and sources of support.** Family and community connection and support are integral to recovery.
- **Reject the gender binary.** It is helpful to understand that gender is multidimensional and that the traditional binary of male/female will not apply to all TGD persons.
- **Recognize your own gender and body privilege.** This is especially important if you are part of the dominant culture, and increases sensitivity, empathy, and understanding.
- **Be comfortable discussing coming out and transition.** Being knowledgeable about the basics will support clients as they explore options. Provide information and support that will help TGD persons and their families to make informed decisions.
- **Accept that surgeries and other ways of affirming gender may be necessary for full body acceptance.** Such surgeries as corrective/affirming rather than "cosmetic."
- **Be an active ally that works to disrupt cisgender privilege across multiple systems**. Therapy boundaries may need to be less rigid (e.g., advocating for clients in unfair situations, working to rectify bullying, providing letters to surgeons).

- **Partner with other sources of support, such as ED and trans health organizations.** These sources may be invaluable to your clients.

Limitations and Future Study

Working with TGD clients with EDs is a burgeoning field, and one needing further study. The TGD umbrella is vast, with many identities, some binary and some nonbinary. This is also a diverse group with multiple intersectional identities, many of them marginalized. It will be important to expand our research to consider such factors. One clinical challenge is the use of growth charts based on natal sex. These are inappropriate for TGD clients and especially youth.

DISCUSSION QUESTIONS

1. Take a moment to journal and reflect on your understanding of your gender identity. Remember that "male-ness" and "femaleness" do not have to balance one another but can stand on their own spectrums.
2. Think about your own gender journey. What were the most important influences (early memories) on your own gender identity development?
3. If you have not already done so (and think the label fits), develop a plan for coming out as a trans ally. What would you need to consider? Who would you come out to?
4. As community connectedness and pride in one's identity serve as resiliency factors for TGD individuals, it is important to know local resources for connecting clients within the community. Look up and jot down support and therapy groups for TGD individuals, as well as pride festivities, so you have them on hand as a reference for future clients.
5. What changes will you make in your practice after reading this chapter?

REFERENCES

Ålgars, M., Alanko, K., Santtila, P., & Sandnabba, N. K. (2012). Disordered eating and gender identity disorder: A qualitative study. *EDs: The Journal of Treatment & Prevention*, *20*(4), 300–311. https://doi.org/10.1080/10640266.2012.668482

American Psychiatric Association. (2013). *Diagnostic and statistical manual of mental disorders* (5th ed.). https://doi.org/10.1176/appi.books.9780890425596

American Psychological Association. (2015). Guidelines for psychological practice with transgender and gender nonconforming people. *American Psychologist, 70*(9), 832–864. https://doi.org/10.1037/a0039906

Bandini, E., Fisher, A. D., Castellini, G., Lo Sauro, C., Lelli, L., Meriggiola, M. C., Casale, H., Benni, L., Ferruccio, N., Faravelli, C., Dettore, D., Maggi, M., & Ricca, V. (2013). Gender identity disorder and eating disorders: Similarities and differences in terms of body uneasiness. *Journal of Sexual Medicine, 10*(4), 1012–1023. https://doi.org/10.1111/jsm.12062

Bell, K., Rieger, E., & Hirsch, J. K. (2019). Eating disorder symptoms and proneness in gay men, lesbian women, and transgender and gender non-conforming adults: Comparative levels and a proposed mediational model. *Frontiers in Psychology, 9*, 2692. https://doi.org/10.3389/fpsyg.2018.02692

Bockting, W., & Coleman, E. (2007). Developmental stages of the transgender coming out process: Toward an integrated identity. In R. Ettner, S. Monstrey, & E. Eylered (Eds.), *Principles of transgender medicine and surgery* (pp. 185–208). The Haworth Press.

Bockting, W., Coleman, E., Deutsch, M. B., Guillamon, A., Meyer, I., Meyer W., III., Reisner, S., Sevelius, J., & Ettner, R. (2016). Adult development and quality of life of transgender and gender nonconforming people. *Current Opinion in Endocrinology, Diabetes, and Obesity, 23*(2), 188–197. https://doi.org/10.1097/MED.0000000000000232

Bockting, W. O., Miner, M. H., Swinburne Romine, R. E., Dolezal, C., Robinson, B., Rosser, B., & Coleman, E. (2020). The Transgender Identity Survey: A measure of internalized transphobia. *LGBT Health*, 7(1), 15–27. https://doi.org/10.1089/lgbt.2018.0265

Cash, T. F. (2011). Cognitive-behavioral perspectives on body image. In T. F. Cash & L. Smolak (Eds.), *Body image: A handbook of science, practice, and prevention* (pp. 39–47). Guilford.

Coleman, E., Bockting, W., Botzer, M., Cohen-Kettenis, P., DeCuypere, G., Feldman, J., Fraser, L., Green, J., Knudson, G., Meyer, W. J., Monstrey, S., Adler, R. K., Brown, G. R., Devor, A. H., Ehrbar, R., Ettner, R., Eyler, E., Garofalo, R., Karasic, D. H., … Zucker, K. (2012). Standards of care for the health of transsexual, transgender, and gender-nonconforming people, Version 7. *International Journal of Transgenderism, 13*(4), 165–232. https://doi-org.10.1080/15532739.2011.700873

Coleman, E., Radix, A. E., Bouman, W. P., Brown, G. R., De Vries, A. L. C., Deutsch, M. B., Ettner, R., Fraser, L., Goodman, M., Green, J., Hancock, A. B., Johnson, T. W., Karasic, D. H., Knudson, G. A., Leibowitz, S. F., Meyer-Bahlburg, H. F. L., Monstrey, S. J., Motmans, J., Nahata, L., … Arcelus, J. (2022). Standards of care for the health of transgender and gender diverse people, version 8. *International Journal of Transgender Health, 23*(sup 1), S1–S259. https://doi.org/10.1080/26895269.2022.2100644

Connolly, M. D., Zervos, M. J., Barone C. J., II., Johnson, C. C., & Joseph, C. L. (2016). The mental health of transgender youth: Advances in understanding. *Journal of Adolescent Health, 59*(5), 489–495. https://doi.org/10.1016/j.jadohealth.2016.06.012

Conner, M., Johnson, C., & Grogan, S. (2004). Sexuality, body image and eating behaviors. *Journal of Health Psychology*, *9*(4), 505–515. https://doi.org/10.1177/1359105304044034

Craig, S. L., Austin, A., Levenson, J., Leung, V. W. Y., Eaton, A. D., & D'Souza, S. A. (2020). Frequencies and patterns of adverse childhood events in LGBTQ+ youth. *Child Abuse & Neglect, 107*, https://doi.org/10.1016/j.chiabu.2020.104623

Dalzell, H. J., & Protos, K. (2020). *A clinician's guide to gender identity and body image*. Jessica Kingsley.

Dalzell, H. J., Protos, K., & Hunt, S. K. (2022). EDs, body image, and body positivity. In A.S. Keuroghlian, J. Potter, & S. L. Reisner (Eds.), *Transgender and gender diverse healthcare: The Fenway Guide* (pp. 170–182). McGraw-Hill. https://accessmedicine.mhmedical.com/content.aspx?bookid=3104&sectionid=259325830

Diemer, E. W., Grant, J. D., Munn-Chernoff, M. A., Patterson, D. A., & Duncan, A. E. (2015). Gender identity, sexual orientation, and eating-related pathology in a national sample of college students. *Journal of Adolescent Health, 57*(2), 144–149. https://doi.org/10.1016/j.jadohealth.2015.03.003

Grant, J. M., Mottet, L. A., Tanis, J., Harrison, J., Herman, J. L., & Keisling, M. (2011). *Injustice at every turn: A report of the National Transgender Discrimination Survey*. National Center for Transgender Equality and National Gay and Lesbian Task Force. https://www.thetaskforce.org/wp-content/uploads/2019/07/ntds_full.pdf

Grunewald, W., Convertino, A. D., Safren, S. A., Mimiaga, M. J., O'Cleirigh, C., Mayer, K. H., & Blashill, A. J. (2021). Appearance discrimination and binge eating among sexual minority men. *Appetite, 156*(32), 104819. https://doi.org/10.1016/j.appet.2020.104819

Guss, C. E., William, D. N., Reisner, S. L., Austin, S. B., Katz-Wise, S. L. (2017). Disordered weight management behavior, nonprescription steroid use, and weight perception in transgender youth. *Journal of Adolescent Health*, *60*(1) 17–22. https://doi.org/10.1016/j.jadohealth.2016.08.027

Hernando, A., Pallás, R., Cebolla, A., García-Campayo, J., Hoogendoorn, C. J., & Roy, J. F. (2019). Mindfulness, rumination, and coping skills in young women with eating disorders: A comparative study with healthy controls. *PloS One*, *14*(3), e0213985. https://doi.org/10.1371/journal.pone.0213985

Hodge, L., & Baker, A. (2021). Purification, punishment, and control: Eating disorders, self-harm, and child sexual abuse. *Qualitative Health Research*, *31*(11), 1963–1975. https://doi.org/10.1177/10497323211017490

Hook, J. N., Davis, D. E., Owen, J., Worthington E. L., Jr., & Utsey, S. O. (2013). Cultural humility: Measuring openness to culturally diverse clients. *Journal of Counseling Psychology, (60)*3, 353–366. https://doi.org/10.1037/a0032595

Hosseini, S. A. & Padhy, R. K. (2021, September 9). *Body image distortion*. StatPearls. https://www.ncbi.nlm.nih.gov/books/NBK546582/

Kamody, R. C., Grilo, C. M., & Udo, T. (2019). Disparities in DSM-5 defined EDs by sexual orientation among U.S. adults. *International Journal of EDs, 53*(2), 278–287. https://doi.org/10.1002/eat.23193

McClain, Z.. & Peebles, R. (2016). Body image and EDs among lesbian, gay, bisexual, and transgender youth. *Pediatric Clinics of North America, 63*(6), 1079–1090. https://doi.org/10.1016/j.pcl.2016.07.008

Meneguzzo, P., Collantoni, E., Gallicchio, D., Busetto, P., Solmi, M., Santonastaso, P., & Favaro, A. (2018). Eating disorders symptoms in sexual minority women: A systematic review. *European Eating Disorders Review, 26*(4), 275–292. https://doi.org/10.1002/erv.2601

Meyer, I. H. (2003). Prejudice, social stress, and mental health in lesbian, gay and bisexual populations: Conceptual issues and research evidence. *Psychological Bulletin, 129*(5), 674–697. https://doi.org/10.1037/0033-2909.129.5.674

Monteleone, A. M., Tzischinsky, O., Cascino, G., Alon, S., Pellegrino, F., Ruzzi, V., & Latzer, Y. (2021). The connection between childhood maltreatment and ED psychopathology: A network analysis study in people with bulimia nervosa and with binge ED. *Eating and Weight Disorders, 27*(1), 253–261. https://doi.org/10.1007/s40519-021-01169-6

Nagata, J. M., Murray, S. B., Compte, E. J., Pak, E. H., Schauer, R., Flentje, A., Capriotti, M. R., Lubensky, M. E., Lunn, M. R., & Obedin-Maliver, J. (2020). Community norms for the ED Examination Questionnaire (EDE-Q) among transgender men and women. *Eating Behaviors, 37*, 101381. https://doi.org/10.1016/j.eatbeh.2020.101381

Narang, P., Sarai, S. K., Aldrin, S., & Lippmann, S. (2018). Suicide among transgender and gender-nonconforming people. *The Primary Care Companion for CNS Disorders, 20*(3), 18nr02273. https://doi.org/10.4088/PCC.18nr02273

Rabito Alcón, M. F., & Rodríguez Molina, J. M. (2015). Body image in persons with gender dysphoria. *Medwave, 15*(4), e6138. https://doi.org/10.5867/medwave.2015.04.6138

SAMHSA. (2019, December). *Cultural humility: Where being human matters the most in serving others.* National Hispanic and Latino Mental Health Technology Transfer Center Network. https://mhttcnetwork.org/sites/default/files/2019-12/GallardoMHfinal.pdf

Singh, A. A., Hays, D. G., & Watson, L. S. (2011). Strength in the face of adversity: Resilience strategies of transgender individuals. *Journal of Counseling & Development, 89*(1), 20–27. https://doi.org/10.1002/j.1556-6678.2011.tb00057.x

Stice, E., & Shaw, H. E. (2002). Role of body dissatisfaction in the onset and maintenance of eating pathology: A synthesis of research findings. *Journal Psychosomatic Research, 53*(5), 985–993. https://doi.org/10.1016/S0022-3999(02)00488-9

Tervalon, M., & Murray-Garcia, J. (1998). Cultural humility versus cultural competence: A critical distinction in defining physician-training outcomes in multicultural education. *Journal of Health Care for the Poor and Underserved, 9*(2), 117–125. https://doi.org/10.1353/hpu.2010.0233

Testa, R. J., Rider, G. N, Haug, N. A., & Balsam, K. F. (2017). Gender confirming medical interventions and eating disorder symptoms among transgender individuals. *Health Psychology, 36*(10), 927–936. https://doi.org/10.1037/hea0000497

Wacker, E. C., & Dolbin-MacNab, M. L. (2020). Feminist-informed protective factors for subthreshold eating disorders. *Qualitative Health Research, 30*(10), 1546–1560. https://doi.org/10.1177/1049732320921832

Watson, R. J., Veale, J. F., & Saewyc, E. M. (2017). Disordered eating behaviors among transgender youth: Probability profiles from risk and protective factors. *International Journal of Eating Disorders, 50*(5), 515–522. https://doi.org/10.1002/eat.22627

CHAPTER 9

COUNSELING MEN WITH EATING DISORDERS

Dominic Denning, Jordan Alvarez, Jorge Castro Lebrón, Eli Gebhardt, and Tiffany A. Brown

In this chapter, we present a review of the epidemiological literature for eating disorders in men. We also aggregate evidence from previous studies concerning eating disorder prevention and treatment in male populations. Importantly, we provide an overview of eating disorder literature for men broadly, and more specifically, in men with diverse and intersectional identities. In addition to our summary of the existing literature regarding eating disorders in men, we also provide a case summary and analysis for a cisgender male with intersectional identities (gay and Black) who presented for treatment for an eating disorder. At the end of the chapter, we outline key future directions as well as some questions to consider regarding the basic and applied research and clinical work for men struggling with eating disorders.

INTRODUCTION

Eating disorders (EDs) are common psychiatric conditions associated with high mortality and significant impairment (Smink et al., 2012). EDs are commonly stereotyped as being a "female disorder," which has led to a dearth of literature regarding the condition in men (Murray et al., 2017).

Counseling Individuals With Eating Disorders: An Intersectional Approach, pp. 191–225

Indeed, most EDs are more common in women than in men (American Psychiatric Association, 2013); however, subpopulations of men (i.e., sexual minority men) are more likely to present with EDs than heterosexual males (Calzo et al., 2017). Given that men may experience different pressures and body ideals than women (i.e., leanness and muscularity; Tylka, 2011), appearance concerns and ED phenomenon in men may not be well captured by existing diagnostic systems (Murray et al., 2017); thus, leading to underdiagnosis. Considering these gender differences, recent research has focused on developing assessments and etiological models to address treatment and prevention gaps in this population. While there has been an increase in ED literature for men over the past decade (Brown & Keel, 2023), the epidemiology, treatment, and prevention of EDs in men remains poorly understood (Lavender et al., 2017).

Epidemiology of Eating Disorders in Men

Twelve-Month and Point Prevalence

Table 9.1 presents point/12-month and lifetime prevalence rates for EDs in men. Pooled prevalence rates based on the Diagnostic and Statistical Manual (DSM)-IV and –5 criteria are as follows: unspecified feeding or eating disorder (UFED) 0.5% (Nagl et al., 2016); sub-ED diagnosis 0.98% (0–12.2%; Chua et al., 2022); binge eating disorder (BED) 0.42% (0–0.8%; Chua et al., 2022; Hudson et al., 2007); BN 0.2% (.01–1.5%; Preti et al., 2009; Chua et al., 2022); AN 0.02% (0–0.03%; Mohler-Kuo et al., 2016; Chua et al., 2022); and avoidant restrictive food intake disorder (ARFID) 5.2% (Chua et al., 2022). The pooled prevalence rates suggest that UFED, ARFID, and sub-ED diagnoses may be the most common ED presentations in men.

Lifetime Prevalence

Consistent with findings from point/12-month prevalence for EDs in men, literature also suggests that EDs are common across the lifespan. Pooled prevalence rates for the DSM-IV and –5 are as follows: UFED 0.96% (0.16–0.7%; Nagl et al., 2016; Silén et al., 2020); OSFED 0.16% (Silén et al., 2020); sub-ED diagnosis 2% (0.91–9.3%; Preti et al., 2009; Feldman & Meyer, 2007); BED 1% (0.26–5.2%; Preti et al., 2009; Feldman & Meyer, 2007); BN 0.48% (0.12–6.2%; Preti et al., 2009; Feldman & Meyer, 2007); AN 0.57% (0–1%; Altwaijri et al., 2020; Feldman & Meyer, 2007). Lifetime prevalence of ARFID in adult men was not reported in any studies in our review. In sum, our findings suggest that lifetime prevalence of sub-ED, BED, and UFED diagnoses may be more common in men than other ED presentations.

Diversity Reporting in Epidemiological Studies

Within the scarce literature relevant to EDs in men, few studies report race/ethnicity, sexual orientation, and gender identity. In our review, only 20% of studies reported participants' racial/ethnic background, 13.3% sexual orientation, and 6.7% transmasculine identity. Furthermore, 80% of the studies were conducted in United States, European, or Australian populations. Given that 12-month prevalence rates for sexually diverse or unsure men are estimated to be 4 to 7 times higher compared to heterosexual men (2.06% and 3.66% respectively; Diemer et al., 2015) and lifetime ED prevalence is estimated to be 8.8% in sexual minority men (SMM; Feldman & Meyer, 2007), epidemiological studies for men have limited generalizability. . Moreover, previous studies estimate the point prevalence of AN and BN to be 4.1% in transmasculine individuals (Diemer et al., 2018), suggesting that this population may also be at elevated risk for EDs. Importantly, none of the studies in this review reported the prevalence of EDs in men across racial/ethnic groups besides Feldman and Meyer (2007), who suggest that full syndrome EDs may be more common in Latinx sexual minority men (SMM) than in White or Black SMM and that subclinical diagnoses on average are comparable across race/ethnicity in SMM.

Eating Disorder Prevention in Men

Prevention Programs and Outcomes for Men

Despite the nascency of ED literature for men, an increasing number of prevention programs have been developed and evaluated recently. These programs may not be considered true ED prevention programs (i.e., programs that reduce the onset of an ED compared to a control condition), but rather, they focus on attenuating putative ED or muscle dysmorphia (MD) risk factors (see Table 9.3). These prevention programs have employed universal strategies (i.e., that address the entire population), selective strategies (i.e., targeting members in a particular population segment known to be at-risk), and indicated strategies (i.e., that concentrate on population segments of high risk or individuals who are already exhibiting symptoms).

The Body Project (Stice et al., 2000), a cognitive dissonance-based program originally designed to target and diminish the internalization of the thin ideal in women, has served as the foundation for the majority of mixed-gender and male-specific ED prevention programming. In young women, these programs have shown a significant decrease in body dissatisfaction, disordered eating symptoms, and likelihood of developing an ED through 3-year follow-up (Becker & Stice, 2017). Consistent with this finding, men in a mixed-gender program (the Body Project 4 All) randomized controlled trial (RCT) demonstrated improvements in their general body image and muscularity dissatisfaction post-intervention and at 2- and 6-month follow-up (Kilpela et al., 2016). Despite these promising findings, body-ideal internalization and ED psychopathology did not significantly decrease. The authors concluded that separate programming for men may be beneficial for outcomes as previous literature concerning dissonance-based prevention were superior for women in women-only programs compared to mixed-gender programming.

The Body Project M (BPM; Jankowski et al., 2017), a selective program, and the Body Project: More Than Muscles (MTM; Brown et al., 2017), an indicated prevention program, were both developed for men with body dissatisfaction and both have evaluated program outcomes. BPM used an open trial design and reported significant within condition differences in muscularity dissatisfaction and internalization of appearance ideals at post-intervention, but these were not significant at 3-month follow-up (Jankowski et al., 2017). In contrast, a RCT for MTM found significant improvements pre- to post-intervention and at 1-month follow-up in eating pathology, MD symptoms, body-ideal internalization, and satisfaction with body fat and muscularity compared to the assessment-only control (Brown et al., 2017). These outcomes are consistent with the broader literature for ED prevention that affirms the greater efficacy of targeted prevention programs (Stice et al., 2007). The effects of MTM have been replicated in a RCT for Brazilian men in terms of reducing internalization of the body-ideal, disordered eating, MD symptoms, drive for muscularity, appreciation of the body, and dissatisfaction with muscularity and body fat through 6-month follow-up (Almeida et al., 2021).

Prevention programs have also been developed for male subgroups that are at increased risk for developing an ED (e.g., SMM). One such program is the PRIDE Body Project, a dissonance-based preventative program for SMM (Brown & Keel, 2015). SMM in the PRIDE Body Project experienced significantly greater reductions in bulimic symptoms, restraint, body dissatisfaction, drive for muscularity, and body ideal internalization compared to assessment-only controls post-intervention. These effects were largely maintained at 1-month follow-up. HIV positive SMM have also been the focus of preventative programs, including the Cognitive Behavioral

Treatment for Body Image and Self Care (Blashill et al., 2017), which aims to improve quality of life and body image. This RCT showed significant and large effects on depression at 6-month follow-up and on body image disturbance at 3-month and 6-month follow-up.

As male athletes are also at increased risk for EDs, the Male Athlete Body Project was developed to help reduce risk in this population (Perelman et al., 2022). In a RCT, male athletes reported increased body satisfaction and reductions in drive for muscularity and athletic body-ideal internalization relative to controls post-intervention and at 1-month follow-up. At follow-up, male athletes also reported increased body satisfaction, reductions in drive for muscularity, and reductions in male athlete's use of performance-enhancing supplements (Perelman et al., 2022).

Diversity Reporting in Prevention Outcomes for Men

The first ED prevention trial specifically for men was published in 2015; thus, ED prevention for men is still in its infancy. Because of this, randomized controlled trials evaluating the efficacy of ED prevention in men have benefitted from transparency regarding participant diversity. In adherence to the 2010 Consolidated Standards of Reporting Trials (CONSORT) checklist, most studies in our review included participants' racial/ethnic background (85.7%) and sexual orientation (71.4%). However, transmasculine individuals to our knowledge were not included in these prevention studies; thus, future prevention work should prioritize inclusivity of male-identifying individuals. Furthermore, most studies (71.4%) were comprised completely or primarily of college students and were solely conducted in the U.S.—limiting the generalizability of these findings. Future trials will need to evaluate the efficacy of these programs across ethnically and racially diverse groups as White participants comprised 32.2–82.4% of participants in our review. Moreover, effectiveness and implementation studies are needed for men, progressing similarly to programs for women (Becker & Stice, 2017).

Treatment Outcomes in Men With Eating Disorders

Treatment Outcomes for Men With EDs

The treatment literature for men with EDs is sparse, in part due to the stigma and barriers men with EDs are confronted with (Bomben et al., 2022). Most studies utilized small samples of men (M = 55.7, median = 27), were naturalistic (93.3%), and used different methods, which creates challenges when trying to compare outcomes and when attempting to identify treatments that may be advantageous for men. Table 9.2 presents an overview of treatment outcomes for men with EDs. A majority (60%) of treatment outcome studies on men were from residential/inpatient settings, and the most commonly reported therapeutic modality was cognitive behavioral therapy (CBT, 46.7%). However, it is important to note that 33.3% of studies did not report what treatment was used, obfuscating what interventions may be salubrious for male populations.

Notwithstanding these limitations, the literature suggests that most studies (60%) found better outcomes for men compared to women with EDs regarding weight restoration. Furthermore, most studies (75%) indicated higher remission rates in male compared to female patients. Studies examining ED symptoms, BMI, and quality of life demonstrate comparable outcomes between men and women. Taken together, these findings suggest that while the treatment literature is minimal for men with EDs, preliminary evidence suggests that bulimic and anorexic symptoms and syndromes may be responsive to traditional ED treatments regardless of gender. Despite these promising preliminary findings, the literature may only be applicable to a small subset of men with EDs. This is, in part, due to differences in body ideals for men (i.e., mesomorphic bodies—lean muscular bodies), which may result in different cognitive and behavioral patterns that are not consistent with prototypical AN and BN diagnoses. Thus, these unique pressures (from partners, friends, family, and media) and body change behaviors may require different treatments (Murray & Griffiths, 2015) as most treatments have been female-focused (Bomben et al., 2022). While prevention programs have been developed to target these novel concerns, evidence-based treatments have yet to be established for these concerns in men.

While there are many confounds when examining treatment effectiveness for men, male patients receiving CBT for EDs on average had comparable or better outcomes compared to female patients, though additional research is needed to confirm this. It is crucial for future studies to examine the efficacy of third wave CBTs (i.e., acceptance and commitment therapy [ACT], dialectical behavior therapy [DBT], etc.) in male populations as these outcomes have not been reported in previous literature, despite ACT and DBT demonstrating preliminary efficacy in treating EDs in female populations (Ben-Porath et al., 2020; Juarascio et al., 2013) and DBT in mixed gender samples (Brown et al., 2018; Denning et al., 2022; Denning et al., 2023) and sexually diverse clients (Donahue et al., 2020).

Diversity Reporting in Outcomes for Men With EDs

Consistent with our findings from our review of the epidemiology of EDs in male populations, treatment studies suffer from similar limitations, which limit the generalizability of findings. As mentioned above, most studies comprised patients with AN or BN (93.3%); however, male participants were characterized as younger, single, educated, and White. Importantly, 46.7% of studies did not report any participant demographics or characteristics aside from age. Of the studies that reported demographic characteristics, only 10.2% of research participants were racially/ethnically diverse. Furthermore, no studies to our knowledge included transmasculine individuals, and only one study reported participants' sexual orientation. The treatment literature for men is small and it may not generalize to men from diverse backgrounds. Future treatment studies should prioritize recruitment of diverse samples (i.e., racial/ethnic, sexual orientation, and gender identity) to bridge knowledge gaps for providers as best practices cannot be established with the existing literature.

CASE VIGNETTE

Given concerns regarding treatments having not been evaluated in diverse samples of men, we include a sample case to illustrate how an existing treatment could be adapted to incorporate intersectional identities.

Case Summary

Jason is a 22-year-old Black, gay male college student who sought outpatient treatment for concerns about his eating and perfectionism regarding his body and level of muscularity. Jason came from a low-income background and was attending a predominantly White institution (PWI) as an undergraduate student. He reported that his decision to seek treatment was a result of his friends' concerns about his physical and mental health. While Jason did have friends who identified as LGBTQ+, few were also from racially minoritized backgrounds. Outside of these friendships, most of his interactions with the LGBTQ+ community came primarily from bars and clubs for SMM men.[1]

In the 6 months prior to treatment, Jason reported that he had been engaging in restrictive eating on a daily basis (restricting processed foods, eating a high protein and low carbohydrate diet), excessive exercise (going to the gym for >2 hours/day) and daily use of muscle enhancing supplements (creatine and fat burners). Jason also experienced occasional food insecurity, which also led him to unintentionally restrict his food intake, although he noted that he appreciated the effects of this on his weight. Over this 6-month period, he lost 40 pounds (treatment baseline BMI = 23.0), which he attributed to his "clean eating" and exercise routine. Jason stated that the main motivation for his weight loss and increase in muscularity was to achieve a body that he felt would gain more attention from other men in the SMM community outside of his PWI. Indeed, he reported that he felt like he received positive attention and reinforcement at the gym and bars/clubs since his weight loss, which he reported he had not experienced at his prior weight. In this 6-month period, his frequency of going out to bars and "clubbing" increased, and he also reported engaging in binge drinking behavior 4–5 nights per week (drinking > 6 drinks per night). After these nights out, Jason would eat a large amount of food (e.g., 3 fast food cheeseburgers and 3 servings of French fries), which he noted felt inevitable after going out. Consequently, these episodes resulted in feelings of intense guilt and shame and longer gym sessions to compensate. After completing a semi-structured clinical interview and self-report assessments, the therapist diagnosed Jason with atypical anorexia nervosa, given his significant weight loss, which may be even more severe given the flaws of BMI and his level of muscularity; and restrictive eating/exercise behavior, with notable low frequency binge eating behavior and aspects of muscularity-oriented disordered eating.

Enhanced CBT for EDs

Enhanced CBT for EDs (CBT-E; Fairburn, 2008) has demonstrated efficacy in improving ED symptoms in adults (Atwood & Friedman, 2020). CBT-E is based on the transdiagnostic cognitive behavioral theory of EDs and suggests that overvaluation of shape and weight and/or control over eating are the core symptoms that drive individuals to engage in maladaptive body change behavior (Fairburn, 2008). The theory asserts that mood intolerance, interpersonal problems, perfectionism, and low self-esteem also maintain ED psychopathology (Fursland & Watson, 2015).

CBT-E follows a 20-session structure over 20 weeks if patients are not underweight, with 40 recommended sessions for individuals who need to restore weight (Fairburn, 2008). The treatment includes four stages. Stage I (first four weeks of therapy) introduces the client to therapy and understanding the history of their ED and any psychosocial variables (e.g., ethnicity, sexual orientation) that have influenced their disorder (Fairburn, 2008). Although CBT-E does not explicitly include adaptations for males or sexual minority populations, the flexibility of the case conceptualization allows clinicians to incorporate personalized factors for clients with intersecting identities. For example, the clinician may consider how sexual minority (SM) identity and/or minority stress reactions may influence overvaluation of weight and shape, food restriction, compensatory behaviors, and other putative maintenance factors (e.g., mood intolerance, interpersonal problems, perfectionism, and low self-esteem). Minority stressors may also exacerbate shape and weight concerns in SM clients because of the pressure to conform to social norms of attractiveness both within and outside of the SM community (Pachankis et al., 2020; Pachankis & Hatzenbuehler, 2013). Relatedly, among those that identify as a SM and racial minority, there may be additional pressure to conform to a community that is often White (Pachankis et al., 2020). It is also important when working with male populations to consider how appearance ideals and performance enhancing substance use (e.g., protein supplements, creatine, steroids) fit in the conceptualization as this is a common weight and shape control behavior among men generally and particularly in SMM populations (Calzo et al., 2017; Murray et al., 2017). During this stage, the therapist works to develop a strong therapeutic relationship, emphasizes self-monitoring and regular eating, and addresses any ambivalence the client may have about treatment (Fursland & Watson, 2015). Fairburn (2008) highlighted that due to high dropout rates, the therapist should strive to be both empathic and firm while emphasizing the importance of homework outside of session (e.g., trying new food-related behaviors and self-monitoring). Finally, helping the client understand that weight changes may occur is essential, as this can be distressing for individuals with EDs.

During the next two weeks of treatment (Stage II) the therapist works with the client to review progress and identify treatment barriers. Notably, therapists should continue to update their case conceptualization throughout treatment as additional barriers or ED maintenance factors are identified. During the next eight weeks of treatment (sessions 6–14; Stage III) the therapist should continue to address the cognitions and behaviors that are maintaining the disordered eating while being attentive to the client's emotions. With sexual minority men, the clinician should address cultural factors (e.g., socioeconomic status, age, outness, and education level) throughout treatment, but especially in Stage III. For example, if a client has difficulty planning for grocery shopping and few cooking skills that would preclude them from eating within their budget, the therapist could help them or direct them towards resources to meal plan. The last phase (Stage IV) focuses on termination and relapse prevention strategies. In this stage, the clinician may highlight ways that sociocultural pressures in the SM community to be lean may be a relapse risk factor, while a supportive social group may be a protective factor (Calzo et al., 2017; Pachankis et al., 2020).

CBT-E With Jason

In **Stage I** the therapist provided psychoeducation regarding Jason's ED and worked with him to construct a conceptual model to demonstrate the factors that maintain and contribute to his ED. As a gay, Black man Jason experienced discrimination both for being Black and for being gay. Jason presented with a strong desire to be more muscular because he felt he was not given attention by the gay community unless he "overcame" being Black and had the "perfect body." The therapist discussed how these cognitions influenced his supplement use, excessive exercise, and restrictive eating. The therapist also worked to understand the triggers that reinforced his belief that he needed to have the "perfect body" and his subsequent ED behaviors. Jason reported that using Grindr and going out frequently made him feel pressure to increase his exercise and restrictive eating. However, during this phase, the therapist emphasized his strengths, such as his involvement with the gay community at his college campus and his close friends who advocated for his treatment.

Jason was encouraged to self-monitor his disordered eating, as well as his alcohol use. Additionally, Jason was encouraged to establish a consistent eating schedule (i.e., 3 meals and 2–3 snacks) to decrease restrictive eating. He reported food insecurity due to his low income and was provided with psychoeducation regarding shopping practices to maximize his resources (e.g., cooking instead of eating out, evaluating less expensive food options) and was directed to local food banks and campus resources. Lastly, while Jason was hesitant to abstain from exercise during treatment, he ultimately agreed.

Stage II involved working with Jason to continue to monitor his eating and exercise habits as well as barriers to treatment. He reported decreased binge drinking due to conversations that highlighted how going out clubbing preceded his ED, which subsequently led to decreases in his binge eating behaviors. However, Jason continued to struggle with eating three meals a day due to fears of gaining body fat and the potential judgment from community members. Jason reported that he was often pressured to send full body photos to acquaintances on Grindr and would often get complimented for his physique, which he was concerned about "losing." However, after further discussion, Jason began to develop an understanding of how he was objectified for being Black in the gay community and that this was a source of discrimination. Consequently, his decreased use of Grindr was associated with fewer compliments and he felt less attractive. Together, the therapist and Jason determined that it would be helpful to interact with the gay community in other ways to help him feel valued outside of his appearance. Jason decided to join the gay section of the Black student union, where he was able to explore his intersectional identities. This increased his belongingness and decreased his feeling of being unattractive by allowing him to focus on other important, valued social activities.

Jason entered **Stage III** of treatment when he no longer had clinically significant restrictive eating and had increased awareness of how his intersectional identities and sociocultural pressures influence his ED. With therapist support, Jason reintegrated functional movement into his routine that was not appearance-focused (e.g., recreational sports), was eating regularly, and decreased his use of muscle enhancing supplements. Lastly, Jason and the therapist continued to highlight his strengths, such as his participation in positive community activities such as cooking with his friends and participating in activities that did not involve going to bars with members of the gay community. Jason also reported decreasing his use of Grindr and added an app time limit.

Jason continued therapy to challenge his beliefs about how his physical appearance is central to finding a partner and Jason was encouraged to note examples of individuals he knew in the gay community that were coupled but did not have the "perfect" body. Jason and the therapist continued to process his racial and sexual identity development, which decreased the cognitive distortions and automatic thoughts he had related to his body image. Jason entered **Stage IV** of treatment when he had subclinical ED symptoms and an awareness of sociocultural pressures that may trigger his disordered eating. Jason created a relapse prevention plan including monitoring signs (e.g., eating less, working out more) that would indicate that he was engaging in disordered eating patterns again and would need to obtain some booster sessions.

FUTURE DIRECTIONS

In sum, the ED literature for men has been growing over the past decade, but still remains sparse for men with diverse and intersectional identities. In reviewing the existing literature, we propose three key priority areas for future ED research in male populations. First, robust epidemiological studies concerning EDs in men are needed, especially those that examine sociodemographic factors. While there is evidence that sexual minority populations are more likely to present with ED behaviors and meet for ED diagnoses (Calzo et al., 2017; Feldman & Meyer, 2007), additional investigations in ethnically and racially diverse populations is needed, as these groups may also be vulnerable to EDs due to experiences of prejudice and stigma.

Second, we suggest that future ED prevention work in men to evaluate whether these programs can actually prevent ED onset, rather than reduce

ED risk factors. Prior work suggests that prevention programs for men have demonstrated preliminary efficacy in reducing risk factors for EDs and often screen for ED diagnoses for eligibility purposes, but none to our knowledge have used diagnostic interviews through long-term follow-up to determine whether these programs prevent ED onset.

Finally, treatments that have demonstrated effectiveness and/or efficacy in treating primarily female populations should be tested in men through both randomized controlled trials and naturalistic outcome studies. However, outcomes should also measure cognitive and behavioral ED symptoms that are prototypical for males (e.g., muscularity oriented disordered eating). Moreover, no treatments to our knowledge have been developed specifically for men with EDs; thus, future research should prioritize treatment development for this population.

DISCUSSION QUESTIONS

1. How does intersectionality play a role in EDs for male-identifying individuals?
2. Are existing ED and body image assessments culturally sensitive and inclusive of men?
3. Do current ED prevention programs prevent ED onset in men or just attenuate risk factors?
4. How can we incorporate intersectional identities into ED treatments for men?

Table 9.1

Extended Epidemiology Review of Eating Disorders in Men From Brown and Keel (2023)

Author & Country	Diagnosis & 12-Month/Point Prevalence	Diagnosis & Lifetime Prevalence	N men	Reported Sample Characteristics
Allen et al. (2013) *Australia*	DSM-5 Any ED = .03		679	Full Mixed Sex Sample Age = 19 – 22 years *Male participant demographics not reported*
Hudson et al. (2007) *United States*	DSM-IV AN = 0 BN = .1 BED = .8 Sub-BED = .8	DSM-IV AN = .3 BN = .5 BED = 2.0 Sub-BED 1.9	1,220	Full Mixed Sex ED Sample M_{age} = 18.9 – 25.4 years *Male participant demographics not reported*
Preti et al. (2009) *Belgium, France, Germany, Italy, Netherlands, & Spain*	DSM-IV AN = 0 BN = .01 BED = .07 Sub-BED = .19 Any ED = .26%	DSM-IV AN = 0 BN = .12 BED = .26 Sub-BED = .91 Any ED = 1.22	1,742	Full Mixed Sex Sample M_{age} = 47.1 years *Male participant demographics not reported*
Carta et al. (2014) *Italy*		DSM-IV AN = 0 BN = .3 BED = .3 Any ED = .6	1,437	Male Participants Age 18+ years *Male participant demographics not reported*
Udo & Grilo (2018) *United States*	DSM-5 AN = .05 BN = .14 BED = .44	DSM-5 AN = .8 BN = .28 BED = .85	36,309	Full Mixed Sex ED Sample M_{age} = 39.1 – 45.2 years *Male participant demographics not reported*

(Table continued on next page)

Table 9.1 (Continued)

Extended Epidemiology Review of Eating Disorders in Men From Brown and Keel (2023)

Author & Country	Diagnosis & 12-Month/Point Prevalence	Diagnosis & Lifetime Prevalence	N men	Reported Sample Characteristics
Silen et al. (2020) *Finland*		DSM-5 AN = .3 BN = .16 BED = .3 OSFED = .16 UFED = 1.6 Any ED = 2.4	638	Full Mixed Sex Sample Age = 21 – 26 years (M_{age} = 22.4 years) *Male participant demographics not reported*
Chua et al. (2022) *Malaysia*	DSM-5 AN = 0 BN = 1.5 BED = 0 AAN = 0 Sub-BN = 12.2 Sub-BED = 0 PD = 0 ARFID = 5.2		338	Male Participants (M_{age} = 36.09 years) Marital Status: Married 46%, Living with partner 1.4%, In relationship but not living with partner 5.1%, Widowed 2.5%, Divorced 2%, Separated .3%, Single 42.7% Ethnicity: Chinese 292%, Malay 63%, Indian 7.5%, Other .3% Income Group: Low 41.8%, Middle 26.1%, High 7.4%, Missing 24.7% Education: Primary .5%, Secondary 27.6%, Diploma/University 63.6%, Post graduate 8.2% Employment: Full time 61.9%, Part time 11.1%, Student 15%, Retired/Unemployed/Not working 9.7%, Other 2.3%

(Table continued on next page)

Table 9.1 (Continued)

Extended Epidemiology Review of Eating Disorders in Men From Brown and Keel (2023)

Author & Country	Diagnosis & 12-Month/Point Prevalence	Diagnosis & Lifetime Prevalence	N men	Reported Sample Characteristics
Nagl et al. (2016) *Germany*	DSM-IV AN or BN = 0 EDNOS = .5 Any ED = .8	DSM-IV AN or BN = .1 EDNOS = .7 Any ED = 1.5	1,543	Full Mixed Sex Sample Age = 14 – 24 years Male participant demographics not reported
Mohler-Kuo et al. (2016) *Switzerland*	DSM-IV AN = .03 BN =.5 BED = .3 Sub-BED = .5 Any ED = .8	DSM-IV AN = .2 BN = .9 BED = .7 Sub-BED = 1.6 Any ED = 1.5	4,423	Full Mixed Sex Sample Age = 15 – 60 years *Male participant demographics not reported*
Huang et al. (2019) *China*	DSM-IV AN < .01 BN < .01 Any ED < .01		14,784	Full Mixed Sex Sample 18+ years *Male participant demographics not reported*
Altwaijri et al. (2020) *Saudi Arabia*		DSM-IV AN = 0 BN = 3.1 BED = 2.7 Any ED = 6.3	4,004	Full Mix Sex Sample Age = 18 – 65 years *Male participant demographics not reported*

(Table continued on next page)

Table 9.1 (Continued)

Extended Epidemiology Review of Eating Disorders in Men From Brown and Keel (2023)

Author & Country	Diagnosis & 12-Month/Point Prevalence	Diagnosis & Lifetime Prevalence	N men	Reported Sample Characteristics
Bagaric et al. (2020) *South Australia*	DSM-5 BN = .4 BED = .03	DSM-5 BN = 1.21 BED = .74	1,453	Full Mixed Sex Sample Age = 15+ years (M_{age} = 53.9 years) *Male participant demographics not reported*
Feldman & Meyer (2007) *United States*		DSM-IV AN = 1 BN = 6.2 BED = 5.2 Any ED = 8.8 Sub-AN = 3.1 Sub-BN = 9.3 Sub-BED 9.3	SMM = 193	SMM Participants M_{age} = 32 years (18 – 59 years) Race/Ethnicity: Black/African American 33%, Latino 33%, White 34%

(Table continued on next page)

Table 9.1 (Continued)

Extended Epidemiology Review of Eating Disorders in Men From Brown and Keel (2023)

Author & Country	Diagnosis & 12-Month/Point Prevalence	Diagnosis & Lifetime Prevalence	*N* men	Reported Sample Characteristics
Diemer et al. (2018) *United States*	DSM-5 AN or BN = 4.1		FTM = 142	Transmasculine Participants Age = 18 – 75 years Race/Ethnicity: White non-Hispanic 80.2%, Black 3.5%, Hispanic 7.7%, Multiracial 6.3%, Other 2.3% Education: < High school 2.8%, High school diploma 12%, Some college 26.1%, Four year college 40.1%, Graduate school 22.5%
Diemer et al. (2015) *United States*	DSM-IV SMM Any ED = 2.06 Unsure Sexual Orientation Any ED = 3.66 Heterosexual Any ED = .55		SMM (*n* = 5,977) Unsure (n = 1,662) Heterosexual (*n* = 91,599)	Cisgender Male Participants Median Age = 20 years College Student = 100% *Male participant demographics not reported*

Notes. AN = Anorexia Nervosa, BN = Bulimia Nervosa, BED = Binge Eating Disorder, AAN = Atypical Anorexia Nervosa, PD = Purging Disorder, ARFID = Avoidant Restrictive Food Intake Disorder, OSFED = Other Specified Feeding/Eating Disorder, UFED = Unspecified Feeding/Eating Disorder, ED = Eating Disorder, EDNOS = Eating Disorder Not Otherwise Specified, SMM = Sexual Minority Male, FTM = Female to Male (transmasculine), DSM = Diagnostic & Statistical Manual.

Table 9.2

Extended Review of Eating Disorder Treatment Outcomes in Men From Brown and Keel (2023)

Author	Dx	Treatment (level of care)	Design	Sample Characteristics	Follow-up	*N* men (comparison)	Outcome
Burns & Crisp (1984)	AN	Refeeding, individual & family psychotherapy (Inpatient)	Naturalistic	*Not reported*	M = 8 years	27 (none)	Good: 12(44%) Intermediate: 7 (26%) Poor: 8 (30%)
Fichter et al. (1986)	AN	Not reported (inpatients/ outpatient)	Naturalistic	*Not reported*	3 years	22 (23 matched F)	Good: 9 (41%) Intermediate: 3 (14%) Poor: 4 (18%) M < F on ED pathology
Oyebode et al. (1988)	AN	Not reported (not reported)	Naturalistic	*Not reported*	9.22 years	13 (13 matched F)	Good: 2 (20%) Intermediate: 3 (30%) Poor: 5 (50%) M < F

(Table continued on next page)

Table 9.2 (Continued)

Extended Review of Eating Disorder Treatment Outcomes in Men From Brown and Keel (2023)

Author	Dx	Treatment (level of care)	Design	Sample Characteristics	Follow-up	*N* men (comparison)	Outcome
Deter et al. (1998)	AN	Not reported (inpatient/ outpatients)	Naturalistic	M_{age} = 17.7 years Marital Status: 82.4% single, 11.8% married, 5.9% other Education: ≤ high school 35.3% Class: Lower 5.9%, lower middle 17.7%, average middle 35.3%, upper middle 17.7%, upper class 23.5%	12 years	12 (91 F)	Good: 7(64%) Intermediate: 1 (9%) Poor: 0 (0%) M > F outcome; M = F ED symptoms
Herpertz-Dahlmann et al. (2001)	AN	Refeeding, individual, group, & family (inpatient)	Naturalistic	*Not reported*	10 years	7 (32 F)	Remitted: 7 (100%) M > F

(*Table continued on next page*)

Table 9.2 (Continued)

Extended Review of Eating Disorder Treatment Outcomes in Men From Brown and Keel (2023)

Author	Dx	Treatment (level of care)	Design	Sample Characteristics	Follow-up	*N* men (comparison)	Outcome
Grabhorn et al. (2003)	AN	Not reported (inpatient)	Naturalistic	M_{age} = 31 years Marital status: single 30.3%, married 69.7% Education: < high school 3% Employment: trade unemployed 0%	2.5 years	13 (342 F)	Successful outcome: 2 (29%) M = F
Bean et al. (2004)	AN	CBT (residential)	Naturalistic	M_{age} men = 18 (13 – 29 years) *Not reported*	1.25 years	7 (26 F)	> 85% IBW = 4 (57.1%) M > F weight gain
Fernandez-Aranda et al. (2009)	BN	Group CBT (outpatient)	Naturalistic	M_{age} = 22.4 years Single 100%	1 year	19 (150 F)	EOT Remained ill: 33.3% Follow-up Remained ill: 28.6% M = F

(*Table continued on next page*)

Table 9.2 (Continued)

Extended Review of Eating Disorder Treatment Outcomes in Men From Brown and Keel (2023)

Author	Dx	Treatment (level of care)	Design	Sample Characteristics	Follow-up	*N* men (comparison)	Outcome
Shingleton et al. (2015)	BED	CBT (outpatient)	Systematic review	M_{age} = 47.7 years Race/Ethnicity: Caucasian 89.4%, Black 4.8%, Hispanic/Latino 5.8% Education: <High school .5%, High school/GED 12%, Some college 30.3%, 4-year degree 33.2%, Post grad 18.8%, Missing 5.3%	EOT (12-24 wks)	208 (1,117 F)	n/a M = F remission and ED symptoms
Woodside & Kaplan (1994)	Mixed (7 AN, 8 BN)	Not reported (day hospital)	Naturalistic	*Not Reported*	EOT (8-14 wks)	15 (334 F)	Good: 4 (28.6%) Poor: 10 (71%) M = F

(Table continued on next page)

Table 9.2 (Continued)

Extended Review of Eating Disorder Treatment Outcomes in Men From Brown and Keel (2023)

Author	Dx	Treatment (level of care)	Design	Sample Characteristics	Follow-up	*N* men (comparison)	Outcome
Stoving et al. (2011)	Mixed (17 AN, 5 BN, 16 EDNOS)	Psychodynamic (inpatient)	Naturalistic	*Not reported*	4.6 years AN & EDNOS 6.2 years BN	38 (997 F)	AN Remission: 59% BN Remission: not reported EDNOS Remission: 77% M > F on time to remission
Weltzin et al. (2012)	Mixed (64 AN 24 BN, 23 EDNOS)	CBT (residential)	Naturalistic	M_{age} adults = 26.7 years M_{age} = 15.2 years Relationship status: Single 30.4%, Partnered 56.5%, Partnered-married 10.9% Sexual Orientation: Heterosexual 48.6%, Gay 5.4%, Unsure 1%, Unknown 45%	EOT only	111 (none)	Significant improvements in BMI, eating pathology (EDEQ-Global); EDE-Q scores fell to outpatient levels

(Table continued on next page)

Table 9.2 (Continued)

Extended Review of Eating Disorder Treatment Outcomes in Men From Brown and Keel (2023)

Author	Dx	Treatment (level of care)	Design	Sample Characteristics	Follow-up	*N* men (comparison)	Outcome
				Education/ Employment: High school 46.8%, College 28.8%, Working 2.7%, Unknown 21.6%			
Aguera et al. (2017) Spain	Mixed (39 AN, 40 BN, 14 BED, 38 OSFED)	CBT (inpatient)	Naturalistic	M_{age} = 26.7 years Civil Status: Single 74.8%, Married-partner. 19.1%, Divorced-separated 6.1% Education: Primary 44.3%, Secondary 39.7%, University 16% Employment Status: Unemployed 28.2%, employed 71.8%	EOT (16 wks)	131 (131 matched F)	AN: Full remission: 17 (43.6%) Partial Remission: 9 (23.2%) Non-remission: 5 (12.8%) BN: Full remission: 19 (47.5%) Partial Remission: 5 (12.5%) Non-remission: 0 (0%) BED: Full remission: 8 (57.1%) Partial Remission: 3 (21.4%) Non-remission: 0 (0%)

(Table continued on next page)

Table 9.2 (Continued)

Extended Review of Eating Disorder Treatment Outcomes in Men From Brown and Keel (2023)

Author	Dx	Treatment (level of care)	Design	Sample Characteristics	Follow-up	*N* men (comparison)	Outcome
							OSFED: Full remission: 17 (44.7%) Partial Remission: 8 (21.1%) Non-remission: 1 (2.6%) M > F on remission from BN & OSFED M = F AN & BED remission
Weltzin et al. (2015)	Mixed (16 AN, 8 BN, 10 EDNOS)	CBT (residential)	Naturalistic	M_{age} = 23.1 years *M* years of Education = 13.1 years Race: 97% Caucasian Relationship: 94% single	7 months	34 (111 F)	Significant improvement in health-related quality of life at EOT and follow-up M = F quality of life

(Table continued on next page)

Table 9.2 (Continued)

Extended Review of Eating Disorder Treatment Outcomes in Men From Brown and Keel (2023)

Author	Dx	Treatment (level of care)	Design	Sample Characteristics	Follow-up	*N* men (comparison)	Outcome
Strobel et al. (2019)	Mixed (119 AN, 60 BN)	CBT (inpatient)	Naturalistic	M_{age} = 27.49 – 34.60 years Education: < 12 years (53 – 71%) Relationship: No partner (58 – 73%), Never married (69 – 90%)	5.8 years AN years BN	179 (179 matched F)	AN Remained ill: 70 (60%) Remitted: 47 (40%) BN Remained ill: 33 (56%) Remitted: 26 (44%) M = F remission

Notes. Morgan-Russell criteria for AN are defined as 1) Good: body weight within 15% of average body weight, appropriate for age and height; 2) Intermediate: body weight within 15% of average weight for age and height but not constantly sustained; 3) Poor: body weight below 15% of average. AN = anorexia nervosa; BN = bulimia nervosa; BED = binge eating disorder; EDNOS = eating disorder not otherwise specified; CBT = cognitive behavioral therapy; M = male; F = female

Table 9.3

Extended Eating Disorder Prevention Programs for Men From Brown and Keel (2023) Review

Study	*N* men	Program	Study Design	Sessions (Duration)	Sample Characteristics	Follow-Up	Results Summary
Brown & Keel (2015) *United States*	87	PRIDE Body Project	RCT (Tx v. Ax Only)	2 sessions (2 hrs/session)	M_{age} = 21.48 years (18 – 30 years) Sexual Orientation: Gay 100% Race/Ethnicity: Caucasian 56.9%, Hispanic/Latino 22.2%, Black 16.7%, Indigenous American 2.8%, "Other" 1.4% Education: Current colleges student 91.7%	1-month	• Greater decreases in body dissatisfaction, drive for muscularity, self-& partner-objectification, dietary restraint, and bulimic symptoms at post and 1-month follow-up • Body-ideal internalization was lower post-intervention
Brown et al. (2017) *United States*	93	Body Project: More than Muscles	RCT (Tx v. Ax Only)	2 sessions (2 hrs/session)	M_{age} = 20.37 years (18 – 27 years) Sexual Orientation: Heterosexual 88.1% Race/Ethnicity: Caucasian 55.9%, Hispanic/Latino 17.2%, Black 9.7%, Asian 7.5%, "Other" 9.7% Education: College Student 95.7%	1-month	• Greater decreases in body-ideal internalization, dietary restraint, drive for muscularity, bulimic symptoms, and MD symptoms at post and 1-month follow-up • Greater improvements in body fat & muscularity dissatisfaction at 1-month follow-up

(Table continued on next page)

Table 9.3 (Continued)

Extended Eating Disorder Prevention Programs for Men From Brown and Keel (2023) Review

Study	*N* men	Program	Study Design	Sessions (Duration)	Sample Characteristics	Follow-Up	Results Summary
Jankowski et al. (2017) *English*	110	Body Project M	Non-randomized Control Trial (Tx v. Ax Only)	2 sessions (1.5 hrs/ session)	M_{age} = 20.67 – 20.81 Education: Current undergraduates 100% Sexualized 7.8 – 10.2% Racialized 8.5 – 17.6%	3-month	• Greater improvements in body-ideal internalization and muscularity dissatisfaction at post-intervention. • No significant differences in eating pathology
Blashill et al. (2017) *United States*	44	CBT-Body Image Self-Care	RCT (Tx v. Enhanced TAU)	12 sessions (50 min/ session)	M_{age} = 46.18 years Race: Black 34.1%, White 63.6%, Native American 4.5%, Other 4.5% 22.7% Latinx Sexual Orientation: 97.7% gay, 2.3% bisexual Education: ≤ HS 23.8%, partial college 34.1%, college graduate 43.2%	6-month	• Body image, depressive symptoms, and global functioning significantly improved through 6-month follow-up

(Table continued on next page)

Table 9.3 (Continued)

Extended Eating Disorder Prevention Programs for Men From Brown and Keel (2023) Review

Study	*N* men	Program	Study Design	Sessions (Duration)	Sample Characteristics	Follow-Up	Results Summary
Almeida et al. (2021) *Brazil*	180	Body Project: More than Muscles	RCT (Tx v. Ax Only)	2 sessions (2 hrs/session)	M_{age} = 20.51 year Race/Ethnicity: White 32.2%, Yellow .6%, Black 9.4%, Brown 57.2%, Indigenous .6% Relationship Status: Single 97.7% Income: Low 37.2%	6-month	• Greater improvements in body appreciation post-intervention • Greater improvements in body-ideal internalization, disordered eating, MD symptoms, drive for muscularity, body appreciation, and muscularity and body fat dissatisfaction through 6-month follow-up
Perelman, et al. (2022) *United States*	112	Male Athlete Body Project	RCT (Tx v. Ax Only)	3 sessions (80 min/ session)	M_{age} = 19.47 College Athletes 100% Race/Ethnicity: Asian 7.5%, Black 15.1%, White 73.1%, "Other" 4.3%, Hispanic/Latino 6.5%, Sexual Orientation: Heterosexual 95.7%	1-month	• Greater improvements in body area satisfaction, drive for muscularity, and athletic ideal internalization post-intervention • Greater improvements in body area satisfaction, drive for muscularity, and performance-enhancing substance use at 1-month follow-up

(Table continued on next page)

Table 9.3 (Continued)

Extended Eating Disorder Prevention Programs for Men From Brown and Keel (2023) Review

Study	*N* men	Program	Study Design	Sessions (Duration)	Sample Characteristics	Follow-Up	Results Summary
Kilpela et al. (2016) *United States*	70	The Body Project 4 All	RCT (Tx v. F Only v. Ax Only)	2 sessions (2 hrs/session)	M_{age} = 19.9 years Undergraduate Students 100% 76.2% Caucasian	6-month	• Lower negative affect post-intervention in the DB group compared to men in assessment only condition but not at 2- or 6-month follow-up • BPSS-R greater improvement in DB condition compared to assessment only and maintained at 2- and 6-month follow-up • Muscularity attitudes lower in DB group compared to assessment only post and 2-month follow-up only • Attitudes towards low body fat post-intervention, 2- and 6-month follow-up

Notes. RCT = randomized controlled trial; CBT = cognitive behavioral therapy; F = female; Ax = assessment; Tx = treatment; TAU = treatment as usual.

REFERENCES

Agüera, Z., Sánchez, I., Granero, R., Riesco, N., Steward, T., Martín-Romera, V., Jimenez-Muricia, S., Romero, X., Caroleo, M., Segura-Garcia, C., Menchon, J.M., & Fernández-Aranda, F. (2017). Short-term treatment outcomes and dropout risk in men and women with eating disorders. *European Eating Disorders Review, 25*(4), 293–301. https://doi.org/10.1002/erv.2519

Allen, K. L., Byrne, S. M., Oddy, W. H., & Crosby, R. D. (2013). DSM–IV–TR and DSM-5 eating disorders in adolescents: Prevalence, stability, and psychosocial correlates in a population-based sample of male and female adolescents. *Journal of Abnormal Psychology, 122*(3), 720–732. https://doi.org/10.1037/a0034004

Almeida, M., Brown, T. A., Campos, P. F., Amaral, A. C. S., & de Carvalho, P. H. B. (2021). Dissonance-based eating disorder prevention delivered in-person after an online training: A randomized controlled trial for Brazilian men with body dissatisfaction. *International Journal of Eating Disorders, 54*(3), 293–304. https://doi.org/10.1002/eat.23423

Altwaijri, Y. A., Al-Subaie, A. S., Al-Habeeb, A., Bilal, L., Al-Desouki, M., Aradati, M., ... & Kessler, R. C. (2020). Lifetime prevalence and age-of-onset distributions of mental disorders in the Saudi National Mental Health Survey. *International Journal of Methods in Psychiatric Research, 29*(3), e1836. https://doi.org/10.1002/mpr.1836

Alvarez, J. C., Denning, D. M., Castro Lebron, J., Ho, V., Chen, S., & Brown, T. A. (2023). Differential effects of community involvement on eating disorder prevention outcomes in sexual minority men. *Eating Disorders: The Journal of Treatment and Prevention*. Advance online publication. https://doi.org/10.1080/10640266.2024.2319946

American Psychiatric Association. (2013). *Diagnostic and statistical manual of mental disorders* (5th ed.). https://doi.org/10.1176/appi.books.9780890425596

Atwood, M. E., & Friedman, A. (2020). A systematic review of enhanced cognitive behavioral therapy (CBT-E) for eating disorders. *International Journal of Eating Disorders, 53*(3), 311–330. https://doi.org/10.1002/eat.23206

Bagaric, M., Touyz, S., Heriseanu, A., Conti, J., & Hay, P. (2020). Are bulimia nervosa and binge eating disorder increasing? Results of a population-based study of lifetime prevalence and lifetime prevalence by age in South Australia. *European Eating Disorders Review, 28*(3), 260–268. https://doi.org/10.1002/erv.2726

Bean, P., Loomis, C. C., Timmel, P., Hallinan, P., Moore, S., Mammel, J., & Weltzin, T. (2004). Outcome variables for anorexic males and females one year after discharge from residential treatment. *Journal of Addictive Diseases, 23*(2), 83–94. https://doi.org/10.1300/J069v23n02_06

Becker, C. B., & Stice, E. (2017). From efficacy to effectiveness to broad implementation: Evolution of the Body Project. *Journal of Consulting and Clinical Psychology, 85*(8), 767–782. https://doi.org/10.1037/ccp0000204

Ben-Porath, D., Duthu, F., Luo, T., Gonidakis, F., Compte, E. J., & Wisniewski, L. (2020). Dialectical behavioral therapy: an update and review of the existing treatment models adapted for adults with eating disorders. *Eating Disorders, 28*(2), 101–121.

Blashill, A. J., Safren, S. A., Wilhelm, S., Jampel, J., Taylor, S. W., O'Cleirigh, C., & Mayer, K. H. (2017). Cognitive behavioral therapy for body image and self-care (CBT-BISC) in sexual minority men living with HIV: A randomized controlled trial. *Health Psychology, 36*(10), 937–946. https://doi.org/10.1037/hea0000505

Bomben, R., Robertson, N., & Allan. S. (2022). Barriers to help-seeking for eating disorders in men: a mixed-methods systematic review. *Psychology of Men Masculinity, 23*(2), 183–196.

Brown, T. A., & Keel, P. K. (2015). A randomized controlled trial of a peer co-led dissonance-based eating disorder prevention program for gay men. *Behaviour Research and Therapy, 74*, 1–10. https://doi.org/10.1016/j.brat.2015.08.008

Brown, T. A., Forney, K. J., Pinner, D., & Keel, P. K. (2017). A randomized controlled trial of The Body Project: More Than Muscles for men with body dissatisfaction. *International Journal of Eating Disorders, 50*(8), 873–883. https://doi.org/10.1002/eat.22724

Brown, T. A. & Keel, P. K. (2023). Eating disorders in men. *Annual Review of Clinical Psychology*, 19, 177–205.

Brown, T. A., Cusack, A., Anderson, L. K., Trim, J., Nakamura, T., Trunko, M. E., & Kaye, W. H. (2018). Efficacy of a partial hospital programme for adults with eating disorders. *European Eating Disorders Review, 26*(3), 241–252.

Burns, T., & Crisp, A. H. (1984). Outcome of anorexia nervosa in males. *The British Journal of Psychiatry, 145*(3), 319–325. https://doi.org/10.1192/bjp.145.3.319

Calzo, J. P., Blashill, A. J., Brown, T. A., & Argenal, R. L. (2017). Eating disorders and disordered weight and shape control behaviors in sexual minority populations. *Current Psychiatry Reports, 19*(8), 1–10. https://doi.org/10.1007/s11920-017-0801-y

Carta, M. G., Preti, A., Moro, M. F., Aguglia, E., Balestrieri, M., Caraci, F., Dell'Osso, L., Di Sciascio, G., Drago, F., Faravelli, C., Hardoy, M.C., D'Aloja, E., Cossu, G., Calo, S., Palumbo, G., & Bhugra, D. (2014). Eating disorders as a public health issue: Prevalence and attributable impairment of quality of life in an Italian community sample. *International Review of Psychiatry, 26*(4), 486–492. https://doi.org/10.3109/09540261.2014.927753

Chua, S. N., Fitzsimmons-Craft, E. E., Austin, S. B., Wilfley, D. E., & Taylor, C. B. (2022). Estimated prevalence of eating disorders in Malaysia based on a diagnostic screen. *International Journal of Eating Disorders*, 55(6), 763–775. https://doi.org/10.1002/eat.23711

Denning, D. M., Perry, T. R., Reilly, E. E., Berner, L. A., Velkoff, E. A., Kaye, W. H., ... & Brown, T. A. (2022). Associations of suicide risk with emotional reactivity, dysregulation, and eating disorder treatment outcomes. *Suicide and Life-Threatening Behavior, 52*(6), 1126–1139.

Denning, D. M., Ciotti, V., Gioia, A., Viranda, T., Reilly, E. E., Berner, L. A., Velkoff, E. A., Anderson, L. K., Kaye, W. H., Wierenga, C. E., & Brown, T. A. (2023). Effects of borderline personality disorder symptoms on dialectical behavior therapy outcomes for eating disorders. *Personality Disorders: Theory, Research, and Treatment*. https://doi.org/10.1037/per0000641

Deter, H. C., Köpp, W., Zipfel, S., & Herzog, W. (1998). Male anorexia nervosa patients in long-term follow-up. *Der Nervenarzt*, *69*(5), 419–426. https://doi.org/10.1007/s001150050291

Diemer, E. W., Grant, J. D., Munn-Chernoff, M. A., Patterson, D. A., & Duncan, A. E. (2015). Gender identity, sexual orientation, and eating-related pathology in a national sample of college students. *Journal of Adolescent Health*, *57*(2), 144–149. https://doi.org/10.1089/trgh.2017.0043

Diemer, E. W., White Hughto, J. M., Gordon, A. R., Guss, C., Austin, S. B., & Reisner, S. L. (2018). Beyond the binary: Differences in eating disorder prevalence by gender identity in a transgender sample. *Transgender Health*, *3*(1), 17–23. https://doi.org/10.1016/j.jadohealth.2015.03.003

Donahue, J. M., DeBenedetto, A. M., Wierenga, C. E., Kaye, W. H., & Brown, T. A. (2020). Examining day hospital treatment outcomes for sexual minority patients with eating disorders. *International Journal of Eating Disorders*, *53*(10), 1657–1666.

Fairburn, C. G. (2008). *Cognitive behavior therapy and eating disorders*. Guilford Press.

Feldman, M. B., & Meyer, I. H. (2007). Eating disorders in diverse lesbian, gay, and bisexual populations. *International Journal of Eating Disorders*, *40*(3), 218–226. https://doi.org/10.1002/eat.20360

Fursland, A., & Watson, H. J. (2015). Enhanced Cognitive–Behavioral Therapy approach to counseling clients with eating disorders. In A.F. Choate (Eds). *Eating Disorders and Obesity: A Counselor's Guide to Prevention and Treatment*, 285–308. https://doi.org/10.1002/9781119221708.ch13

Fernández-Aranda, F., Krug, I., Jiménez-Murcia, S., Granero, R., Núñez, A., Penelo, E., Solano, R., & Treasure, J. (2009). Male eating disorders and therapy: A controlled pilot study with one year follow-up. *Journal of Behavior Therapy and Experimental Psychiatry*, *40*(3), 479–486. https://doi.org/10.1016/j.jbtep.2009.06.004

Fichter, M. M., Daser, C., & Postpischil, F. (1986). Anorexic syndromes in the male. In G. I. Szmukler, P. D. Slade, P. Harris, D. Benton, G. F. M. Russell (Eds.), *Anorexia nervosa and bulimic disorders* (pp. 305–313). Pergamon. https://doi.org/10.1016/B978-0-08-032704-4.50037-1

Grabhorn, R., Köpp, W., Gitzinger, I., von Wietersheim, J., & Kaufhold, J. (2003). Differences between female and male patients with eating disorders: Results of a multicenter study on eating disorders (MZ-Ess). *Psychotherapie, Psychosomatik, Medizinische Psychologie*, *53*(1), 15–22. https://doi.org/10.1055/s-2003-36479

Herpertz-Dahlmann, B., Hebebrand, J., Müller, B., Herpertz, S., Heussen, N., & Remschmidt, H. (2001). Prospective 10-year follow-up in adolescent anorexia nervosa—course, outcome, psychiatric comorbidity, and psychosocial adaptation. *The Journal of Child Psychology and Psychiatry and Allied Disciplines*, *42*(5), 603–612. https://doi.org/10.1111/1469-7610.00756

Huang, Y., Wang, Y. U., Wang, H., Liu, Z., Yu, X., Yan, J., Yu, Y., Kou, C., Xu, X., Lu, J., Wang, Z., He, S., Xu, Y, He, Y., Li, T., Gui, W., Tian, H., Xu, G., Xu, X., … & Wu, Y. (2019). Prevalence of mental disorders in China: A cross-sectional epidemiological study. *The Lancet Psychiatry*, *6*(3), 211–224. https://doi.org/10.1016/S2215-0366(18)30511-X

Hudson, J. I., Hiripi, E., Pope, H. G., Jr., & Kessler, R. C. (2007). The prevalence and correlates of eating disorders in the National Comorbidity Survey Replication. *Biological Psychiatry*, *61*(3), 348–358. https://doi.org/10.1016/j.biopsych.2006.03.040

Jankowski, G. S., Diedrichs, P. C., Atkinson, M. J., Fawkner, H., Gough, B., & Halliwell, E. (2017). A pilot controlled trial of a cognitive dissonance-based body dissatisfaction intervention with young British men. *Body Image*, *23*, 93–102. https://doi.org/10.1016/j.bodyim.2017.08.006

Juarascio, A., Shaw, J., Forman, E., Timko, C. A., Herbert, J., Butryn, M., Bunnell, D., Matteucci, A., & Lowe, M. (2013). Acceptance and commitment therapy as a novel treatment for eating disorders: An initial test of efficacy and mediation. *Behavior modification*, *37*(4), 459–489.

Kilpela, L. S., Blomquist, K., Verzijl, C., Wilfred, S., Beyl, R., & Becker, C. B. (2016). The body project 4 all: A pilot randomized controlled trial of a mixed-gender dissonance-based body image program. *International Journal of Eating Disorders*, *49*(6), 591–602. https://doi.org/10.1002/eat.22562

Lavender, J. M., Brown, T. A., & Murray, S. B. (2017). Men, muscles, and eating disorders: An overview of traditional and muscularity-oriented disordered eating. *Current Psychiatry Reports*, *19*(6), 1–7. https://doi.org/10.1007/s11920-017-0787-5

Mohler-Kuo, M., Schnyder, U., Dermota, P., Wei, W., & Milos, G. (2016). The prevalence, correlates, and help-seeking of eating disorders in Switzerland. *Psychological Medicine*, *46*(13), 2749–2758. https://doi.org/10.1017/S0033291716001136

Murray, S. B., & Griffiths, S. (2015). Adolescent muscle dysmorphia and family-based treatment: A case report. *Clinical Child Psychology and Psychiatry*, *20*(2), 324–330. https://doi.org/10.1177/1359104514521639

Murray, S. B., Nagata, J. M., Griffiths, S., Calzo, J. P., Brown, T. A., Mitchison, D., Blashill, A.J., & Mond, J. M. (2017). The enigma of male eating disorders: A critical review and synthesis. *Clinical Psychology Review*, *57*, 1–11. https://doi.org/10.1016/j.cpr.2017.08.001

Nagl, M., Jacobi, C., Paul, M., Beesdo-Baum, K., Höfler, M., Lieb, R., & Wittchen, H. U. (2016). Prevalence, incidence, and natural course of anorexia and bulimia nervosa among adolescents and young adults. *European Child & Adolescent Psychiatry*, *25*(8), 903–918. https://doi.org/10.1007/s00787-015-0808-z

Oyebode, F., Boodhoo, J. A., & Schapira, K. (1988). Anorexia nervosa in males: Clinical features and outcome. *International Journal of Eating Disorders*, 7(1), 121–124. https://doi.org/10.1002/1098-108X(198801)7:1<121::AID-EAT2260070113>3.0.CO;2-U

Pachankis, J. E., Clark, K. A., Burton, C. L., Hughto, J. M. W., Bränström, R., & Keene, D. E. (2020). Sex, status, competition, and exclusion: Intraminority stress from within the gay community and gay and bisexual men's mental health. *Journal of Personality and Social Psychology, 119*(3), 713–740. https://doi.org/10.1037/pspp0000282

Pachankis, J. E., & Hatzenbuehler, M. L. (2013). The social development of contingent self-worth in sexual minority young men: An empirical investigation of the "Best Little Boy in the World" hypothesis. *Basic and Applied Social Psychology, 35*(2), 176–190. https://doi.org/10.1080/01973533.2013.764304

Perelman, H., Schwartz, N., Yeoward-Dodson, J., Quiñones, I. C., Murray, M. F., Dougherty, E. N., Townsel, R., Arthur-Cameselle, J., & Haedt-Matt, A. A. (2022). Reducing eating disorder risk among male athletes: A randomized controlled trial investigating the male athlete body project. *International Journal of Eating Disorders, 55*(2), 193–206. https://doi.org/10.1002/eat.23665

Preti, A., de Girolamo, G., Vilagut, G., Alonso, J., de Graaf, R., Bruffaerts, R., Demyttenaere, K., Pinto-Meza, A., Haro, J.M., Morosini, P., & ESEMeD-WMH Investigators. (2009). The epidemiology of eating disorders in six European countries: Results of the ESEMeD-WMH project. *Journal of Psychiatric Research, 43*(14), 1125–1132. https://doi.org/10.1016/j.jpsychires.2009.04.003

Shepherd, B. F., Denning, D. M., Elbe, C. I., Maki, J. L., & Brochu, P. M. (2023). Status, sexual capital, and intraminority body stigma in a size-diverse sample of gay men. *Body Image, 45*, 219–228. https://doi.org/10.1016/j.bodyim.2023.03.005

Shingleton, R. M., Thompson-Brenner, H., Thompson, D. R., Pratt, E. M., & Franko, D. L. (2015). Gender differences in clinical trials of binge eating disorder: An analysis of aggregated data. *Journal of Consulting and Clinical Psychology, 83*(2), 382–386. https://doi.org/10.1037/a0038849

Silén, Y., Sipilä, P. N., Raevuori, A., Mustelin, L., Marttunen, M., Kaprio, J., & Keski-Rahkonen, A. (2020). DSM-5 eating disorders among adolescents and young adults in Finland: A public health concern. *International Journal of Eating Disorders, 53*(5), 790–801. https://doi.org/10.1002/eat.23236

Smink, F. R., Van Hoeken, D., & Hoek, H. W. (2012). Epidemiology of eating disorders: Incidence, prevalence and mortality rates. *Current Psychiatry Reports, 14*(4), 406–414. https://doi.org/10.1007/s11920-012-0282-y

Stice, E., Mazotti, L., Weibel, D., & Agras, W. S. (2000). Dissonance prevention program decreases thin-ideal internalization, body dissatisfaction, dieting, negative affect, and bulimic symptoms: A preliminary experiment. *International Journal of Eating Disorders, 27*(2), 206–217.

Stice, E., Shaw, H., & Marti, C. N. (2007). A meta-analytic review of eating disorder prevention programs: Encouraging findings. *Annual Review of Clinical Psychology, 3*, 207–231. https://doi.org/10.1146/annurev.clinpsy.3.022806.091447

Støving, R. K., Andries, A., Brixen, K., Bilenberg, N., & Hørder, K. (2011). Gender differences in outcome of eating disorders: A retrospective cohort study. *Psychiatry Research, 186*(2–3), 362–366. https://doi.org/10.1016/j.psychres.2010.08.005

Strobel, C., Quadflieg, N., Naab, S., Voderholzer, U., & Fichter, M. M. (2019). Long-term outcomes in treated males with anorexia nervosa and bulimia nervosa—A prospective, gender-matched study. *International Journal of Eating Disorders, 52*(12), 1353–1364. https://doi.org/10.1002/eat.23151

Tylka, T. L. (2011). Refinement of the tripartite influence model for men: Dual body image pathways to body change behaviors. *Body Image, 8*(3), 199–207. https://doi.org/10.1016/j.bodyim.2011.04.008

Udo, T., & Grilo, C. M. (2018). Prevalence and correlates of DSM-5–defined eating disorders in a nationally representative sample of US adults. *Biological Psychiatry, 84*(5), 345–354. https://doi.org/10.1016/j.biopsych.2018.03.014

Weltzin, T. E., Cornella-Carlson, T., Fitzpatrick, M. E., Kennington, B., Bean, P., & Jefferies, C. (2012). Treatment issues and outcomes for males with eating disorders. *Eating Disorders, 20*(5), 444–459. https://doi.org/10.1080/10640266.2012.715527

Weltzin, T., Bean, P., Klosterman, E., Lee, H. J., & Welk-Richards, R. (2015). Sex differences in the effects of residential treatment on the quality of life of eating disorder patients. *Eating and Weight Disorders-Studies on Anorexia, Bulimia and Obesity, 20*(3), 301–310. https://doi.org/10.1007/s40519-014-0162-z

Woodside, D. B., & Kaplan, A. S. (1994). Day hospital treatment in males with eating disorders—Response and comparison to females. *Journal of Psychosomatic Research, 38*(5), 471–475. https://doi.org/10.1016/0022-3999(94)90108-2

ENDNOTE

1. Previous research suggests that appearance-based community involvement activities such as going out to bars and clubs are associated with greater body dissatisfaction in SMM (Alvarez et al., 2023). Moreover, experiences of intraminority body stigma (i.e., negative body comments from other SMM) are more commonly experienced by SMM who are young men of color (Shepherd et al., 2023).

CHAPTER 10

EATING DISORDERS IN THE ORTHODOX JEWISH COMMUNITY

Devorah Levinson, Sara Fruchter, Katherine L. Loeb, and Catherine R. Drury

In 2010, media outlets began to report a concerning increase in eating disorder (ED) pathology among Orthodox Jewish adolescent females (Kennedy, 2010; Rabin, 2011). Within the more Orthodox denominations of Judaism, some assume that the insularity of Orthodox community members, their separation from secular society, and their level of religious observance confer protection from ED risk. Even when EDs are identified in such communities, stigma associated with mental illness and distrust of secular institutions make Orthodox Jewish individuals less likely to seek mental health treatment (Popovsky, 2010; Schnall et al., 2014). As a result, the Jewish community, specifically the ultra-Orthodox (UO) Jewish community, remains an underserved population in need of specialized ED services (Schnall et al., 2014). This chapter offers insights and recommendations for increasing access to care for Jewish populations and adapting intervention efforts to meet Jewish patients' religious, cultural, and spiritual needs.

Existing literature on EDs in the Jewish community is lacking in breadth, depth, and specificity, particularly with regard to the UO Jewish sect. This chapter will include four main sections. The first will provide an overview

Counseling Individuals With Eating Disorders: An Intersectional Approach, pp. 227–250

of the research that has been conducted in this area, with a particular focus on its methodological limitations. The second section will review data from Relief Resources, a mental health organization that was founded specifically to increase knowledge of and access to treatment among UO Jewish individuals, thereby adding valuable information to the little that is known about EDs in this community. The third section will focus on cultural considerations for working with a UO population, informed by qualitative information gathered from relief resources as well as current research. We will intersperse this section with case material and examples of Orthodox Jewish patients in ED treatment. The final section reviews ED prevention programs implemented in the UO community. By exploring EDs in the Jewish community through these different lenses (i.e., quantitative, descriptive, and clinical), this chapter will paint a fuller picture of what is known, and which areas warrant further investigation.

WHAT IS AN "ORTHODOX" JEW?

It is important to note that the Jewish community includes a variety of religious sub-denominations ranging from Orthodox to secular, with the Orthodox sect of Judaism including both the ultra-Orthodox/Haredi community and the modern Orthodox (MO) community. Although there are many Jewish laws and customs, Jews who identify as "Orthodox"' observe the following core components: *Kashrus*[1] (dietary restrictions), the Sabbath (Jewish day of rest on the seventh day of the week), and laws of family purity (i.e., laws pertaining to the sexual relationship between a husband and wife). While the UO follow a very strict interpretation of Jewish law and separate themselves from secular society, MO populations adhere to the core Jewish laws and traditions (to varying degrees) while also assimilating into secular society. At the other end of the spectrum, secular or traditional Jewish individuals are less observant of the Jewish law and very assimilated into the secular world (Latzer et al., 2008), with some identifying as Reform, Conservative, or "culturally Jewish" such that they acknowledge their Jewish heritage but are not religious. Cultural differences between these groups relevant to ED risk, prevention, and treatment will be clarified throughout this chapter.

RESEARCH ON EATING DISORDERS IN ORTHODOX JUDAISM

Prevalence

Few studies have examined ED prevalence rates among Jewish populations in the United States (U.S.). Although the results of this limited body of literature suggest a higher ED prevalence among Jewish individuals compared to the general population, these conclusions were drawn from very small samples (Rayworth et al., 2004; Sykes et al., 1988). More often, researchers have explored risk for disordered eating among Jewish females by administering self-report measures (e.g., Eating Attitudes Test-26) and comparing the scores of non-clinical Jewish samples to those of non-Jewish controls or previously established norms (Latzer et al., 2019; Pinhas et al., 2008). The results of these studies are inconsistent, with some finding higher rates of disordered eating problems in Jewish samples and others lower. The variability of these findings appears to be related to a myriad of factors, including heterogeneity in participants' religious observance level, age, and geographic location (Latzer et al., 2007, 2008; Lokech-Fisher, 2016).

Pinhas and colleagues (2008) compared rates of disordered eating among two groups of Canadian adolescents (male and female): Jewish individuals of varied religious observance levels and non-Jewish individuals. They found significantly higher rates of disordered eating in Jewish adolescent females, with 25% of Jewish adolescent females and 18% of non-Jewish adolescent females determined to be at risk for an ED. Jewish adolescent males also reported significantly higher rates of dieting activity than non-Jewish adolescent males; however, there was no difference between Jewish and non-Jewish adolescent males regarding rates of overall eating pathology.

Many studies of ED pathology in the Jewish community have been conducted in Israel, where there are generally higher rates of ED symptoms than in western countries (Latzer et al., 2008). Israel has a large Jewish population (i.e., 73% Jewish with 12% identifying as UO), which makes it conducive to studying ED risk in this religious demographic (Central Bureau of Statistics, 2020; Malach & Cahaner, 2021). However, sociocultural differences between Israel and Western countries might account for differences in ED pathology, rather than religion. As evidence, a greater percentage of secular females (adolescent and adult) in Israel score in the high-risk category for disordered eating (Latzer et al., 2019; Latzer & Tzischinsky, 2003) compared to their U.S. counterparts (Latzer et al., 2015; Loketch-Fisher, 2016).

Risk and Resilience

Most of the research on EDs in Jewish populations has centered around the question of whether religion acts as a protective factor in relation to ED risk, with mixed results. Several studies have found that greater religiosity is associated with fewer ED symptoms and more positive body image (Handelzalts et al., 2017; Latzer et al., 2007, 2015; Loketch-Fisher, 2016).

Gluck and Gelieber (2002) compared Orthodox and secular American Jewish college students and found that secular Jewish females were more likely to fear becoming fat and engage in bulimic behaviors than Orthodox Jewish females. In contrast, some studies reported no relationship between the level of religious observance and ED pathology among Jewish women (Aival Naveh et al., 2021; Feinson & Meir, 2012; Frenkel et al., 2018), and one study found that UO Jewish females endorsed more ED symptoms than MO Jewish females (Lazar-Feigenbaum, 2014).

This conflicting literature highlights what is likely a complex relationship between ED pathology and religiosity, and the need to investigate different aspects of this relationship. Based on cross-sectional research, it appears that faith and religiosity can positively or negatively correlate with ED pathology, depending on an individual's motivations for religion and the nature of their relationship with God (Akrawi et al., 2015; Bachner-Melman & Zohar, 2019; Weinberger et al., 2016). Among Jewish women, intrinsic religious beliefs (i.e., an internal and personal relationship with God) are associated with lower levels of disordered eating than extrinsic religious beliefs (i.e., religious commitments motivated by social pressures and expectations; Weinberger et al., 2018). Furthermore, expressing frustration with God and religion during challenging times (or, negative religious coping) is associated with increased ED pathology among adolescent Orthodox Jewish women, while positive religious coping, or finding meaning through religion, appears not to be associated with ED pathology (Latzer et al., 2015).

Jewish laws of modesty have also been proposed as a possible ED protective factor for the members of the Orthodox Jewish community who observe these laws. These modesty laws (i.e., *Tznius*) are based on the concept of humility and require women to dress and conduct themselves in ways that do not attract unnecessary attention. For example, women are typically required to conceal parts of their bodies by wearing stockings and skirts that cover their knees, shirts that cover their collarbone and elbows, and a hair covering if they are married. According to objectification theory (Fredrickson & Roberts, 1997), laws of modesty may protect women from EDs by covering their bodies such that they are less likely to feel objectified (Bachner-Melman & Zohar, 2019; Tiggemann, 2013). Additionally, it has been suggested that high levels of religiosity help women internalize values of modesty over external beauty ideals (Lazter et al., 2007), thereby making them less susceptible to the potential negative effects of those ideals. For example, Loketch-Fischer (2016) found that higher levels of modesty were associated with lower levels of body shame and fewer ED symptoms in Jewish groups that endorsed greater religiosity. This study encompassed a range of religious observance among their participant pool, including UO women. Other researchers have hypothesized that modesty laws may increase an individual's risk for EDs by causing feelings of shame and guilt regarding their body and sexual urges (Bachner-Melman & Zohar, 2019; Fisherman, 2016; Forta, 2020). Further research is needed to better clarify the ways in which Jewish teachings surrounding modesty relate to women's feelings about their bodies.

The role of food in Jewish religion and culture and its relationship to ED pathology also warrants additional study. Many Jewish holidays and customs center around meals, which women are typically responsible for preparing and serving. This ongoing exposure to food and the strict laws surrounding kosher food preparation may affect the progression and manifestation of ED symptoms (Bachner-Melman & Zohar, 2019). Several authors have also proposed that the focus on conformity in Orthodox Jewish communities may lead some women to assert their own individuality and control through food, especially during adolescence (Bachner-Melman & Zohar, 2019; Forta, 2020). At the same time, Jewish law emphasizes the importance of ritualized, routine, and mindful eating, an approach that could regulate eating behavior (Shafran & Wolowelsky, 2013). Before and after eating, Jewish individuals are required to say blessings (i.e., *Brachos)* as a way of thanking God for their food, praising God for his creations, and asking permission from God to eat. Thus, eating is a spiritual act through which individuals can connect with their religion and show gratitude for the food they eat. Future research should explore how these Jewish customs surrounding food may influence disordered eating behaviors in the Jewish community.

Pressure to fulfill multiple roles has been hypothesized as another factor that may increase ED risk among Jewish women. For example, MO women encounter dual expectations from both the secular and religious worlds, as they are more readily exposed to secular beauty standards and may value career and academic success, but also must fulfill religious standards surrounding marriage and motherhood. This pressure for perfection in multiple roles and responsibilities has been termed the "superwoman ideal," and is associated with increased ED risk among Orthodox Jewish women (Weinberger et al., 2018). Furthermore, in many UO households, women are expected to have many children and manage the daily household tasks while also being the primary financial provider for the family so their husbands can study the *Torah* (i.e., Jewish texts) full time (Frenkel et al., 2018). Frenkel and colleagues (2018) examined the 'superwoman ideal' in relation to EDs and found that UO Jewish women who endorsed internalization of this ideal reported higher levels of ED pathology.

Some preliminary research has begun to explore the relationship between religious fervency and disordered eating symptoms amongst men. Fisher (2013) considered three case studies of young Orthodox Jewish men who experienced rapid weight loss related to religious zeal. These men had interpreted a Jewish law too strictly (i.e., that a person should not indulge themselves) and began to limit their food intake to meet this religious demand. These behaviors are also consistent with religious scrupulosity, a subtype of obsessive-compulsive disorder (OCD) involving religious or moral obsessions (Greenberg & Huppert, 2010). As there is comorbidity between OCD and EDs (Mandelli et al., 2020), additional information would be needed to clarify whether the weight loss these men experienced was strictly related to religious scrupulosity or a comorbid ED diagnosis.

Limitations in Existing Research

It is difficult to draw broad conclusions from the current literature on EDs and Jewish populations due to the many subgroups within the Jewish community and further divides within each subgroup according to geographic location, religious observance level, and specific belief system (Popovsky, 2010). For example, even within the UO Jewish community, there is a wide spectrum of religiosity and great variability in the customs followed by each sub-group (e.g., Yeshivish, Chabad, Hassidic; Loketch-Fischer, 2016). Thus, research findings in one Jewish community may not generalize to another.

Currently, little is known about ED prevalence and risk among UO Jewish populations, with many studies recruiting participants who identify as being on the Orthodox spectrum instead of UO specifically (Gluck & Geliebter, 2002; Pinhas et al., 2008). The majority of studies describe participants as "Orthodox" without specifying the subgroup of orthodoxy of their sample or defining how this term is being used. Additionally, it is difficult to conduct ED research in UO communities due to the insularity of the community and distrust regarding working with secular institutions (Bachner-Melman, & Zohar, 2019). As previously described, anecdotal reports from Rabbis and newspaper articles indicate that there is increasing concern over the alarming rates of EDs in these communities (Kennedy, 2010; Rabin, 2011); however, more research is needed to corroborate these accounts. Additionally, only one study has examined ED risk among Orthodox Jewish men (Fisher, 2013). Future research should explore the various cultural and religious factors that may make Orthodox Jewish men susceptible to EDs.

Specific recommendations for conducting research in UO communities include partnering with UO organizations, utilizing UO interviewers, and administering culturally appropriate measures (Rier-Schwartzbaum & Heller, 2008). It is also crucial for researchers to establish trust with community members by seeking support from community leaders and including Orthodox Jewish individuals as members of the research team. Additionally, ensuring the privacy and confidentiality of research participants' data is of particular importance within UO Jewish communities due to the mental health stigma that exists.

Finally, another important gap in the literature is the lack of research examining degree of religious observance as a moderator of ED treatment outcome, across feasibility, acceptability, engagement, and symptom indices. Such data are critical in identifying when an intervention needs a cultural adaption, and how the revised protocol should differ from the original (Lau, 2006). Some have gone as far as proposing that integrating religious and spiritual goals into treatment may promote ED recovery: as an individual with an ED reconnects with their religious identity and relationship with God, they may shift their attention and the source of their self-worth away from disordered eating and appearance-based criteria (Richards et al., 2020).

RELIEF RESOURCES: OBSERVATIONS OF EATING DISORDERS IN THE UO COMMUNITY

History of Relief Resources

While the need for ED treatment for Orthodox Jewish communities has increased, there remains a limited number of programs that cater to this population. In 2001, Relief Resources (Relief) was created to help fill this gap. Founded by a member of the UO community, Relief is a not-for-profit mental health referral agency serving Orthodox Jewish communities and primarily UO Jewish communities, where it has established itself as a trusted resource. Individuals contacting Relief complete a detailed telephone intake with a referral specialist before being connected with mental health resources that best meet their specific needs. Over the past 20 years, Relief has expanded and currently receives calls from around the world, with offices in four countries: United States, Canada, Israel, and the United Kingdom. Recognizing the unique complexities of EDs and ED treatment, the organization created a separate ED Division in 2006 to provide specialized referrals and ED resources. For the past 14 years, this division has been documenting data on the referral calls it receives.

Trends in ED Presentations—Past Five Years

Treatment-Seeking Rates

Over the past 5 years, Relief has experienced a consistent yearly increase in ED-related calls, though these referrals remain a small percentage of the total inquiries received for the full spectrum of mental health concerns (e.g., in 2021, 3.5% of total calls were ED-related). Prior to 2021, there had been between 228 and 267 new ED-related calls per year, but this number increased 40% in 2021. This trend may be attributed to the COVID-19 pandemic, which has been posited to heighten ED risk (Zipfel et al., 2022) due to stressors that can exacerbate existing weight and shape concerns (e.g., social isolation, disruption to daily routines, fears of health, consumption of appearance-related media; Rodgers et al., 2020). Additionally, COVID-19 social restrictions and increased parental contact in the home may have made it more likely that parents would notice eating and behavior changes in their children.

Age

Over 60% of ED-related calls received in the past 5 years were for individuals aged 13 to 25, with 40% of calls for individuals aged 13 to 18. This reflects existing research in the general community reporting higher rates of ED pathology among adolescents and young adults (Stice, Marti, et al., 2013). It is also possible that the adolescent and young adult age group is more likely to present for treatment via their parents, whereas adults must independently overcome the ambivalence intrinsic to restrictive EDs and make that first call.

Gender

In the past 5 years, almost 85% of ED-related callers to Relief were seeking a referral for a female prospective patient, mirroring the higher prevalence of EDs among females than males in the general population (Udo & Grilo, 2018). However, this disparity may be intensified by the stigma associated with males seeking ED treatment and limited awareness that EDs do occur in males. Moreover, most adolescent and young adult UO males are away from their families at *yeshivas* (i.e., Judaic studies-focused boarding schools), reducing opportunities for parents to notice weight loss or changes in eating behavior.

Diagnosis

At Relief, unofficial diagnoses are assigned during referral calls based on an individual's endorsed symptoms, or on a parent's observations of their child. The following frequencies were reported for ED calls in 2021: 37%

anorexia nervosa (AN), 25% binge eating/overeating, 6% bulimia nervosa (BN), 6% avoidant/restrictive food intake disorder (ARFID), 26% other (i.e., other specified feeding or eating disorder [OSFED], or disordered eating that would not meet criteria or severity for any ED category). The majority of calls were for referrals for adolescent females with restrictive ED symptoms. While these diagnoses were not confirmed following the referral, this information does shed some light on ED pathology among treatment-seeking individuals or families in the UO community.

CULTURAL CONSIDERATIONS FOR UO PATIENTS

There are many factors and influences to consider when applying a diversity-based framework to the provision of mental health services for Orthodox Jewish patients. This is especially the case in the treatment of UO Jewish individuals, who follow a stricter interpretation of the Jewish law and use its instructions to guide all areas of their lives (e.g., family, social life, work; Bachner-Melman & Zohar, 2019). To conduct culturally-informed clinical practice with this population, clinicians should try to familiarize themselves with basic core Jewish laws and adapt interventions according to patients' sociocultural context (Clauss-Ehlers et al., 2019; Latzer et al., 2019), taking caution not to dilute any of the active mechanisms of treatment in doing so. While the following considerations provide a baseline understanding of the types of issues that may present in the assessment and treatment of EDs within Jewish communities, each patient's relationship to Judaism, God, and their community is uniquely complex and interwoven with other cultural influences and identities. Thus, it is incumbent upon clinicians to invite patients to describe the role of religion in their life, rather than rely on preconceived conceptualizations or assumptions.

Barriers to Care

Despite the efforts of organizations such as Relief, mental illness likely remains underreported and undertreated in Orthodox Jewish communities (Schnall et al., 2014). The barriers to care that are relevant to this population are multifaceted and a nuanced understanding of these issues is essential to better serving these communities and improving prevention and treatment outcomes. Perhaps most notably, there exists wariness and stigma among Orthodox Jewish individuals surrounding mental health services provided by secular institutions (Hofman & Ben Shalom, 2011). As discussed further below, parents may fear that secular clinicians will influence their children by promoting non-religious values during sessions.

Furthermore, mental health stigma in some UO Jewish communities may deter individuals from seeking treatment out of fear that any association with mental illness will affect their ability to marry or ruin their family's reputation. As evidence, one of the ED treatments programs that collaborates with Relief has noted that Orthodox Jewish patients tend to arrive to the facility at a later and more severe stage of illness than secular patients.

Cost of ED treatment is a major barrier to care in the general population (Ali et al., 2017) that may be especially salient to UO Jewish communities. UO families tend to be larger, and parents have increased financial responsibilities, especially in homes where the wife is the sole financial supporter. As a result, UO families often struggle to afford mental health services (Schnall et al., 2014), which may lead them to delay seeking ED treatment or discontinue treatment prematurely.

Finally, a barrier unique to UO communities relates to the limited access most households have to technology and the internet. While the increased use of telehealth and remote therapy services has reduced barriers to mental health care (e.g., transportation, scheduling constraints) for many groups (Gajarawala & Pelkowski, 2021) this may not be the case for all UO Jewish communities. Many UO Jewish homes do not have consistent internet access, computers, or smart phones, which are required to access telehealth platforms. This relates to the insularity of the community and the desire to limit exposure from secular influences. Although many UO families are trying to adapt to this new wave of telehealth interventions and may be able to attend weekly virtual sessions, higher level of care programs are more challenging, particularly for adolescents whose parents do not want them using a smart phone or device for long periods of time. Other factors that make telehealth interventions difficult for this population include that some clients may struggle with learning how to use different technological platforms or may not have consistent access to the internet. Furthermore, as most mental health clinicians and resources promote their services and conduct outreach via websites and social media, UO Jewish individuals may not be as aware of how to find services or navigate the mental healthcare system as those who regularly use such technology.

Kashrus

The laws of *Kashrus* refer to the strict dietary laws that dictate what foods are eaten and how they are prepared within religious Jewish communities. The main laws of Kashrus are: only animals with split hooves and that chew their cud are to be consumed as food (i.e., no pig), and only after a ritual slaughter; fish must have fins and scales; and meat and dairy are forbidden to be eaten together. When following the laws of *Kashrus*, community members require that the processed or prepared foods they buy are labeled as kosher. The kosher symbol on packaging indicates that the food preparation was supervised by a religiously observant Jewish individual, known as a *mashgiach*. Just as within the Orthodox community there is a wide range of subgroups and varying degrees of observance, so too are there many different kosher supervision entities, each with its own certification symbol, and each of which may or may not be recognized as adequate by a particular segment of the Jewish community. Understanding the laws of *Kashrus* and each patient's personal observance level can help clinicians create an ED treatment plan that is respectful of these rules. Clinicians can also support individuals in balancing the need for a varied, flexible diet as part of treatment with adherence to the laws of *Kashrus*. Fortunately, in recent years, there has been an increase in ED treatment programs that offer kosher food to accommodate Jewish patients.

Case Example. Sarah, a 12-year-old UO patient with ARFID, was participating in a targeted course of cognitive behavioral therapy (Thomas & Eddy, 2018). This intervention includes in-session exposure exercises with foods that elicit a fear that, if consumed, it will lead to a negative outcome, such as gagging or vomiting. Sarah had avoided all sticky or gummy foods for three years, since an incident in which she found it difficult to fully swallow a piece of caramel candy and felt like she was choking. She was responding very well to treatment and had reached a point where she was able to tolerate all feared foods except the one that had triggered the ARFID to begin with. The plan for the upcoming session was to finally begin exposures with caramel. While typically only one parent was able to bring her to sessions, both her mother and father attended this visit to support Sarah and celebrate her anticipated success with the first steps in the process.

When it was time to begin the exposure, the therapist asked the parents for the box of caramels that they had planned to bring, and each parent looked at the other expectantly. They quickly realized there had been a misunderstanding about who was responsible for buying them earlier in the day.

The therapist, an observant Jew from the MO community, was eager to help and offered the parents access to her stash of packaged items she kept on hand for exposure work and therapeutic family meals. Because she only purchased certified kosher foods, she was confident that Sarah and her parents could find a suitable and acceptable option among the variety of items, including candy.

As the family looked through the choices, they became quiet and visibly uncomfortable, and the therapist quickly realized her mistake: the foods were kosher to her community's standards, but not theirs. She immediately apologized for her error, explaining that her excitement over Sarah's progress had momentarily eclipsed her attention to detail. Sarah's father smiled and said he was just relieved that she had figured it out on her own, as he had not wanted to offend her by explaining why they were declining the food. The awkwardness in the room dissipated, and they all planned for when and how this exposure could be accomplished.

In recounting this incident in supervision, the therapist and supervisor reflected on whether a strong therapeutic alliance could buffer the sting of a culturally insensitive or ignorant mistake, whether an established trust might elucidate a clearer distinction between a therapist's intent versus impact, and how to be attuned to indicators that this trust had been breached.

Shabbos and Jewish Holidays

Each week, from Friday at sundown to Saturday when the stars come out (25 hours), Orthodox Jewish communities celebrate the Sabbath (Shabbos), during which women typically prepare at least two large meals for their families, one served Friday evening, and one served Saturday mid-day. In so doing, they are heavily involved in everything from grocery shopping to cooking, serving, and eating large meals with others, all activities that can be exceedingly stressful for an individual with an ED. Jewish holidays and religious events often include family gatherings for formal meals that require extensive preparation. Certain holidays, such as Passover, can be especially difficult as they forbid eating certain foods (e.g., grains), thus requiring a person to alter much of their diet for over a week-long period.

Moreover, there are six religious fast days throughout the Jewish year, two during which one cannot eat or drink for 25 hours. For individuals with EDs, the religious reasons for fasting can become complicated by weight-loss motivations; also, ED treatment may prohibit them from fasting with the rest of their community. Patients in treatment for a restrictive ED are never required to fast and Jewish laws forbid individuals from fasting when sick.

Case Example. Shifra, a 45-year-old woman who identified as part of the UO community, had presented for cognitive-behavioral treatment of binge eating disorder (CBT-E; Fairburn, 2008). She was engaged with and responsive to early change strategies, including a structured pattern of eating, advanced planning of meals and snacks, and self-monitoring. The frequency of her binge eating episodes began to markedly decrease, with one exception: Shabbos.

Shabbos posed multiple challenges for Shifra that extended before Shabbos, on Thursday evening and Friday when she typically cooked, to after Shabbos until going to bed Saturday night. She blamed herself for these lapses, citing diet-culture reasoning to frame them as personal failures, and correspondingly experiencing significant shame. The therapist reinforced an alternative perspective from Shifra's earlier-created personalized CBT-E case formulation, identifying how her Shabbos experience ignites a cycle that echoes the broader maintaining mechanisms of her binge eating disorder. For Shifra, these included: an emphasis on appearance and the thin ideal (Orthodox individuals wear their finest clothes on Shabbos, and Shifra refused herself new items until she could once again fit into her older, smaller dresses); dissatisfaction with shape and weight (she therefore wore clothes on Shabbos that were uncomfortably tight, over which she wore oversized toppers to hide her shape and to remain modest); dietary restraint and restriction (Shifra would try to circumvent her anticipated Shabbos binge eating episodes by promising herself that she would "be good" and refrain from indulging in her favorite foods); reactive loss-of-control eating; and negative affect and self-appraisal.

The therapist inquired about the feasibility of implementing stimulus control techniques, and Shifra explained how the feast-like environment of Shabbos renders such measures extraordinarily difficult. In addition, because writing is not permitted on Shabbos, she could not benefit from the therapeutic aspects of self-monitoring. (Electronics are also forbidden on Shabbos, which precludes the use of self-monitoring apps. These would not be accessible anyway as most UO Jewish individuals do not own smart phones to avoid the temptation of accessing secular material via the internet.) The therapist thanked Shifra for amplifying her understanding of this weekly holy day.

Returning to the formulation, Shifra and the therapist focused on modifying dietary restraint and created a plan to expose Shifra to Shabbos foods in limited quantities to facilitate habituation and behavioral experimentation. For example, Shifra would serve herself a small portion of each of her preferred Shabbos food as she made it before Shabbos, in lieu of snacks or lunch, with another portion set aside for a pre-lunch exposure/snack Saturday morning. This helped Shifra begin meals without undo hunger, enjoy the special Shabbos foods in a stimulus-controlled manner while also observing them losing their "forbidden" charm, learn that these foods could be disassociated from loss-of-control eating behavior, and end Shabbos without the self-disgust and binary stance that contributed to her continuing binge eating on Saturday nights. Shifra worked to plan her meals and snacks for Thursday evening through Saturday night carefully to reduce the likelihood of binge eating. The therapist also suggested that during these high-risk days of the week, Shifra put a marble in a jar for every meal or snack that went as planned, or that was flexibly altered to accommodate an unexpected circumstance or food preference. In addition to circumventing Shabbos restrictions on self-monitoring methods, Shifra enjoyed the visual of the jar filling faster as the weeks of treatment went on.

Shidduchim

Shidduchim is a cultural tradition in the UO Jewish population in which families seek the services of a matchmaker, relative, or friend who arranges dates for men and women with the sole purpose of marriage. While the dates are arranged, marriages are not, and an engagement requires the interest and consent of both members of the couple. According to Jewish law, men and women are forbidden from touching prior to marriage, and the *shidduch* process often moves quickly, with most individuals marrying within months of meeting. Women often begin the *shidduch* process around the age of 18 and there is pressure for a woman to be married by her early 20s.

While the *shidduch* system is not known to increase ED risk (while there are hypotheses to this effect, there is no research to support them), it appears that thin-ideal beauty standards have started to influence the process. Specifically, anecdotal reports from community members suggest that young women experience pressure to obtain a slimmer body shape to thereby increase the likelihood that they will be successfully matched. Some young men or their parents may specifically aim to date and marry a woman whose body shape fits the thin-ideal, and request this from the matchmaker.

Community members often submit personal resumes during this process, which includes references for prospective suitors to call to learn more about them and their families. Stigma associated with mental illness in UO Jewish communities may make it more difficult for an individual with a history of mental illness to find a *shidduch*. As a result, many young people, families, and even adults may delay treatment for a mental health issue out of fear that knowledge of their mental health problem in the community will interfere with their or their siblings' *shidduch* process.

Case Example. A secular therapist treating a 19-year-old patient with AN, now nearing remission, received an unexpected voicemail soon after the patient began the *shidduch* process. The Rabbi of the potential groom's family had called to inquire about the patient's current mental health status. In their investigatory efforts about the potential bride, the groom's family had heard that the patient had an ED in the past. The matchmaker had asked for verification of the patient's recovery, and the patient's mother gave her the therapist's phone number.

By the time the therapist had finished with her next patient, there was a second message, this one from the patient's mother. The mother anxiously asked the therapist to give her daughter a clean bill of health in light of how much better she was at this point.

Aside from collecting the multiple releases of information required (each with its own restrictions on content), the therapist also had to consider how she would represent the patient's current clinical status. While the patient had made remarkable progress, she still had a few recommended pounds to gain, shape and weight were still disproportionately influential in her self-evaluation (although much less so than at baseline), and she had held on to a small subset of her food rules and restrictions. While the patient might not have been diagnosed with an ED had she presented initially with only these concerns, the therapist knew that this clinical picture, in the context of recovering from AN, could represent a state of fragility and risk of relapse. Moreover, the patient had been below the diagnostic threshold for only a brief period.

After consulting with a colleague who specializes in ethical issues in ED treatment, the therapist met with the patient and parents and spoke to them candidly about what she could and could not say with accuracy in response to this inquiry, and in response to several hypothetical follow-up questions that might arise. The therapist then left it up to the patient to decide if and how she would like the therapist to proceed within those parameters; the patient, in turn, deferred the decision to her parents.

Role of the Rabbi

It may be beneficial for mental health providers to collaborate with rabbinical authority when treating UO Jewish individuals (Popovsky, 2010). Certain UO Jewish communities are organized around the Rabbi (the religious leader of the community's synagogue [i.e., place of worship]), where community members regularly seek both religious and personal advice from the Rabbi. Prior to seeking mental health services, UO individuals may consult with the Rabbi for his approval to work with a mental health professional. By partnering with a patient's Rabbi, a clinician can help that patient resolve any conflicts between their treatment and religious observance. For example, patients and therapists may seek a Rabbi's approval to refrain from observing a religious fast day because of the risks of fasting to a patient's mental or physical health (Rabin, 2011). However, individuals vary with regard to their relationship with their Rabbi and their personal preferences, and it is important to determine with each patient whether contacting their Rabbi would be beneficial for their treatment.

Adolescent Patients

As previously discussed, ED prevalence is higher among Jewish female adolescents than adults, which reflects the typical age of ED onset in the general population (Smink et al., 2012; Stice, Rohde, et al., 2013). It is important to note that UO parents may be hesitant to send their children to therapy and especially to inpatient or residential treatment programs. Oftentimes, adolescent patients from UO communities have never spoken to someone who is not UO, and parents may be concerned about their exposure to secular influences.

Parents are also likely to be protective of the subject matter discussed in therapy sessions, and it is important for clinicians to communicate frequently with parents to keep families engaged in treatment. Clinicians may find it helpful to establish a communication policy whereby parents are updated on their child's progress regularly and informed of ways they can facilitate their child's recovery at home. Female adolescents in these communities tend to live at home until they are married, and so, their parents are very much involved in their daily lives.

Family Size

In response to the Jewish commandment "be fruitful and multiply," UO Jewish families tend to be large, with seven children being the average (Hofman & Ben Shalom, 2011). This tradition not only contributes to the financial and household stress in this community but also has important implications for ED treatment. Specifically, ED interventions such as Family Based Treatment (FBT) for adolescents with AN can be adapted to the circumstances of each family. While FBT traditionally recommends that all family members living in the home attend FBT sessions, this may not be feasible with larger families. Moreover, parents sometimes try to keep the diagnosis and treatment process private from siblings, whom they fear may reveal the situation to their friends, thereby risking tarnishing the family's reputation. Other challenges related to family size include regular attendance of appointments as it can be stressful for parents to find the time and resources to bring their child to treatment consistently and at the same time find childcare for the younger children at home.

Case Example. After moving her ED-focused practice from the Upper East Side of Manhattan to a town near a large UO community, a therapist observed that her assumptions about family size impeding the successful delivery of FBT were unfounded. Specifically, she reflected that parents in wealthy, single-earner, highly-resourced small families could have difficulty with the intense level of parental responsibility required in treatment, while parents in low-income, dual-earner, large UO families could harness internal and extended-family resources to attend to each of 10 children as if they were the only child at home. She recognized some underlying biases that fueled her prior assumptions and brought these to the attention of her supervisor so they could understand and address them.

Gender and Sexuality

Patients may feel uncomfortable seeing therapists of a different gender due to the laws in the Jewish religion regarding interactions between unrelated males and females. For example, there is a Jewish law that forbids men and women from being alone together in a room with the door closed; thus, patients working with therapists of a different gender may feel uncomfortable attending sessions in a closed space. Likewise, in FBT family sessions, husbands may feel uncomfortable speaking to a female therapist and making eye contact with her.

Sexuality is generally not discussed in UO families or schools. Girls learn about their reproductive organs when they start menstruating, without any linkage to sex or sexuality. Information about sex between a husband and wife is delivered by a teacher in a one-to-one or group format during the weeks before a wedding. Thus, adolescents and unmarried young adult patients are likely to be uncomfortable or confused if such issues are referenced in treatment (e.g., in a demographic question about sexual orientation, or in assessing body avoidance, including avoiding physically intimate encounters because of shape concerns).

Beauty Ideals

UO communities place great focus on insularity and separating themselves from secular society. To this end, many UO households have been encouraged to limit access to the television, internet, or smart phones to reduce secular influences in the home. Even with limited access to media, Jewish women are not entirely protected from the thin-ideal and beauty standards of the broader culture. UO individuals are still seeing the appearance ideal when it is promoted by models on billboards, advertisements on public transportation, and in the body shapes and sizes of store mannequins. Over the years, stringency related to internet usage has become more challenging to uphold, and each UO household varies regarding their level of internet exposure. With the onset of COVID-19, there has been a greater necessity for internet access and videoconferencing, which has required more community members to spend time online for appointments and shopping, possibly increasing their exposure to secular media. Additionally, thin-ideal beauty standards are promoted within UO communities just as they are outside of them: through focused advertisements for weight loss programs and low-calorie foods in Orthodox Jewish magazines.

PREVENTION OF ED IN THE UO COMMUNITY

As this chapter has emphasized, the Jewish community, including the UO, are not immune from EDs and are exposed to similar risk factors (e.g., thin-ideal media) as the broader community. With this in mind, prevention programs that have been successful in the general population should also be helpful for the Orthodox community; however, they must be packaged in an acceptable way and adapted to be more applicable to the community's lifestyle. In general, prevention programs for EDs have traditionally targeted adolescent females whose age and gender put them at heightened risk for developing ED pathology (Rhode et al., 2015). ED prevention programs for UO Jewish populations should ideally address risk factors that are specific to the UO community; however, research is not yet available to guide that effort. The prevention studies that have been conducted show promising potential for adaptations of existing prevention programs to reduce ED symptoms and improve body esteem among Jewish adolescents (Casasnovas et al., 2019; Glovinsky, 2018). Only one study thus far has assessed for progress at follow up (Casasnovas et al., 2019).

The Body Project is an ED prevention program targeting the sociocultural pressures women experience to achieve a thin and slender body type and other appearance ideals (Stice et al., 2001). Rooted in cognitive dissonance theory (Festinger, 1957), this 4–6-week program leads participants in actively challenging and critiquing thin-ideal pressures in verbal and written activities to induce dissonance and thereby change beliefs. Extensive research on the Body Project has demonstrated this program's effectiveness in reducing ED pathology among high school- and college-age females (Ghaderi et al., 2020; Stice et al., 2011, 2013).

The Body Project has been successfully adapted for the UO community (Casasnovas et al., 2019), specifically for delivery in UO Jewish all-female high schools. In this tested adaptation, stimulus materials were modified to be better aligned with the participants' life experiences (e.g., using images to which participants were more likely to be exposed). Another aspect of the adaptation addressed how Jewish laws of modesty and humility might intersect with negative body image. Furthermore, the adapted Body Project explained how the tenets of the prevention program were consistent with certain Jewish laws and values. Finally, facilitators of the program in the school were Orthodox Jewish individuals. At the end of the program, students demonstrated significant reductions in risk factors associated with EDs, including body dissatisfaction and negative affect, which were sustained over a 6-month period (Casasnovas et al., 2019).

As with ED treatment, ED prevention programs encounter barriers to implementation in UO institutions because of mental health stigma and distrust of secular institutions. When searching for a school in which to conduct the pilot study of the adapted Body Project, Casasnovas and colleagues (2019) noted that many schools rejected the program because they were uncomfortable with its secular origins and concerned about working with individuals from secular institutions. Even after the pilot study was complete and there were data supporting the adaptation, several schools expressed hesitancy with the program because of its subject matter. Ultimately, to increase schools' comfort with the program, its name was changed from the "The Body Project" to "Project Everybody" (there were concerns that leading with the word "Body" was both misleading and suggestive of inappropriate content). To partner with UO institutions, it is crucial that prevention programs collaborate with Orthodox mental health professionals and religious leaders in their adaptation of program materials.

CONCLUSION

There is increasing demand for ED treatment in the UO Jewish community, and yet multiple barriers (e.g., insufficient research, mental health stigma, and fear of secular influence) limit or complicate the development and provision of adequate and targeted services. Clinicians and researchers working with Jewish individuals in the Orthodox spectrum should seek information about the cultural variables that may require adaptations in both ED prevention and treatment models. Given the significant risk and morbidity associated with EDs in the general population (van Hoeken, & Hoek, 2020), it is imperative that additional efforts be made to address the barriers to specialized care that persist among UO Jewish communities, and to tailor interventions to meet their unique needs.

DISCUSSION QUESTIONS

1. How do you think some of the cultural considerations for the Orthodox Jewish community might complicate certain aspects of eating disorder treatment? As a clinician, how would you balance a patient's treatment goals with these cultural influences?
2. This chapter has emphasized the methodological limitations of the quantitative research about eating disorders in Jewish populations.

What patterns do you see in the data that do exist? How might they inform your perspective and approach to treating members of these communities, considering both similarities and differences compared to the general population of individuals with eating disorders?

3. How would you respond to a clinical situation in which you believe an adolescent Orthodox Jewish patient requires a higher level of care? However, her parents do not want her to be admitted to a secular inpatient facility?

REFERENCES

Akrawi, D., Bartrop, R., Potter, U., & Touyz, S. (2015). Religiosity, spirituality in relation to disordered eating and body image concerns: A systematic review. *Journal of Eating Disorders, 3*(1), 1–24. https://doi.org/10.1186/s40337-015-0064-0

Ali, K., Farrer, L., Fassnacht, D. B., Gulliver, A., Bauer, S., & Griffiths, K. M. (2017). Perceived barriers and facilitators towards help-seeking for eating disorders: A systematic review. *International Journal of Eating Disorders, 50*(1), 9–21. https://doi.org/10.1002/eat.22598

Aival-Naveh, E., Rothschild-Yakar, L., & Kurman, J. (2021). The moderating effects of self and other mentalizing on the relationship between distress and disordered eating: A cross-cultural examination. *Journal of Clinical Psychology, 77*(9), 1937–1953, https://doi.org/10.1002/jclp.23121

Bachner-Melman, R., & Zohar, A. H. (2019). Potential risk and protective factors for eating disorders in Haredi (UO) Jewish women. *Journal of Religion and Health, 58*(6), 2161–2174. https://doi.org/10.1007/s10943-019-00854-2

Cahaner, L., Malach, G., & Choshen, M. (2017). 2017 Statistical Report on UO Society in Israel Jerusalem. Jerusalem, Israel: The Israel Democracy Institute.

Casasnovas, A. F., Huryk, K. M., Levinson, D., Markowitz, S., Friedman, S., Stice, E., & Loeb,

K. L. (2019). Cognitive dissonance-based Eating disorder prevention: Pilot study of a cultural adaptation for the Orthodox Jewish Community. *Eating Disorders, 29*(2), 192–204. https://doi.org/10.1080/10640266.2019.1644797

Central Bureau of Statistics. (2020, December 31). *Population of Israel on the eve of 2021*. הקיטסיטטסל תיזכרמה הכשלה. Retrieved April 27, 2022, from https://www.cbs.gov.il/en/mediarelease/Pages/2020/Population-of-Israel-on-the-Eve-of-2021.aspx

Clauss-Ehlers, C. S., Chiriboga, D. A., Hunter, S. J., Roysircar, G., & Tummala-Narra, P. (2019). Apa Multicultural Guidelines executive summary: Ecological approach to context, identity, and intersectionality. *American Psychologist, 74*(2), 232–244. https://doi.org/10.1037/amp0000382

Fairburn, C. G. (2008). *Cognitive behavior therapy and eating disorders*. Guilford Press.

Feinson, M. C., & Meir, A. (2012). Disordered eating and religious observance: A focus on ultra-Orthodox Jews in an adult community study. *International Journal of Eating Disorders*, *45*(1), 101–109. https://doi.org/10.1002/eat.20895

Festinger, L. (1957). *A theory of cognitive dissonance* (Vol. 2). Stanford University Press.

Fisher, M. (2013). Weight loss as a result of religious zeal in young Orthodox Jewish males. *International Journal of Adolescent Medicine and Health*, *25*(2), 181–183. https://doi.org/10.1515/ijamh-2013-0028

Fisherman, S. (2016). Body image and wellbeing in religious male and female youth in Israel. *Gender and Diversity Issues in Religious-Based Institutions and Organizations*, 51–79. https://doi.org/10.4018/978-1-4666-8772-1.ch003

Forta, M. L. (2020). *Community healthcare stakeholders on risk factor description for eating disorder prevention for Jewish orthodox adolescent females* (Publication No. 28157831) [Doctoral dissertation, Grand Canyon University). ProQuest Dissertations Publishing.

Frenkel, T. D., Latzer, Y., & Lev-Wiesel, R. (2018). Relationship between the ideal woman model, self-figure drawing, and disordered eating among Jewish ultra-orthodox women and national religious women. *Israel Journal of Psychiatry*, *55*(1), 73–84.

Fredrickson, B. L., & Roberts, T. A. (1997). Objectification theory: Toward understanding women's lived experiences and mental health risks. *Psychology of Women Quarterly*, *21*(2), 173–206. https://doi.org/10.1111/j.1471-6402.1997.tb00108.x

Gajarawala, S. N., & Pelkowski, J. N. (2021). Telehealth benefits and barriers. *The Journal for Nurse Practitioners*, *17*(2), 218–221. https://doi.org/10.1016/j.nurpra.2020.09.013

Ghaderi, A., Stice, E., Andersson, G., Enö Persson, J., & Allzén, E. (2020). A randomized controlled trial of the effectiveness of virtually delivered Body Project (vBP) groups to prevent eating disorders. *Journal of Consulting and Clinical Psychology*, *88*(7), 643–656. https://doi.org/10.1037/ccp0000506

Glovinsky, A. (2018). *Implementing a culturally-adapted eating disorder prevention program in an Orthodox Jewish high school* (Publication No. 10819972) [Doctoral Dissertation, Rutgers, the State University of New Jersey, Graduate School of Applied and Professional Psychology]. ProQuest Dissertations Publishing.

Gluck, M. E., & Geliebter, A. (2002). Body image and eating behaviors in orthodox and secular Jewish women. *The Journal of Gender-Specific Medicine*, *5*(1), 19–24.

Greenberg, D., & Huppert, J. D. (2010). Scrupulosity: A unique subtype of obsessive-compulsive disorder. *Current Psychiatry Reports*, *12*(4), 282–289. https://doi.org/10.1007/s11920-010-0127-5

Handelzalts, J. E., Geller, S., Levy, S., Vered, T., & Fisher, S. (2017). Body image among three denominations of Jewish women in Israel. *International Journal of Culture and Mental Health*, *10*(2), 206–216. https://doi.org/10.1080/17542863.2017.1290126

Hofman, S., & Ben Shalom, H. (2011). Reflections on working in an UO mental health clinic. *International Journal of Psychotherapy*, *15*(3), 79–92.

Kennedy, K. (2010, December 10). *Eating disorders on rise for Orthodox Jewish girls.* The Associated Press. https://www.nbcnews.com/id/wbna40607997

Lazar-Feigenbaum, T. C. (2014). *Social control, age, religiosity, and symptoms of eating disorders in Orthodox Jewish girls.* (Publication No. 3624683) [Doctoral dissertation, Hempstead: Hofstra University]. ProQuest Dissertations Publishing.

Latzer, Y., Orna, T., & Gefen, S. (2007). Level of religiosity and disordered eating psychopathology among modern-Orthodox Jewish adolescent girls in Israel. *International Journal of Adolescent Medicine and Health,19*(4), 511–522. https://doi.org/10.1515/ijamh.2007.19.4.511

Latzer, Y., Spivak-Lavi, Z., & Katz, R. (2015). Disordered eating and media exposure among adolescent girls: The role of parental involvement and sense of empowerment. *International Journal of Adolescence and Youth, 20*(3), 375–391. https://doi.org/10.1080/02673843.2015.1014925

Latzer, Y., & Tzischinsky, O. (2003). Weight concern, dieting and eating behaviors. A survey of Israeli high school girls. *International Journal of Adolescent Medicine and Health, 15*(4), 295–306. https://doi.org/10.1515/ijamh.2003.15.4.295

Latzer, Y., Weinberger-Litman, S. L., Spivak-Lavi, Z., & Tzischinsky, O. (2019). Disordered eating pathology and body image among adolescent girls in Israel: The role of sense of coherence. *Community Mental Health Journal, 55*(7), 1246–1252. https://doi.org/10.1007/s10597-019-00446-0

Latzer, Y., Witztum, E., & Stein, D. (2008). Eating disorders and disordered eating in Israel: An updated review. *European Eating Disorders Review, 16*(5), 361–374. https://doi.org/10.1002/erv.875

Lau, A. S. (2006). Making the case for selective and directed cultural adaptations of evidence-based treatments: Examples from parent training. *Clinical Psychology: Science and Practice, 13*(4), 295–310. https://doi.org/10.1111/j.1468-2850.2006.00042.x

Loketch-Fischer, M. (2016). *The relationships among modesty, self-objectification, body shame, and eating disorder symptoms in Jewish women.* (Publication No. 10158441) [Doctoral dissertation, Hempstead: Hofstra University). ProQuest Dissertations Publishing.

Malach, G., & Cahaner, L. (2021, January 1). *Statistical report on UO Society in Israel.* Statistical Report on UO Society in Israel—The Israel Democracy Institute. Retrieved April 27, 2022, from https://en.idi.org.il/haredi/2020/?chapter=34272#:~:text=In%202020%2C%20the%20ultra%2DOrthodox,2%20million%20people%20by%202033.

Mandelli, L., Draghetti, S., Albert, U., De Ronchi, D., & Atti, A. R. (2020). Rates of comorbid obsessive-compulsive disorder in eating disorders: A meta-analysis of the literature. *Journal of Affective Disorders, 277*, 927–939. https://doi.org/10.1016/j.jad.2020.09.003

Pinhas, L., Heinmaa, M., Bryden, P., Bradley, S., & Toner, B. (2008). Disordered eating in Jewish adolescent girls. *The Canadian Journal of Psychiatry, 53*(9), 601–608. https://doi.org/10.1177/070674370805300907

Popovsky, M. A. (2010). Special issues in the care of UO Jewish psychiatric in-patients. *Transcultural Psychiatry, 47*(4), 647–672. https://doi.org/10.1177/1363461510383747

Rabin, R. C. (2011, April 11). *Rabbis sound an alarm over eating disorders.* The New York Times. https://www.nytimes.com/2011/04/12/health/12orthodox.html

Rayworth, B. B., Wise, L. A., & Harlow, B. L. (2004). Childhood abuse and risk of eating disorders in women. *Epidemiology*, 271–278. https://doi.org/10.1097/01.ede.0000120047.07140.9d

Rier, D. A., Schwartzbaum, A., & Heller, C. (2008). Methodological issues in studying an insular, traditional population: A women's health survey among Israeli haredi (UO) Jews. *Women & Health*, *48*(4), 363–381. https://doi.org/10.1080/03630240802575054

Rodgers, R. F., Lombardo, C., Cerolini, S., Franko, D. L., Omori, M., Fuller-Tyszkiewicz, M., Linardon, J., Courtet, P., & Guillaume, S. (2020). The impact of the COVID-19 pandemic on eating disorder risk and symptoms. *International Journal of Eating Disorders*, *53*(7), 1166–1170. https://doi.org/10.1002/eat.23318

Richards, P. S., Weinberger-Litman, S., Berrett, M. E., & Hardman, R. K. (2020). Spirituality, religion, and eating disorders. In D.H, Rosmarin, & H.G, Koenig, (Eds.), *Handbook of spirituality, religion, and mental health* (2nd ed., pp. 99–118). Academic Press.

Rhode, P., Stice, E., & Marti, C. N. (2015). Development and predictive effects of eating disorder risk factors during adolescence: Implications for prevention efforts. *International Journal of Eating Disorders*, *48*(2), 187–198. https://doi.org/10.1002/eat.22270

Schnall, E., Kalkstein, S., Gottesman, A., Feinberg, K., Schaeffer, C. B., & Feinberg, S. S. (2014). Barriers to mental health care: A 25-year follow-up study of the Orthodox Jewish community. *Journal of Multicultural Counseling and Development*, *42*(3), 161–173. https://doi.org/10.1002/j.2161-1912.2014.00052.x

Shafran, Y., & Wolowelsky, J. B. (2013). A note on eating disorders and appetite and satiety in the orthodox Jewish meal. *Eating and Weight Disorders-Studies on Anorexia, Bulimia and Obesity*, *18*(1), 75–78. https://doi.org/10.1007/s40519-013-0011-5

Smink, F. R., van Hoeken, D., & Hoek, H. W. (2012). Epidemiology of eating disorders: Incidence, prevalence and mortality rates. *Current Psychiatry Reports*, *14*(4), 406–414. https://doi.org/10.1007/s11920-012-0282-y

Stice, E., Chase, A., Stormer, S., & Appel, A. (2001). A randomized trial of a dissonance-based eating disorder prevention program. *International Journal of Eating Disorders*, *29*(3), 247–262. https://doi.org/10.1002/eat.1016

Stice, E., Rohde, P., Durant, S., Shaw, H., & Wade, E. (2013). Effectiveness of peer-led dissonance-based eating disorder prevention groups: Results from two randomized pilot trials. *Behaviour Research and Therapy*, *51*(4–5), 197–206. https://doi.org/10.1016/j.brat.2013.01.004

Stice, E., Marti, C. N., & Rohde, P. (2013). Prevalence, incidence, impairment, and course of the proposed DSM-5 eating disorder diagnoses in an 8-year prospective community study of young women. *Journal of Abnormal Psychology*, *122*(2), 445–457. https://doi.org/10.1037/a0030679

Stice, E., Marti, C. N., Rohde, P., & Shaw, H. (2011). Testing mediators hypothesized to account for the effects of a dissonance-based eating disorder prevention program over longer-term follow-up. *Journal of Consulting and Clinical Psychology*, *79*(3), 398-405. https://doi.org/10.1037/a0023321

Sykes, D. K., Leuser, B., Melia, M., & Gross, M. (1988). A demographic analysis of 252 patients with anorexia nervosa and bulimia. *International Journal of Psychosomatics, 35*(1–4), 5–9.

Tiggemann, M. (2013). Objectification theory: Of relevance for eating disorder researchers and clinicians? *Clinical Psychologist, 17*(2), 35–45. https://doi.org/10.1111/cp.12010

Thomas, J. J., & Eddy, K. T. (2018). *Cognitive-behavioral therapy for avoidant/restrictive food intake disorder: Children, adolescents, and adults*. Cambridge University Press. https://doi.org/10.1017/9781108233170

Udo, T., & Grilo, C. M. (2018). Prevalence and correlates of DSM-5–defined eating disorders in a nationally representative sample of US adults. *Biological psychiatry, 84*(5), 345–354. https://doi.org/10.1016/j.biopsych.2018.03.014

van Hoeken, D., & Hoek, H. W. (2020). Review of the burden of eating disorders: Mortality, disability, costs, quality of life, and family burden. *Current Opinion in Psychiatry, 33*(6), 521–527. https://doi.org/10.1097/yco.0000000000000641

Weinberger-Litman, S. L., Latzer, Y., Litman, L., & Ozick, R. (2018). Extrinsic religious orientation and disordered eating pathology among MO Israeli adolescents: The mediating role of adherence to the superwoman ideal and body dissatisfaction. *Journal of Religion and Health, 57*(1), 209–222. https://doi.org/10.1007/s10943-017-0443-8

Weinberger-Litman, S. L., Rabin, L. A., Fogel, J., Mensinger, J. L., & Litman, L. (2016). Psychosocial mediators of the relationship between religious orientation and eating disorder risk factors in young Jewish women. *Psychology of Religion and Spirituality, 8*(4), 265–276. https://doi.org/10.1037/a0040293

Zipfel, S., Schmidt, U., & Giel, K. E. (2022). The hidden burden of eating disorders during the COVID-19 pandemic. *The Lancet Psychiatry, 9*(1), 9–11. https://doi.org/10.1016/S2215-0366(21)00435-1

ENDNOTE

1. This chapter will be using some of the pronunciations and dialects of the broader UO community. There are other variations in pronunciations and terminology across communities. For example, this chapter will be saying "kashrus" while some Jewish communities use the term "kashrut."

CHAPTER 11

EATING DISORDERS IN ASIAN AMERICANS

Addressing Racism and Other Contextual Considerations in Care

Norman Kim

While long considered disorders that primarily affected affluent, young White women, there is a growing understanding that eating disorders can and do affect people of all ethnicities, nationalities, genders and gender identities, ages, or body sizes. Using data from the NIMH Collaborative Psychiatric Epidemiological Studies (CPES), Marques and colleagues (2011) found (a) no significant differences in the prevalence rates of anorexia nervosa across all ethnic groups that were studied, (b) significantly higher prevalence rates of bulimia nervosa in Latino and African American groups, and (c) significantly higher prevalence rates of binge eating disorder for all ethnic groups studied. Even though eating disorder prevalence rates were similar or greater than those of their White peers, people in ethnic minority groups with a lifetime history of any eating disorders were significantly less likely to utilize mental health services than their non-Latino White peers. The authors emphasized that these data represent an important need in communities of color that is currently going unmet—namely, a need for providers to better understand the specific experiences of communities of color.

Counseling Individuals With Eating Disorders: An Intersectional Approach, pp. 251–262

This echoes a larger pattern of disparities in mental health care utilization that have long been known and, unfortunately, have not changed much in recent decades. Black Americans, Latinx Americans and Asian Americans have consistently underutilized mental health care services (Hall et al., 2021) compared to their White peers. People from minority communities experience greater difficulty in accessing mental health care, report multiple barriers to care, and are significantly more likely to receive poorer quality care (U.S. Department of Health and Human Services, 2001; Satcher Health Leadership Institute at Morehouse School of Medicine, 2022). Asian Americans continue to demonstrate the lowest utilization rates for mental health services due to myriad barriers, including stigma around acknowledging mental health issues, the particular salience of shame within Asian communities, and lack of culturally appropriate treatment approaches and culturally attuned providers (Sue et al., 2012). This chapter will focus on Asian Americans and eating disorders.

ASIAN AMERICANS

Asian Americans have become the fastest growing ethnic minority group in the United States, recording an 81% increase from 2000 to 2019, according to U.S. Census data (U.S. Census Bureau, 2021). The population of Asian Americans has nearly doubled since 2000 and is projected to double again by 2060 (Budiman & Ruiz, 2021). To further characterize this group, as of the 2020 census, 19.9 million people (a total of 7.2% of the U.S. population) identified as Asian alone, 4.1 million people identified as Asian with another ethnic group, 1.6 million people identified as Native Hawaiian or as Pacific Islanders, and more than 70% of Asian American adults were born in another country. As defined in the United States, by convention, if not strictly speaking by geographic accuracy, the Asian American diaspora comprises dozens of ethnic groups and nationalities speaking well over 100 languages (Budiman & Ruiz, 2021). This group is generally aggregated as those people with origins or family roots in East Asian, South Asian, and Southeast Asian countries, and those with origins or roots in the Pacific Islands. While geographically part of Asia, in the United States, those people with origins or family roots in the Middle East or Central Asian countries are generally not referred to as Asian.

Despite this growing presence of Asian Americans and the fact that since the 16th century there has been Asian immigration to the territories that would become the United States (Borah, 1995), there is a concerning lack of understanding of the diversity and nuances of the Asian American experience, which is reflected and further magnified in existing disparities in the healthcare system. Although often treated as a monolithic group,

Asian Americans' diversity reflects the range of countries and groups of the diaspora, each with its own history, culture, language, religion, and circumstance (Liu et al., 2022). This immense diversity and range of experiences and backgrounds is essential to keep in mind in any discussion of Asian Americans as a group.

Until recently, Asian Americans have also largely been absent in discussions about racism and the impacts of systemic racism on healthcare. Although anti-Asian sentiment has always been a part of the history of Asians in America, it has not necessarily been a part of the national conversation and in the national consciousness in the way that it has during the COVID-19 pandemic. Due in part to the increasingly xenophobic and racist rhetoric around COVID-19, 2021 saw a 167% increase in hate crimes targeting Asian people (Federal Bureau of Investigation, 2021). Because many anti-Asian hate crimes are not reported or counted as hate crimes, these numbers are almost certainly undercounting the actual increase and extent of the problem. This increase in vitriol and verbal and physical violence targeting Asian people has revived the "yellow peril" racist metaphor from the 19th century warning of the danger to the dominance of the Western world by Asian people, which has always been present in the undercurrent of anti-Asian racism.

This is one of the most pernicious consequences of the "model minority" myth, which purports that Asians are inherently endowed with qualities that allow them to be more likely to succeed relative to other minority groups, ostensibly because of a cultural emphasis on education and strong work ethic (Poon et al., 2016; Yoo et al., 2010). One implication of this stereotype is that Asian-Americans are somehow immune from the impacts of systemic racism, which is demonstrably false, such that there is therefore not a need to more closely examine disparities, barriers, or other elements of inequities.

The larger problem with this myth is that its intent is not to elevate Asians by pointing at their successes. The intent of the model minority myth is to alleviate Whites of the responsibility of systemic racism by shifting the blame for racist policies and institutions to the inability of Black and Brown peoples to be successful like Asian people purportedly have been. The model minority myth is not pro-Asian, as Asian Americans are still perpetually foreign, othered, and ostracized. The model minority myth is anti-Black, as it serves to devalue and denigrate Black and Brown peoples by pointing out the manufactured contrast of Asian success. It serves to drive a wedge between Asians and other minoritized groups in support of maintaining White supremacy.

The model minority stereotype has also supported the bias that Asian Americans are less likely to suffer from mental health struggles because Asian Americans are less likely to report problems (Le et al., 2020). The relative lack of research on various elements of Asian Americans' well-being clearly reflects this bias. As the model minority stereotype is internalized by Asian Americans, attempting to seek care is itself something that could be viewed as a failure, implying that one is not successfully embodying the expectations of the myth. This is particularly true for those whose family history includes immigration. In order to deal with the stresses of assimilation into a new and different culture, many immigrant families must adopt a survival mentality with a focus on the basics, which does not include well-being or mental health. Along with other elements of stigma, structural racism, and systemic bias, the consequences of this stereotype are but one of the many factors that have resulted in inadequate recognition of eating disorders in Asian Americans.

Acculturative Stress

As acculturation impacts and informs the experiences of many Asian Americans, it is crucial to integrate this construct into the conceptualization of eating disorders in this population (Zhou et al., 2022). Acculturation refers to the process of change and adaptation that an individual from a different culture undergoes when adapting to a host culture, characterized by two domains: the degree to which the individual embraces or rejects their own culture, and the degree to which the individual desires to interact with the host culture (Berry, 1992). The specific psychosocial stress associated with this process of adapting is referred to as acculturative stress (Berry, 1998). Distinct from general experiences of stress, the impact of acculturative stress appears related to the degree of distance from the culture of origin and the host culture (Fox et al., 2017). This is a particularly salient construct for many Asian Americans, especially those whose families may have recently immigrated. There is a marked distance between most Asian languages and English, Asian customs and practices and American ones, and other elements of more collectivistic Asian cultures and a mythically individualistic American culture. In addition, within Asian American communities and families, there are often conflicting pressures to "fit-in" to American culture and society to maximize chances of economic security and success, and a simultaneous pressure to hold on to cultures of origin (Castillo et al., 2012).

Acculturative stress has also been posited to be associated with disordered eating behaviors and increased body dissatisfaction in Asian American samples (Davis & Katzman, 1999; Perez et al., 2002; Smart et al., 2011) through the mechanism of exposure to Western norms and values leading to internalizing these norms and values and their commensurate attractiveness ideals. Eating disorder behaviors appear to function as a necessary coping mechanism that provides relief from the impacts of acculturative stress (Kalantzis et al., 2022). The process of acculturation and the resulting distress appear to be significant factors in body dissatisfaction, self-esteem, and disordered eating behaviors.

Beyond Thinness

Sociocultural models for the development of eating disorders (Cheng, 2014; Stice, 2001; Striegel-Moore & Bulik, 2007) involve the internalizing of societal standards of attractiveness and worth and their association with thinness. Ubiquitous, unrelenting messages about thinness and virtue sets the stage upon which body image disturbances and dissatisfaction arise, in part, from perceived discrepancies between oneself and these societal ideals.

But these models do not adequately capture the nuances of the experiences of people of color, including Asian Americans, whose intersectional identities develop in a sociocultural context that values not just thinness, but more specifically, thinness and Whiteness. The thin ideal has embedded within it messages about Whiteness as the aspirational default which necessitates the denigration of other identities. Whiteness is an important qualifier which is always implicitly there when we discuss thinness, whether we make it explicit or not (Strings, 2019). The "thin ideal" is, in reality, the "White, thin ideal." In any discussion of body image, but especially when discussing body image in communities of color, it is imperative that we acknowledge and incorporate the problematic nature of this messaging that values certain bodies (i.e., White bodies) and sets them as the default, and devalues other bodies (i.e., those of non-White people). For Asian Americans, the clear message is that Asian bodies and Asian-ness are not desired and of lesser value (Zhou et al., 2022).

For many Asian people, faces are the most notable contrast that distinguishes Asian bodies from White bodies, the specificity of which is not necessarily captured in Western conceptualizations of body image. Frederick et al. (2016) summarized and supported the argument for the construct of face image as distinct from a body image as a particularly salient feature for Asian American women. They outline several elements of face image, including perceptions about one's own face and facial appearance, as well as feelings about the ethnically specific, phenotypic features of one's face. More Western appearing facial features (e.g., more Caucasian looking eyes, more defined nose and jawline, whiter skin) are associated with greater attractiveness and, by extension, with greater opportunities socially and in business (Frederick et al., 2016). Face image appears to be an ethnically specific element of appearance surveillance and evaluation which, in turn, are related to risk for eating pathology.

Western-centric facial ideals and the resulting dissatisfaction with face image among Asian Americans can lead to insecurity, impaired self-worth and, in some cases, compensatory measures such as cosmetic surgery. South Korea, for example, leads the world in cosmetic surgery procedures per capita (Holliday & Elfving-Hwang, 2012), and among the most common procedures, as it is in other Asian countries, is the blepharoplasty, or "double-eyelid" surgery, which creates more Caucasian appearing, larger appearing eyes. Rhinoplasties, or "nose jobs," to create more defined, Western-appearing noses are also common procedures in Asian countries (Kwon et al., 2021). In contrast, White recipients of cosmetic procedures rarely have procedures to change their racial identity (Davis, 2003).

According to Yu and colleagues (2019), other elements of body image with specific salience for Asian Americans are height, shape of arms and legs, and breasts and hips. Like face image, these features are explicitly compared against their White counterparts with White features being perceived as more desirable and attractive. There is also a strong influence of colorism, valuing those within a culture with lighter skin and devaluing those with darker skin, within Asian cultures. Lighter skin is associated with wealth, refinement, purity, and femininity, but also, most directly, aspirational Whiteness. In all of these examples, there is an unambiguous message here about whose bodies are valued and whose bodies need to be "fixed."

Applicability of Sociocultural Model to Asian Americans

Existing models that inform the conceptualizing of the posited sociocultural pathology of eating disorders have been derived from White/European samples and, more importantly, from White European theories. Pedagogy and subsequent praxis continue to reflect their Western European, individualistic context as well as the establishment of a clear default (or normal), namely White, cis-male, and heteronormative. To some extent, pathology has always been defined by one's distance from that default condition and all the biases contained within them. This has certainly been true of our understanding of the development of eating disorders. At best, there have been discussions about and attempts to adapt these ideas to non-European persons, but there remains the core problematic nature of having the basis and foundation of even these adaptations deeply biased and prejudiced by their provenance in Whiteness. For example, there are gendered and racialized messages that are present in the ways that American culture views Asian people. Asian women, in particular, tend to be fetishized and hypersexualized (Kawamura, 2011), objectified and cast as submissive. Asian men are viewed as passive, nonsexual, and not traditionally masculine (Chua & Fujino, 1999; Poon & Ho, 2008).

Using structural equation modeling (SEM), Cheng (2014) tested a theoretical, causative model of factors related to race/racism, culture, and sociocultural influences as they predict disordered eating behaviors. In examining disordered eating behaviors in Asian American women, they found that greater affiliation with Western beauty ideals was correlated with worse body image and greater degrees of disordered eating behaviors. Their model also demonstrated a direct relationship between Asian American women's experiences of discrimination and disordered eating behaviors, mediated by lower self-esteem, confirming the broader conceptualization of disordered eating behaviors in people of color as resulting from experiences of racism and discrimination, which themselves result in greater degrees of negative self-evaluations. More specifically, having a history of experiencing race/ethnicity-based teasing appears to potentiate internalization of the Western ideal, resulting in greater impacts on negative self-esteem and increased levels of body dissatisfaction.

In another study of Asian American women, internalization of the thin ideal and acculturative stress were positively related to disordered eating behaviors (Akoury et al., 2019), supporting the notion that a clearer understanding of cultural factors is key to elucidating disordered eating in Asian Americans. Of note, a greater degree of biculturalism, proficiency and comfort with both one's culture of origin and the dominant culture appeared to protect individuals from developing disordered eating. Tsong and Smart (2015) found that the pressures of navigating dual cultures and having trouble meeting the often-conflicting expectations of dual cultures actually increase the risk for developing disordered eating.

Conclusions and Recommendations

While the presumptive truth of who can be affected by an eating disorder is relatively clear, disparities remain in part due to larger societal prejudices which result in discrimination and marginalization. More directly, these disparities are also reflective of an ontological question regarding the nature of eating disorders. If they are primarily psychologically driven by wanting to be thinner, then thinking some groups might be protected from such pressures might make some sense. However, if eating disorders are instead psychologically rooted in a profound sense of being lesser-than, being inadequate, being broken (which they are), in the wake of genetic vulnerability and predisposition, it makes little sense to presume anyone immune.

As a starting point, it is essential to acknowledge that Asian Americans' experiences of eating disorders emanate from the intersection of race/ethnicity, and gender, among other overlapping identity factors (Le et al., 2020). The lived experiences of racism and misogyny, just to name two, for Asian Americans are different from the experiences of their White peers because of the interconnected nature of having multiple minoritized identities. Decades of research on Minority Stress (Meyer, 2003) for those with multiple marginalized identities have firmly established the confluence of chronic, daily stressors related to minority status and consequent negative health outcomes. Asian communities, as well as the world at large, deluge Asian Americans with messages about the relative worth of Asian-ness and of Whiteness, and the meaning of the distance of definably Asian characteristics and features from the White, thin ideal.

Providers hoping to work with Asian Americans who have eating disorders must have a more complex understanding of the acculturative process and associated stressors as experienced by the Asian diaspora. In a survey of therapists treating Asian American women with eating disorders (Smart et al., 2011), common themes emerge related to therapists' conceptualization of ED in the cultural context and approaches to treatment. The former includes achieving at all costs and family dynamics. The latter includes cultural adaptations to mainstream therapy and specific therapeutic emphases. Therapists reported having direct conversations, challenging differing cultural norms and involving the parents of adult clients in a culturally appropriate manner. These recommendations reflect the need for clinicians to understand their own biases and stereotypes and more routinely inquire about issues related to culture and experiences of discrimination and racism. They found that a more nuanced understanding of intergenerational cultural expectations, internal conflicts around existing in dual cultures, and the resultant stress was also vital. In addition, the specific meaning of thinness and the messages received about thinness from both the culture of origin and the mainstream culture should be explored as a crucial factor in eating pathology.

To better capture the particulars of the experience of Asian Americans, clinicians must more routinely ask about daily and chronic racial traumas. The fetishization and objectification of Asian women and desexualization of Asian men are potent microaggressions experienced by Asian Americans. Even seemingly innocuous questions about other elements of Asian identities can feel like a questioning of our American-ness given the history of treating Asians in America as perpetual foreigners and outsiders to be treated with suspicion.

The collectivistic cultures from which many Asian Americans come result in some vital differences from Western American families. While in a Western context, the main focus might be on individuation from the family of origin, in an Asian context, there must be an understanding of different family structures and dynamics. Familial interdependence may be an expectation or normative value. The notion of Filial piety (respect for elders) increases the pressure that can be experienced when attempting to assert one's own needs. Consistent with previous findings, Tsong and Smart (2015) found that the need for Asian Americans to please parents through achievements was associated with disordered eating. This pressure is in part based on the notion that one's actions not only reflect upon one's self but also upon one's family, community, and ancestors. These manifestations of cultural conflict are essential to incorporate into conceptualizations of eating disorders in this population.

Finally, typical assessments must be expanded to reflect a more specific understanding of the salient forces that manifest as eating pathology in Asian Americans. Yu et al. (2019) recommend assessing interdependence and independence as constructs, as well as the client's identification with individualistic or collectivistic values and beliefs. Given the clear association between face image and risk of eating disorders, providers should be asking more detailed questions about perceptions and meaning of various elements of face image and body image for Asian American patients. It is imperative that clinicians obtain a clear, longitudinal history of teasing (especially when race-based), marginalization, discrimination and other experiences of systemic, chronic racism. Culturally relevant and specific beliefs about mental health, stigma, and food should also be explored and incorporated into treatment approaches.

The dominance of Western European ideas and perspectives on the nosology of mental illness, not to mention the development of interventions and treatments, has created and perpetuated a system wherein Whiteness is the default condition and against which pathology or deviance is defined (Sue et al., 2012). This built in bias requires not merely an adaptation, but a substantive change in the approach to prevention, assessment, and treatment of eating disorders in Asian Americans to more closely reflect the most current understanding.

DISCUSSION QUESTIONS

1. What is the relationship between the model minority myth, acculturation stress, and eating disorders in the Asian American community?
2. What might sociocultural models for the development of eating disorders miss when considering the experiences of the Asian American community?

3. How would you consider the role of collectivistic cultures when treating a patient in a Western individualistic context?
4. What questions would you ask when assessing an Asian American man for an eating disorder?

REFERENCES

Akoury, L. M., Warren, C. S., & Culbert, K. M. (2019). Disordered eating in Asian American women: Sociocultural and culture-specific predictors. *Frontiers in Psychology, 10*, 1950.

Berry, J. W. (1992). Acculturation and adaptation in a new society. *International Migration, 30*, 69–85.

Berry, J. W. (1998). Acculturative stress. In P. B. Organista, K. M. Chun, & G. Marín (Eds.), *Readings in ethnic psychology* (pp. 117–122). Taylor & Frances/ Routledge.

Borah, E. G. (1995). Filipinos in Unamuno's California Expedition of 1587. *Amerasia Journal, 21*(3), 175–184.

Budiman, A., & Ruiz, N. G. (2021, May 16). *Asian Americans are the fastest-growing racial or ethnic group in the U.S.* Pew Research Center. https://www.pewresearch.org/fact-tank/2021/04/09/asian-americans-are-the-fastest-growing-racial-or-ethnic-group-in-the-u-s/

Castillo, L. G., Zahn, M. P., & Cano, M. A. (2012). Predictors of familial acculturative stress in Asian American College Students. *Journal of College Counseling, 15*(1), 52–64. https://doi.org/10.1002/j.2161-1882.2012.00005.x

Cheng, H. L. (2014). Disordered eating among Asian/Asian American women: Racial and cultural factors as correlates. *The Counseling Psychologist, 42*(6), 821–851.

Chua, P., & Fujino, D. C. (1999). Negotiating new Asian-American masculinities: Attitudes and gender expectations. *The Journal of Men's Studies,* 7(3), 391–413. https://doi.org/10.3149/jms.0703.391

Davis, K. (2003). Surgical passing: Or why Michael Jackson's nose makes us uneasy. *Feminist Theory, 4*(1), 73–92.

Davis, C., & Katzman, M. A. (1999). Perfection as acculturation: Psychological correlates of eating problems in Chinese male and female students living in the United States. *International Journal of Eating Disorders, 25*(1), 65-70.

Federal Bureau of Investigation (2021). *Hate crime data.* National Incident-Based Reporting System (NIBRS). https://cde.ucr.cjis.gov/LATEST/webapp/#/pages/explorer/crime/hate-crime

Fox, M., Thayer, Z., & Wadhwa, P. D. (2017). Acculturation and health: the moderating role of socio-cultural context. *American Anthropologist, 119*(3), 405–421. https://doi.org/10.1111/aman.12867

Frederick, D. A., Kelly, M. C., Latner, J. D., Sandhu, G., & Tsong, Y. (2016). Body image and face image in Asian American and White women: Examining associations with surveillance, construal of self, perfectionism, and sociocultural pressures. *Body Image, 16*, 113–125.

Hall, G. C. N., Berkman, E. T., Zane, N. W., Leong, F. T., Hwang, W. C., Nezu, A. M., Nezu, C. M., Hong, J. J., Chu, J. P., & Huang, E. R. (2021). Reducing mental health disparities by increasing the personal relevance of interventions. *American Psychologist*, *76*(1), 91.

Holliday, R., & Elfving-Hwang, J. (2012). Gender, globalization and aesthetic surgery in South Korea. *Body & Society*, *18*(2), 58–81.

Kalantzis, M. A., Lim, S., Dauber, A. K., Studer-Perez, E. I., Silverman, Z. J., & O'Brien, W. H. (2022). Acculturative stress and eating disorder psychopathology: A meta-analysis. *Eating Behaviors*, 101694.

Kawamura, K. Y. (2011). Asian American body images. In T. F. Cash & L. Smolak (Eds.), *Body image: A handbook of science, practice, and prevention* (pp. 229–236). Guilford Press.

Kwon, S. H., Lao, W. W., Lee, C. H., Hsu, A. T., Koide, S., Chen, H. Y., Cho, K. H., Tanaka, E., Cheon, Y. W., & Chang, T. N. (2021). Experiences and attitudes toward aesthetic procedures in East Asia: a cross-sectional survey of five geographical regions. *Archives of Plastic Surgery*, *48*(6), 660–669. https://doi.org/10.5999/aps.2020.02565

Le, T. P., Kuo, L., & Yamasaki, V. (2020). Gendered racial microaggressions, feminism, and Asian American women's eating pathology: An intersectional investigation. *Sex Roles*, *83*, 127–142.

Liu, T., Liu, C., & Chang, Y. J. (2022). Asian American mental health amidst COVID-19 anti-Asian racism: Internalized racism and generational status as moderators. *Asian American Journal of Psychology*, *13*(4), 328.

Marques, L., Alegria, M., Becker, A. E., Chen, C. N., Fang, A., Chosak, A., & Diniz, J. B. (2011). Comparative prevalence, correlates of impairment, and service utilization for eating disorders across U.S. ethnic groups: Implications for reducing ethnic disparities in health care access for eating disorders. *International Journal of Eating Disorders*, *44*(5), 412–420.

Meyer, I. H. (2003). Prejudice, social stress, and mental health in lesbian, gay, and bisexual populations: Conceptual issues and research evidence. *Psychological Bulletin*, *129*, 674–697.

Perez, M., Voelz, Z. R., Pettit, J. W., & Joiner, T. E., Jr. (2002). The role of acculturative stress and body dissatisfaction in predicting bulimic symptomatology across ethnic groups. *International Journal of Eating Disorders*, *31*(4), 442–454.

Poon, M. K. L., & Ho, P. T. T. (2008). Negotiating social stigma among gay Asian men. *Sexualities*, *11*(1-2), 245-268. https://doi.org/10.1177/1363460707085472

Poon, O., Squire, D., Kodama, C., Byrd, A., Chan, J., Manzano, L., Furr, S., & Bishundat, D. (2016). A critical review of the model minority myth in selected literature on Asian Americans and Pacific Islanders in higher education. *Review of Educational Research*, *86*(2), 469–502. https://doi-org.avoserv2.library.fordham.edu/10.3102/0034654315612205

Satcher Health Leadership Institute at Morehouse School of Medicine. (2022). *The Economic Burden of Mental Health Inequities in the United States Report*. Satcher Health Leadership Institute.

Smart, R., Tsong, Y., Mejía, O. L., Hayashino, D., & Braaten, M. E. T. (2011). Therapists' experiences treating Asian American women with eating disorders. *Professional Psychology: Research and Practice*, *42*(4), 308.

Stice, E. (2001). A prospective test of the dual-pathway model of bulimic pathology: Mediating effects of dieting and negative affect. *Journal of Abnormal Psychology, 110*, 124–135.

Striegel-Moore, R. H., & Bulik, C. M. (2007). Risk factors for eating disorders. *American Psychologist, 62*, 181–198.

Strings, S. (2019). Fearing the black body. In *Fearing the Black body*. New York University Press.

Sue, S., Cheng, J. K. Y., Saad, C. S., & Chu, J. P. (2012). Asian American mental health: A call to action. *American Psychologist, 67*(7), 532.

Tsong, Y., & Smart, R. (2015). The role of cultural beliefs in disordered eating among Asian-American women. *Asian American Journal of Psychology, 6*(4), 342.

U.S. Census Bureau. (2021, August 12). *2020 U.S. Population More racially and ethnically diverse than measured in 2010*. https://www.census.gov/library/stories/2021/08/2020-united-states-population-more-racially-ethnically-diverse-than-2010.html

U.S. Department of Health and Human Services. (2001). *Mental health: Culture, race, and ethnicity—a supplement to mental health: A report of the surgeon general*. U.S. Department of Health and Human Services, Substance Abuse and Mental Health Services Administration, Center for Mental Health Services.

Yoo, H. C., Burrola, K. S., & Steger, M. F. (2010). A preliminary report on a new measure: Internalization of the Model Minority Myth Measure (IM-4) and its psychological correlates among Asian American college students. *Journal of Counseling Psychology, 57*(1), 114–127. https://doi.org/10.1037/a0017871

Yu, K. Y., Pope, S. C., & Perez, M. (2019). Clinical treatment and practice recommendations for disordered eating in Asian Americans. *Professional Psychology: Research and Practice, 50*(5), 279–287. https://doi.org/10.1037/pro0000244

Zhou, Z., Liew, J., & Luo, W. (2022). Acculturation and disordered eating among Asian American college students: The role of objectification through a sociocultural lens. *International Journal of Environmental Research and Public Health, 19*(21), 13967.

CHAPTER 12

PREVENTING AND TREATING EATING DISORDERS AND DISORDERED EATING AMONG ATHLETES

Sasha Gorrell, Rachael Flatt, Prim Siripipat, and Danielle Chapa

Athletic participation has many benefits, including improved physical and psychological health among athletes compared to non-athlete peers (Weight et al., 2016), and positive impact on adolescent academic outcomes (Videon, 2002). However, research also suggests that participation in competitive sports can increase the likelihood of developing eating disorders (EDs) and disordered eating behaviors (DEBs; Bratland-Sanda & Sundgot-Borgen, 2013; Chatterton & Petrie, 2013; Greenleaf et al., 2009). By definition, EDs are serious mental illnesses that are characterized by unhealthy eating patterns and weight control behaviors (American Psychiatric Association, 2013), and are associated with psychiatric and medical morbidity (Gibson et al., 2019; Swanson et al., 2011) and elevated mortality (van Eeden et al., 2021). In contrast, DEBs are a collection of abnormal eating patterns that are quite common (Neumark-Sztainer et al., 2006) and although they may pose a threat to physical health, they do not meet the clinical diagnosis of an ED (Thompson & Sherman, 2014). Unique features of both the athlete mindset (e.g., Arthur-Cameselle & Baltzell, 2012; Gorrell & Anderson,

Counseling Individuals With Eating Disorders: An Intersectional Approach, pp. 263–288

2018) and the sporting environment (e.g., Davis et al., 2018; Scott et al., 2022) can place athletes at greater risk for both EDs and DEBs, and their associated negative physical and psychological consequences (Gibson et al., 2019; Mountjoy et al., 2014). In particular, eating pathology among athletes can lead to a range of serious metabolic and physiologic consequences, including relative energy deficiency in sport (REDS), a condition that results from insufficient caloric intake and energy over-expenditure (Carson et al., 2022; Holtzman et al., 2019; Mountjoy et al., 2014; Torstveit et al., 2019). Given these considerable psychological and physical health risks, continued efforts to better understand and treat EDs and DEBs among athletes within competitive sports is of great importance.

This chapter begins with an overview of research evidence regarding the interplay between athletics, eating pathology, and intersectional identity. Here, risk factors for EDs and DEBs are identified as prevalence estimates across various athlete sub-groups. A discussion of evidence-based treatment (EBT) and prevention efforts that have been tested to date follows. Finally, a case study analysis is included. The chapter concludes with suggestions for future treatment and research directions, with a particular emphasis on ways in which clinicians and researchers must continue to consider intersectional factors within their work.

SPECIFIC RISK FOR EATING PATHOLOGY AMONG ATHLETES

Research examining risk factors associated with EDs and DEBs among athletes has considered intersecting factors specific to the athlete and the sporting environment. For example, one survey study that explored explicit and implicit teammate influences found that athletes who had received a critical comment from a teammate had significantly greater eating and exercise pathology, higher anxiety, and lower self-esteem compared to those who had not (Scott et al., 2022). Other work has compared vulnerability for EDs and DEBs across different sport-type classifications such as leanness, aesthetic, or weight-class sports (de Bruin, 2017). While definitions differ, leanness sports emphasize a thin physique (e.g., distance running; Carson et al., 2022), aesthetic sports include artistic appeal as a basis for evaluation (e.g., figure skating; Voelker et al., 2014), and weight-class sports stipulate weight criteria for participation (e.g., wrestling, rowing; Bratland-Sanda & Sundgot-Borgen, 2013; Gorrell et al., 2021; Krauss et al., 2018). Research generally suggests that individuals participating in leanness, aesthetic, or weight-class sports are at a greater risk for eating psychopathology than their other sport-type counterparts (Anderson & Petrie, 2012; Bratland-Sanda & Sundgot-Borgen, 2013; de Bruin, 2017).

In many sport contexts, there is a perception that "a thin/lean body shape equates to success." This message may be communicated directly or indirectly to athletes (Arthur-Cameselle & Baltzell, 2012; Thompson & Sherman, 2014). Context matters; one recent study found that elite female athletes were able to differentiate between their body image ideal in daily life and their body image in sports, identifying the latter as the key factor in the development of their ED (de Bruin & Oudejans, 2018). Some sports (e.g., tennis) may qualify as both lean and non-lean, depending on the measures and criteria used. Further, one's position on the team (e.g., offense or defense) may necessitate a different body ideal, and therefore increase risk for DEBs. One study found that 9% of rugby players had DEBs, but within this sample, 52.2% of the forwards endorsed objective binge-eating, compared to 31.4% among backs (Compte et al., 2018).

Although female athletes may report improved body image compared to non-athletes (Varnes et al., 2013), a sport-specific body ideal (e.g., striving to achieve leanness) may motivate engagement in DEBs (Homan, 2010; Kerr et al., 2006), which may be exacerbated in aesthetic or weight class sports (Flatt et al., 2021). Such behaviors may be positively reinforced by coaches, peers, and family, which can hinder acknowledgment of the problem and reduce help-seeking (Flatt et al., 2021). Even when symptoms are observable, within the sports context, they may be misinterpreted as performance-enhancing behaviors (Martinsen & Sundgot-Borgen, 2013). For example, weight loss, dieting, excessive training, and achieving a specific body type are often associated with perceived improvements in performance (Sundgot-Borgen & Torstveit, 2010). In addition, some high-performance sporting environments promote a culture of "mental toughness" (Walton et al., 2019), whereby fear of consequences, including loss of selection or judgment from coaches or teammates, can inhibit help-seeking (Castaldelli-Maia et al., 2019). We note this issue to highlight how the prevalence estimates that we discuss below may reflect under-reporting among athletes who may be reluctant to seek help for emergent eating pathology.

Prevalence and Incidence Estimates of Eating Pathology Among Athletes

In general, the risk of having a subclinical or clinical ED is higher among elite athletes (13.5%) compared to the general population (4.6%; Sundgot-Borgen & Torstveit, 2004). Elite status, which is generally characterized by high-level athletes who compete nationally, internationally, and/or professionally, has also been shown to increase risk for EDs and DEBs compared to community controls (Byrne & McLean, 2002), and to more recreational athlete counterparts (Smolak et al., 2000; Youngman & Simpson, 2014). However, rates of EDs and DEBs vary, due in part to other factors mentioned above such as type of sport (e.g., leanness, aesthetic sports) and, as highlighted above, whether athlete status is a risk or protective factor in regard to risk for EDs or DEBs. For instance, one study found that ED prevalence was 7% vs. 2.3% among adolescent athletes compared with controls, and higher for female than male athletes (14% vs. 3.2%, respectively; Martinsen & Sundgot-Borgen, 2013). Furthermore, an early systematic review of 26 studies of female athletes concluded that athletes were slightly more at risk for eating pathology than non-athletes (Smolak et al., 2000). However, findings from at least two studies suggest the opposite, whereby among adolescent elite athletes, a higher prevalence of peer control subjects reported DEBs (15–26%) compared to the athletes (11–15%; Martinsen et al., 2010; Rosendahl et al., 2009). Further, in a recent meta-analysis of 56 studies of female athletes, mean differences between athletes and non-athletes were non-significant for overall ED pathology as measured by self-report, loss-of-control eating, restricting, and drive for thinness (Chapa et al., 2022). In this study, body dissatisfaction was higher among non-athletes compared to athletes. However, sport type was a significant moderator of body dissatisfaction differences between athletes and non-athletes, such that effect sizes were larger in studies with aesthetic or leanness sports. These results underscore the aforementioned risk of EDs and DEBs among those participating in these two sport types (e.g., Anderson & Petrie, 2012; de Bruin, 2017; Voelker et al., 2014).

The entire spectrum of ED diagnoses and different types of DEBs appear to be represented across athlete samples (Bratland-Sanda & Sundgot-Borgen, 2013; Gorrell et al., 2021; Greenleaf et al., 2009; Petrie et al., 2008) with one recent study showing that percentages across all probable ED diagnoses in a large survey sample of athletes in the United States were similar (Flatt et al., 2021). For example, based on symptom report, 29% of athletes in this sample likely had subclinical bulimia nervosa, compared with 27% of non-athletes (Flatt et al., 2021). Prevalence estimates of certain behaviors, such as excessive exercise, also appear to be higher among athletes (11%), compared with non-athletes (5.5%; Flatt et al., 2021); several studies show elevated rates of those who were considered "symptomatic" relative to excessive exercise (along with other DEBs) in collegiate male athlete samples (16–25%; Chatterton & Petrie, 2013; Gorrell et al., 2021; Petrie et al., 2008). Notably, there are several commonly used terms for problematic exercise in the field, including "excessive," in part due to complexities around conceptualization and differentiation from high-level training and across diagnoses (e.g., Mond & Gorrell, 2021). More research is indicated in this domain in order to better capture the compulsive and driven nature of this behavior to compensate for caloric intake—above and beyond training.

More ED and DEB research has been conducted with majority female athlete samples compared to male or nonbinary samples, and research is very limited when considering the intersectionality of gender and other identities. There is relatively consistent evidence that estimates of EDs and DEBs are lower in male compared to female athletes (Kristjánsdóttir et al., 2019; Martinsen et al., 2010; Petrie et al., 2008; Schaal et al., 2011; Sundgot-Borgen & Torstveit, 2004). While again, rates vary, overall estimates suggest that up to 45% of female athletes and up to 19% of male athletes experience EDs or DEBs (Bratland-Sanda & Sundgot-Borgen, 2013). Of note, in a meta-analytic review specific to male athletes, male athletes did not differ from non-athlete controls in rates of DEBs (Chapman & Woodman, 2016); however, in this review, significant moderator effects emerged for sport type, specific to higher rates of DEBs among males participating in wrestling.

These findings also support that risk for EDs and DEBs is relative to sport type (Bratland-Sanda & Sundgot-Borgen, 2013; Byrne & McLean, 2002; Schaal et al., 2011; Sundgot-Borgen & Torstveit, 2004), however, results are not consistent. For example, one study of elite female athletes found that more athletes in leanness sports (46.7%) reported EDs than athletes in non-leanness sports (19.8%), or controls (21.4%); however, when adjusting for age, there were no differences between athletes and controls with respect to rates of EDs or DEBs (Torstveit et al., 2007). Further, in another study, no differences in dieting or DEBs were found between athletes in leanness and non-leanness sports (Martinsen et al., 2010).

Perhaps as a result of sport-specific body dissatisfaction (Krentz & Warschburger, 2011), higher rates of EDs and DEBs have also been evidenced among those participating in aesthetic sports compared to non-aesthetic sport counterparts or controls. Several studies have specifically highlighted elevated prevalence estimates of EDs and DEBs in ballet (Arcelus et al., 2014), figure skating (Voelker et al., 2018), and gymnastics (Tan et al., 2016), relative to other non-aesthetic activities. In one sample of female figure skaters, 13% of the sample reported DEBs; this prevalence did not differ from adolescent age-matched controls. Similar estimates were evidenced in a sample of professional adult female ballet dancers, where 11% of those surveyed met clinical status for an ED (Gorrell et al., 2019). Among elite collegiate female gymnasts, 29% and 6% evidenced subclinical or clinical EDs, respectively (Anderson & Petrie, 2012). Findings are also a bit mixed here, in that while prevalence estimates were not delineated within one systematic review, reported effect sizes indicate higher prevalence of eating pathology among dancers, with no significant effects emergent for gymnasts (Smolak et al., 2000).

Few studies to date have focused on eating pathology in retired athletes or directly considered how intersecting identities might impact vulnerability for DEB. One recent qualitative study noted that participants shared how they had come to understand post-retirement that reconciliation between sport-related body ideals (e.g., muscular) and more socially constructed thin-ideals was nearly impossible (i.e., aligning with a conception of "the female athlete paradox"; Krane et al., 2004), whereby femininity and muscularity were juxtaposed (Barrett et al., 2022). Incidence estimates among retired athletes have only been reported in one study thus far, citing a rate of 8.3% for any ED across 6 months (Gouttebarge & Kerkhoffs, 2017). Among gymnasts and swimmers (i.e., two leanness sports), prevalence estimates range from 9.3–20.0% (Kerr et al., 2006; Thompson et al., 2021) and point prevalence estimates range from 3.1–27.4% among retired gymnasts, hockey players, and swimmers (Gouttebarge & Kerkhoffs, 2017; Thompson et al., 2021).

In summary, risk factors for EDs and DEBs among athletes that appear to be the most robust and consistent to date include participation in leanness, aesthetic, or weight class sports; and emphasis on achievement of a sport-specific ideal. How different identities and demographics within the sports context and their intersections may interact and impact prevalence and incidence estimates of ED-related features such as body dissatisfaction, perceived ideal physiques, and other identified risk factors has not been studied sufficiently.

EVIDENCE-BASED TREATMENTS (EBTs)

Athletes comprise a unique population with specific clinical needs (de Bruin, 2017). Although some intervention research has addressed how to reduce symptoms of DEBs among athletes (Gorrell et al., 2019; Perelman et al., 2022; Stewart et al., 2019; Tomalski et al., 2019), research devoted specifically to the *treatment* of EDs among athletes is still growing (Stranberg et al., 2020; Thompson & Sherman, 2014) and only a small number of interventions have been implemented with athletes (Sandgren et al., 2020). Recent commentary and qualitative work provide a rationale for athlete-specific treatment programs that address risk factors within the athletic environment, and unique characteristics of athlete status that impact onset and maintenance of symptoms and treatment response (Arthur-Cameselle & Baltzell, 2012; de Bruin, 2017; Plateau et al., 2017; Stranberg et al., 2020). In the United States, some ED treatment centers feature an "athlete track" and a limited number of programs are dedicated specifically to athlete ED care (Conviser et al., 2018; Fewell et al., 2018a, 2018b; Stranberg et al., 2020). The International Olympic Committee, among other large governing bodies that interface with athletes, have published positions regarding prevention, early identification, and treatment of EDs (Mountjoy et al., 2018). In a systematic review of 13 studies and 9 different ED interventions, the most successful were conducted face-to-face, had a longer duration with higher session frequency, and targeted varying concepts such as self-esteem and ED pathology (Sandgren et al., 2020). A specific consideration that may be important when formulating an EBT plan for an athlete with an ED includes forming a multidisciplinary treatment team where all involved personnel represent different fields (i.e., athletic, medical, psychological, nutrition), and are positioned to provide collaborative care. At a minimum, this team includes a psychotherapy clinician with an ED specialty, a dietitian with experience in athlete nutrition, and a primary medical doctor who can monitor physical health on a regular basis. Other key stakeholders include coaching staff/athletic trainers who engage with the athlete, parents/spouses/family, and athletic administrative staff members, as indicated (Conviser et al., 2018).

Practical Considerations in Referral to ED Care

Early detection and expedient referral to ED treatment is essential to ensuring optimal treatment outcomes (Treasure & Russell, 2011). Effective screening and determination of an appropriate referral depends on sensitively evaluating the presenting concerns through a biopsychosocial framework and identifying factors that trigger and maintain EDs and DEBs (de Bruin, 2017). For some athletes, seeking treatment can be challenging considering frequent lack of ED literacy among athletes and coaches (Plateau et al., 2017) and support may be lacking when the onset of eating pathology jeopardizes the athlete's ability to participate in certain competitive events. In addition, if an athlete is traveling when monitoring is indicated, medical resources specific to ED care may need to be sought and some resources that are typically available to an athlete when "in season" may not be an option in the "off season." For some at an elite or professional level, the timing of referral to treatment may negatively impact their career, or prevent them from qualifying for certain milestone events (e.g., the Olympics). In these instances, protecting the privacy of the athlete may also be important, and nuanced clinical judgment and consultation within the treatment team about how to best support the athlete is indicated. Given that participation in ED treatment may require significant alterations to the athlete's training regimen, competition, school, employment, and/or team obligations, personnel from various settings should be involved in facilitating the athlete's treatment (Conviser et al., 2018).

EBTs used to treat EDs include cognitive-behavioral therapy enhanced for EDs (CBT-E), dialectical behavior therapy (DBT), acceptance and commitment therapy (ACT), and family-based treatment (FBT), all of which should also be considered for the care of athletes when appropriate (Conviser et al., 2018). Global international guidelines support FBT as the first-line treatment approach for children and adolescents with anorexia or bulimia nervosa; here, caregivers are considered essential supports as the youth navigate the treatment process with their family (Gorrell et al., 2019). For adolescents for whom FBT is ineffective or contraindicated (e.g., should caregivers be unable to participate in treatment) CBT is additionally recommended (Gorrell et al., 2019). Although there are no recommended treatments for adults with anorexia nervosa, there is considerable empirical support for CBT across transdiagnostic EDs (Fairburn et al., 2003; Linardon et al., 2017) and growing support for the use of third-wave approaches like DBT and ACT (Ben-Porath et al., 2020; Juarascio et al., 2017). Further discussion of the principal components of CBT are included just below in a case vignette. In addition to addressing the ED, a tailored treatment plan might also address comorbid presentations that frequently co-occur with EDs (e.g., anxiety and mood disorders; Drakes et al., 2021; Ferrell et al., 2022; Swanson et al., 2011) and include other intersectional factors, such as (when applicable) familial dynamics, interpersonal relationships, sexuality, identity development, and trauma history.

Practical Considerations When Enrolled in ED Care

Many concerns highlighted above extend to when an athlete is participating in treatment. For example, clinical decision-making about when an athlete may be ready to discharge from a higher level of ED care may include prioritization of their traveling or seasonal schedule (e.g., an athlete may stay on tour with modified activity in the off season, when dedicated rest is planned). Athletes may also have sport-specific nutritional needs above and beyond general metabolic recovery from an ED, which underscores the importance of having this expertise as part of the multidisciplinary treatment team. Given the known practice of body comparison in group treatment settings, it might also be difficult for some athletes to assimilate into non-specialized treatment milieus as they might feel out of place (Plateau et al., 2017). This concern may be further exacerbated for nonbinary or transgender athletes given that few higher-level-of-care ED treatment centers are able to provide care in a group setting where individuals who are not women-identifying feel equally represented.

Domains to Address During ED Care

For the athlete who is enrolled in care and addressing their ED, the function of DEBs may hold additional complexity. For example, self-induced vomiting may serve a general emotion-regulation purpose; it may occur secondary to binge eating; and it may be motivated by a desire to lose weight to enhance sport performance. These are only three of many possibilities. Supporting an athlete to understand the intersection of their ED and athletic identity is critical in helping them to begin to make effective behavior change. Other aspects of athlete identity may need to be explicitly addressed in the context of psychotherapy. For instance, rigid internalization of identity may prevent an athlete from thinking more flexibly about their ability to participate in that sport, even with a different training regimen or body type. It is common early in treatment to observe patients with high athletic identity, particularly those with anorexia nervosa, who hold strong beliefs that their success in the sport is directly tied to their current physique, and as a result are less motivated and engaged in treatment out of fear that performance will be negatively impacted. Relatedly, although body image is typically addressed within evidence-based ED treatments, it is important that athletes engage in thinking about body image in the sport context. For example, to what extent does the athlete formulate their self-concept and body satisfaction based on sport-specific ideals, typical cultural ideals, and/or other ideals within their immediate awareness (e.g., gender), and how do these ideals potentially interact and contribute to their ED? (Barrett et al., 2022; Krane et al., 2004). It is also important to address pressures that are specific to the athletic environment, such as performance pressures (e.g., determining if a coach has instructed the athlete to lose weight), and relationships and communication styles with teammates and coaches (e.g., critical comments; Scott et al., 2019; 2022). Each of the above domains is impacted by the intersection of the patient's personal identities and athlete identity, which will be a substantive area of future research around tailoring ED treatment.

Return to Activity

An important aspect of treating an athlete with an ED includes their relationship with exercise. Athlete identity may impact willingness to decrease activity level in the acute phase of illness (Thompson & Sherman, 2014). These internal pressures to continue athletics at a high level, despite negative consequences, can be compounded by external pressure and messaging from coaching staff. Accordingly, it is typically helpful to designate one provider on the team—typically the treating therapist—to oversee return to exercise. Return to activity should be graded, shared with all team members, supervised, and dependent on psychological readiness and compliance with other treatment goals. Of note, some work suggests that supervised activity in the context of athlete ED treatment may yield improvements in strength and power (Fewell et al., 2018b).

Not all athletes are motivated to return to activity or to competitive sports; oftentimes, negative self-evaluation or fear of judgment from others (e.g., teammates, coaches) related to having a different body shape or being deconditioned leads an athlete to avoid re-engagement in the sport (Plateau et al., 2017). In these cases, careful evaluation of the function of avoidance is indicated and often warrants a discussion about whether the athlete wants to continue playing their sport. Further, sometimes the recovered body may no longer fit the perceived ideal of the specific sport, or be suitable for performance at the level at which the athlete had been performing. Here again, measured discussion about the relative values of ED recovery versus risk for relapse may be indicated.

STRATEGIES FOR PREVENTION

Given the unique risk factors and serious medical consequences of DEBs and EDs among athletes, prevention efforts are critical. Prevention targets include athletes themselves, as well coaches/trainers and other members of sport organizations, with strategies that include psychoeducation on nutrition and EDs; challenging body ideals; and improving body image and self-esteem. A recent review suggests that the formation of DEBs among athletes might not be associated with sport pressures as much as other ED features, such as body image dissatisfaction (Stoyel et al., 2020). To address these risk factors directly, prevention programs to date have generally attempted to intervene with athletes as the primary target audience, and many of these programs have led to reductions in DEBs. For example, the Female Athlete Body Project (FAB; Stewart et al., 2017, 2019), previously the Athlete Modified Healthy Weight Intervention (Becker et al., 2012) is a peer-led program for female athletes. FAB focuses on: (a) reconciling the sport-specific body ideal relative to a healthy-ideal, (b) providing psychoeducation and support for behavior change related to improved nutrition and energy balance, and (c) creating space for athletes to participate in activities designed to improve body image. At 18-month follow-up, athletes who participated in FAB reported lower levels of thin-ideal internalization and dietary restraint, and fewer episodes of loss-of-control eating compared to controls (Stewart et al., 2019). Subsequent modification of FAB specifically for ballet dancers also demonstrated reductions in overall ED pathology, dietary restraint, and body dissatisfaction (Gorrell et al.,

2019). Although initially designed for female athletes, Perelman and colleagues (2022) tested an adapted FAB for male athletes, the Male Athlete Body Project (MABP), with modified gender language and more program content pertaining to the muscularity ideal. At one-month follow-up, athletes who participated in MABP maintained post-treatment improvements in body satisfaction and reductions in drive for muscularity (Perelman et al., 2022). At this time, it is unclear how genderqueer/gender-fluid individuals would respond to programs like FAB and MABP, given unique concerns that can arise as a result of the important intersection of sport/athlete identity, sport-specific body ideals, desired gender appearance, and societal ideals about preferred bodies for different genders.

Other prevention programs include coaches/trainers and other organizational staff. For example, Piran (2013) integrated a prevention program within a ballet school whereby psychoeducation was provided to staff in an effort to reduce body-focused language, and dancers were consulted to identify action they could take to improve the school environment as it pertained to weight/shape pressures. Similar to the systemic approach taken by Piran (2013), Martinsen et al. (2014) implemented a school-based prevention program for male and female high school athletes which included coaches, staff, and parents. It focused on increasing athlete self-esteem and self-efficacy, and educating coaches on nutrition and ED-identification and resulted in no new ED cases among the female athletes (relative to 13% increase in controls) at one-year follow up, and a reduction in self-reported DEBs. More recently, a program designed to educate coaches about how to promote healthy ideals within their sports/training context showed significant improvement in coaches' confidence and knowledge regarding warning signs and how to approach an at-risk athlete, and positive change in attitudes about their own rule-driven exercise behavior (Selenius et al., 2022).

Continued efforts to prevent EDs among athletes are necessary and should include a way to more efficiently identify athletes who may most benefit from early intervention efforts. Further, when systemic issues related to ED risk within a sport are suspected, it may be particularly important to ensure that the burden of preventing EDs in athletes is not solely placed on the athletes themselves but more appropriately on the entire system, including increasing coaches' and trainers' knowledge about appropriate screening and identification of ED risk.

CASE VIGNETTE

To illustrate key aspects of addressing EDs in athletes, the following case vignette is followed by a discussion of intersecting multicultural- and athlete-related factors. All identifying information has been either removed or changed to protect client privacy.

A 19-year-old collegiate athlete at a southern university in the United States presented for mental health screening per the university's standard annual wellness protocol. In this initial meeting, they self-identified as nonbinary and multiracial and reported that they had competed on the women's lightweight rowing team for two seasons. They were currently considering taking a medical leave of absence due to increasingly severe eating concerns. Asked to complete the Counseling Center Assessment of Psychological Symptoms-62 (CCAPS-62; Samlan et al., 2021), they reported "elevated" levels of distress related to eating concerns and "moderate" levels of distress related to generalized anxiety concerns. Consequently, the athlete was asked to schedule a more comprehensive intake with an athletic department mental health team member.

During the intake 2 weeks later, the assigned treating clinician conducted a structured clinical interview based on the Eating Disorder Examination (EDE; Cooper & Fairburn, 2011). Here, reported concerns were severe caloric restriction (< 1,000 kcal/day), strict food rules, and pervasive thoughts around food, weight, and shape that negatively impacted their ability to concentrate, complete academic work, and participate in training. They denied any current binge eating or compensatory behaviors, but endorsed a history of excessive exercise (compulsive cardio workouts 2–4x/week for 3–5 hours outside of regular training hours) during athletic off-seasons in high school. When queried further, they reported that this exercise was beyond what would have been expected of other athlete peers, and motivated by a desire to prevent weight gain. They reported a recent weight loss of 20 pounds over the past 3 months, with current BMI (measured in light clothing during this intake) of 20.2 kg/m^2. Historically, they described long-standing severe body image concerns since middle school and onset of restriction of calories and types of foods (e.g., carbohydrates and fats) around the time they started rowing as a high-school freshman. Finally, they described competing pressures related to physique: they experienced distress around internal and environmental pressures to maintain a low weight to row. They also expressed a desire to present a more androgynous physique that aligned with their gender identity, which they felt could be achieved through maintaining DEBs. Based on recent weight loss, and clinical symptom report from the EDE, it was determined that the athlete met criteria for atypical anorexia nervosa. The athlete agreed with this diagnosis, and together, the clinician and athlete identified the following collaborative treatment goals, to: (a) restore and stabilize weight, (b) establish a neutral relationship with food and shape, and (c) reconsider the role that athletics played in their life.

Of note, during the required appointment with the team physician, their vitals were within normal ranges. Still, the athlete opted to postpone their return to training in order to prioritize treatment. They participated in 15 weeks of outpatient CBT-E (Fairburn et al., 2003) with a clinical psychologist trained in EBTs for EDs and met weekly with a dietitian specializing in athlete EDs. Consistent with CBT-E, the therapist, dietitian, and athlete collaboratively worked to establish regular eating, reintroduce feared foods, stabilize weight, and address triggers. These treatment targets were captured in a treatment contract, which the treatment team and athlete signed during the fourth week of treatment; this aided the athlete in successfully adapting eating habits and caloric intake for several weeks. After 2 months of treatment, the athlete expressed interest in restarting training in the hopes of competing one more season before retiring. The treatment team (therapist, dietitian, team physician, team athletic trainer) met regularly to discuss treatment progression and, with the athlete, collaboratively developed return-to-play (RTP) and exercise plans (see Cook et al., 2016 for recommendations) based on meeting treatment milestones. The team closely oversaw a graded exercise plan that slowly reincorporated cardio and weight training, followed by ergometer training, and eventually training on the water with the rowing team. With the athlete's consent, the treatment team also coordinated with the athletics department and coach to ensure the athlete was supported. The athlete made the rowing team and competed one more season. Meetings with the therapist, dietitian, and team physician were reduced to bi-monthly as long as the athlete met treatment targets.

The therapist and athlete continued to discuss weight and shape concerns while monitoring regular eating during the competition season. Shortly after the season ended and the athlete retired from sports to focus on health and academics, they experienced a relapse of restrictive eating and a few excessive exercise episodes. They connected this to a sense of loss of their athlete identity and expected physique changes. In particular, they experienced intense fear of developing more feminine physical characteristics when no longer training. The therapist and athlete discussed the intersection of athlete and gender identities, acceptance of their physique, and their desire to connect more with the queer community on campus while maintaining connections to former teammates. Following the CBT-E manual, final sessions were spent on how to maintain treatment gains and prevent relapses.

At termination 2 months later, the client had increased their caloric intake, expanded food options, and had successfully challenged their "no processed sugar" rule. They had also not engaged in any DEBs in over a month and had weight restored to a BMI of 23 kg/m2. They reported feeling "more confident in [their] physique" and fostered meaningful connections through both their athletic and queer communities, which they reported "helped to bridge the transition out of sport."

CASE STUDY ANALYSIS

The case vignette presented several unique challenges. First, the nature and progression of using an EBT model warrants discussion given that there are limited/no EBTs specifically designed for athletes with EDs, particularly those with excessive exercise as a key DEB. Second, multicultural and environmental complexities will be incorporated as the client's approach to and feelings toward their body are addressed. Third, the importance of both cultural competence and humility will be highlighted, as members of a treatment team should be sensitive to shared/divergent aspects of identity and their impact on rapport and clinical progress.

EBT Considerations for Case Study

When the athlete presented for intake after CCAPS screening, the therapist used evidence-based screening tools and frameworks to capture a holistic view of the athlete and develop an informed case conceptualization. In particular, the EDE-Q (Fairburn et al., 2003) was used to assess ED pathology, the Athlete Identity Measurement Scale (AIMS; Brewer et al., 2012) was used to assess athlete identity, and the therapist used a multicultural ecological framework to assess identity, relationships, community, and broader context. Taking this approach allowed the treatment team and athlete to collaboratively identify and prioritize treatment targets, leverage their strengths, and use an EBT that would best match their presenting concerns, severity of illness, and stage of life.

Outpatient level of care was selected based on numerous factors. First, BMI was in the "normal" range, and upon physical examination, the athlete did not present with indicators that warranted a higher level of care (i.e., vital sign concern). The athlete was consistently monitored to evaluate any negative changes in these parameters in case a higher level of care needed to be introduced. The treatment team opted to use CBT-E for this athlete in part due to their desire and motivation to change, suggesting they could engage well in an individual EBT. Although FBT for EDs is another first-line treatment (Lock & Le Grange, 2019), the team did not opt for this model because the athlete's family lived out of state and was not easily accessible or connected to the athlete. Furthermore, they had not yet disclosed their gender identity to their family due to concerns about acceptance and psychological safety, and the intake clarified that one of the

ED maintaining factors was the client's desired physique, based on their gender identity. In reviewing the combination of these factors, including client motivation, the team felt it best to use CBT-E as a first-line treatment.

Decisions about exercise titration were overseen by the therapist, and regulated by the whole treatment team, including the dietitian, physician, and athletic trainer. This team approach was necessary to ensure that the athlete's RTP was safe in terms of psychological and medical risk. The treatment contract and RTP were adapted to fit the client as an individual and their status as an athlete, and required regular meetings with staff, elimination of DEBs, meeting meal plan requirements specified by the dietician, and monthly check-ins with the ED team and athletics department. The athlete would need to meet > 75% of the contract requirements and adherence was evaluated monthly. In this particular case, the family was not involved in contract check-ins, per the client's request. The coach was also not included at this step, given that they were asked to seek educational and training opportunities to better support the rowing team. To bolster motivation and compliance, the team also included specifics about the athlete's goals and their vision for life post-treatment (e.g., hopes of being able to return to rowing, improve social connection with friends, and explore a new relationship with their body) alongside next steps if milestones were not attained (e.g., higher level of care if weight was lost/client became medically unstable/was not abstaining from DEBs). The plan detailed a graded return to exercise with close monitoring by the athletic trainer and physician to ensure medical stability; training began with low-volume and low-intensity activity, monitored weight-lifting sessions, and conditioning. Short, low-intensity ergometer pieces were added, which were eventually lengthened as caloric demands were met. Once the athlete (a) met caloric demands based on training load > 85% of the time, and (b) met times to be slated for a boat, the coach added the athlete to a boat roster for full training on the water. The treatment contracts and RTP plans were uniquely leveraged to serve as a motivation; contracts were not designed to be punitive, but rather informative, motivating, and collaborative so the client would feel ownership over their treatment progression and return to sport.

A final treatment consideration was the sport-related risk and maintaining factors inherent to the sport context. Participation in lightweight rowing is associated with a high degree of weight monitoring and frequent weigh-ins due to stringent requirements for competition. In addition to weight requirements for competition, the client reported often hearing, "A lighter boat is a faster boat." Thus, athletes in lightweight rowing, including this client, often experience additional pressure to weigh less, while maintaining strength/endurance, to give their team a competitive edge and improve performance. Additionally, the client reported unhealthy team locker room dynamics including body checking and body comparison, especially in the context of wearing fitted uni-suit team uniforms. They also noted conversations about additional exercise and training above-and-beyond recommendations from coaches/trainers, and negative messaging from coaches about eating "junk food," not exercising, and gaining weight as the rowers prepared for off-season breaks and summer activities. Over the course of treatment, the client and therapist identified and targeted these sport-related ED risk and maintaining factors while simultaneously addressing the overarching importance of identifying as an elite athlete and its intersection with their other identities (discussion to follow).

Multicultural and Identity Considerations

This case highlighted how intersecting identities, internal pressures, and perceived and known external pressures reinforced the ED and created tension. Although CBT-E has not been explicitly adapted for individuals who identify as nonbinary or for athletes, the treatment framework can flexibly incorporate discussions about risk and maintaining factors, particularly as they relate to background and lived experience. A primary multicultural consideration was the delicate balancing and integration of their genderqueer and athlete identities as they each related to two different "perceived ideal physiques." Far from family, the athlete felt as though they were within a space and community that would be more accepting of a less feminine and more androgynous presentation. Their college environment felt empowering, but it reinforced a desire to lose weight and keep feminine physical characteristics at bay. On the other hand, they felt an internal desire to be "more muscular and bulkier" to mirror their rowing teammates, but also to stay thin enough to maintain their lightweight rower status.

As a first step, the treatment team sought to identify the function of the DEBs (in this case, restriction and excessive exercise). Restriction compensated for caloric intake and helped them to achieve a thinner, more androgynous physique, in line with their gender. The function of their excessive exercise was more complex: weight and shape concerns related to the sport context, and the associated excessive exercise episodes served to (a) maintain muscular physique for rowing, which was reinforced by teammates and the coach; and (b) mitigate anxiety related to rowing and performance concerns. Within the CBT-E framework, the team worked with the client to identify the DEB functions and triggers and abstain from engaging in these behaviors while developing and honing skills to navigate their distress.

Second, the team worked to address body image and tension between perceived body ideals. The athlete felt as though they "were being pulled in two different directions," and identified different body ideals for rowing ("muscular and sinewy") and gender identity ("thinner with no curves or really defined muscles"). There was a tertiary pressure to present more femininely to family; however, this became less influential as treatment progressed and connections with their gender identity and the campus queer community were deepened, and the therapist introduced communication and acceptance strategies in preparation for future conversations and interactions with their family. The athlete was encouraged to challenge unhelpful cognitive distortions (e.g., "I'm a failure if I don't achieve this body ideal") and to accept current societal norms despite disagreeing with them (e.g., "I can acknowledge that most people expect me to look feminine, especially if they knew me growing up, and I don't need to fit into one of two boxes anymore"). The therapist also worked with the client to celebrate what their body could do both as an athlete and in life more generally, rather than experiencing their body as a consistent reminder of "failure" at reconciling two competing body ideals. The therapist encouraged the client to connect with their long-term goals and vision for life after sports, which further motivated them to take the necessary steps to fully recover and work toward acceptance of their body in the current moment.

SUGGESTIONS FOR THE FUTURE

Virtually none of our athlete research to date has specifically investigated intersectional factors that may differentially contribute to onset and maintenance of clinical symptoms. This may in part explain why prevalence estimates of EDs and DEBs vary so greatly, depending on characteristics that are unique to the study sample. Selecting athlete samples to reflect a broader range of demographics should be an essential focus in future research, and will be critically important in understanding risk for EDs and DEBs specific to racial/ethnic groups, trans or nonbinary athletes, sexual orientation, and other minoritized identities.

In regard to screening, our current measures of ED pathology have all been developed and normed on primarily White, cisgender female samples. Therefore, although some research suggests that, for example, Black collegiate athletes do not have lower self-esteem or greater ED pathology compared to White athlete counterparts (Johnson et al., 2004), these findings may reflect the limitations of assessment tools that lack cultural sensitivity. Calls have arisen within the ED field in recent years, underscoring the importance of inclusivity and intersectionality in our research (Burke et al., 2020; Goel et al., 2022); these broader efforts within the ED field must include athletes, with a full embrace of best practices in conducting screening, recruitment, and assessment that is culturally informed.

In regard to treatment, we also acknowledge that, to date, no athlete-specific ED treatments have been developed and rigorously tested. Although efforts are made to integrate evidence-based approaches into treatment sites (either those with athlete tracks, or dedicated to serving athletes only), it remains to be seen whether these approaches systematically contribute to improved outcomes. It could be the case that specified training for clinicians in treating athletes is needed at the graduate or postdoctoral level. It could also be the case that a specific training manual could be used to efficiently disseminate athlete-specific treatment modules as an adaptation to pre-existing EBTs. To answer these questions, targeted outcomes research is needed, both to test existing as well as potential novel treatments in development.

To inform all of these efforts, recent commentary highlights how important a culturally humble approach is when both assessing and treating EDs and DEBs in the context of sport (Perelman & Reel, 2022). For example, current body-image interventions in use may not be suitable for a broader range of body ideals, and may lie outside of the historic perspective that assumes a dichotomy of internalization of a thin ideal or an athletic ideal (Homan, 2010). Particular attention should be placed on adapting body image interventions for athletes who may fall outside of two separable genders, and include multi-faceted cultural considerations. Further, recent work highlights the intersection of food insecurity and DEBs (Abbey et al., 2022); for young athletes across various contexts (e.g., partial college scholarship), directly addressing access to adequate nutrition is an important focus for future clinical and policy interventions.

In summary, athletes are a unique population, who require additional support to prevent and treat eating pathology (de Bruin, 2017), and much lies ahead in improving our ability to successfully mitigate their risk and suffering. Best practices in the future of improved care of athletes will optimally acknowledge individual variability in clinical presentations, and promote culturally sensitive care that can address the intersection of both general and athlete-specific features of ED pathology.

DISCUSSION QUESTIONS

1. If we aim to better support athletes in ED treatment, what training opportunities should be prioritized for clinicians who intend to provide services for these patients?

2. How do systemic/cultural values interact with athlete-specific cultural values to increase the risk of and maintenance of ED pathology among athletes?
3. With limited resources, should intervention and prevention efforts prioritize the athlete or the athletic environment within which they engage in their sport?

REFERENCES

Abbey, E. L., Brown, M., & Karpinski, C. (2022). Prevalence of food insecurity in the general college population and student-athletes: A review of the literature. *Current Nutrition Reports, 11*(2), 185–205. https://doi.org/10.1007/s13668-022-00394-4

American Psychiatric Association. (2013). *Diagnostic and statistical manual of mental disorders* (5th Ed.). https://doi.org/10.1176/appi.books.9780890425596

Anderson, C., & Petrie, T. A. (2012). Prevalence of disordered eating and pathogenic weight control behaviors among NCAA Division I female collegiate gymnasts and swimmers. *Research Quarterly for Exercise and Sport, 83*(1), 120–124. https://doi.org/10.1080/02701367.2012.10599833

Arcelus, J., Witcomb, G. L., & Mitchell, A. (2014). Prevalence of eating disorders amongst dancers: A systemic review and meta-analysis. *European Eating Disorders Review, 22*(2), 92–101. https://doi.org/10.1002/erv.2271

Arthur-Cameselle, J. N., & Baltzell, A. (2012). Learning from collegiate athletes who have recovered from eating disorders: Advice to coaches, parents, and other athletes with eating disorders. *Journal of Applied Sport Psychology, 24*(1), 1–9. https://doi.org/10.1080/10413200.2011.572949

Barrett, S., Petrie, T., Voelker, D., & Jackson, R. (2022). The body satisfaction and psychological well-being of retired women athletes: A long-term qualitative analysis of bodies in motion. *Body Image, 43*(3), 143–153. https://doi.org/10.1016/j.bodyim.2022.08.009

Becker, C. B., McDaniel, L., Bull, S., Powell, M., & McIntyre, K. (2012). Can we reduce eating disorder risk factors in female college athletes? A randomized exploratory investigation of two peer-led interventions. *Body Image, 9*(1), 31–42. https://doi.org/10.1016/j.bodyim.2011.09.005

Ben-Porath, D., Duthu, F., Luo, T., Gonidakis, F., Compte, E. J., & Wisniewski, L. (2020). Dialectical behavioral therapy: An update and review of the existing treatment models adapted for adults with eating disorders. *Eating Disorders, 28*(2), 101–121. https://doi.org/10.1080/10640266.2020.1723371

Bratland-Sanda, S., & Sundgot-Borgen, J. (2013). Eating disorders in athletes: Overview of prevalence, risk factors and recommendations for prevention and treatment. *European Journal of Sport Science, 13*(5), 499–508. https://doi.org/10.1080/17461391.2012.740504

Brewer, B. W., Van Raalte, J. L., & Linder, D. E. (2012). *Athletic Identity Measurement Scale* [Data set]. American Psychological Association. https://doi.org/10.1037/t15488-000

Burke, N. L., Schaefer, L. M., Hazzard, V. M., & Rodgers, R. F. (2020). Where identities converge: The importance of intersectionality in eating disorders research. *International Journal of Eating Disorders*, *53*(10), 1605–1609. https://doi.org/10.1002/eat.23371

Byrne, S., & McLean, N. (2002). Elite athletes: Effects of the pressure to be thin. *Journal of Science and Medicine in Sport*, *5*(2), 80–94. https://doi.org/10.1016/S1440-2440(02)80029-9

Carson, T. L., West, B. T., Sonneville, K., Zernicke, R. F., Clarke, P., Harlow, S., & Karvonen-Gutierrez, C. (2022). Identifying latent classes of relative energy deficiency in sport (RED-S) consequences in a sample of collegiate female cross country runners. *British Journal of Sports Medicine* *57*(3), 153–159. https://doi.org/10.1136/bjsports-2021-104083

Castaldelli-Maia, J. M., Gallinaro, J. G. de M. e, Falcão, R. S., Gouttebarge, V., Hitchcock, M. E., Hainline, B., Reardon, C. L., & Stull, T. (2019). Mental health symptoms and disorders in elite athletes: A systematic review on cultural influencers and barriers to athletes seeking treatment. *British Journal of Sports Medicine*, *53*(11), 707–721. https://doi.org/10.1136/bjsports-2019-100710

Chapa, D. A. N., Johnson, S. N., Richson, B. N., Bjorlie, K., Won, Y. Q., Nelson, S. V., Ayres, J., Jun, D., Forbush, K. T., Christensen, K. A., & Perko, V. L. (2022). Eating-disorder psychopathology in female athletes and non-athletes: A meta-analysis. *International Journal of Eating Disorders*, *55*(7), 861–885. https://doi.org/10.1002/eat.23748

Chapman, J., & Woodman, T. (2016). Disordered eating in male athletes: A meta-analysis. *Journal of Sports Sciences*, *34*(2), 101–109. https://doi.org/10.1080/02640414.2015.1040824

Chatterton, J. M., & Petrie, T. A. (2013). Prevalence of disordered eating and pathogenic weight control behaviors among male collegiate athletes. *Eating Disorders*, *21*(4), 328–341. https://doi.org/10.1080/10640266.2013.797822

Compte, E. J., Murray, S. B., Sepúlveda, A. R., Schweiger, S., Bressan, M., & Torrente, F. (2018). What position do you play? Eating disorder pathology among rugby players, and the understudied role of player position. *International Journal of Eating Disorders*, *51*(8), 1015–1019. https://doi.org/10.1002/eat.22933

Conviser, J. H., Schlitzer Tierney, A., & Nickols, R. (2018). Essentials for best practice: Treatment approaches for athletes with eating disorders. *Journal of Clinical Sport Psychology*, *12*(4), 495–507. https://doi.org/10.1123/jcsp.2018-0013

Cook, B. J., Wonderlich, S. A., Mitchell, J. E., Thompson, R., Sherman, R., & McCallum, K. (2016). Exercise in eating disorders treatment: Systematic review and proposal of Guidelines. *Medicine and Science in Sports and Exercise*, *48*(7), 1408–1414. https://doi.org/10.1249/MSS.0000000000000912

Cooper, Z., & Fairburn, C. (2011). *Eating Disorder Examination* [Data set]. American Psychological Association. https://doi.org/10.1037/t03975-000

Davis, L., Appleby, R., Davis, P., Wetherell, M., & Gustafsson, H. (2018). The role of coach-athlete relationship quality in team sport athletes' psychophysiological exhaustion: Implications for physical and cognitive performance. *Journal of Sports Sciences*, *36*(17), 1985–1992. https://doi.org/10.1080/02640414.2018.1429176

de Bruin, A. P. K. (2017). Athletes with eating disorder symptomatology, a specific population with specific needs. *Current Opinion in Psychology*, *16*, 148–153. https://doi.org/10.1016/j.copsyc.2017.05.009

de Bruin, A. P. K, & Oudejans, R. R. D. (2018). Athletes' body talk: The role of contextual body image in eating disorders as seen through the eyes of elite women athletes. *Journal of Clinical Sport Psychology*, *12*(4), 675–698. https://doi.org/10.1123/jcsp.2018-0047

Drakes, D. H., Fawcett, E. J., Rose, J. P., Carter-Major, J. C., & Fawcett, J. M. (2021). Comorbid obsessive-compulsive disorder in individuals with eating disorders: An epidemiological meta-analysis. *Journal of Psychiatric Research*, *141*, 176–191. https://doi.org/10.1016/j.jpsychires.2021.06.035

Fairburn, C. G., Cooper, Z., & Shafran, R. (2003). Cognitive behaviour therapy for eating disorders: A "transdiagnostic" theory and treatment. *Behaviour Research and Therapy*, *41*(5), 509–528. https://doi.org/10.1016/S0005-7967(02)00088-8

Ferrell, E. L., Russin, S. E., & Flint, D. D. (2022). Prevalence estimates of comorbid eating disorders and posttraumatic stress disorder: A quantitative synthesis. *Journal of Aggression, Maltreatment & Trauma*, *31*(2), 264–282. https://doi.org/10.1080/10926771.2020.1832168

Fewell, L. K., Nickols, R., Schlitzer Tierney, A., & Levinson, C. A. (2018a). Eating disorders in sport: Comparing eating disorder symptomatology in athletes and non-athletes during intensive eating disorder treatment. *Journal of Clinical Sport Psychology*, *12*(4), 578–594. https://doi.org/10.1123/jcsp.2018-0046

Fewell, L. K., Nickols, R., Schlitzer Tierney, A., & Levinson, C. A. (2018b). Strength and power improvements in athletes and non-athletes during intensive eating disorder treatment. *Journal of Clinical Sport Psychology*, *12*(4), 562–577. https://doi.org/10.1123/jcsp.2018-0014

Flatt, R. E., Thornton, L. M., Fitzsimmons-Craft, E. E., Balantekin, K. N., Smolar, L., Mysko, C., Wilfley, D. E., Taylor, C. B., DeFreese, J. D., Bardone-Cone, A. M., & Bulik, C. M. (2021). Comparing eating disorder characteristics and treatment in self-identified competitive athletes and non-athletes from the National Eating Disorders Association online screening tool. *International Journal of Eating Disorders*, *54*(3), 365–375. https://doi.org/10.1002/eat.23415

Gibson, D., Workman, C., & Mehler, P. S. (2019). Medical complications of anorexia nervosa and bulimia nervosa. *Psychiatric Clinics of North America*, *42*(2), 263–274. https://doi.org/10.1016/j.psc.2019.01.009

Goel, N. J., Jennings Mathis, K., Egbert, A. H., Petterway, F., Breithaupt, L., Eddy, K. T., Franko, D. L., & Graham, A. K. (2022). Accountability in promoting representation of historically marginalized racial and ethnic populations in the eating disorders field: A call to action. *International Journal of Eating Disorders*, *55*(4), 463–469. https://doi.org/10.1002/eat.23682

Gorrell, S., & Anderson, D. A. (2018). Athlete identity and eating pathology in distance runners: When compulsive exercise matters. *Journal of Clinical Sport Psychology*, *12*(4), 647–657. https://doi.org/10.1123/jcsp.2018-0016

Gorrell, S., Loeb, K. L., & Le Grange, D. (2019). Family-based treatment of eating disorders: A narrative review. *Psychiatric Clinics*, *42*(2), 193–204. https://doi.org/10.1016/j.psc.2019.01.004

Gorrell, S., Nagata, J. M., Hill, K. B., Carlson, J. L., Shain, A. F., Wilson, J., Alix Timko, C., Hardy, K. K., Lock, J., & Peebles, R. (2021). Eating behavior and reasons for exercise among competitive collegiate male athletes. *Eating and Weight Disorders—Studies on Anorexia, Bulimia and Obesity*, *26*(1), 75–83. https://doi.org/10.1007/s40519-019-00819-0

Gorrell, S., Schaumberg, K., Boswell, J. F., Hormes, J. M., & Anderson, D. A. (2019). Female athlete body project intervention with professional dancers: A pilot trial. *Eating Disorders*, *29*(1), 56–73. https://doi.org/10.1080/10640266.2019.1632592

Gouttebarge, V., & Kerkhoffs, G. M. M. J. (2017). A prospective cohort study on symptoms of common mental disorders among current and retired professional ice hockey players. *The Physician and Sportsmedicine*, *45*(3), 252–258. https://doi.org/10.1080/00913847.2017.1338497

Greenleaf, C., Petrie, T. A., Carter, J., & Reel, J. J. (2009). Female collegiate athletes: Prevalence of eating disorders and disordered eating behaviors. *Journal of American College Health*, *57*(5), 489–496. https://doi.org/10.3200/JACH.57.5.489-496

Holtzman, B., Tenforde, A. S., Parziale, A. L., & Ackerman, K. E. (2019). Characterization of risk quantification differences using female athlete triad cumulative risk assessment and relative energy deficiency in sport clinical assessment tool. *International Journal of Sport Nutrition and Exercise Metabolism*, *29*(6), 569–575. https://doi.org/10.1123/ijsnem.2019-0002

Homan, K. (2010). Athletic-ideal and thin-ideal internalization as prospective predictors of body dissatisfaction, dieting, and compulsive exercise. *Body Image*, *7*(3), 240–245. https://doi.org/10.1016/j.bodyim.2010.02.004

Johnson, C., Crosby, R., Engel, S., Mitchell, J., Powers, P., Wittrock, D., & Wonderlich, S. (2004). Gender, ethnicity, self-esteem and disordered eating among college athletes. *Eating Behaviors*, *5*(2), 147–156. https://doi.org/10.1016/j.eatbeh.2004.01.004

Juarascio, A. S., Manasse, S. M., Schumacher, L., Espel, H., & Forman, E.M. (2017) Developing an acceptance-based behavioral treatment for binge eating disorder: Rationale and challenges. *Cognitive and Behavioral Practice*. *24*(1), 1–13. https://doi.org/10.1016/j.cbpra.2015.12.005

Kerr, G., Berman, E., & Souza, M. J. D. (2006). Disordered eating in women's gymnastics: Perspectives of athletes, coaches, parents, and judges. *Journal of Applied Sport Psychology*, *18*(1), 28–43. https://doi.org/10.1080/10413200500471301

Krane, V., Choi, P. Y. L., Baird, S. M., Aimar, C. M., & Kauer, K. J. (2004). Living the paradox: Female athletes negotiate femininity and muscularity. *Sex Roles*, *50*(5/6), 315–329. https://doi.org/10.1023/B:SERS.0000018888.48437.4f

Kraus, U., Holtmann, S. C., & Legenbauer, T. (2018). Eating disturbances in competitive lightweight and heavyweight rowers. *Journal of Clinical Sport Psychology*, *12*(4), 630–646. https://doi.org/10.1123/jcsp.2016-0042

Krentz, E. M., & Warschburger, P. (2011). Sports-related correlates of disordered eating in aesthetic sports. *Psychology of Sport and Exercise*, *12*(4), 375–382. https://doi.org/10.1016/j.psychsport.2011.03.004

Kristjánsdóttir, H., Sigurðardóttir, P., Jónsdóttir, S., Þorsteinsdóttir, G., & Saavedra, J. (2019). Body image concern and eating disorder symptoms among elite Icelandic athletes. *International Journal of Environmental Research and Public Health*, *16*(15), 2728. https://doi.org/10.3390/ijerph16152728

Linardon, J., de la Piedad Garcia, X., & Brennan, L. (2017) Predictors, moderators, and mediators of treatment outcome following manualised cognitive-behavioural therapy for eating disorders: A systematic review. *European Eating Disorders Review*. *25*(1), 3-12. https://www.doi.org/10.1002/erv.2492

Lock, J., & Le Grange, D. (2019). Family-based treatment: Where are we and where should we be going to improve recovery in child and adolescent eating disorders. *International Journal of Eating Disorders*, *52*(4), 481–487. https://doi.org/10.1002/eat.22980

Martinsen, M., Bahr, R., Børresen, R., Holme, I., Pensgaard, A. M., & Sundgot-Borgen, J. (2014). Preventing eating disorders among young elite athletes: A randomized controlled trial. *Medicine & Science in Sports & Exercise*, *46*(3), 435–447. https://doi.org/10.1249/MSS.0b013e3182a702fc

Martinsen, M., Bratland-Sanda, S., Eriksson, A. K., & Sundgot-Borgen, J. (2010). Dieting to win or to be thin? A study of dieting and disordered eating among adolescent elite athletes and non-athlete controls. *British Journal of Sports Medicine*, *44*(1), 70–76. https://doi.org/10.1136/bjsm.2009.068668

Martinsen, M., & Sundgot-Borgen, J. (2013). Higher prevalence of eating disorders among adolescent elite athletes than controls. *Medicine & Science in Sports & Exercise*, *45*(6), 1188–1197. https://doi.org/10.1249/MSS.0b013e318281a939

Mond, J., & Gorrell, S. (2021). "Excessive exercise" in eating disorders research: Problems of definition and perspective. *Eating and Weight Disorders-Studies on Anorexia, Bulimia and Obesity*, *26*, 1017–1020. https://doi.org/10.1007/s40519-020-01075-3

Mountjoy, M., Sundgot-Borgen, J., Burke, L., Ackerman, K. E., Blauwet, C., Constantini, N., Lebrun, C., Lundy, B., Melin, A., Meyer, N., Sherman, R., Tenforde, A. S., Torstveit, M. K., & Budgett, R. (2018). International Olympic Committee (IOC) consensus statement on relative energy deficiency in sport (RED-S): 2018 update. *International Journal of Sport Nutrition and Exercise Metabolism*, *28*(4), 316–331. https://doi.org/10.1123/ijsnem.2018-0136

Mountjoy, M., Sundgot-Borgen, J., Burke, L., Carter, S., Constantini, N., Lebrun, C., Meyer, N., Sherman, R., Steffen, K., Budgett, R., & Ljungqvist, A. (2014). The IOC consensus statement: Beyond the female athlete triad—relative energy deficiency in sport (RED-S). *British Journal of Sports Medicine*, *48*(7), 491–497. https://doi.org/10.1136/bjsports-2014-093502

Neumark-Sztainer, D., Wall, M., Guo, J., Story, M., Haines, J., & Eisenberg, M. (2006). Obesity, disordered eating, and eating disorders in a longitudinal study of adolescents: How do dieters fare 5 years later? *Journal of the American Dietetic Association*, *106*(4), 559–568. https://doi.org/10.1016/j.jada.2006.01.003

Perelman, H., & Reel, J. J. (2022). Using a culturally humble approach to examine and address disordered eating in sport. *Journal of Applied Sport Psychology*, *35*(4), 643–657. https://doi.org/10.1080/10413200.2022.2078904

Perelman, H., Schwartz, N., Yeoward-Dodson, J., Quiñones, I. C., Murray, M. F., Dougherty, E. N., Townsel, R., Arthur-Cameselle, J., & Haedt-Matt, A. A. (2022). Reducing eating disorder risk among male athletes: A randomized controlled trial investigating the male athlete body project. *International Journal of Eating Disorders*, *55*(2), 193–206. https://doi.org/10.1002/eat.23665

Petrie, T. A., Greenleaf, C., Reel, J., & Carter, J. (2008). Prevalence of eating disorders and disordered eating behaviors among male collegiate athletes. *Psychology of Men & Masculinity*, *9*(4), 267–277. https://doi.org/10.1037/a0013178

Piran, N. (2013). *Preventing eating disorders: A handbook of interventions and special challenges* (1st ed.). Routledge. https://doi.org/10.4324/9780203778081

Plateau, C. R., Arcelus, J., Leung, N., & Meyer, C. (2017). Female athlete experiences of seeking and receiving treatment for an eating disorder. *Eating Disorders*, *25*(3), 273–277. https://doi.org/10.1080/10640266.2016.1269551

Rosendahl, J., Bormann, B., Aschenbrenner, K., Aschenbrenner, F., & Strauss, B. (2009). Dieting and disordered eating in German high school athletes and non-athletes. *Scandinavian Journal of Medicine & Science in Sports*, *19*(5), 731–739. https://doi.org/10.1111/j.1600-0838.2008.00821.x

Samlan, H., Hawley McWhirter, E., & Clark, B. A. M. (2021). The counseling center assessment of psychological symptoms-62 (CCAPS-62) and college academic outcomes. *The Counseling Psychologist*, *49*(6), 882–906. https://doi.org/10.1177/00110000211010301

Sandgren, S. S., Haycraft, E., & Plateau, C. R. (2020). Nature and efficacy of interventions addressing eating psychopathology in athletes: A systematic review of randomised and nonrandomised trials. *European Eating Disorders Review*, *28*(2), 105–121. https://doi.org/10.1002/erv.2704

Schaal, K., Van Loan, M. D., & Casazza, G. A. (2011). Reduced catecholamine response to exercise in amenorrheic athletes. *Medicine and Science in Sports and Exercise*, *43*(1), 34–43. https://doi.org/10.1249/MSS.0b013e3181e91ece

Scott, C. L., Haycraft, E., & Plateau, C. R. (2019). Teammate influences on the eating attitudes and behaviours of athletes: A systematic review. *Psychology of Sport and Exercise*, *43*, 183–194. https://doi.org/10.1016/j.psychsport.2019.02.006

Scott, C. L., Haycraft, E., & Plateau, C. R. (2022). The impact of critical comments from teammates on athletes' eating and exercise psychopathology. *Body Image*, *43*, 170–179. https://doi.org/10.1016/j.bodyim.2022.08.013

Selenius, S., Birgegård, A., & Forsén Mantilla, E. (2022). Preliminary evaluation of the online course "I Care" targeting eating disorder knowledge and attitudes among sports coaches and fitness instructors. *Journal of Eating Disorders*, *10*(1), 142. https://doi.org/10.1186/s40337-022-00663-1

Smolak, L., Murnen, S. K., & Ruble, A. E. (2000). Female athletes and eating problems: A meta-analysis. *The International Journal of Eating Disorders*, *27*(4), 371–380. https://doi.org/10.1002/(sici)1098-108x(200005)27:4<371::aid-eat1>3.0.co;2-y

Stewart, T. M., Pollard, T., Hildebrandt, T., Beyl, R., Wesley, N., Kilpela, L. S., & Becker, C. B. (2017). The Female Athlete Body (FAB) study: Rationale, design, and baseline characteristics. *Contemporary Clinical Trials*, *60*, 63–71. https://doi.org/10.1016/j.cct.2017.06.005

Stewart, T. M., Pollard, T., Hildebrandt, T., Wesley, N. Y., Kilpela, L. S., & Becker, C. B. (2019). The Female Athlete Body project study: 18-month outcomes in eating disorder symptoms and risk factors. *The International Journal of Eating Disorders*, *52*(11), 1291–1300. https://doi.org/10.1002/eat.23145

Stoyel, H., Slee, A., Meyer, C., & Serpell, L. (2020). Systematic review of risk factors for eating psychopathology in athletes: A critique of an etiological model. *European Eating Disorders Review*, *28*(1), 3–25. https://doi.org/10.1002/erv.2711

Stranberg, M., Slager, E., Spital, D., Coia, C., & Quatromoni, P. A. (2020). Athlete-specific treatment for eating disorders: Initial findings from the Walden GOALS Program. *Journal of the Academy of Nutrition and Dietetics*, *120*(2), 183–192. https://doi.org/10.1016/j.jand.2019.07.019

Sundgot-Borgen, J., & Torstveit, M. K. (2004). Prevalence of eating disorders in elite athletes is higher than in the general population. *Clinical Journal of Sport Medicine*, *14*(1), 25–32. https://doi.org/10.1097/00042752-200401000-00005

Sundgot-Borgen, J., & Torstveit, M. K. (2010). Aspects of disordered eating continuum in elite high-intensity sports: Disordered eating in elite athletes. *Scandinavian Journal of Medicine & Science in Sports*, *20*, 112–121. https://doi.org/10.1111/j.1600-0838.2010.01190.x

Swanson, S. A., Crow, S. J., Grange, D. L., Swendsen, J., & Merikangas, K. R. (2011). Prevalence and correlates of eating disorders in adolescents: Results from the national comorbidity survey replication adolescent supplement. *Archives of General Psychiatry*, *68*(7), 714–723. https://doi.org/10.1001/archgenpsychiatry.2011.22

Tan, J. O. A., Calitri, R., Bloodworth, A., & McNamee, M. J. (2016). Understanding eating disorders in elite gymnastics. *Clinics in Sports Medicine*, *35*(2), 275–292. https://doi.org/10.1016/j.csm.2015.10.002

Thompson, A., Petrie, T., Tackett, B., Balcom, K., & Watkins, C. E. (2021). Eating disorder diagnosis and the female athlete: A longitudinal analysis from college sport to retirement. *Journal of Science and Medicine in Sport*, *24*(6), 531–535. https://doi.org/10.1016/j.jsams.2020.12.004

Thompson, R. A., & Sherman, R. (2014). Reflections on athletes and eating disorders. *Psychology of Sport and Exercise*, *15*(6), 729–734. https://doi.org/10.1016/j.psychsport.2014.06.005

Tomalski, J., Clevinger, K., Albert, E., Jackson, R., Wartalowicz, K., & Petrie, T. A. (2019). Mental health screening for athletes: Program development, implementation, and evaluation. *Journal of Sport Psychology in Action*, *10*(2), 121–135. https://doi.org/10.1080/21520704.2019.1604589

Torstveit, M. K., Fahrenholtz, I., Lichtenstein, M., Stenqvist, T. B., & Melin, A. (2019). Exercise dependence, eating disorder symptoms and biomarkers of relative energy deficiency in sports (RED-S) among male endurance athletes. *BMJ Open Sport & Exercise Medicine*. https://doi.org/10.1136/bmjsem-2018-000439

Torstveit, M. K., Rosenvinge, J. H., & Sundgot-Borgen, J. (2007). Prevalence of eating disorders and the predictive power of risk models in female elite athletes: A controlled study: Eating disorders in athletes and controls. *Scandinavian Journal of Medicine & Science in Sports*, *18*(1), 108–118. https://doi.org/10.1111/j.1600-0838.2007.00657.x

Treasure, J., & Russell, G. (2011). The case for early intervention in anorexia nervosa: Theoretical exploration of maintaining factors. *British Journal of Psychiatry*, *199*(1), 5–7. https://doi.org/10.1192/bjp.bp.110.087585

van Eeden, A. E., van Hoeken, D., & Hoek, H. W. (2021). Incidence, prevalence and mortality of anorexia nervosa and bulimia nervosa. *Current Opinion in Psychiatry*, *34*(6), 515–524. https://doi.org/10.1097/YCO.0000000000000739

Varnes, J. R., Stellefson, M. L., Janelle, C. M., Dorman, S. M., Dodd, V., & Miller, M. D. (2013). A systematic review of studies comparing body image concerns among female college athletes and non-athletes, 1997–2012. *Body Image*, *10*(4), 421–432. https://doi.org/10.1016/j.bodyim.2013.06.001

Videon, T. M. (2002). Who plays and who benefits: Gender, interscholastic athletics, and academic outcomes. *Sociological Perspectives*, *45*(4), 415–444. https://doi.org/10.1525/sop.2002.45.4.415

Voelker, D. K., Gould, D., & Reel, J. J. (2014). Prevalence and correlates of disordered eating in female figure skaters. *Psychology of Sport and Exercise*, *15*(6), 696–704. https://doi.org/10.1016/j.psychsport.2013.12.002

Voelker, D. K., Petrie, T. A., Reel, J. J., & Gould, D. (2018). Frequency and psychosocial correlates of eating disorder symptomatology in male figure skaters. *Journal of Applied Sport Psychology*, *30*(1), 119–126. https://doi.org/10.1080/10413200.2017.1325416

Walton, C. C., Purcell, R., & Rice, S. (2019). Addressing mental health in elite athletes as a vehicle for early detection and intervention in the general community. *Early Intervention in Psychiatry*, *13*(6), 1530–1532. https://doi.org/10.1111/eip.12857

Weight, E. A., Navarro, K. M., Smith-Ryan, A., & Huffman, L. T. (2016). Holistic education through athletics: Health and health-literacy of intercollegiate athletes and active undergraduate students. *Journal of Higher Education Athletics & Innovation*, *1*, 38–60. https://doi.org/10.15763/issn.2376-5267.2016.1.1.38-60

Youngman, J., & Simpson, D. (2014). Risk for exercise addiction: A comparison of triathletes training for sprint-, Olympic-, half-ironman-, and ironman-distance triathlons. *Journal of Clinical Sport Psychology*, *8*(1), 19–37. https://doi.org/10.1123/jcsp.2014-0010

ABOUT THE AUTHORS

Robbi K. Alexander, APN, PMHCNS-BC, is a registered nurse whose entire career has been spent in psychiatric/mental health nursing, with the last 14 years devoted to the treatment of those with eating disorders. She was the Director of the Princeton Center for Eating Disorders, Administrative Director of Psychiatry at Penn Medicine Princeton Health, and is currently the Assistant Vice President for Behavioral Health Nursing, Penn Medicine, Princeton. Dr. Alexander is an affiliate member of the Penn Medicine Princeton Medical Staff, affiliated nursing faculty at the University of Delaware, and Clinical Associate in the Academic Support Staff, University of Pennsylvania School of Nursing. Her research interests include psychiatric-mental health nursing workforce development and best practices for treatment of those with eating disorders.

Jordan Alvarez, MA, currently conducts mental health outreach for eating disorders in Atlanta Georgia. He also conducts body image and disordered eating research in the ACCEPT lab at Auburn University with Dr. Tiffany Brown. He has a bachelor's degree from Skidmore College in Psychology and a master's degree from Auburn University in Counseling Psychology. Lastly, he works with LGBTQ clients and their parents in the Atlanta community.

Tatyana Bidopia, MA, is currently a doctoral student in clinical psychology at Fordham University. She holds a Bachelor of Science degree from Duke University and completed her Master of Arts degree at Fordham University. Tatyana's research focuses on employing both quantitative and qualitative methods to explore sociocultural risk and protective factors related to disordered eating and body image issues within marginalized populations. She has a particular interest in utilizing an intersectionality framework to comprehend how individuals facing intersecting forms of oppression are differentially affected by disordered eating. Tatyana's future career aspirations involve providing clinical support to individuals diagnosed with eating disorders and other comorbid conditions, alongside advancing her research program dedicated to reducing mental health disparities in underserved populations.

Allegra Borghese, PhD, completed her doctoral training in Counseling Psychology at Fordham University and developed a specialized focus on eating disorders from working at the University of Pennsylvania, VA Healthcare System, and multiple outpatient ED clinics in New York and New Mexico. Her research projects seek to understand the multicultural factors that impact minority women who experience overeating and eating disorders. She is currently based in New York, where she worked as a clinical psychologist at Wellbridge Addiction Treatment & Research and now is in private practice.

Tiffany A. Brown, PhD, is a clinical psychologist and Assistant Professor within the Department of Psychological Sciences at Auburn University, where she directs the AppearanCe Concerns, Eating, Prevention, & Treatment (ACCEPT) Lab and co-directs the Auburn Eating Disorders Clinic. Her research focuses on developing and evaluating interventions for appearance-based and eating disorders in populations that have been traditionally overlooked, including LGBTQ+ and male populations. Her research has been funded by the Arlene and Michael Rosen Foundation, the Academy for Eating Disorders, the Global Foundation for Eating Disorders, and the National Institute of Health. Additional research interests include understanding factors related to treatment outcome across gender and sexual identity, the effectiveness of dialectical behavior therapy for eating disorders, and how interoception and gastric specific anxiety sensitivity can be targeted in eating disorder treatment.

Natasha L. Burke, PhD, is a psychology professor at Fordham University and a licensed clinical psychologist. She earned her BS and MA degrees from New York University and her PhD from the University of South Florida. She completed her clinical psychology residency at the Warren Alpert Medical School of Brown University and her postdoctoral training at the Uniformed Services University of the Health Sciences and the *Eunice Kennedy Shriver* National Institute of Child Health and Human Development. Intersectionality is infused in all aspects of her work. She makes inroads into eating disorder-related disparities by addressing risk, measurement, models, and interventions for multiple marginalized individuals. She also examines the complex interplay among eating, weight, sociodemographic characteristics, psychological comorbidities, and associated risk factors. Her goal is to continue to inform research and interventions in racial/ethnic minority and economically disadvantaged populations and to highlight the disparate risk at the intersections of those identities.

Danielle Chapa, PhD, completed her doctoral degree in clinical psychology at the University of Kansas and her predoctoral clinical psychology internship at Western Psychiatric Hospital. She is completing her postdoctoral training on a T32 fellowship in the Department of Psychiatry at the University of Pittsburgh. Her research focuses broadly on better understanding the function of maladaptive and compulsive exercise among individuals with eating disorders in order to identify novel treatment approaches. She is particularly interested in the presentation of eating disorders in athletes and worked with a team of researchers to develop a self-report assessment of maladaptive training behaviors.

Catherine Cook-Cottone, PhD, C-IAYT, is a licensed psychologist, certified yoga therapist, and professor at University at Buffalo, SUNY. She is creator and director of the Mindful Counseling Advanced Certificate program and co-founder and president of Yogis in Service, Inc. a not-for-profit organization that creates access to yoga. Catherine's research specializes in embodied self- regulation (i.e., yoga, mindfulness, and mindful self-care) and psychosocial disorders (e.g., eating disorders, substance use, and trauma). Catherine has written ten books and over 85 peer reviewed articles and book chapters. She was awarded the American Psychological Association's Citizen Psychologist Presidential Citation. She is co-editor in chief of *Eating Disorder: Journal of Treatment and Prevention* and author of *Embodiment and the Treatment of Eating Disorders: The Body as a Resource in Recovery* (W.W. Norton), *Mindfulness and Yoga for Self-Regulation* (Springer), and *Mindfulness and Yoga for Schools* (Springer).

Maya Cottone, BA, is a doctoral student studying counseling psychology at Fordham University. Her research interests surround trauma, utilization of trauma-informed practices, eating disorders, mindfulness and embodiment practices, and psychological disorders. Maya is dedicated to serving children and adolescents in her work. She is a seminar presenter for Elevate Education, working with grade school students throughout the metropolitan area to learn study and self-regulation skills, and a volunteer at NexGen Scholars, a program dedicated to supporting underrepresented undergraduate students interested in applying to doctoral programs in psychology. Her current research focuses on investigating the lived experiences of emerging adults who decline the use of therapeutic mental health services. She plans to use this work to inform therapeutic outreach and better understand existing narratives surrounding therapeutic mental health services throughout emerging adult populations.

Melinda Parisi Cummings, PhD, is a licensed psychologist with over 25 years of experience in working with those with eating disorders. She is currently an Associate Professor in the APA-accredited doctoral program in Counseling Psychology at Holy Family University, with primary teaching responsibilities in the areas of assessment, psychopathology, and clinical practice. Prior to her faculty appointment, she served for 15 years as Program Director of the Princeton Center for Eating Disorders at Penn Medicine Princeton Medical Center. She continues to serve as a consultant to the program and is an affiliate member of the Penn Medicine-Princeton medical staff. She has written and presented extensively on assessment and treatment of eating disorders, the impact of eating disorders on families, and ethical issues in providing care. She maintains a part-time psychotherapy and supervision/consultation practice and is a Certified Eating Disorders Specialist and Approved Consultant through the International Association of Eating Disorder Professionals.

Heidi Dalzell, PhD, is a licensed clinical psychologist with over 25 years of clinical experience in working with and serving as an ally to the queer, transgender, and nonbinary community. Dr. Dalzell maintains a busy private practice specializing in eating disorders, trauma, and mid-life eating disorders. She also served as the clinical director of a group psychotherapy practice in the Philadelphia area. Dr. Dalzell is a prolific author covering subjects such as eating disorders, addiction, gender identity, mindfulness, racial justice and spirituality. She has spoken nationally and internationally on these topics. Dr. Dalzell is the co-author of *A Clinician's Guide to Gender Identity and Body Image*, a groundbreaking work on the intersection of body image, eating disorders, and gender identity.

Dominic Denning is a graduate student and University Graduate Fellow in the Clinical Psychology Doctoral Program at University of Massachusetts, Amherst. He graduated from the University of Nevada, Reno with a bachelor's degree in Psychology-Research and Anthropology. Subsequently, he completed a post-baccalaureate research coordinator position at University of California, San Diego Eating Disorder Center for Treatment and Research under the mentorship of Dr. Tiffany A. Brown. His program of research aims to understand the course, phenomenology, treatment and prevention of borderline personality disorder, transdiagnostic emotional dysfunction, and self-damaging behaviors (e.g., suicide, nonsuicidal self-injury, and disordered eating) in traditionally underrepresented groups (i.e., male, sexual minority, and gender minority populations).

Catherine Drury is a PhD student in Clinical Psychology at Fairleigh Dickinson University and a predoctoral clinical psychology fellow at UCSF. Her research interests center around improving eating disorder assessment and treatment for at-risk and underserved populations, particularly dancers and athletes. She previously worked for 8 years as a licensed clinical social worker (LCSW) in clinic, hospital, and agency settings throughout New York City, serving primarily adolescents and young adults with histories of trauma. She also delivered specialized programs and services designed to meet the mental health needs of professional dancers and pre-professional dance students. She has a Master of Science in Social Work from Columbia University.

Rachael Flatt, MA, is a UNC-Chapel Hill Clinical Psychology doctoral candidate under the mentorship of Dr. Cynthia Bulik. Prior to graduate school, she served as the Programs Director at the Center for m2Health at Palo Alto University and worked on digital eating disorder intervention research with Dr. Barr Taylor at Stanford University. She completed her undergraduate degree at Stanford University in 2015. She also placed seventh in the 2010 Olympic Winter Games in women's figure skating and was the 2010 US National Champion and the 2008 World Junior Champion. She continues to be active in the sports community by serving on several committees for the US Olympic and Paralympic Committee and US Figure Skating. Her long-term interests include furthering eating disorder research and digital mental health technology and developing tailored interventions for use with athletes.

Sara Fruchter PhD, graduated from the Clinical Psychology Ph.D. program at Fairleigh Dickinson University and is currently a postdoctoral fellow at New York Presbyterian Hospital. . Her research interests involve focusing on the relationship between social media usage, specifically the use of photo-editing applications, and body image concerns in college students. Sara has also been involved in research efforts focusing on improving healthy eating in college students and adapting interventions for youth with obesity. Sara has worked in schools, community clinics and hospitals, providing clinical services to patients across the lifespan with a range of mental health concerns.

Eli Gebhardt is a PhD graduate student and Presidential Graduate Research Fellow in the Clinical Psychology Program at Auburn University. He acts as a graduate research assistant in the AppearanCe Concerns, Eating, Prevention and Treatment (ACCEPT) Lab. Eli graduated from Sam Houston State University with his bachelor's degree in psychology in 2017. He then served two years as a post-baccalaureate research coordinator in the Anxiety & Health Behaviors (AHB) Lab directed by Dr. Jasper A. J. Smits and the Laboratory for the Study of Anxiety Disorders (LSAD) under the direction of Dr. Michael J. Telch at the University of Texas at Austin. In the ACCEPT lab, Eli investigates how body image concerns, minority stressors, and attention bias influences emotional distress and the development of anxiety and stress-related disorders among LGBTQ+ individuals. He aims to adapt extant treatments, using technological advances, to enhance treatment accessibility and adherence among LGBTQ+ individuals.

Francesca Gomez is currently a graduate student in the Clinical Psychology PhD program at Arizona State University (ASU). At ASU, Francesca works with Dr. Marisol Perez in the Body Image Research and Health Disparities (BIRHD) Lab. Francesca's research interests aim to understand the aggregate risk for eating disorders among individuals in minority populations and identify points of intervention to address healthcare disparities. In particular, she is interested in understanding the role and experience of eating disorders within diverse populations experiencing multiple minority stressors.

Sasha Gorrell, PhD, is an Assistant Professor in the Department of Psychiatry and Behavioral Sciences at the University of California, San Francisco. Her clinical focus is in the treatment of adolescents with restrictive eating disorders, specifically in supporting their recovery in family-based treatment, and in intervention and prevention efforts that promote the well-being of athletes. Her current NIMH-funded research leverages behavioral data and neuroimaging to investigate specific neurobiological risk and maintenance factors for problematic exercise behavior in the context of eating pathology. Her overall research interests include exploration of biobehavioral mechanisms that promote our understanding of motivated behavior. This work includes better characterizing maintenance mechanisms and shared features of anxiety and eating disorders and using this knowledge to adapt and develop evidence-based treatment for eating disorders.

Yvette E. Karvay, MA, is a doctoral candidate in Fordham University's Clinical Psychology doctoral program. She previously earned her BA and MA degrees from Stony Brook University. Her research lives at the intersections of eating disorders, weight stigma, and diagnostic classification, especially as these areas impact populations that have been traditionally marginalized and underserved in the eating disorder field. Her most recent work also examines the relationship between food insecurity and disordered eating. Her overarching goal is to inform eating disorder research and interventions for individuals with marginalized identities.

Merle A. Keitel, PhD, is a professor in the Counseling Psychology doctoral program and former chair of the Division of Psychological and Educational Services at Fordham University's Graduate School of Education. Her primary teaching responsibilities are in the areas of individual psychotherapy and counseling theory and process. Dr. Keitel is proud of the accomplishments of the many doctoral students she has mentored over the past 38 years. She is the co-author with Mary Kopala of *Counseling Women with Breast Cancer* (SAGE, 2000) and the co-editor of the *Handbook of Counseling Women* (SAGE, 2003, 2017). She has written numerous book chapters and articles on topics related to women's issues and health psychology, such as eating disorders, cancer, infertility and miscarriage, and PCOS. She was given the James C. Hansen Humanitarian award from the University of Buffalo, the Katherine J. Scanlon Award for "extraordinary contribution to Fordham University and to the field of Psychology," and was represented in the Oral History of Feminist Psychologists (Division 35, APA).

Norman Kim, PhD, is the Diversity, Equity, and Inclusion Officer for the Center for Practice Innovation at the Columbia Department of Psychiatry, and the founder of the Institute for Antiracism and Equity, a social justice focused consultancy. He completed his BA at Yale and his PhD in psychology at UCLA. Norman has developed expertise in psychiatrically complex populations, the application of a transdiagnostic framework for eating disorders, taking an evolutionary approach to shame and anxiety, and minority mental health. He is a regular national and international speaker, educator, and passionate advocate with a particular focus on minority status and barriers to mental health care. Norman serves on a number of advisory boards; most recently he was the Deputy Director of a tech startup focused on providing culturally intelligent, adapted, and accessible care to marginalized communities, and was the co-founder of Reasons Eating Disorder Center.

Jorge Castro Lebrón, BS, is a research coordinator in the AppearanCe Concerns, Eating, Prevention, & Treatment (ACCEPT) Lab at Auburn University managing a study about a dissonance-based eating disorder prevention program aimed to treat young men. He graduated from Auburn University in May 2022 with his BS in neuroscience and has previously worked in research examining the effects of cannabis use on neurological processes as well as stigma against mental disorders. He aims to further his education and career and eventually enter a Clinical Psychology PhD program. In his future research endeavors, he hopes to investigate how different factors may affect diagnosis and treatment of mood and/or anxiety disorders in historically marginalized groups.

Devorah Levinson is a Referral Specialist and the Director of Eating Disorders Division at Relief Resources; a mental health referral service that caters to the needs of the Orthodox community. Her role at Relief is to provide mental health referrals and information to families and patients, and she serves as a conduit to appropriate and effective care. She has presented on the topics of mental health and eating disorders in the Jewish community at schools and hospitals. Mrs. Levinson also has a strong focus on eating disorder prevention and, in that vein, was part of a team that adapted The Body Project for the Orthodox Jewish Community.

Katharine L. Loeb, PhD, FAED, is Director of Research and Training at the Chicago Center for Evidence Based Treatment. She is a retired Professor of Psychology in the PhD Program in Clinical Psychology at Fairleigh Dickinson and was the founding Director of the Mount Sinai Eating and Weight Disorders Program. Dr. Loeb earned her PhD in Clinical Psychology from Rutgers and completed her fellowship at Columbia University. She is a faculty member of the Training Institute for Child and Adolescent Eating Disorders, and on the medical advisory board of Relief Resources, an international referral service for the Orthodox Jewish community.

Erin E. Ott, PhD, is a licensed counseling psychologist in New York. Dr. Ott earned her PhD in Counseling Psychology from Fordham University, where she also earned her master's in Mental Health Counseling. Her graduate research and dissertation focused on boys and men with eating disorders and the experiences of parents caring for a child with anorexia nervosa. Currently, Dr. Ott provides outpatient psychotherapy to older adolescents and adults across the gender and sexuality spectrum, with a specialization in supporting individuals impacted by trauma, anxiety, body image distress, disordered eating, and complex family dynamics. Based on both clinical and research experience, Dr. Ott also specializes in stressors unique to individuals caring for a loved one with a chronic mental health and/or medical condition, especially those caring for individuals with eating disorders. Dr. Ott also has worked as an adjunct professor at Fordham University.

Jennie Park-Taylor, PhD, is an Associate Professor and the Director of Training of the APA-accredited doctoral program in Counseling

Psychology at Fordham University's Graduate School of Education in New York City. Her primary teaching responsibilities are in the areas of multicultural counseling, qualitative research methods and family counseling and assessment. Dr. Park-Taylor has written numerous articles and book chapters on topics related to intersectional social identities, the health and wellness of minoritized individuals and threats to identity and healthy development (e.g., racism, stereotype threat).

Marisol Perez, PhD, is a Professor in the Department of Psychology at Arizona State University. Her program of research encompasses both theoretical and applied studies in the area of eating behaviors and disorders, often using a focus on Hispanic/Latinx populations. Dr. Perez has over 90 publications, and consistently been granted funded over the past 10 years. She currently serves as Editor of *Clinician's Research Digest*, and was the President for the Society for a Science of Clinical Psychology.

Carly Pershyn is a doctoral fellow in Counseling Psychology at University at Buffalo. She is a pleasure activist and former Women's Health Advocate at Planned Parenthood in Buffalo, NY. She has received several awards for her research and scholarship, including the 2017 SUNY Chancellor's Award for Student Excellence, Outstanding Psychology Student Award, Outstanding Philosophy Student Award, and Who's Who Among Students in American Universities Award. She is the recipient of several scholarships, including The President's Circle Scholarship. Her research is on sexuality, intimacy, yoga, trauma, self-care, collective care, and eating behavior. She is a certified yoga instructor and mindfulness therapist and often uses yoga principles to inform her counseling practice, emphasizing embodiment, interoceptive awareness, and self-care.

Tamique Ridgard, PhD, is an Assistant Professor in the School Psychology program at Fordham University. She is a licensed psychologist in New York State and a Nationally Certified School Psychologist (NCSP). Dr. Ridgard earned her Bachelor of Science in psychology at Yale University and her Doctor of Philosophy in school psychology at Lehigh University. Dr. Ridgard's research interests focus on creating systems-level change to improve the mental health and well-being of children and families from minoritized backgrounds. Dr. Ridgard is particularly interested in providing evidence-based, culturally responsive services to children through indirect models of service delivery, such as two-generational parenting programs. In her clinical work, Dr. Ridgard has provided assessment and intervention services for children from birth through adolescence in a variety of settings, including schools, school-based health clinics, outpatient mental health clinics, pediatric primary care centers, home visiting programs, child welfare services, and private practice.

Prim Siripipat, MSEd, is a PhD student at Fordham University's Counseling Psychology Doctoral Program. She obtained her MEd from the University of Missouri and MSEd in Mental Health Counseling from Fordham University. The former top 10 nationally ranked junior tennis player graduated from Duke University, where she was a member of the national champion Blue Devils Women's Tennis Team. Prior to joining the counseling profession, Prim spent nearly two decades as a leader in the field of sports broadcasting, including six years at ESPN as an award-winning TV/radio personality, journalist, play-by-play tennis announcer, and producer. Today, she is the host of "The Next Chapter with Prim Siripipat," which explores how athletes cope with retirement and the transition from sport. A long-time advocate for mental health, Prim hopes to combine her athletic and broadcasting experiences with her doctoral training to help educate athletes, coaches, parents, and governing bodies about the importance of athlete mental health and well-being.

Kate Terranova, PhD, is a licensed clinical psychologist who has been involved in eating disorder research for 10 years. Prior to receiving her PhD, she worked as a research coordinator for an NIMH-funded longitudinal multimodal imaging study of the structural and functional development of frontostriatal neural systems in adolescents with bulimia nervosa. While in doctoral training, she conducted a qualitative study focusing on the interpersonal, societal, and cultural factors of bulimia nervosa recovery and a quantitative study examining the relationship between binge eating disorder, race-related stress, social support, and attachment style. She is currently working in a group private practice in New York where she specializes in the treatment of trauma-related disorders and continues to counsel individuals with body image concerns and disordered eating.

Jessica Lennon Whitney, PhD, is an educator and consulting psychologist to public and private sector organizations on issues of leadership development, workplace mental health, and diversity and inclusion. She is on faculty at University of North Carolina, Wilmington, where she teaches courses on the theory and practice of counseling and psychotherapy. Before becoming a psychologist, Dr. Whitney worked in the corporate sector in revenue generating and internal consulting roles at Ernst & Young LLP (now EY) and Time Warner (now Warner Media), focused on firm-wide leadership development, gender equity, and diversity and inclusion strategy development and workplace culture change. Dr. Whitney was born and raised in Washington, DC, and completed her undergraduate studies at the University of Pennsylvania. She earned a MEd and MA from Teachers College, Columbia University, and a PhD in counseling psychology from Fordham University, both in New York, NY.

Julia Yermash, BS, is a graduate student in Clinical Psychology at Fordham University working under the mentorship of Dr. Natasha Burke. She earned her BS from New York University and completed post-baccalaureate training at Brown University's School of Public Health. Her current research primarily focuses on sociocultural influences (e.g., generational status, socioeconomic status, and acculturation) on eating behaviors in marginalized populations. Other research interests include weight stigma in healthcare settings and the relationship between food insecurity and disordered eating. She hopes to increase the dissemination and implementation of culturally-tailored eating disorder treatments for adolescents and young adults in community-based settings.

www.ingramcontent.com/pod-product-compliance
Lightning Source LLC
LaVergne TN
LVHW052044200926
848481LV00005B/1727